Shackled Spirits Broken Hearts

URSULA MATTHEWS

Britain's Next
BESTSELLER

Britain's Next Bestseller
An imprint of Live It Ventures Ltd
www.bnbsbooks.co.uk

All enquiries should be addressed to:
Live It Ventures Ltd,
27 Old Gloucester Road
London, WC1N 3AX

Cover design by A.J
Photographs courtesy of
Ursula Matthews and Jane Read

ISBN: 978 1910565537

To my wonderful, loving grandparents,
Lorenz and Anna Renges
and my supportive
Auntie Anni and Uncle Thomas.

To my beloved children,
Mark and Jane
for their never ending support and love.

To my beautiful grandchildren,
Michael, Matthew, Lara and Thomas.

And last but not least, my dear friend,
Daphne Rossiter
Without whom this book may never
have been published.

"Love is based on our capacity to
trust in a reality beyond fear,
to trust a timeless truth bigger than
all of our difficulties"

The Art of Forgiveness, Loving Kindness and Peace
- Jack Kornfield

Maria and Lorenz Renges Wedding Day Feb 5th 1941
In traditional Saxon costume

Maria and Lorenz Renges Wedding Party, Feb 5th 1941

Prologue

Maria

It's January 1944. Maria is walking down the deserted lane in the small village of Kerz in Transylvania where she was born and grew up.

It's a very cold winters day with lots of snow on the ground. Maria hurries along wrapped in a thick warm winter coat. With every step she takes her warm lined winter boots make a crunching noise on the packed snow. Maria is on her way to get some bread from another villager who's baked that day.

As she walks along looking at the majestic snow covered peaks of the Carpathian Mountains in the distance, her thoughts wander back through the last few years and the happiness she's known.

She was only 17 years old when she met Lorenz at the Baptist Church in Hermannstadt. He was 24 and a fully qualified gents tailor. They started seeing each other and fell in love. Maria and Lorenz married in the winter of 1941, she was just 20 years old.

They decided to live in Kerz with Maria's elderly mother. Her father had been dead for some years, and her only brother had died at the age of 14, before Maria was born. She'd also had a sister, who had died at the age of 20, giving birth to a baby girl, about the same time as Maria was born. Her mother and niece were the only close family she had.

How quickly things had changed and all Maria's happiness had been taken away. The Second World War was on when she got married, but everybody lived in the hope that it would end soon, and people could get on with their lives.

Her husband Lorenz had been conscripted into the German army. Transylvania was part of the Austro-Hungarian Empire, which had an alliance with Germany and therefore the men in Transylvania went into the German forces.

In the 11th and 12th centuries, Transylvania belonged to Hungary. The

King of the day gave Saxon settlers, from Central Europe, land to farm and cultivate, build cities and villages and make new lives for themselves.

The Saxons and Hungarians lived peacefully side by side for centuries. During the latter periods, Romanians from Moldavia in the East and Valachia in the South settled in Transylvania as well, the Carpathian Mountains forming a natural border between that country, Moldavia and Valachia. Until the 20th century, Transylvania remained under the rule of the Austro-Hungarian Empire.

The Transylvanian Saxons never lost their allegiance to the German fatherland. They remained true to their traditions and way of life.

Lorenz was stationed in Bucharest for his army training but came home on leave regularly.

Their first born was a baby boy, whom they named Christian after Maria's father. Christian was born on the 1st of January 1942. Maria's mother died soon after the baby's birth.

In July 1943 their second child, a baby girl, was born.

They named her Ute.

The only time Lorenz saw his baby girl was when she was 3 months old and he was home on leave. Then he was sent to the front in Italy to fight against the British and their allies.

Walking along absorbed in deep thought, Maria wonders what the future has in store for her and her family. She's thinking about Lorenz, who she assumes is somewhere in Italy and wonders how he is. Her thoughts and prayers are with him constantly in the hope that he is safe and well and that he'll return to her soon.

No one in the village has a radio, so there's very little news about the war. She hasn't heard from Lorenz for a long time. That in itself is a good omen. Families are notified very quickly when a loved one is wounded or killed in action. Every day that passes without receiving a telegram is a blessing.

As Maria turns the corner into the main street of the village, she sees a tarp covered truck parked further along the street. When she reaches the truck, two soldiers with rifles jump out of the truck and block her way.

One of the soldiers orders Maria to get into the back of the truck. Alarm bells immediately go off in her head. She recalls the rumours going around about people in other villages being taken by force and not seen again.

She refuses to get in the truck and tells the soldiers that she's left a baby and a toddler with neighbours and must get back to them. This makes no difference. The soldiers grab one arm each and drag her towards the back of the truck.

Maria struggles and resists with all her might, begging and pleading with the soldiers to let her go home to her children. She tells them her baby is only 6 months old and is still nursing. She can't possibly go anywhere and leave her children, there's no one to take care of them. Her begging and pleading are to no avail.

One of the soldiers slaps her several times across the face and tells her to shut her mouth. Two soldiers in the back of the truck grab Maria under both arms and heave her up into the back.

She's thrown onto a huddled mass of people who are in the back of the truck. Their faces are all familiar to Maria. They are all young men and women from the village. She asks what's happening but gets no response. Everybody looks completely terrified. They are all her Saxon friends and neighbours.

The soldiers keeping guard in the back of the truck tell Maria to sit down and be quiet.

She has no option and relents.

The truck moves off and after a short time comes to a stop. With guns pointing at the prisoners, the two soldiers in the rear of the truck, tell everybody to get off and not speak to each other.

Maria realises that they're at the railway stop. A very long cattle train is standing there, with lots of soldiers, mulling about, guns at the ready.

She hopes that maybe they have been brought here to help load cattle onto the train. She asks one of the soldiers what's happening and why they've all been brought here.

A gruff man's voice from behind yells at Maria that she was told to shut up and then slams the rifle into her back. Maria collapses on her hands and knees. The soldier screams at her "You Saxon whore, shut your mouth and don't move."

She is in absolute agony.

A fear like she's never experienced before grips Maria.

She can only think of her babies and what will happen to them if she's taken away. She stays doubled up on the ground and tries to collect her thoughts. The pain in her back is excruciating, but all she can think about is how she can escape from this nightmare.

A Saxon man nearby starts to shout and attack one of the soldiers. Other Saxons join in the fray. Soldiers from all directions come running, firing shots into the air. Orders are being shouted by an officer and soon the offending Saxons are on the ground being beaten and kicked until they're senseless.

While all this is happening, Maria seizes her opportunity to make a run for it. She does not get very far as the crack of a bullet and a shout stops her dead in her tracks. She's petrified and frozen to the spot. A soldier holds a gun to her chest while another one puts chains round her ankles.

Maria is dragged over to the train. The sliding door of a cattle wagon is opened and she's hoisted up by strong arms and thrown into the wagon. She lies on the floor which is covered in a thin layer of straw. The other villagers from the truck are forced into the wagon at gun point and then the door is shut and bolted behind them.

Everybody's in a panic. Women and girls start to weep. Men are shouting and cursing and demand to be released. Shots are fired outside and everybody's ordered to be quiet or be shot.

It dawns on all the prisoners that this nightmare is for real and a complete quiet settles over them, with just an occasional sob to be heard.

Eastern Europe is now under Soviet Communist rule. All able bodied men and women between the ages of 16 and 40 are being rounded up and taken to Russia for slave labour. Many of the prisoners are Saxons, Hungarians and Gypsies.

The Romanian army is on the Russian side and is charged, by the communists, to do all their dirty work of taking the people by force and transporting them to the Russian gulags.

The cattle train remains in the village for 24 hours, while more people are abducted and loaded in the wagons.

The remaining villagers are threatened to be shot if they come anywhere near the train. The train is guarded at all times by soldiers.

On the way to Russia, the train stops at many other villages and towns, where the cattle wagons are filled to capacity with more abductees. The bodies are so densely packed into the wagons, there's barely room to sit in a crouched position on the floor.

The train finally starts its long journey, which takes a week to get to Russia. The prisoners rations are black bread and water and barely enough to keep them alive. On their arrival in Russia, the prisoners must endure further trips in cattle wagons to the coal and salt mines in Siberia,

Some people died before they reached their destination. They only had the clothes they were captured in. They were dying of hypothermia and pneumonia in the harsh Siberian winter.

The cattle wagons were draughty and the only warmth was from the body heat of the other people. They swapped places and tried to keep each other warm by having a turn at being in the middle of the body mass.

The ones that did survive the horrendous trip, in the depths of the Russian winter, had to endure the hard labour, starvation and lack of medical care in the labour camps where thousands died.

Stalin killed 20 million of his own people and millions more from other countries that worked in the gulags. He killed millions more than

Hitler did, but that part of history remains untold and forgotten.

Maria was in Russia for 3 years working in a coal mine. The conditions were antiquated and sub-human. She was in a mine accident and had her pelvis and thighs crushed between two coal wagons.

Of no further use to the communists, Maria was sent home in 1947 and spent one year recovering from her horrific injuries, before she could have her children back.

Most prisoners were kept in the Russian gulags until the late 40s, years after the war was over.

Maria's brother-in-law was not released until 1951 from the Siberian salt mines. He'd been captured in 1939, at the beginning of the war, and hadn't been heard of for 12 years. His family thought he was dead.

After their ordeals in the Soviet gulags, men and women came home physically and emotionally crippled. They had to come to terms with their ruined lives, which they had to endure in the oppressive communist regime that Transylvania was now under. They had to live with their mangled bodies and broken spirits. In turn they inflicted untold misery on wives, husbands and children.

They were tormented by the horrors and ghosts of the past, which they could never forget.

Many wished they had perished in the camps.

Maria with her children, Ursula, 3 months old and her brother
Christian, almost 2 years old

Chapter One

One of my very first childhood memories goes back to when I am about 2 years old. I'm in Groysie's arms, being carried to the stables. Groysie is the Saxon name for Granny. She's my father's mother. My brother Christian is trotting along behind us. We are both carrying a small tin mug.

As we enter the stable, I see Granddad, sitting on a small three legged stool near the rear end of the cow, bucket between his legs, milking it. He stops and looks at us all. Christian and I hand him our mugs and he fills them both with warm frothy fresh milk from the bucket.

This is one of our favourite treats and we always want more. Groysie is firm and says it will spoil our evening meal, if we have too much milk.

Christian and I are much too young to know about the war, that's been going on for the past six years. Our lives have been very sheltered, we've been looked after and had all our needs met by my wonderful Grandparents and their youngest son Tummy, who is only ten years older than me. He's more like a big brother than an uncle.

My Grandfather is a farmer and farms the land his forefathers cultivated for generations and centuries before him. They were Saxons from Central Europe, who settled in Transylvania in the 12th century. They made a good life for themselves, working the fertile land and raising their cattle and sheep. They built beautiful cities and villages, and made Transylvania into a prosperous country.

My Grandparents' small farmhouse is in the village of Stolzenburg, about 15km from Hermannstadt, one of the bigger cities in Transylvania.

Granddad owned farmland, vineyards, cattle and sheep. He sold his produce at the farmers market in Hermannstadt.

My Grandparents had six children, five sons and one daughter. Lorenz, my father, was the eldest, born in 1914, he was named after my grandfather. Hans was the second eldest, born 1916, then came Misch, short for Michael, born 1918.

Martin was their fourth son born 1922. He joined the army when he was only 17 years old. He lied about his age so he could join up. Martin was blown up by a land mine and killed in the first year of the war.

Then came Anni, their only daughter, born 1925. She was named after my Granny. In 1943 when she was only 18 years old, she was taken for slave labour to Russia, the same as our mother.

Thomas the youngest, whom we all called Tummy, didn't come along until 1933. He was my grandparents' only child to remain at home.

Life in the village was quiet and uneventful. Farmers were working very long hours to get the work done. They'd lost more than half of the workforce to the war or to the labour camps, in Russia.

Most days Christian and I were taken to the fields, and left to play under a bush or tree, while my grandparents and Tummy worked the land. Occasionally we were left at home with Tummy, or with a niece of my grandfathers, who was Tummy's age.

The spring, summer and autumn were the busiest times around the farm. Everything had to be done manually. There were no modern mechanical machines.

The harvest was the busiest time of all. There was a limited time to bring in the crops and the grape harvest, spending days at the farmers market selling the produce, preparing and storing food for the winter. The jobs were never ending and Tummy had to help most of the time.

Christian and I had to amuse ourselves. We had no toys to play with but were happy to run around the yard chasing the chickens and playing with anything we could find. Our favourite playmate was Nero, the great St. Bernard. He was a beautiful dog and enjoyed being around us. We climbed on him and rode him like a pony. He was so good natured and let us do anything to him.

The memories from that summer, when I was three, are very vivid. Granddad made several trips with the cart and horses into the hills, to collect cheese from the shepherd who looked after his flock of sheep.

On several occasions, Granddad took Christian and me with him. I loved riding in the wagon with Granddad. The ride seemed to be quite long and on the way home we always stopped in a forest. Granddad spread out a blanket and we'd eat in the shade of a tree. Then we'd pick mushrooms to take home to Groysie to cook.

I don't remember ever playing with other children in those early days. Everybody was so busy with their work, people didn't have the time to get together. Sunday was just like any other day with lots to do.

When all the land work was finished and everything stored away and

Groysie had done all the pickling and preserving, things got a little easier.

One day that autumn, Granddad came home very agitated. He told Groysie to get together food, clothes, bedding and cooking equipment and start putting it all in the wagon. A lot of quiet talk went on, but no one told us what was happening. The adults rushed around, trying to do everything very quickly. When they were done, we all got into the cart and drove out of the village, towards the hills. There were lots of other wagons, with all their families, taking the same route out to the forest.

When I was a lot older, Groysie told me why we'd left the village. The Russian armies were retreating from Europe, after the war. People from other villages had fled, to save their lives, whilst soldiers pillaged, raped and murdered the villagers. Understandably, people just packed up and fled.

We lived in the forest, by a stream, for several weeks with all the other villagers, until the mass retreat was over. A posse of men went back to the village every night to feed the animals. Eventually everybody returned home.

Men were returning from the war, in dribs and drabs, now that it was over. Michael was my grandparents' only son who returned from the war.

My father, had been captured by the British in Italy and had spent the last part of the war, in a P.O.W. camp in East Anglia, England.

There'd been no news of Hans, who'd been captured at the beginning of the war by the communists. We didn't know if he was dead or alive.

Nothing had been heard of Anni or my mother and we didn't know if they were still alive. Michael got married, soon after his return from the war, to a girl he'd known since childhood. Michael had been in the same unit as his brother, Martin, and had been with him at the end, when Martin was killed.

Early December, Granddad would slaughter a couple of pigs and life was hectic again for a week or so. Granddad smoked whole sides of bacon. Groysie made strings and strings of sausages. Some were cooked and stored in huge jars in their own fat and some were smoked and hung in a storage space in the loft with the bacon, where it was very cold during the winter months and everything was kept fresh.

Christian and I, were happy to try and help, and generally watched all the goings on, with childhood fascination.

I loved the winter when we were all at home. Only the animals, in the barn, had to be taken care of and the rest of the time was spent indoors,

After Christmas, Groysie spent most of her time spinning wool, flax and hemp. When that was all done, she dyed some of the yarn. Granddad then put up the wooden loom and Groysie wove different kinds of cloth for weeks on end.

Granddad spent his time feeding and looking after the animals and mending farm equipment. He was a good handyman and could turn his hand to anything. Tummy helped him and learned how to do things.

Groysie made Tummy sit and read and write. He'd only been to school for a couple of years at the beginning of the war. The school had been closed down, as the male teachers had been called up and the female teachers taken to the labour camps in Russia. Poor old Tummy had missed most of his schooling and Groysie tried very hard to at least get him to read and write fluently and do basic arithmetic.

Both Christian and I adored Tummy. He was a quiet boy, but liked to play with us and tease us. He never went anywhere or did anything. There was nothing in the village for people or children to do, so everybody just stayed at home.

On those cosy winter days, we liked sitting and listening to Groysie telling us Bible stories. My grandparents were very religious. They belonged to a very strict sect of the Baptist church, where they occasionally went on a Sunday, when they had time. We were always left at home with Tummy.

The Bible was the only book allowed into our house. We had no children's books of fairy tales or rhymes. Christian and I, didn't know about such books, and were very happy for Groysie to tell us Bible stories. She had a way with telling the stories and made them come to life for us.

Granddad was very strict. All his children had to abide by his puritan ways. Smoking and drinking were strictly forbidden. Going to dances, the cinema or theatre, was out of bounds. Going to any public place, for any kind of enjoyment, was absolutely prohibited. On some of those winter days, Groysie got out photographs. She'd point out each member of the family and tell us who they were. She had several pictures of my father and mother. Christian seemed to know who they were. I think it was just from Groysie telling us again and again, that my brother remembered them.

He'd only been one year and nine months old, when he last saw my father and only two, when my mother was taken.

Groysie said that our father and mother would come home one day and then we'd go and live with them.

I used to get very upset and tell Groysie that I always wanted to live with her, Granddad and Tummy, not with those people in the photos.

Granny would laugh, give me a big hug and say that all children should live with their parents. I loved my Groysie so much, even as a three year old, I couldn't imagine life without her.

Chapter Two

In the spring, of 1947 big changes came to Transylvania. All the Saxon land, properties and businesses were taken and became the property of communist Romania.

No one received a penny of compensation.

People became paupers overnight, with nowhere to go.

Granddad got his notification that his land, livestock and house would be taken over by the state and we would have to move out of our house and find somewhere else to live. I can still see Granddad, sitting at the kitchen table, head in his hands, crying like a baby. Groysie, trying to comfort Granddad and saying that surely even the communists couldn't be that cruel and take everything and throw us out on the street.

But that's exactly what happened.

Over the next couple of weeks, we saw terrible changes take place. Men came and led the cows and horses away to the collective farm, which had been set up at the outskirts of the village. Then, they loaded the pigs, chickens and animal fodder into carts and took everything away.

My Grandparents watched in dismay and disbelief. Granddad's mood changing from anger to despair. Everything he and his forefathers had worked for and achieved, to make a better life for their families, had been taken from them, like candy from a baby. There was absolutely nothing they could do or anyone to go to for help.

The final insult came, when men turned up and took the barn down and dismantled the stables brick by brick. Everything was hauled away by wagons and horses and erected somewhere else. Nero, our beautiful dog, was taken and Christian and I were very upset. It took Groysie a long time to console us.

Finally, the day came when we all had to vacate our home. We were only allowed to take what we could physically carry. My grandparents were laden down with the bare essentials. Christian and I carried what little we could and Tummy had a pretty good load as he was bigger and stronger than us. All the furniture and household goods had to be left.

Groysie's sister lived in the village and had not been kicked out of her house yet, so we moved in with her. A few days later we had to move again as her house had now been taken too.

We had nowhere to go. Granddad was an elder in the Baptist community in the village. The Baptist meeting place was in one of the village houses. This was taken by the state too, but the Baptists had been allowed to carry on using it for the time being.

Granddad partitioned a small section of the meeting room off, by knocking a few bits of wood together and covering it with sacking. The rest of the room was still used for their meetings.

There was a small, wood burning stove, in the corner of our bit where Groysie could cook a one pot meal.

Groysie stitched some sacking into big bags and they were allowed to fill them with straw, which became our beds on the floor.

Granddad managed to find an old wooden table and we used the chairs from the meeting room. He put some nails into a wooden plank and nailed it to the wall. This served to hang the few belongings we managed to carry away from the house. Groysie said we should be thankful to the Lord that we had a roof over our heads and were all together.

The biggest problem now was food. We'd always had plenty of good food and now that was all gone.

Granddad, Groysie and Tummy all had to work on the collective farm. They didn't get paid, but received weekly rations of maize flour, potatoes and a few vegetables in season. We never ever got meat, eggs or dairy products.

The village shop had been closed down and there was only a kiosk where people could get paraffin for their lamps.

From having had good farm food throughout the war, we now had to survive on the meagre rations that were doled out. Groysie did her best to stretch the little food out for the week.

We kids complained about eating polenta and potatoes every day. Sometimes Groysie was so upset and cried. She felt sorry for us and didn't like to see such depravation.

Granddad and Groysie talked about the unfairness of the system. The communists, that were in charge at the collective farm, had good lives. They lived in our houses, and took home all kinds of food: meat, eggs, cheese, milk and anything else they wanted.

Granddad talked about the huge lorries, being loaded on a regular basis, with animals, grain and fresh produce. They were all destined for the

Soviet Union and the general population was left to survive on starvation rations.

Granddad often looked very sad. He prayed more than ever, asking God to deliver us from this communist plague. He hated working on the land that had been his, and looking after the animals, that had belonged to him. Some days he'd come home and tell us that he'd seen Nero chained up at the collective farm. He'd be very upset and said the dog was always so pleased to see him. After a while, he stopped telling us, because we got upset every time too.

Groysie had to work 6 days a week, like Granddad and Tummy. Our neighbour, who was very old, was at home all day and kept an eye on us. At least, that's what she was supposed to do. Most of the time, during the summer months, she dozed on her verandah all day.

During the summer and autumn, Christian and I were left on the verandah, all day. We had a couple of chairs, with an old blanket thrown over, which was our little house. We didn't have toys, so we gathered sticks and stones and made up games.

Sometimes, we'd go out to the street and play with other kids in the neighbourhood. We lived on the main road, that went through the village. There was no danger of being knocked down by a car or lorry, as these were very rarely seen. We would just stand and watch them go by with fascination.

Life was pretty uneventful. We never did anything or went anywhere. The summer was better, as we could play outside in the dusty street, where all the kids looked like street urchins, including us.

The winter days were long and boring, cooped up in our little space with nothing to do. Tummy brought a piece of cardboard home one day and drew Ludo on it. He taught us how to play. We used different coloured pebbles and Tummy made a wooden die, and burnt spots into all the sides.

Bible stories were always a favourite, with Christian and me, and we could sit for hours listening to the same stories, over and over.

When there was a funeral, during the warm summer months, all the little kids in the street, would gather and gawp at the funeral procession going by. The local brass band marched in front of the hearse, blasting out soulful and sombre music.

All the little kids, barefoot and tattered looking, would join behind the mourners and follow the procession, all the way to the cemetery. At the cemetery gates we'd all be told to get lost. I loved looking at the ornate and gilded hearse. I'd never seen such a pretty wagon. The music made me hop and skip, I thought the whole event was a lot of fun.

Sunday, was my favourite day. Nobody went to work and we were all at home together. The Baptist community gathered in the bigger part of the room, where we lived. The congregation was divided. The men sat on the right side of the room and the women on the left facing the pulpit.

My Granddad or one of the other elders preached the sermon from the pulpit at the front of the room. At times the preaching got louder and louder. I was under the impression we were being shouted at, which always scared me.

I found having to sit still for so long very hard. During the warm weather Groysie sent us out to play. The winter months were bitterly cold with lots of snow, so we had to sit still and be patient.

I liked it when we sang hymns, but prayers went on and on and everybody wanted their turn to say their bit.

One evening, during the summer months a lot of people gathered in the street near where we lived.

We all went out to see what was happening.

A little while later, two policemen marched a woman out of a house nearby. As they came closer to us, I saw a necklace with bits of raw meat, hanging down the front of the woman's body.

I started to scream when I saw a chickens head, dangling on this woman's chest, with blood dripping down her front and onto the ground. Groysie grabbed both my brother and me and rushed us into our house. This image stayed with me, for a long time. I couldn't sleep and had nightmares.

The woman had stolen the chicken from the collective farm. Her husband had been killed, in the war, and she was raising 4 children on her own.

People said she was desperate.

Granddad told Groysie that the woman had been sent to prison and her children had been put into an orphanage.

Winter came and life was tough.

We had very little to eat and not enough wood to burn, to keep us warm. We'd often sit huddled up, on our straw mattresses, hungry and cold. Groysie got very upset to see us like this. We'd had such a good life on the farm. There was plenty of all kinds of food. Behind the barn my grandparents had a big vegetable garden, where, from spring to autumn, every kind of vegetable was grown. Beyond that, there was an orchard, with many different kinds of fruit trees, supplying us with all our needs and more.

In the farm yard there was a huge mulberry tree. For several weeks during the summer, mulberries rained down, laying thick and dark on the ground. Tummy often climbed up on the tree and shook a branch, while my grandparents held a blanket stretched out for the mulberries to fall onto.

Groysie loved telling me, when I was a little older, how when I was just a toddler and ran around in the yard, I'd pick up what I thought were mulberries and pop them in my mouth. Unfortunately the chickens also ran around in the yard and loved eating the mulberries. Their poop looked the same as the berries. I'd often pick up the poop and eat it.

Christian found this highly amusing to watch, then run off in glee telling Groysie that I was eating poop again.

The other thing we really missed was milk. We drank fresh, raw milk on a daily basis and we hadn't had a drop since we were kicked out of our house.

When Granddad made wine in the autumn, he always made grape juice for the children and that was a favourite tipple of ours.

The winter finally turned into spring and the weather started to get better.

Groysie had been at home most of the time during the winter months. Granddad and Tummy worked at the collective farm, doing the jobs that needed doing. Now they were all going back to the land work and we were left all day.

Both Christian and I, loved our little family so much. My grandparents were the kindest people and loved us so dearly. There were never any cross words. Tummy always played with us, when he had time, and we just adored him.

One day the postman brought us a letter. We never received mail. I didn't know what a letter was. Groysie turned it over, while Christian and I both watched.

"It's from your mother" she said.

She opened the letter and read it, then told us our mother was back from the labour camps and wanted us to be returned to her.

I still remember, asking Groysie all kinds of questions, about my mother and what she looked like. Groysie had often shown us pictures of our parents, but they were black and white. I wanted to know how tall she was. What colour eyes and hair she had? If she was kind and loving like Groysie and Granddad?

Groysie assured me that all mothers were kind and loved their children.

I'd always been a chatterbox and asked questions nonstop. Whereas Christian was quiet and not at all inquisitive. I just assumed that we'd all go to mother and live together.

The day before we left, to go back to my mother, a neighbour took a family picture of my grandparents, Tummy, Christian and me outside in the street, in front of the house we lived in.

The following morning, Granddad, Groysie, Christian and I were leaving on a horse and cart, which belonged to the collective farm, to the train station in Hermannstadt. There we would get the train to Kerz, where my mother lived and where Christian and I, had been born.

I had never seen a train but was very excited to be going on one. Groysie had explained that trains ran on iron tracks. It all seemed rather incredible to me. I'd chattered excitedly to my brother, but he didn't seem interested, he looked bored and just shrugged his shoulders.

The money for the train fare had to be requested from the collective farm. Only Groysie and Granddad were allowed to take us. Poor Tummy was so disappointed. He never went anywhere and would have loved to go on the trip. He was fourteen and a half now and had to work hard at the collective farm. He had no time to have friends and was very lonely and shy.

When the man with the horse drawn cart came to pick us up, I hugged Tummy so hard. I didn't want to let him go. He'd been a part of my life since I could remember, and I couldn't contemplate leaving him.

As the cart drove away, I looked back at my dear Tummy and waved. He just stood outside the house looking sad and forlorn with tears running down his face.

The trip to Hermannstadt took a long time.

Only one horse drew the cart at a slow and sedate pace. Granddad sat at the front with the driver. Groysie, Christian and I sat on the floor in the back of the cart.

When we entered the city, there was so much to see and we didn't know where to look first. We passed beautiful enormous houses, the like of which I'd never seen. Groysie said before the war very rich people lived there. We drove down long wide tree lined streets. It was all so new and exciting to me.

The journey took us across a big square with statues and lots of massive buildings several storeys high. They all had big red flags flying from them with a white sickle and hammer painted in the middle.

We passed many different churches. Some had very pointed towers and others were shaped like onions. We drove past very high thick walls with several towers built into the walls at regular intervals. Groysie said that was part of the old city wall, which had been built in the Middle Ages to protect the town and its people from the Turks. These people wanted to invade and take away our land, towns and villages. The war had lasted a long time, but the Saxon people had managed to keep the invaders out.

Granddad said that nothing had stopped Stalin and the communists taking everything away from us.

We saw a two carriage train. I asked Groysie if this was the train we were going on. She said it was a kind of train called a tram. The tram only ran in the city and took people to all different parts of Hermannstadt.

There were lots of people in the city, walking and hurrying in all directions. We saw ladies pushing funny things with babies and toddlers in them. We didn't have anything like that in our village. Groysie told us that our mother had pushed us around in one of these contraptions when we were babies.

Here in the city, people were dressed very differently from those in our village. The women wore colourful dresses and coats and very nice shoes. The men wore very smart jackets and trousers and most people wore hats. Groysie said that's how city people dressed.

In the village where we'd lived, the women wore long gathered drab skirts, white shirts and dark scarves on their heads. They always wore aprons to protect their skirts. The men wore equally dull clothes and heavy boots. Only on Sundays the villagers wore their traditional Saxon costumes. These varied from village to village. They were all beautifully handmade and embroidered in rich and wonderful colours. They were handed down through the generations. It took weeks and months to make some of these traditional clothes.

Groysie said the city ladies wore modern, fashionable and elegant clothes. Some of the women wore lipstick which made their lips very red. Some ladies also curled their hair.

I was fascinated by it all and thought it all wonderful. I told Groysie that's what I wanted to do when I was a big girl, but Groysie said that it was a sin and God wouldn't like it.

The horse and cart finally pulled up outside an enormous building many storeys high, which Granddad said was the railway station.

We said goodbye to the driver and walked through massive open doors into a gigantic hall with very high ceilings, where people seemed to rush in all directions.

Granddad went to a window in a wall and came back with four bits of paper, which were the tickets for the train trip to Kerz.

As the train was not leaving for a while, we all sat on a slatted wooden bench watching people, eating our cold pieces of polenta which Groysie had brought for us.

Christian and I were getting impatient with the long wait.

At long last Granddad said it was time and we walked across the big hall to the opposite side we'd come in and went out through large double doors onto the platform.

I couldn't believe how big the train was when I first saw it. The locomotive was enormous. The big iron wheels were much higher than Granddad and he was tall.

The big round chimney on the locomotive was belching out black smoke, which seemed to go everywhere. Every so often a loud shrill whistle came from the locomotive, which made me jump every time.

We walked along the train and Granddad opened a door to a carriage and helped Groysie up the ladder that came down to the platform. He then lifted me up into the carriage and then Christian. He followed carrying the cloth bag with our few belongings. A gangway ran down the middle of the carriage with wooded slatted benches either side, two benches facing each other all along.

We found two free seats. Christian and I immediately commandeered the two either side by the window. Not long after a long shrill whistle came from the locomotive and the train started to slowly move.

This was a whole new world to me and I could hardly contain my excitement. Christian on the other hand was sitting quietly pressing his nose against the window, watching everything fly by.

The train stopped many times at all the small villages on the way before we reached Kerz, where it was time for us to get off. I wanted to stay on the train forever as I was having so much fun.

The railway station in Kerz, like all the other villages we'd passed through, had no cement platform, just hard packed dirt. There was a long drop from the bottom of the ladder to the ground. Granddad lifted both Christian and me off the train and then helped Groysie get down.

We all stood and watched the train pull away and when it became smaller and smaller and disappeared round a bend in the distance, we started to walk along the tracks towards a dirt road, that lead to the village.

This was just a railway stop. There was no big fancy building, only a small wooden hut where tickets were sold.

The houses were the same as the houses in Stolzenburg where my grandparents lived. They were tiny compared to the beautiful villas in Hermannstadt.

The houses stood in neat rows with high walls connecting one house to the next at the front. Big double doors were set in each wall, when opened, a horse or oxen drawn wagon could pass through. A smaller door was built in closer to the house for people to enter. All the yards were hidden from view.

We walked along four streets to reach the other end of the village where my mother lived. We passed quite a lot of people on the way who all greeted us. I think they all knew who we were. The village was small and everybody knew each other.

We rounded a corner into another street which had a few houses on the left and one house on the right at the very end. Beyond that there were fields and hills in the distance.

Groysie told us this was called the Little Lane and it was where our mother lived.

It was late afternoon and still sunny and quite warm. Half way down the lane we saw two young women sitting on a bench in front of a house. When they saw us they both got up and started walking towards us.

One of the women was walking with the aid of crutches and the other one was walking slowly beside her.

They didn't walk very far before they stopped and watched our approach.

I recognise the woman on crutches from her picture.

It's my mother.

She's not dressed like Groysie. She's wearing similar clothes I saw the women in the city wear. Her hair is brown and curly down to her shoulders, with some fancier bits held with pins on the top of her head.

The lady with her is similarly dressed but is plumper with a fuller face.

Christian is already hiding behind Groysie's skirt, which he always does with strangers. The adults greet each other, then my mother ruffles the top of my head and says I've grown and changed so much since I was a baby, she'd never recognise me.

Christian is still hiding behind Groysie. Mother tries to coax him out. Groysie gently pulls him in front of her and he gets the same treatment as I did. Neither of us get a hug or a kiss from my mother. Maybe it's hard for her to bend down on crutches.

She tells us to call her mother, in Saxon it is Mudder. I say I want to call her mammy or mamma, the same as I've heard other children call their mothers. Mother tells me that I'm not a baby anymore and therefore I have to call her Mudder, which seems very formal.

I feel slightly wary of this woman. She's seems cold and aloof, not at all how I imagined her to be.

The lady with my mother is her niece Grete who's been helping to look after her and will be there to look after us until Mudder's legs and hips are completely healed.

We're told to call her niece Gretchen Tante. She's actually our cousin but the same age as Mudder.

We all go into the house.

The adults chat and exchange news.

Later on we all sit down to a vegetable stew. Christian and I pick at the food. He doesn't like cooked carrots and I don't like cooked peppers, which happen to be most of the ingredients in the stew. Mudder says Groysie has obviously spoilt us and that will definitely have to change. Groysie comes to our defence and says we're only little and bound not to like everything, so not to be too hard on us.

Both Christian and I stick to Groysie like glue and follow her everywhere, even to the wooden outhouse in the back of the garden.

My mother's house is a typical village dwelling. Twelve wide concrete steps lead up to an open verandah. My grandparents also had a verandah in their house, but it was enclosed with windows and had double doors at the bottom of the stairs. It made a nice sunny room, where Christian and I often played.

My mother's verandah leads into a room with a kitchen table and chairs. Quite a modern cooking range stands along one wall. Nearby is a dresser with pretty china displayed in the top half. There's also a double divan along another wall. A window overlooks the back yard.

Opposite the window a door leads to a much bigger room with two windows facing the street and another one at the side overlooking the yard. The windows are covered in pretty embroidered net curtains.

In the farthest corner on the left side of the room, stands a lovely double bed covered in fine bedding. I'm told that every young girl, when she reaches her teenage years, learns to sew and embroider. They all spend years making and embroidering household linen for when they marry and set up home. Some of these items are also handed down from mother to daughter. Everything is of such good quality and lasts for decades.

Groysie had also had nice linen, china and furniture, but everything had remained in the house when we were kicked out.

A big highly polished table stands in the centre of the room with lots of chairs around it. A very long chest with back runs nearly all the way along the right side of the room. It's painted dark green and adorned with flowers on the seat and the front.

I learn later that this belonged to my grandparents Christian and Elisabeth. Both their names are written on the front of the chest with the year they got married. Alongside the same wall stands a wardrobe in the same style as the chest. On the same wall, and close to the double bed, is a lovely dresser which looks the same. All in dark green with flowers painted on. Groysie says it is all Tyrolean style furniture.

A child's cot, made of plain wood and slatted sides, stands in the corner on the left. It was much bigger than the baby cots of today. This was to be the bed Christian and I would share.

Christian is nineteen months older than me, but throughout our childhood years we were about the same height. He isn't much taller than me today.

So at four and a half and six years old we could just about fit in the cot, stretched out, with our heads and feet touching each end.

We both slept in that cot for two years.

There was no electricity or plumbing in the villages back in those days. Each house had a deep well in the yard and a wooden outhouse at the back of the garden.

My mother had also had her house and land taken from her and nationalised. When mother came back from the labour camps, she was allowed to live in her house.

The following year a Romanian couple with 3 children were moved into the smaller of our two rooms.

The morning after we arrived, my grandparents had to leave and return home. Christian looked morose and very unhappy and wouldn't speak to anybody.

I was in floods of tears and completely mortified. I clung onto Groysie's skirt and begged her to stay or else take me back with them. Groysie was very kind and loving. I sat on her lap and she tried to explain why things had to be this way. She said we belonged with my mother not old grandparents. Our father would come home soon and we'd all be together again.

I wouldn't accept any of her explanations and just cried more and more.

It seemed like Christian had accepted his fate, but I was going to fight every inch of the way.

Still, it made no difference. When the time came for Granddad and Groysie to leave, Gretchen Tante had to prise me off Groysie and physically restrain me while they walked down the lane, round the corner and out of sight. Everybody in the neighbourhood must have heard my pleading and anguished screams. I really thought I would die. I was dragged into the house balling my eyes out.

Christian just stood all alone, forlorn looking and sad with tears streaming down his face. The only people I'd ever known and loved so much had gone. I felt completely abandoned and alone.

Mudder had no patience. She was very cross and told me I was bad and to start being a good girl and behaving myself. She said she'd have to teach us how to behave, because clearly, we'd been badly spoiled by our grandparents and not taught any manners.

The days that followed were absolutely unbearable.

Gretchen Tante was very nice and kind to both Christian and me. Mudder was intolerant and shouted at us a lot. Neither of us were able to please her. She never spoke kindly or gave us a loving hug or kiss.

Christian and I became even closer than we had been. We tried to comfort and find solace in each other.

I thought about Granddad, Groysie and Tummy all the time and missed them so much but dare not breathe their names when Mudder was around as she would really lose her temper.

I still hoped each day that Groysie would come back and take us home.

Chapter Three

Mother's health gradually improved. She got stronger and started walking without crutches. Gretchen Tante moved back to her own home, which she shared with her father and grandparents. She married about the same time as my parents. Her husband was killed in the war. She'd spent several years in the Russian labour camps as well.

Gretchen Tante was loving and kind to us. On many occasions she stepped in and stopped my mother from hitting us. When she left Christian and I really missed her.

Things changed drastically afterwards.

Mother had no patience and lashed out at the slightest thing that annoyed her.

Both Christian and I started wetting the bed at night, which absolutely infuriated Mudder. She screamed, shouted and lashed out and said we were nothing but dirty little animals and should sleep outside. We became very frightened and kept our distance from her whenever we could.

One day she came home carrying two long green willow wands. They were as thick as a finger one end and tapered into a fine point the other end. Mudder said this was what she would use to punish us with if we disobeyed, misbehaved and carried on wetting the bed. She rested the two wands on the top of a picture frame, where we could see them at all times.

I don't ever remember being hit or punished by my grandparents and had no idea what was in store for us but was frightened nevertheless.

I was the first to experience the fiery sting of the willow wand in one of her mad rages.

Christian and I slept in the nude as we had no nightclothes. One night I was woken up being hoisted over the railings of the cot and dragged to the other side of the room. I thought I must be having a nightmare, then realised Mudder was hauling me by the arm. She reached for one of the willow wands above the picture and started lashing me across the back of my body and legs. She was screaming abusive words at me and kept on hitting me with the wand. I could hear my own shrill, horrified screams above everything. My body felt as if it were on fire, the pain was beyond endurance.

I couldn't get away. Mudder was holding on tight to my arm and the blows were raining down on me.

Christian was woken up by the screams and started shouting at Mudder to stop hitting me. She turned on him and told him to shut up or he'd get the same treatment. She finally stopped beating me, left me in a heap on the floor and went outside.

Christian climbed out of bed and came over to me and embraced me in his arms. He was only 6 years old. We held each other tight and cried for a long time. I told him I didn't know why she did it. He led me back to our cot and when I got in I knew the reason for the beating. I'd wet the bed. Mudder must have checked the bed in the night and just gone insane.

I couldn't sleep I was in too much pain. When it got light, Mudder had not returned to the room. The bed was not just wet but stained with blood. I had thick swollen welts all over my back and legs. They were like multicoloured snakes, oozing and crawling all over my body.

Mudder didn't take us out for days after that. She didn't want anybody to see what she'd done to me.

As time went on these beating became the norm. I always had sores on my back and legs.

The bed wetting got worse.

Christian got away with less beatings as he didn't wet the bed as often as me.

I was absolutely terrified of Mudder. At night I lay awake too scared to sleep in case I wet myself. This only made me more tired and perpetuated the bed wetting.

On many occasions I'd woken in the night and found the bed was wet. I'd be beside myself with fear. I'd wake Christian and ask him to help me blow on the sheet to dry it, but of course that didn't work and the hiding would come anyway.

At the age of fourteen my mother had been apprenticed to a housekeeper and cook in a wealthy industrialist's villa in Hermannstadt.

The apprenticeship was for 4 years and she learned all about housekeeping, cooking and how to run this wealthy home.

After meeting my father, getting married and having two children Mudder was happy. It all ended though when my father went to war and she was taken to the labour camps in Russia.

After her horrendous ordeal in the coal mine, her accident and the yearlong recovery from her injuries, Mudder still held out hope that when my father came back from the war they would have a good life and be happy again.

During the first summer back with my mother, she received some letters from my father in England. She never read any of them to us but was very cross at times after reading the letters.

She showed us the photographs he sent of himself taken by professional photographers. He was dressed to the nines as though he'd just stepped out of a fashion magazine.

My mother ranted and raved about my father spending good money on these pictures and living like a king in England and us starving back home.

Mother now had a job as a housekeeper and cook in a big house in the village. The manager of the flax factory near the village lived there with his family.

It was a very demanding job. She left the house early in the morning and got back in the evening. Sometimes as late as 9 or 10 o'clock. She had no one to leave us with as everybody worked.

We had strict instructions never to leave the yard and when it rained we went onto the verandah, but the house was always locked.

In the mornings before she left, she gave us a piece of polenta and sometimes black bread. Occasionally we got a glass of milk, which she brought home from the big house. Normally we just drank water from a bucket on the verandah.

For our midday meal Mudder left us each a piece of polenta or black bread in a chest on the verandah. There was never anything to go with the polenta or bread. By 6 in the morning she was gone. We'd still be hungry and eat the meagre rations left for us long before midday. The rest of the day we were ravenous and hunting for anything edible.

We'd often sneak into the neighbours' gardens, stealing unripe fruit from their trees and then end up with tummy ache and diarrhoea.

Our garden was overgrown with weeds. Mudder didn't have time to plant any vegetables. Other people planted all types of vegetables in their gardens, we'd sneak in over the fence or through a gap and pull up carrots and pinch tomatoes and cucumbers and anything else we could find to eat. If the neighbours were around and saw us they chased us away.

Failing that Christian and I picked sorrel stalks and leaves from our garden and ate them.

We knew the big house where Mudder worked. One day when we were very hungry, Christian said we should go to the big house and ask Mudder for something to eat.

When we got there and knocked on the door, the lady of the house opened the door. We must have looked like a couple of street urchins and she just told us to get lost.

Christian said our mother worked there and we wanted to see her. She got angry and told us to leave and not come back.

That evening when Mudder got home we both got a hell of a beating. We told her we got very hungry and wanted something to eat. She said she didn't want to hear it. We'd disobeyed her by leaving the house and embarrassed her at work. We were never to do it again. We were too afraid to ever go to that house again and end up being thrashed.

A friend of mothers was a dressmaker. She made me a pretty skirt and a white puffed sleeved blouse from some of mother's old clothes. Christian got a pair of short trousers and a shirt made from father's old clothes. We were only allowed to wear our new things on Sundays.

Mudder said the clothes we arrived in were like paupers' clothes and she was ashamed to be seen with us.

Some Sundays Mudder took us to visit an aunt of hers, who lived the other end of the village in a street called The Clay Pit. She had two daughters and a son who were still living at home. Her husband was dead.

In the back garden they had several beehives. We always got bread and honey to eat. It was a real treat. We'd never had honey before and absolutely loved it.

Their front room had a massive table in the middle with a frame all around the sides. The table was alive and crawling with cream coloured silkworms as thick as a finger. We liked picking mulberry leaves in the garden and covering the silkworms with them. Then we sat for ages, watching these fat, creepy worms slither over each other to get to the fresh leaves. I loved watching them.

Over the weeks Christian and I visited this aunt most Sundays. Mudder didn't come with us very often. We loved going and always looked forward to our treat of bread and honey. Mudder always gave us strict instructions to be back by noon.

This particular Sunday, the aunt lost track of time and we got home a little late. Christian told Mudder why we were late and the aunt had said it was her fault. After that we were not allowed to visit again.

Late that summer we got the first parcel from my father in England. Mudder had to go to Hermannstadt by train to pick the parcel up and we had to stay at home.

When she got back she told us father had sent a lot of lovely things. Unfortunately she had to sell most of the things to pay the duty on the parcel.

I remember and can still see the red crepe soled sandals I got. I also received white socks, under panties and a multi coloured jumper.

All the things were so fine and beautiful.

Christian also got crepe soled sandals, but his were dark blue. He also had socks, underpants and a jumper. Years later he told me he hated wearing his sandals as they hurt him a lot, but he never said so at the time.

Mudder had kept some chocolate and sweets for us.

During the latter part of the war and the communist era that followed, chocolate and sweets were never seen in the shops. So for Christian and me this was a whole new experience and we loved these wonderful treats.

A few weeks before Christmas Mudder went to Hermannstadt again to pick up another parcel father had sent. Christian and I were very excited as we knew there would be chocolates and sweets in the parcel for us.

Mudder again kept just a few things and sold the rest to pay the duty on the parcel.

Both Christian and I got winter coats. Mine was a terracotta colour with the collar and trim round the pockets a darker shade. I'd never seen anything so beautiful and stylish, let alone been the proud owner of such a garment. Christian's coat was air force blue and just as lovely as mine.

We both got brown ankle boots. The leather was so soft and the boots were lined with a warm and soft material. The boots had a special smell and I loved to just sniff in the scent. To this day, when I smell new shoes, it takes me right back to when I was little.

Mudder gave us each a box. I couldn't imagine what could be inside. I took the lid of the box and there was the most exquisite doll imaginable. She looked like a princess fast asleep. Her dark eyelashes rested on her pink cheeks. I was so nervous, I didn't know what to do. Mudder told me to pick the doll up. As I did so, her eyes opened and big blue eyes looked straight at me. I was dumbstruck. The doll had long dark hair and and rose bud lips, I thought I'd died and gone to heaven. Surely such a wonderful doll couldn't belong to me.

I examined her closely. She wore a pretty floral dress and a red coat. On her feet she wore white socks and black patent shoes. Under her dress she even had on lacy under panties. As I turned the doll on her tummy to examine the back of her, she said MAMA. Not just any doll, but a talking doll no less. I really thought I was the luckiest child alive. In all the excitement over my doll, I'd completely forgotten my brother. When I turned to show him my doll, he seemed every bit as excited as me.

Mudder was sitting on the floor putting together a miniature railway track. Christian was clinging to a small locomotive and four equally tiny carriages as though he was being threatened to have them taken from him. The locomotive and carriages were painted red and green and had some writing along the side. Our toys were just magical and Christian was lost for words.

When the track was finished it was an oval shape and covered a fair bit of the floor. Mudder placed the four carriages on the track which all hooked together. We were both enthralled and watched with fascination as Mudder now put a key in the side of the locomotive and wound it up. She then placed it and hooked it to the carriages. Lo and behold the little train started to move and pick up speed, pulling the carriages along behind.

Christian and I sat captivated, watching this magical little train go round and round the track. Mudder pressed a button on the top of the locomotive and it gave a shrill whistle.

I could have sat there all day, hugging my dolly and watching the little train. It gradually slowed as the mechanism wound down and then stopped. Mudder wound the locomotive up twice more and then the train was packed up and put back into its box.

My doll also had to go back in her box. I just thought of her as lying in her bed asleep. Neither Christian or I had ever owned a toy of any sort. Here we were now and each had a toy so wonderful and magical, that any child would have given anything to see, let alone possess.

Over the next few days, kids from the neighbourhood came and admired our precious toys. I didn't like it when Mudder made me give the doll to other kids to hold.

After a few days the doll and the train were packed away and put on top of the wardrobe. Mudder said we could only play with them on special occasions.

On Christmas Eve, Mudder dressed us in our beautiful coats and shoes and took us to church for the evening service. A big Christmas Tree stood in the front of the church, near the altar, decorated with garlands and white candles.

After the service the candles were lit on the tree by the choir boys. All the younger children stood in a line in front of the altar. Christian and I stood in the line too. We slowly walked round the altar and each child was given a brown paper bag. In the bag was a homemade biscuit shaped like a Christmas tree, an apple and two walnuts. We were delighted with our gift.

When we got home Mudder had another surprise for us. She held both her hands, which were made into fists, out in front of her and told Christian to choose a hand. When she opened her fist, there in her palm was a red, sparkling, shiny square, which she gave to my brother.

She opened her other hand and there was a sparkling, shiny square too, but it was green. My heart sank. Red was my favourite colour and I wanted red too.

I'd learnt a lot in the past few months and knew I couldn't voice my disappointment, as I would lose the present and get a good hiding for being ungrateful.

The hidings were as frequent as ever, mostly for wetting the bed, but sometimes we were beaten and had no idea why.

The little parcels each had a sweet inside. We treasured the pretty shiny paper for a long time afterwards, smoothing it out with our fingers until the paper was tattered and torn and fell apart.

After church that Christmas Eve, Mudder let us play with the doll and train for a while and then the toys were packed away and we didn't get to play with them for another year, until the following Christmas.

The next day, which was Christmas Day, Mudder had to go to work. Christmas was not celebrated in the communist countries.

After Christmas things got a lot worse. The letters that came from my father in England, sent Mudder into hysterical and uncontrollable rages.

I remember her ranting and raving at us, as though it was our fault. She called my father all kinds of nasty names, telling us he didn't love us and was never coming home.

All her anger was directed at us. She was shouting and ranting and throwing things about the room. She should never have come back home from Russia, she yelled. She could have gone to Germany instead with a German officer she'd met in the labour camp.

Christian and I were absolutely terrified and we huddled together for comfort. Her tirade subsided for short periods and then Mudder would start ranting again. She looked so mad that at times when she came close to us screaming and shouting, we thought she'd pick us up and hurl us across the room.

After a long time she calmed down, went out and didn't come home for hours.

My mother had a beautiful singing voice. In the past we'd hear her sing from time to time. I loved listening to her singing and often wandered how someone who sang so beautifully could turn into a monster the next minute. I liked one song in particular. It was called La Paloma and she sang it in German. I didn't understand German at the time only Saxon, but as I got older I learned the words to the song. It was a love song. The words were all about love, longing and desire and the melody was hauntingly beautiful. At the time Christian and I were much too young to understand how Mudder must have felt and the pain she must have suffered. The love of her life had betrayed her. My father had deserted her. He'd left and forsaken her, in this terrible place to bring their children up on her own. He should have come home like most of the other men and faced his responsibilities and shared the hardship we were all going through.

I never ever heard Mudder sing again.

Every little thing became vexing to Mudder. She never talked to us apart from when she was giving us orders. The beatings intensified. We were rarely let out of the yard and she never took us anywhere in fear of being judged about the welts and the marks on our bodies.

Mudder often screams at me and tells me to get out of her sight. You look just like that deserter of a father of yours, she shouts and I don't want to be reminded of him. How she must hate me. There's never any kindness or affection shown to either of us by Mudder and we're not allowed to see anybody else. Christian and I just learn to depend on each other as much as we can.

We're so terrified of Mudder that we're very happy when she's not around and we're left on our own.

During the long cold winter months, with thick snow everywhere, Mudder lights the fire in the range and we have to put wood on during the day. The wood runs out most days long before Mudder gets home. Christian and I just sit huddled in a blanket and try to keep warm that way.

Mudder is on bad terms with all the neighbours. She's so embittered she refuses help from other people who try to be kind. If anybody says anything to her she tells them to mind their own business.

The bad tempered episodes are getting worse every day. Life is a big struggle and we never get enough to eat. She's renewed the willow wands several times. When they dry out they're not as effective and don't hurt as much.

We're both so frightened of Mudder that we don't function when she's around. I get very clumsy and do things badly and am always wondering when a blow will rain down on me. Both Christian and I shy away from Mudder like nervous little animals. She only has to look at me and I'm reduced to tears but try very hard to swallow my tears and my fear.

Crying really angers Mudder and makes things worse.

Chapter Four

The spring of 1949 is slowly coming and it's getting warmer. The deep winter snow is melting and the rivers and streams from the Carpathian Mountains are swelling more and more every day. The River Alt and all the streams coming down completely flood the village. The water comes almost to the top step of our verandah. I've never seen so much water and I'm sure we're all going to die. Mother can't go to work, and we have no food in the house. A neighbour comes in a small boat and brings us some polenta.

We're so hungry, it tastes good.

After a few days, the water recedes, and the village gets back to normal. A lot of the streets that have had water rushing down them now look like troughs.

Spring brings a lot of work on the land. Mother goes to work on the collective farm. She only works from 6 in the morning till 6 in the evening now. She works on the land with other people and drives a cart with horses. She brings the leather horsewhip home every evening and hangs it on a hook on the back of the door.

The horsewhip frightens both Christian and me.

We both know she will use it.

Our first taste of the horsewhip is when Mudder gets home from work one evening and we've been out in the lane playing with other kids. We'd started to sneak out for a little while every now and then when Mudder's at work. It's nice being with other children. We always go back to the yard well before Mudder comes home.

This particular evening we've lost track of time and are caught out.

Suddenly Mudder is just there, standing like a demon with the horsewhip in her hand. We don't have to be told to get in the yard. Christian and I both scamper through the street door with Mudder following close behind, screaming at us.

She's very good with the whip and controls it like a lion tamer. She can reach her target from quite a distance. We're both running down the yard, but the whip whistles through the air and the fine leather thong licks repeatedly round our bare legs and arms.

It burns like fire. The pain is excruciating.

I buckle at the knees and lay there in a heap. Christian doesn't get much further and collapses too. Mudder stands over us and tells us that's merely a taste. The next time she won't be as lenient.

The next moment a neighbour, who's heard our screams and Mudder's rage, storms into our yard, tears the horsewhip from her hand and threatens to turn the whip on her. Mudder's quite indignant and tells him to mind his own business. He warns her that if he ever hears her using the whip on us again, he will deal with her and then he leaves. After that episode, she only punishes us indoors.

Somebody gives Mudder a broody goose and 10 eggs. In the small shed at the back of the yard, we help make a nest of straw, where the goose will sit on the eggs until they're hatched.

Christian and I are very excited about having baby goslings. We peep into the shed every day to see if they've hatched. Then one day they arrive, one by one until all ten goslings are out. Oh, what joy and excitement. It's so nice to have these little things running around in the yard and we love watching them. They're covered in fluffy yellow down and every time we get too close to them, the mother goose hisses at us.

On one side of the village, a cold clear stream runs from the Carpathian Mountains. The stream splits into several arms and forms a delta just before it reaches the big River Alt. The Alt is a wide, deep fast flowing river, which has claimed many lives over the years.

During the long hot summer months, the local kids spend Sundays, splashing and enjoying the shallow waters. There are a few deeper pools that form in parts of the stream where children can learn to swim.

Willow trees and shrubs grow on the pebbly, grassy banks, where flocks of geese from the village compete with the kids for the open spaces and shallow waters.

In the spring, several canvas covered gypsy wagons settle near the stream outside the village. The gypsies wander round the streets, carrying large sacks on their backs, with wooden clothes pegs, wooden spoons and equipment to mend pots and pans. During the summer months they also make thousands of bricks from clay on the outskirts of the village. The villagers are wary of the gypsies. Given the opportunity, and not watching them closely, they'll steal anything they can get their hands on.

The women are dressed in bright, multicoloured billowing skirts down to their ankles. They're always barefoot. On the upper part of their bodies they wear equally colourful blouses with ample gathered sleeves and fronts. Their skin is dark and swarthy. The jet black hair is worn long with gold and silver coins platted into strands. Some of the women wear beautiful bright scarfs tied pirate fashion round their heads. The intense and shifty black eyes stare out of their artful and calculating faces. They wonder around like apparitions from another planet, knocking on people's doors, trying to sell them stuff or telling them their fortunes.

The men are clad in black and white and very mysterious looking. Their black breeches are tucked into knee length leather boots. Their white shirts are full and gathered round the neck and sleeves. Their appearance is that of pirates with evil dark looking faces and long bushy beards.

All the men wear small black hats that look more like bowler hats. They're so scary looking. Christian and I have never seen gypsies before we came to Kerz and we're very frightened of them.

Mother has told us that the gypsies carry naughty little kids away in their big sacks. She says if we're not good she'll give us to them. The thought of these dark and awful looking people taking us away is even worse than the beatings we regularly get from Mudder.

Spring turns into the hot unbearable long summer days.

It doesn't seem possible, but Mudder's worse than ever. She was never one to smile much. When with us, she's stoney faced and devoid of any emotion. She's so scary, we don't want to be around her.

Every Sunday, Christian and I wear the nice clothes that Mudder's friend made for us and go to church. We haven't been to church since Christmas Eve. Mudder never goes with us and she never visits family or friends anymore.

My brother and I are very happy to go on our own. Being with Mudder makes us too fearful. We think now that I'm nearly 6 and Christian is seven and a half, we're old enough to go to church on our own on a Sunday.

Mudder goes out all day too, but we don't know where she goes, and she never says. We don't see her until the evening.

After church in the morning, we latch onto other kids. Some kind villager always takes us home for something to eat midday. People are sympathetic to our plight and show us real kindness.

We spend the afternoon playing games with the other kids on the village green. Some of the time we walk to the River Alt and watch the flat wooden ferry going to and fro, carrying people and animals, horses and wagons across.

I can sit for hours watching the ferry. When no one wants to cross, the ferryman sits in his little wooden hut. When someone arrives the other side of the river they just shout, "Ferryman ahoy" and the whole process starts again. On Sundays, most people go for walks. A lot of courting couples find quiet little spots by the river and enjoy the simple pleasure of just chatting and being together. Parents are out with their children. Most of them go to the streams and watch the kids splashing and enjoying the water.

Christian and I tag along and join anybody who's there.

We must be home by a certain time. The church bells call people to the evening service and that's our cue. If we miss the toll of the bells and get home late, we're in big trouble.

More often than not, we arrive home before Mudder and must wait for her to come back.

Chapter Five

September arrives, children go back to school and Christian starts his first year. School starts at 7.30. The first year kids finish at 12.30. The morning is always very long on my own and I can't wait till my brother gets home.

Not long after Christian starts school, a Romanian couple with two boys and a girl move into our house. They have the smaller of the two rooms and we must walk through it to get to our room.

The little girl is my age and I now have a play mate and am very happy. One boy is the same age as Christian and the other one is a couple of years older.

The couple both work on the collective farm like Mudder. The little girl is looked after by an old granny who lives in the Romanian part of the village. Some days the woman comes home earlier, and I get to play with the little girl and bit by bit, I start learning Romanian.

A lot of Saxon kids don't learn it until they go to school, unless they have contact with Romanian children early on. In the time the family was living with us, I became fluent in their language. Romanian was the main language, spoken by Saxons and Hungarians alike.

Life for Christian and me remained miserable with lots of physical and emotional punishments.

When the Romanian family was around, Mudder was a little more lenient. She was always so nice to the couple and their children. These children could be very naughty, but their parents never hit them. They got up to all kinds of mischief. Mudder would kind of laugh and pretend it was all very funny.

I watched the interactions between this family. There was a lot of love and affection. These children were not the least bit afraid of their parents. I so much wanted things to be like that with us and Mudder, but it never happened.

There's an epidemic of chicken pox in the village. Christian, myself and the three Romanian kids all get it.

The Romanian woman stays at home and looks after us all. I'm really pleased that Mudder isn't with us all day.

I still wet the bed most nights and receive regular beatings for that. I've learned to swallow my cries, otherwise the punishment lasts longer.

The chicken pox spots are so itchy. We scratch until we're bloody, more so when we're asleep. The bedding gets stained. This infuriates Mudder and she hits us for that as well, but it's so hard not to scratch.

One evening in the autumn, Mudder puts us to bed earlier than usual. She throws a blanket over the cot, so we can't see out. We're told to go to sleep and leave the blanket where it is. If she catches us peeking, we'll taste the sting of the willow wand.

Christian and I lay very still. We can hear Mudder opening a window to the street. Seconds later we hear a man's voice in the room. Mudder and the man talk very quietly in Romanian. They chat and laugh. Our Romanian is limited and we don't understand much. We would love to peek out from behind the blanket but know that it's more than our life is worth and eventually fall asleep.

The following morning there's no sign of the man anywhere and the blanket covering our cot has been removed.

This happens more and more often. On Sunday when Christian and I go to church, the other children talk about Mudder having a Romanian boyfriend. Christian gets very upset and tells the kids not to lie. Mudder would never have a boyfriend, let alone a Romanian one. The Saxons and Romanians don't mix like that and anyway, we have a father so that can't be true.

One of Christian's little friends takes us to our house after church and points to the footprints on the whitewashed front wall of our house. There's no mistake, the footprints are as clear as anything going to one of the windows.

We know somebody's been climbing through the window in the evenings, but being kids and ignorant about such things, haven't made anything of it.

The boy says a young man has been seen on several occasions climbing up the wall and through the window. All the villagers are talking about it.

Christian sits on the bench in front of the house and looks miserable. I join him and wonder what all the fuss is about.

It's Christmas Eve. Christian and I are very excited. There's thick snow on the ground and we'll be going to church later to get our goodie bag.

It's getting dark early now. A bell rings outside. Mudder and the Romanian woman both go out onto the verandah and all five kids follow behind.

At the bottom of the wide stairs stands an old man with a long white beard, holding a small Christmas tree with lots of lit candles.

I can't believe it.

Father Christmas is bringing us our own tree.

The next moment, the old man's beard catches fire and his whole face is engulfed in flames. The women both scream. Mudder dashes into the house and comes running out with the bucket of drinking water. She rushes down the stairs and throws the whole bucket full of water over the old man. The tree has caught fire and is burning on the ground. The old man looks like a drowned rat, he turns and runs out the door, disappearing into the night.

As we all stand and watch, the flames consume our little Christmas Tree. I'm pretty upset.

It would have been so nice to have a Christmas tree in the house.

Christian and I go to church a little later, but Mudder doesn't go with us. After the service, all the young children walk round the altar. We all get a brown paper bag with a Christmas tree shaped biscuit, an apple and two walnuts

We walk home in the snow, very happy with our Christmas present.

That evening when the Romanian children's father comes home, his face is covered in very nasty sores.

His eldest son laughs at his father and says it was very funny when his beard had caught fire. His mother tells him to hush.

The father bravely tries to save the situation by telling us all that Father Christmas had caught him drinking with other men. This was not allowed on Christmas Eve, so Father Christmas had given him and the other men a good beating and that's why he had all the sores.

The story convinced me and the other little girl, but I don't know if my brother and the other Romanian boy believed it.

That evening, as a special Christmas gift, Mudder brought out the boxes with the doll and the train. We hadn't seen them or played with these beautiful toys for a year.

I was so happy to be holding my doll in my arms again. My joy and excitement was every bit as great as it had been the first time.

The Romanian children joined us for a while. The little Romanian girl couldn't take her eyes of my doll. I let her hold the doll for a while but watched like a doting mother and didn't quite trust her with my precious baby.

That evening before going to bed, the doll and train were put into their boxes once more and stored away.

Not very long after Christmas, the Romanian family move out of our house. I'm very sad to see them go. Having had them living in our house was a bit of a buffer against all the terrible treatment from Mudder.

As she was cleaning the room the Romanian family occupied, she found some bedbugs. The three kids had slept in one of Mudder's beds and their parents had brought their own. She dragged the mattress into the yard, poured paraffin all over it and set it on fire. She then did the same with the iron bed frame. She cleaned and scrubbed every surface and crack in the room. Mudder then checked out every crevice in our room too until she was satisfied there were no more bed lice.

One winter morning, not long after the Romanian family moved out, Christian and I were just about to leave the house to go to church. There was a knock on the door. Christian opens the door and a young woman stands there.

Mudder seems rather surprised by our visitor.

She greets her in a friendly fashion and invites her in.

The young woman is our father's sister, Anni. She gives both Christian and me a big hug. It's so long since I've had a hug from an adult and I shy away. Mudder never hugs or gives us any kind of affection. The only physical contact she has with us is when she holds onto our arm as she brings down the willow wand or horsewhip.

Annitante, which is what we call her, tells Mudder that she's come to take me back to my Grandparents. They've all been very worried about our well-being, especially mine. She tells Mudder that my Grandparents have had several letters, sent by Mudder's neighbours, asking them to do something, as there's a lot of concern about the safety and wellbeing of both Christian and me, but especially for me.

Mudder is enraged by these accusations and demands from Annitante the names of the people that have written to my Grandparents. Annitante won't say and a very heated argument follows.

Annitante calls me over and asks if she can take off my dress and stockings. I don't know what's going on and why I need to undress. Mudder tells her to stop. She says Annitante has no right to question how she raises her children.

My aunt pulls down my stockings and lifts my dress. She seems furious. She shouts at Mudder that she should be horse whipped and only a demented person could inflict such terrible punishment on a child.

"She's only six years old for God's sake. What crime could she have committed to deserve the kind of beatings that leave such marks?"

Both Christian and I are terrified and crying. Mudder will throw my aunt out and we'll be left behind. To my surprise, she goes and gets a small cloth, puts my few belongings on it and ties it into a bundle before throwing it at my aunt.

"You take her," she yells at my aunt. "I'm sick of looking at her and constantly being reminded of her father. Take her, I don't ever want to see her again."

Christian stands there looking devastated. "Can I go too?" He whimpers. She tells him to shut up and he's staying where he is. Christian face crumples up and he starts to cry. Suddenly, I think of my beautiful doll and ask to take her with me. Mudder tells me the doll stays where it is, and I too start to cry.

Annitante puts on my lovely coat from England and my warm ankle boots. I embrace Christian and tell him we'll come back for him. He looks utterly dejected and miserable and is in floods of tears.

Annitante hugs my brother and then we leave.

I'm completely bewildered by what's happened. I'm grief stricken by having left my brother behind. I cry all the way through the village, not seeing anything or anybody on the way to the train stop.

It's still winter and the snow is thick on the ground. We go into the wooden hut at the train stop. Annitante buys our tickets. We sit on a wooden bench and wait a long time for the train.

Annitante has managed to calm me down and I've stopped crying. She tells me how much Groysie, Grandad and Tummy are looking forward to seeing me again after nearly two years.

When the train arrives, Annitante helps me climb up the steps into the carriage.

I sit by the window crying. I think of my poor brother and feel very unhappy. I tell Annitante what a monster Mudder is. I tell her about all the beatings we've had and how she frightens and terrifies us.

Annitante holds me closely and promises me that nobody will beat me anymore. They all love me and will look after me.

"But what about Christian?" I ask.

"We'll see," she says.

The trip takes a while. Kerz is only about 50km from Hermannstadt. Every few kilometres, the train stops at a small village, but eventually we get there.

Outside the big railway station in Hermannstadt, horse drawn coaches are lined up along the pavement. We stop at the first coach, Annitante chats to the driver and then we get into the coach. The interior is plush with padded seats. I've never been in anything so fancy.

It's late afternoon and getting dark.

The horses pull away from the pavement and we're off. There are lamps on the end of very long poles along the road, lighting up the whole street. I've never seen anything like it. When we were taken back to mother two years ago, it was during the day and I hadn't noticed these poles with the lamps.

I ask Annitante who lights all these lights every evening and that it must take a long time. She tells me that somebody at the electricity station just turns a switch and all the street lights in the city come on. She says they're called electric lights. I think it's all wonderful, but strange. All the big windows in the big houses and buildings are brightly lit.

I then ask Annitante if all the lights in the houses and buildings are lit by the same person who turns the street lights on.

My aunt finds that funny and laughs. She says, in the houses and the buildings, every room has a switch on the wall. People working or living there can switch the lights on and off when they want. I look at my aunt in wonderment and disbelief and tell her I've never heard of such a thing.

The driver stops outside a single storey building. It has no front garden and is built right next to the pavement. Annitante pays the driver and we go through big wooden double doors into a large oblong courtyard. Single storey buildings go all around the courtyard with doors at regular intervals.

Annitante knocks on one of the doors and an older lady opens it.

Annitante tells me this is Mitzitante, my mother's second cousin. We're going to sleep here for the night and then travel to Stolzenburg the next day where my grandparents still live.

Mitzitante is very nice. I like her a lot. She has a deep voice and smokes a lot. I tell her I thought only men smoked. The only women I'd ever seen smoking were gypsies.

She roars with laughter and finds it very amusing. She says she's definitely not a gypsy, but she does like smoking.

Annitante and Mitzitante sit and chat for a while. My aunt explains why I'm here with her and what's been going on with my mother in Kerz.

Mitzitante is shocked.

Mitzitante tells my aunt that the last time she saw me, I was three months old. My father was home on leave from the army. At that time my parents had been a very happy young couple with two lovely children. She would never have believed that my mother could have turned into the monster my aunt had described.

Mitzitante had never married and lived in this three roomed flat with her sister Grete, who was a little younger than her and unmarried.

Mitzitante is a tailoress and does beautiful embroidery. She has wealthy communist clients and earns a pretty good living.

Grete works at the town hall for the communist government as a secretary and has a lot of good connections. I learn all this when I'm quite a bit older and visit them often.

Mitzitante prepares a meal for the three of us. The food is so good, and I eat a lot. Mizitante remarks on where such a skinny little thing puts so much food.

Annitante tells her that she was shocked to see how malnourished both Christian and I were when she saw us.

After dinner, Mitzitante gives me a lovely red apple. It's been months since I've had a piece of fruit, apart from the apple at Christmas from the church. I savour every bite. She has a cigarette and I think that's really strange.

It's been such an extraordinary day. I can't believe what's happened. One moment I'm so happy, then I think of my brother and feel very sad.

That night I have a single bed all to myself. It's a proper grown up bed, not a cot and I like it very much. Sleep doesn't come for a long time. All kinds of conflicting, worrying thoughts, race through my mind. I'm also worried about going to sleep in case I wet the bed, which I still do quite a lot.

I'm totally exhausted and finally fall asleep. I have terrible nightmares. Annitante is kneeling by the bed hugging and stroking me as she wakes me from my horrors. I tell her I have these terrible dreams all the time and Christian usually cuddles me. Annitante stays with me until I fall asleep.

When I wake up in the morning I'm lying in a wet bed. I'm mortified. I feel so ashamed and utterly bad. Mudder always shouts horrible names at me when she beats me after wetting the bed.

What's going to happen now? Will Annitante or Mitzitante give me a good thrashing?

I don't know what to do and just lie there with my eyes shut. Eventually Annitante walks over to my bed. She speaks to me quietly. I open my eyes and burst into tears. She asks me why I'm crying.

I can't talk. My whole body is shaking. "What is the matter Uta? Tell me what's wrong, are you hurt?"

Between sobs I blurt out "I've... wet... the... bed."

"Oh dear," she says. "Don't cry, we'll sort it out."

"Am... I... going... to... get... a... beating?" I ask through further sobs.

"Of course not," Annitante says, "Whatever makes you think that?"

I'm crying even harder now, with relief I think. I tell Annitante as I'm trying to control my sobs and heaving chest, that Mudder whipped me with the willow wand every time I wet the bed.

My other aunt hears the conversation and comes over to the bed. "Just wait till I see your mother," she says. "I'll give her a good beating." This makes me smile and giggle a bit.

After a delicious breakfast of bread and jam and a glass of warm milk, Annitante thanks Mitzitante for her kind hospitality. Mitzitante gives me a big warm hug and kisses my cheeks. I give her the biggest hug I can muster up and kiss her back. She tells me to come back soon for another visit, as she presses an apple into my hand.

"For the journey," she says.

Annitante tells me the horse drawn coach ride was a special treat last night. Now we'll take the tram to the other end of the city where the road leads to Stolzenburg. She hopes we'll get a ride in a wagon with somebody going that way.

A lot of people were waiting at the edge of the city to get rides to different villages.

After a long wait, we finally got a ride on the back of a horse drawn wagon. It was full with potatoes. The driver threw an old blanket over some of the load and Annitante and I sat on top.

The ride seemed very long. When we got to Stolzenburg, our bottoms were numb, and we were frozen stiff.

We drove past the house, where we'd lived in a small corner of a room, which Granddad had partitioned off. Things had been so hard, and we'd been so poor, but life had been nowhere near as bad as our lives with Mudder in Kerz.

All the memories came flooding back. I couldn't wait to see my grandparents and Tummy. I asked Annitante where we were going. She told me that my Grandparents had moved.

The man dropped us at the end of the street where my Grandparents' house was. I thought they must have moved back to their own house.

Annitante told me that they'd moved into a tiny little one roomed house on the edge of the village, where the Romanian people lived.

We walked through a narrow dirt lane with houses either side and then turned onto a dirt track. We followed a creek, with bushes and trees along the edge. On the right side of the track there were a few tiny houses with small fenced in gardens. There was still a lot of snow on the ground and everything looked very pretty.

The dirt track went up to a small open area and on the other side stood two tiny houses also with fenced in gardens. Quite a steep hill rose to the right, where quite a few more small shack like houses were dotted about.

Annitante led me to the little shack on the left, right next to the creek. A wooden gate in a rickety fence led into a small garden, now covered in snow.

As we approached the little house, the door flew open and Groysie stood there with wide open arms.

I ran to her and threw myself into her big loving embrace. I wrapped my arms around her neck and didn't ever want to let go again. We both cried, and she hugged me very tightly and held me in her arms for a long time.

The little house was warm and welcoming. There was only the one room and it was very small. A wood burning stove stood in one corner. There were two small windows. One faced the front to the dirt track and the other was on the side facing the garden. The windows were bare, no nets or shutters adorning them.

The rickety old table from the other place stood under the window with three wooden chairs. Two rough wooden framed beds with straw mattresses were standing either side of the table along the walls.

In the back corner of the room stood a high wooden stool with an enamelled bowl on the top. Next to that was an enamel bucket for drinking water.

The back of the door had hooks, where some very shabby clothes hung. By the wood stove, were two shelves on the wall where Groysie kept her two pots, tin plates and mugs. One of the pots had a few forks, knives and spoons sticking out the top.

Nothing had changed since we'd gone back to Mudder, but I was so happy to be back. Groysie was still the same, still wearing the same clothes. The dark gathered long skirt with an apron tied round her waist. The white shirt gathered at the neck and around the cuff and her old boots Michael, her son, had made for her before the war.

Groysie wore her greying hair plaited and coiled into a bun at the nape of her neck. She was the most precious thing in the world and I loved her so, so much.

I asked where Granddad and Tummy were.

Tummy is somewhere outside Groysie says. He'd made a sledge and taken it up the hill to try it out. He'll soon be back she says.

No sooner had Groysie spoken and the door opened and there stood Tummy. He was sixteen now and had grown very tall and thin but was still the same old Tummy.

He stood in the doorway. His nose was grazed, and bleeding and his lips were also bleeding and very swollen. He was obviously embarrassed.

"You look like you've been ploughing the ground with your face," Groysie says.

He said the sledge wasn't very good and he ended up in the creek, scraping his face on the stones. We all laugh at the thought of him in the creek and he laughs too. I'm so pleased to see him and give him a big hug.

Groysie tells me that Granddad works in a factory in Hermannstadt as a labourer. He has no other skills outside of farming. He'd become very depressed and disheartened working at the collective farm and watching the mess being made by the people in charge, who knew nothing about farming.

Groysie says Granddad has managed to get an old bike and comes home every Saturday evening and returns to Hermannstadt on Sunday evening. Everybody works six days a week and has one day off. Granddad is renting a room with a family he's met at church there.

Granddad is trying to find a place in the city, so we can move there and all live together. He's about sixty now and the 20km bike ride is especially hard in the winter, when there's lots of snow and the roads are bad.

Annitante stays the night, she shares the bed with Groysie and I sleep head to toe with Tummy in the other bed.

The next morning, Annitante goes back to Hermannstadt where she works as a domestic help for a family with four children.

The man of the house has a very important job in the communist party and they live in a big villa, where Annitante has her own room.

Annitante tells me that there are two bathrooms and two toilets in the villa. They have electric lights not paraffin lamps like us. The kitchen is big with lots of cupboards, a gas range, constant running hot and cold water and a refrigerator. Annitante says she never sweeps the floor but uses a machine to suck all the dirt and dust up.

Annitante must explain to me what all these things are, as I've never seen such things.

It all sounds fantastic.

The most incredible thing though is, each of the 4 children has their own room and each room is bigger than the room in this little house. The floors in the kitchen, bathrooms, hallway and stairs are all pale coloured marble, Annitante says. There are beautiful oriental carpets on all the parquet floors throughout the house. The furniture in the house comes from all different parts of Europe and is beautiful.

I can't imagine such a house and ask Annitante if she'll take me there when we move to the city.

Now that Annitante's gone I get to sleep with Groysie every night, except on Saturday when Granddad's home.

I still have terrible night terrors. I scream and thrash about in my sleep, but Groysie is there now to cuddle and comfort me. She calms me down; reassures me and tells me everything will be all right. Over time the nightmares get less, but never stop all altogether. The bed wetting also gets less over time.

The following Saturday, Groysie tells me Granddad will get home later that day. I can hardly contain myself, because I want to see him so much.

Groysie says Granddad works from 6 in the morning till 3 o'clock and on Saturday he cycles home straight after work.

Groysie asks me if I'd like to walk to the other end of the village and wait for him. I'm so excited. I'm hopping and skipping alongside Groysie, chatting nonstop. I must be making up for the last two years. Mudder hated idle talk and Christian and I had to be very quiet around her.

We walk all the way through the village past the ruins of the fortress on the hill. Then we pass the house where we lived before Christian and I went back to Mudder. I talk and think about my brother a lot. I get upset and feel very sad that he isn't with us.

Groysie and I stop on the edge of the village and wait for Granddad. It's not long before I see a figure on a bike in the distance. As he gets closer I can see that it's Granddad and I start jumping up and down with joy, shouting his name.

He gets off his bike, leans it against a tree. I run to him and he lifts me up in his arms and hugs me tightly. He tells me I've grown a lot, but I am as light as a feather. Groysie says it's because I'm just skin and bones. I look at his beloved face and tell him he still looks the same. His eyes are still as blue and sparkling as ever and his moustache tickled me when he kissed me, which I always liked.

Granddad lifts me onto the bike saddle and pushes me for a while, holding the back of the saddle with one hand the handle bar with the other. I've never been on a bike and am enjoying the ride.

After a while I want to get off and walk between them holding both their hands, whilst Granddad pushes the bike with his free hand.

I'm so happy that I'm with the two people I love most in the whole world.

That evening Granddad, Groysie, Tummy and I sit down to a potato stew and polenta. It's poor man's fare, but I can eat my fill and that feels so good.

Later when I get undressed to go to bed, Granddad is shocked by how skinny I am and all the sores and bruises on my body, which have begun to fade a little and don't look half as bad as when I first arrived, almost a week ago.

He's absolutely furious and says he can't grasp how a mother could subject her children to such cruelty.

The next morning, we all go to church. The room that Granddad partitioned off for us to live in when we were kicked out of our house, is now one big room again. Everybody in the congregation is pleased to see me and I'm pleased to see them all.

After church we go home for our midday meal of vegetable soup and polenta. Tummy plays Ludo with me, while Grandad and Groysie rest on their bed for a while. Later in the afternoon Groysie and I walk through the village with Granddad. He gets on his bike and rides away and I wave until he disappears into the distance.

During the rest of the winter, Groysie's at home until the land work begins. Tummy works at the collective farm.

He helps to feed the animals, clean stables and styes and milk the cows. During the day Groysie and I sometimes go and visit her sister or Granddad's sister or brother. They all have grown up children, so there's never anybody to play with. I'm happy though just sitting and listening to the grown-ups.

Groysie has a goat. Her name is Lisi. In the winter Lisi is shut in a small shed in the garden. We feed her hay and root vegetables. She's having kids soon and so we don't get milk from her. Our diet in the winter consists of root vegetables, potatoes, dried beans and polenta.

It's so good to be able to eat enough and not have to go hungry all the time.

Chapter Six

I always look forward to Saturdays when Granddad is coming home. I love it when we are all together. After our midday meal, I nag Groysie all afternoon to go and meet Granddad. When she eventually tells me I can go, I practically run all the way to the other end of the village.

She lets me go on my own most of the time.

The people who live in the city have ration cards for bread, milk and oil and other essential foods like flour, rice and margarine. Having ration cards doesn't guarantee you get the food you're entitled to. The rations are just enough to keep starvation at bay. Granddad gets rations, but only for himself as we don't live in the city with him.

The village Konsum (general store) doesn't sell any food items at all or clothes. It only sells a few essential household items and paraffin for our lamps.

The villagers get their food rations of vegetables and maize meal from the collective farm. Groysie doesn't even get oil - all our food is cooked in water.

When Granddad comes home on Saturday, he picks his black bread ration of 200 grams up for Sunday and shares it with us all. I look forward to that small piece of bread so much. Granddad always saves me two or three small pieces of bread from the week, which is rock hard by the time he comes home. I don't care though and enjoy nibbling at the hard bread. It lasts and takes longer to eat. I always look forward to my weekend treat.

One very cold and blustery winter afternoon, Groysie has to go and fetch our vegetables from the collective farm. My winter coat is getting very small for me and my boots pinch my toes.

I don't want to go with her.

Groysie gets her box of photographs down from a shelf on the wall and says I can look at them while she's away and that she won't be long. I look at all the old pictures of people and faces that have become familiar over my short life, but only through photographs.

I haven't met most of them. The pictures are of my uncles and aunt, mother and father.

When I look at the face of my mother, an unbelievable fear grips me. I can't bear her looking at me from the photo. Groysie has a short pencil which she keeps on a shelf. I'm not allowed to use it. Groysie says it's hard to get pencils and she must look after it.

I go and get the pencil and systematically scribble out my mother's face from every photograph, until it's beyond recognition. I feel safe again. Where the evil face was, there's just a black blob.

When Groysie comes home and sees what I've done, she sits next to me and asks why I've done that. I told her that I had to do it and that now Mudder couldn't look at me anymore and hurt me. Groysie said that Mudder couldn't hurt me from a photo, but I told her that it hurt every time I looked at her.

"Oh, my child," Groysie said, (which is what she often called me when not calling me by my name). "She won't hurt you while you're with us."

Groysie embraced me and hugged me for a long time. It felt good and safe to be in her arms.

Lisi the goat had two kids in March.

The snow was melting fast and everything was beginning to get green.

We still didn't have any milk as the two kids drank it all.

After the long winter months being shut up in her little hut, Lisi loved being out and enjoyed the new growth on the bushes along the creek and the spring grass.

Groysie and I took Lisi out on a long rope every day, so she could eat her fill. I loved watching the two kids romping and cavorting with each other, then around their mother and us. I often joined in the play and chased them around. They were so sure footed, agile and nimble and a joy to watch. They were my two new playmates and it was good to have them around.

Unfortunately, when they were about 10 weeks old, a man from the collective farm came and took them away. I was very upset and so was Lisi. She cried and looked for her babies for a long time.

I assumed the kids had been given to other people who needed goats.

The day after the kids were taken away, I overheard Groysie tell Tummy to fetch our share of the meat from the kids from the collective farm.

I asked Groysie what she meant. She sat me down and explained how things worked. We were only allowed to have the one goat and Lisi belonged to the collective farm.

When she had babies the collective farm took them and killed them for meat.

I was so upset and just sat there with tears running down my face. Why were people so mean I asked Groysie? She said that was the way of life and animals had to be killed for meat.

We got enough meat for 2 meals and the rest was kept by the collective farm. When Groysie made a goat stew I refused to eat any of it.

After the kids had gone we now had the milk from the goat, which made life a little easier.

Lisi went out to pasture with all the other goats from the village. Groysie and I got up early in the morning and walked Lisi to the main road where we waited for the shepherd boy to come by collecting the goats.

Groysie and I picked Lisi up before sunset at the main road. For the first few days Lisi ran home in front of us and waited at the garden gate. When Groysie let her in, she'd frantically run around the garden, look in the hut and bleat pitifully for her babies.

I felt so sorry for poor Lisi. Groysie said she'd forget about her babies soon and then she'd be okay.

That didn't make me feel any better.

Spring turned into summer.

It was much easier for Granddad to ride his bike home every Saturday. Life in general was better in the summer.

There were no other children in the neighbourhood I could play with. There was no one Groysie could leave me with and so I went to the fields with her and Tummy every day.

In the evenings, Groysie and Tummy dug the earth over in our small vegetable garden and planted potatoes and vegetables, which helped to subsidise our rations.

Most evenings we all went to bed early. Most exhausted were Groysie and Tummy who were worn out from the physical toil and the heat of the unrelenting sun.

There were no books to read before bedtime, so Groysie was happy to tell me a bible story.

Occasionally Groysie and I walked across a big meadow to the hills where a fresh spring came out. We'd collect water in a can and Groysie soaked dried beans in this water overnight. She said this water was softer than that from the well and the beans were better cooked in this water.

One evening I told Groysie I'd go and fetch the water on my own as she was busy in the garden.

As I was getting closer to the hills, where the spring cascaded down and formed into a pool, I saw a big dog drinking at the water's edge.

I thought nothing of it and kept on walking.

Suddenly a lot of shouting and hollering went on behind me. I stopped and turned round. A man was running towards me in the distance waving his arms and shouting in Romanian. He was shouting and telling me to stop and not go any further.

When he caught up with me all out of breath and panting, he said the animal at the spring was a wolf. We weren't very far from the spring.

The man picks up stones and hurls them at the wolf. He's a big creature. He turns and snarls and shows his vicious teeth.

The man throws a few more stones until one of them hits the wolf, who yelps, takes one long leap into the shrubbery above the spring and disappears.

The man walks to the spring with me. I fill my can with water, then start walking home. The Romanian guy insists on accompanying me.

He tells Groysie about the near miss with the wolf and says she should never let me go there by myself. After the man has gone Groysie, tells me that wolves can and have killed young children in the past and if they're desperate enough, they will even attack adults.

Wolves can often be heard howling in the evening and nighttime. Groysie says the wolves come right into the village at night and kill dogs, cats or other small animals they can find.

That scares me, and I never venture out on my own when it starts to get dark and stay close to the house.

Every evening, long before it gets dark, I walk along the dirt track by the creek to the main street to meet Lisi, coming home from the pasture.

Along the track there's all kinds of distractions for a young child.

I slide down the bank of the creek and mess about in the shallow water. The coolness of the water feels good on my bare feet. I throw sticks and leaves from nearby bushes into the creek and watch them float away. I imagine they're little boats drifting down a river.

Groysie has told me that my father lives in England, which is an island and to get there one must go on a big ship across the sea. I don't really understand what she means but think it's fascinating.

The grassy bank is covered in all sorts of wild flowers and is home to all kinds of insects and tiny bugs, which can amuse me for ages.

But after a while, I remember that I have to meet our goat and tear myself away from the coolness of the stream and the fun I'm having. The track is very dusty and the dirt sticks to my wet feet.

I'm not bothered by this.

I run barefoot all summer and have to have my feet washed every evening.

I skip along the track humming and singing. Finally, I turn the corner into the very narrow lane running between two houses, which leads to the main road where I will wait for Lisi.

I've only gone a few paces into the lane, when one of our neighbour's buffalo turns the corner at the other end and charges down towards me.

A huge panic engulfs me and I'm momentarily frozen to the spot… but not for long.

I turn and run back along the track by the creek. I'm absolutely terrified and can hear the huge black snorting beast closing in on me. It will trample me to death and Groysie will find me here, flattened and dead on the track, like a bug that's been squashed underfoot.

As my little legs carry me as fast as they can, I stub my toes on jutting out stones, stumble and fall headlong on the side of the track.

Almost immediately, the black monster thunders past me and disappears in the distance. I can't believe I'm still alive and not trampled to death.

I try to get up, but my legs are shaking like jelly. My chest is heaving, and tears start to run down my dusty, dirty face. I finally manage to sit up. Both my knees are grazed and bleeding. One of my big toes is also bleeding from where I stubbed it on the stone.

I'm alive though, yet still can't stop crying and feel very sorry for myself.

Eventually I pick myself up and start to slowly walk home, having forgotten all about Lisi. All I want is to get back to my Groysie.

When I walk into our little shack, I'm a sobbing blubbering wreck. Groysie looks at me worried and asks what's happened. Why am I bleeding and covered in dirt? She can't understand a single word I'm trying to say through my heaving sobs. She sits me on her lap, cuddles me and tries to calm me down.

After a while, when I've regained my composure, I tell her how the buffalo chased me.

Groysie hugs me tightly and smiles warmly at me. Her embrace is always so calming and such a comfort to me.

Then she tells me that the buffalo was not chasing me. It has a calf at home, which is too young to go out to pasture with the herd and the poor creature was running like a demented thing to get back to its child.

If it ever happens again, Groysie says, just stand aside and it will run right by you. She says buffalo are very gentle, docile creatures and normally amble along quite slowly.

I give Groysie a huge hug and stay on her lap a while longer and think how lucky I am to have her.

Chapter Seven

One day Groysie says we're going to visit our neighbour who is sick. She's an old Romanian woman who lives on her own with her three pigs in a tiny one roomed shack, even smaller than ours.

I've never been in the neighbour's place, but have often passed by her on the dirt track along the creek. She seems a grumpy old thing and walks very slowly, all bent over and propping herself up with a wooden stick.

Whenever I see her, I always greet her in Romanian. Groysie says I must always respect people older than myself and wish them a good day. The most I ever get in return from her is a mutter or a grunt.

She's very poor and wears dirty, tattered old clothes. Her full, ragged old skirt hangs down to her ankles.

On several occasions when I've passed her by, she's stopped on the dirt path, grabbed her skirt at the front and pulled it away from her body. A stream of pee would gush down between her legs, hit the dusty track and splash all over her bare feet. When she finished, she'd just walk on without any regard for anybody having seen her. It reminded me of cows and oxen. When they were pulling a cart and needed to pee, they'd just stop dead in their tracks and open the floodgates.

When I told Groysie about the old woman, she said she is an uneducated, simple old peasant and doesn't know any different. She tells me she has no children or family, and no one ever visits her, so round we go with a jug of vegetable soup and a wedge of cold polenta.

Groysie knocks on the door and we go in. A terrible stench assaults my nostrils. It's very dark in the room. The only tiny window is shuttered and lets hardly any light in.

Three pigs come squealing over to us. They're very friendly and it seems like they're greeting us. I like pigs and give them all a pat on the back.

It takes a while for my eyes to adjust to the dark. Then I see the old woman lying in one corner of the room in her tattered clothes on a bed of straw on the floor. She's half covered with an equally ragged old sheep skin.

The stench in the room is horrendous. I pinch my nostrils shut with finger and thumb and tell Groysie I want to go because I can't breathe.

Groysie tells me not to be silly, the smell won't kill me and to have a little patience and stand by the door and wait.

The old woman calls the pigs. They all go over to her and lie down just like dogs.

The room is bare, with just a small rickety table and an old wooden chair standing in one corner.

A small wood burning stove stands against the wall. A bucket of water and an enamelled tin bowl holding a few bits of tin crockery stand on the floor next to the stove.

The hard-packed earth floor is covered in faeces, displaying various degrees of decomposition. It must be the pigs and the old woman's.

Even the pig sties I've been in as a child never smelt this bad as they were cleaned out regularly.

I can't believe how anybody can live in such a filthy state. Groysie always says that water doesn't cost anything, no matter how poor one is.

Groysie sets the jug of soup and polenta on the table and goes over to the old woman and chats to her in Romanian.

I'm not listening to the conversations. I'm pacing up and down in front of the door, almost suffocating with the stench and whining to Groysie that I want to go home, or I will puke.

Groysie tells the old woman that we'll come back the next day and then we leave.

I refuse to go in to see the old woman again. I sit outside and wait while Groysie takes in food and makes sure the old woman is all right.

I'm standing on the corner of the lane and main street waiting for Lisi to come home with the goat herd. I've been standing there for ages and I'm getting a little worried. I don't like being out on my own when it gets dark. There's no electricity in the village, so it's pitch black at night. The deserted track by the creek is very scary and I know the wolves come into the village at night.

Groysie returns before its completely dark. She wonders why I'm not home yet. We wait a while longer before Groysie says we'll walk home before its completely dark, so we can see a little along the dirt track.

Lisi knows her way home says Groysie, she'll be all right.

It's Friday night and I'm excited about Granddad coming home tomorrow evening. I chatter nonstop to Groysie and she just humours me. I tell her how

I wait at the other end of the village and the minute I see Granddad appear in the distance, I run to him. He always puts me on the crossbar and we ride through the village and home together.

Tummy is at home waiting impatiently. He wants to know why we're so late. He says he nearly came looking for us.

The three of us sit down to our evening meal of vegetable or potato soup or stew with polenta.

Suddenly, a terrible commotion erupts outside. The neighbourhood dogs are barking like crazy.

Tummy jumps up from the table and hurries outside. Groysie and I follow behind. Tummy is running towards the gate, which was left open so that Lisi could come in.

Groysie and I are just behind Tummy. He's already halfway across the little green going to the creek. The moon is rising and casting eerie shadows.

Just as Tummy reaches the bank of the creek, the outstretched leaping silhouette of a wolf passes right in front of him and disappears into the night.

There's a bit of a rise in the land in front of our shack and the bank dips down into the creek.

Tummy stands on the edge of the rise looking down into the creek. As he slides down the bank, Groysie and I get there and follow him down to the water.

It's not until then that we realise that Lisi is lying in a pool of milky red water with her throat ripped open and her udder torn.

We just stand there, in shock, looking at this gruesome scene. Neighbours run out of their homes, wondering what all the noise is about.

I'm clinging onto Groysie's hand, tears are streaming down my face. If only we'd waited for Lisi I say to Groysie between sobs, the wolf wouldn't have got her and she'd still be alive.

Groysie puts her arms around me and hugs me. We were all very fond of Lisi. She was more than just our source of milk, she was a loved and dear pet.

A neighbour helps Tummy carry the goat from the creek into our garden. They put her in her little shed and close the door. It's too late to dig a hole and bury Lisi. She stays in the shed overnight. Her eyes are wide open. Goats have strange eyes, they have long pupils that look weird and now they really look scary and frightening.

We all feel very sad. Groysie tells me that somebody gave her a cup of sugar and she was going to make sweet cornbread the next day. Now she couldn't do it as there was no milk. We would also have to go back to drinking peppermint or linden blossom tea in the mornings.

Late Saturday afternoon I walk to the other end of the village to wait for Granddad. I'm usually very happy and skipping along. Today I'm very sad thinking about poor old Lisi. Even the small piece of black bread Granddad offers me, doesn't make me happy.

Granddad wheels his bike, as I walk beside him holding his hand. I can't stop crying as I tell him about what happened to Lisi the night before.

He's sad about Lisi, but says he's glad I wasn't with the goat, because the wolf could have attacked me instead.

When we got home, Granddad got a spade and with Tummy's help they started digging a hole behind the house. I stood and watched in silence as the hole got deeper and deeper.

Granddad says it's not just to bury the goat but also to catch the wolf. He takes Lisi's shed door off its hinges and balances the door over a rod across the middle of the hole. It fits the hole perfectly with just a tiny gap all around. Before nightfall he gets the dead goat and lays it across the middle of the door.

He says the wolf will smell the goat and come back to get it. If the wolf steps either end on the door, it will tip. The wolf will fall in the hole and the door will come back up and trap him. Then he will kill the wolf.

The following morning, we find the hole empty and part of the goat's remains dragged into the field behind the house. It didn't work. The wolf managed to drag the goat's carcass off the door without being trapped. He had a good feed and left the remains behind. Granddad is cross, but says wolves are clever creatures.

Groysie says that the goat is dead, and nothing will bring it back. Killing the wolf didn't serve any purpose as it only did what it had to do to survive.

I love the summer. The days are long and hot. I run around barefoot in just my underpants. Groysie says it saves on clothes and shoes. I only have my winter boots father sent, which are now much too small for me.

Saturday evenings when Granddad is home, he always reads long passages from the bible after the meal and says long prayers. Groysie also says payers, but hers are much shorter.

I prefer Groysie telling me bible stories, rather than listen to Granddad's reading. She's very good and tells them in a simple way that I can understand.

On Sunday morning we all go to the Baptist meeting hall. I have to sit still for long periods and I find it very boring.

One Saturday in the summer, Granddad says he has good news. He's found a place in the city where we can all live together. He tells Groysie he's already been working on the place to get it ready, but there's still quite a bit of work to do.

I ask Granddad if it's one of those big houses I've seen with electric lights and switches on the wall.

He tells me it's only a tiny little hut that was owned by a family before the war. They used it during the summer months to spend the occasional night when they came out from the city. It's right on the outskirts of the town with lots of fields and woods around.

There are no electric lights, indoor toilet or running water in the place. It's built from slats of wood and mud and he's doing his best to make it cosy for us all.

The important thing is, we will all be together and he won't have to be on his bike during all those bad winter days.

I'm quite disappointed. I thought everybody in the city had electric lights, indoor toilets and water coming out of taps.

One day Groysie tells me that I'm seven years old now and will start school in September. I don't know when my birthday is, all I know that every summer I'm a year older.

I tell Groysie I don't want to go to school unless she goes with me. Groysie laughs and thinks that's funny. She tells me all children must go to school to learn to read and write. Adults have already been to school and don't need to go any more.

I need clothes and shoes for school. My beautiful coat from England is now too small. The sleeves are halfway up my arms and the buttons don't do up any more. The hem only reaches halfway down my thighs. The lovely warm boots are so small I can't even get my feet in any more.

Groysie exchanges my boots for some homespun cloth with a woman in the village. The coarse cloth is made into a coat by a villager, which reaches almost down to my ankles. It's very big on me. I tell Groysie I don't like the coat. It's dark, drab and very ugly, not at all like my beautiful coat father sent.

Groysie tells me I should be thankful to have a coat at all. It was made big, so it would last longer.

Annitante brings a piece of very dull fabric home one weekend which is made into a dress for me. The dress is horrible too and completely drowns me.

Granddad's sister can make shoes of sorts. She makes me a pair of shoes from white goatskin with black patches. Groysie says beggars can't be choosers, which doesn't make sense to me. Even the shoes are too big and feel like boats. That's not bad enough, they're hairy as well. Looking back, I must have looked more like a kid being sent to work in a circus rather than going to school.

I tell Groysie I won't wear the shoes, I'd sooner go barefoot. Just wait and see, when the snow comes you'll be pleased to have any shoes. She says she wished she could buy me nice clothes, but they just haven't got the money.

Annitante has knitted me woollen stockings that reach up to my thighs. Thin elastic bands hold the stockings up above my knees. They're so rough and make my legs itch. The elastic bands are tight and cut into my legs. I take the bands off and end up with the stockings around my calves and ankles. What a sight I must be.

Groysie walks to school with me on the first day. It's early September and still warm, and here I am all bundled up in my winter gear, as this is all I have.

The school house is in the church yard next to the Lutheran Church. We don't go to this church. Granddad says the people in this church are not true believers.

So why am I going to their school I ask Groysie. She tells me it's the only German school in the village. But I don't speak German I tell her. You'll soon learn she says. Why can't I go to a Saxon school I want to know. Because there are no Saxon schools.

Groysie explains to me that the common language of all Saxons is German. Saxon is just a dialect of the German language and practically every village has its own dialect. I find it all rather odd and confusing.

When we get to the school, there are quite a few other boys and girls my age, clinging onto an adult's hand for dear life.

We're all ushered into a big room with funny slanted little tables that have small benches attached to them. Groysie tells me they're the school desks and I will sit at one of them next to another child.

A big table and chair stand in front of all the school desks with a big blackboard on the wall behind.

I have never been in a class room and don't know what to make of it all. The woman who showed us into the room now stands behind the big table. She asks the parents to seat the children at one of the desks. She speaks in Saxon.

I sit next to a little boy who looks frightened and near to tears and every bit as bewildered as I feel.

The woman tells us her name, which I don't remember and tells us she's our teacher. She asks all the adults to stand at the back of the class.

I don't know any of the other children. We all turn around to make sure our parents are still there.

The teacher tells us that for the first week she will speak Saxon to us, but then she will start to talk and teach us in German only.

She also tells us that school is 6 days a week. The first week we'll be there from 8 in the morning until 12 o'clock. After that school will start at 7.30 and finish at 12.30. As I can't tell the time yet, Groysie says that's after breakfast until the midday meal.

The teacher then tells the parents to go and come back at 12 o'clock. As parents leave, pandemonium breaks out. Kids are screaming, crying and making for the door. I stand there bewildered, tears welling up and overflowing.

The teacher stands in front of the door, so no one can escape. She calmly tells the children to sit down and calm down and then just stands and waits. I look around me at all the sad and crumpled up faces, tears and snot running down most them. I pick up the hem of my dress, wipe the tears off my face and then do as the teacher asks.

Apart from the occasional sob, the crying stops and the kids calm down. The teacher sits at the big table. She opens a big book and starts reading a story to us. Every so often she turns the book to the class and shows us pictures related to the story. It's the first time I've heard a story other than from the bible and seen such wonderful pictures. It's the story of Red Riding Hood and I'm absolutely mesmerised, but also a little frightened and completely forget about Groysie for a while.

During that first morning there were a few mishaps. The boy next to me pooped in his pants and several kids peed where they sat. The boy next to me was taken to the outhouse, but still stank to high heaven when he came back.

I was glad to see Groysie at twelve and proudly told her I had neither peed or pooped my pants like some of the kids.

I only went to the village school for a couple of weeks and had learned just a few German words when we moved to Hermannstadt.

Chapter Eight

Granddad came home as usual on Saturday. On Sunday morning an oxen drawn wagon came to our little house. It was full of fresh hay. Groysie had emptied the old hay, which had been in the bags that served as mattresses for the past year and was now filling them with wonderful smelling fresh hay to take to Hermannstadt.

When she was finished, and the wagon was empty, Granddad, Tummy and the driver of the wagon loaded our few meagre belongings. The rickety old table and four wooden chairs, the wooden bed frames, the wood stove and the few household items. The only other set of clothes that we each owned were folded and packed into a cloth bag by Groysie.

Granddad's bike went on the wagon and lastly the hay filled bags for our beds, on which Groysie, Tummy and I sat. Granddad sat on the wooden seat at the front with the driver. And so our journey and adventure began. The trip took forever. The oxen ambled along at a very slow and sedate pace. Groysie says we're in no hurry and have all day. Eventually we reach the outskirts of Hermannstadt. Granddad tells us we must drive all the way through the city to reach the other side where our new home is.

I'm very happy about that, as I get to see all the beautiful big houses and villas. Some of them are just massive with fancy wrought iron fencing all around and enormous big double wrought iron doors. Wide paved or tiled drives lead through landscaped gardens to big impressive front doors.

I wonder what these houses are like inside, I can't even begin to imagine. I just wish we could live in such a place.

We're now driving through streets with fewer houses and a lot of empty spaces between them.

Granddad says this is a new and undeveloped part of the city. The war came, and building stopped and that's why there are so few houses.

All the city streets are asphalt or paved with cobble stones. Here however, the roads and sidewalks are just packed earth.

We're right on the edge of town and I can see mountains in the distance.

The wagon pulls up outside a two storey red brick built house, which has not been rendered or painted.

Granddad takes Groysie and me to meet Frau Friedsam who lives there. She takes us into a large kitchen on the ground floor and offers us all a glass of water.

I wonder why we're here and ask Frau Friedsam where we're going to live. She takes me by the hand and leads me to a big window overlooking a large garden.

At the end of the garden is a wooden fence and the other side of the fence stands a tiny shack with a small window facing our way.

See that little house Frau Friedsam says, that's where you're going to live. I think how nice it would be if we could live in a house like this, but I don't say anything.

Frau Friedsam gives me a biscuit with fancy edges on it. I've never had anything like it and don't know what it is. She tells me I will like it, all children like biscuits. I take a little bite and it tastes so good. I nibble like a little mouse on the remainder, so it will last longer.

On the way out through the hall, I see 3 more doors leading to other rooms and a wide staircase going up to the next floor. I know Granddad has a room in this house and I wonder which room it is.

Groysie and I then go out and follow Granddad through Frau Friedsam's garden to the fence, which has a wooden gate in it. We go through the gate and stand outside the little shack.

Granddad says it's wonderful compared to what it was before. He's mended lots of holes in the walls, put glass in the tiny windows and then whitewashed the walls inside and out, so it looked fresh.

Granddad says we could never afford the rent in one of the big houses. This little place would be cosy and warm during the winter and in the summer, we had the garden where we could plant vegetables.

The little house is at the bottom of a hill. The garden slopes upwards with a grassy area at the top, where trees grow. There are no fences at the side or top of the garden.

We have no neighbours either side.

The house and land belongs to the state, the same as all properties and land in the whole of Romania. All the big houses that I've seen are occupied by many families. Usually a couple of rooms per family and they all pay rent to the state.

Granddad says at least we don't have to share our little home with anybody else.

The door to the house faces the hill and further along the wall there's a very small window.

The inside is tiny, and the ceiling is very low. Granddad had to bend his head to get through the door, but he can stand up inside. He tells Tummy, who's already taller than him not to grow any more or his head would touch the ceiling.

There's just about enough room for our few bits of furniture. Granddad puts one of the beds we've brought with us, which is not very wide, in the far corner along the wall. The other bed which is about the same size, he places across the back wall with the end touching the side of the other bed. It fits in very snugly. Tummy will sleep there, and I will share the other bed with Annitante who will now live with us.

Flush to the end of our bed is our small square table and right up against the table is a small wardrobe Granddad has acquired. On the other wall opposite the table is a small open shelving unit and a wooden bench next to that.

Granddad has also acquired an old iron bed with sagging springs and an old mattress. He's placed that in the corner opposite the entrance door. He and Groysie will share this bed. Right next to the bed along the wall on the right as you go into the house is a small kitchen dresser which Granddad has made. The pots, crockery and food will be stored there. Next to that is our bucket of drinking water

On the left of the door going in is a small table with an enamelled wash bowl.

There's no room along the wall for the wood stove. So, Granddad has placed it in the centre of the room with the smoke pipes going through the ceiling and out of the roof. He says having the stove in the middle of the room will warm the house better.

When Granddad first started work on the hut, the floor was packed earth. Over the months he's been collecting bits of planks and has managed to lay a wooden floor, which looks like patchwork and is very rough. Groysie has a couple of homespun runners which will make the room warmer and cosier.

We have a hanging paraffin lamp over the table and a smaller one hanging on the wall at the other end near Granddad and Groysie's bed.

Outside, a few yards from the house is a well, which is filled with rocks and stones to the very top. We get our water from the Friedsam family's well next door. Granddad says in the spring he will get all the rocks and stones out of the well, clean it out and then we'll have our own water.

Granddad has built a small wooden outhouse, which he's set over a big hole he's dug in the far corner of the garden, away from the house.

Groysie says everything will work out fine now that we're altogether. We are now all entitled to food rations, which will make life a little easier.

Groysie is up at 5 o'clock every morning. She must light the wood stove and boil the water for our herbal tea. Breakfast consists of herbal tea, a piece of cold polenta or a piece of black bread. I'm very happy that I don't have to have polenta every morning. The black bread is such a treat even though we seldom have margarine or anything else to spread onto it.

It's my first day at school in Hermannstadt. Groysie has given me a wash and has taken extra care to comb my long hair, which has never been cut. It's very long and reaches right down to my bottom and I always wear it in two plaits, which Groysie braids for me every morning.

School starts at 7.30 am Groysie and I leave the house at 7 o'clock. It will take about 20 minutes to walk there. It's a cool autumn morning and I'm wearing my new dress, coat and shoes. I've refused to wear the elastic garters to hold up my stockings as they hurt. Groysie says she'll look for wider elastic and make me new ones. My thick, coarse, itchy stockings are crumpled up below my knees and ankles all the time and I'm forever pulling them up. My dress is very long though, which hides them somewhat.

When we get to school, Groysie takes me into the grade one classroom and leaves me with the teacher. Groysie hung my coat outside the classroom, where a lot of other coats were hanging on pegs along the wall.

All the other children in the class look at me as though I'm some kind of alien from another planet. They whisper, giggle and point at me. I feel so bad I want to run out of the classroom and go home.

The children are all dressed very differently from me. All the girls have pretty dresses on that only reach their knees. They all wear nice shoes and fine stockings that stay up and not fall around their ankles. I feel like a freak and know all the kids are making fun of me.

The teacher leads me to the last row of desks in the class and points to a place next to a boy. She lifts the lid of the desk and I assume she wants me to put my satchel inside. I sit down without having understood anything the teacher said. She speaks only German.

When the teacher gives instructions I just watch the boy next to me and copy what he does.

During the break I follow the other children outside and watch them play. There's one group of 3 or 4 girls who come over to me and taunt me. They say things in a nasty way to me. They point at my clothes, make horrible faces at me and laugh.

I don't understand what they're saying, but I know they're being horrible. I just stand there, determined not to cry. This happens during every break. There's no teacher around to stop it.

At 12.30 the bell rings for the end of school. The children gather their things and rush out the classroom. The teacher comes over and speaks to me. I look at her vacantly and shrug.

When I get outside Groysie is waiting for me. I'm so pleased to see her.

There are quite a few mothers there picking up their kids. These young women are all very elegantly dressed, the way city people dress and my Groysie stands there in her long drab clothes, looking like somebody from an era long gone. That's how people in villages dress, it hasn't changed in centuries.

The other kids gawp at us. I take Groysie's hand and pull her along. I just want to get away from there and all the prying eyes.

When I think nobody else can see me I start to cry. I tell Groysie what a horrible day I've had and how some of the kids are very spiteful. I tell her how they made fun of my clothes and pulled my pigtails. I said I wish I had nice clothes like the other children, maybe then they would not be nasty to me.

Groysie says once I learn German it will all be better and I'll make some friends. I feel very sad and tell her I don't want to go back to school.

When we get home, Groysie says Frau Friedsam will take us to visit another family who live in her street. They have a little girl too and hopefully we can play together. We have some soup Groysie made and then we go to see Frau Friedsam.

All three of us walk to Frau Hannich's house and I meet the little girl. Her name is Heide and she is the youngest of three children. Her sister Inge is 15 and Horst her brother is 13. They're hardly ever around, so I don't get to know them very well.

Heidi's mum and dad are very nice people. Over the years they're very kind to me and I spend a lot of time in their home.

They live in a very nice big house, which belonged to them before the war. Now the state owns it. They share the house with a Hungarian family of 5, Heide's paternal grandparents and her maiden aunt.

Food is very scarce. Everyone has rationing cards, but that's no guarantee to get the food one's entitled to. We must queue for everything and that eats up our time and becomes the focus of Groysie's and my life.

Granddad, Annitante and Tummy all work, so the queueing for foods is mostly left to Groysie and me.

After the first week at school I tell Groysie that I can go and come home from school on my own. The bullying from the other kids is ongoing every day. I just have to put up with it. Day by day I understand a little more German and soon I'll be able to talk back to the other kids and defend myself.

Milk is sold from small wooden huts in all parts of town at eight every morning, except Sundays, when all the shops are shut. The nearest milk hut is only a couple of streets from where we live.

The queues start forming at 5 every morning. There's never enough milk for everybody, so people queue early to have a better chance of getting some. Sometimes there's no milk at all and everybody has stood for hours and waited in vain.

We're a family of 5 and are allowed 500 mil of milk a day. The milk comes in big metal churns and is measured and poured into cans people bring with them.

Every morning my job is to get in the lineup for milk by 6 o'clock and stand till 7, when Groysie comes and continues standing and I go to school.

I have to be up by 5.30. Groysie gets me ready for school and gives me breakfast and then I go and keep her place in the milk line-up.

As for the rations for other food, bread, sugar, oil and maize meal, which are considered essential foods, can't be bought either when they are needed. The shops only have these provisions from time to time and then huge queues form and people stand for hours, hoping the food won't run out before it is their turn.

Things can get fraught in these big line-ups. Violence breaks out sometimes and people get stabbed and even killed. Everybody guards their space as if life depended on it and God help anybody who tries to push their way into a queue. If I queue with Groysie she looks out for me and sends me out of the line when it becomes dangerous. She always tells me if I'm on my own to get out and it doesn't matter if I lose my place.

Queuing for bread is another daily chore. If you miss one day or the bread runs out before your turn, you lose that day's ration.

On rare occasions the shops get other food stuff like rice, macaroni or margarine which can be bought without ration coupons. Each person is only allowed 500g of pasta or macaroni or 250g of margarine.

At times like this queues are enormous, and people get extremely aggressive. Fights always break out when ration free food is sold.

Meat was the rarest commodity sold, at most two or three times a year. Whilst being jostled, squashed and sometimes hurt whilst queuing, when your turn came, you didn't get to choose what meat you wanted. You were handed a brown paper bag with hopefully some meat and not all bones inside and you were glad to get that. People made use of every part of the animal, offal, ears, snouts, feet and anything else that was thrown in.

Sometimes Groysie and I went out just looking for food queues. When we found one, we'd just join the lineup. Very often no one knew what would be sold until the shop opened.

We also had ration cards for clothes and footwear. These goods were only sometimes in the shops and big queues would form. If you were lucky enough to get something, you didn't care what colour or size it was, it could always be altered or made into something else.

Toiletries were nonexistent. I never owned a toothbrush, toothpaste or nice soap. We only had washing soap for clothes, which was strong and smelled terrible. I'd never ever seen toilet paper. Granddad brought home newspapers he fished out of bins at work. Groysie cut them into squares and put them in the outhouse.

It was different if you belonged to the communist party or had connections with somebody who did. They had their own special shops, where everything was available.

None of these people had to queue for anything.

They had their own bakeries that baked beautiful bread. It was nothing like the black bread we got with all kinds of rubbish in it.

In the centre of the city there are a couple of delicatessen that sell wonderful looking cakes, ice cream and coffee. These places are always full of party members and army officers accompanied by their women dressed to the nines with bleached or dyed hair and made up like clowns.

The two big old hotels in town have good restaurants in them, which ordinary people can't even dream of going to. They're only frequented by the same people who belong or have connections and their families, or by special visitors from other communist countries.

Now that our family is living together, we all go to Baptist church every Sunday morning.

We walk to the tram near my school, ride into the upper city and then walk down to the lower part. The whole trip takes about an hour.

The church service is very long, and I get so bored, I don't know what to do with myself. I sit with Groysie and all the other women on wooden benches. The congregation is divided. The men sit on the right facing the pulpit and the women on the left.

When we get home, we have our midday meal of a vegetable soup or potato goulash, which Groysie has cooked the day before. Granddad is very strict and doesn't allow any kind of work to be done on Sunday. I'm not allowed to go and play with Heide either.

When I'm a little older and can make my way to church on my own, I have to go back to the meeting hall for Sunday School in the afternoon.

Granddad, Annitante and Tummy usually go to the evening service as well. Groysie and I stay at home, because it gets too late for me.

Heide's house is almost at the end of the street, with just a couple of other houses further along. Beyond there only fields, meadows, forests and hills stretch out to the mountains in the distance. There's a very big fenced in garden with grass and fruit trees. A wooden cabin with a verandah at the front, stands in the garden. A Saxon family with 12 children rent the place. They have an apartment in the city where they live.

The father is the conductor of the Hermannstadt Philharmonic Orchestra. He's rarely seen. The children's ages range from 20 down to 1 year old. The whole family spends a lot of time out here, especially during the spring, summer and autumn. The cabin has several bunk beds and can accommodate quite a few people.

Selma is the same age as me and one of the younger kids in the family. She's thin and lanky and has protruding front teeth. They refer to this place where they live, as their garden. Selma, her sister Ilse and one or two of her older brothers are in the garden more often than the rest of the family. Sometimes they bring one or two of the younger siblings with them.

I get to know them all that first autumn through Heide. They have a ball and we play all kinds of games in the meadows nearby. On other occasions we play hide and seek, which is always a lot of fun. They've all accepted me, and I like being part of this little group.

The boy I'm sitting next to at school also lives in the street and often plays with us all. His name is Ernst. He doesn't have much to do with me at school. Maybe he thinks if he does the kids will pick on him too.

Ernst is the youngest of four children. His father remained in Austria after the war and his mother struggles to bring up 4 children of school age. They also live in a hovel, not much bigger than ours, and are very poor. His mother is a tiny frail woman who cleans houses and does people's laundry. She's always very pleasant when I see her in the street, but always looks tired and downtrodden as though she's carrying the world on her shoulders.

A lot of the time I can't go out to play. There's always queues we must stand in, or I have to help Groysie in the garden.

Heide and the other kids in our little gang have much more time to play. They don't have to queue and help like me. They have parents and older siblings helping.

The family, with the 12 kids, has a much easier life. The father's job as the conductor affords them privileges the rest of us don't get.

I'm always nagging Groysie to let me go and play. She's soft and often gives in and tells me to go for a bit, but not to stay out long. When she says I can go, I get out so fast just in case she changes her mind.

Annitante's the hard one, when she's at home she always finds me something to do. She says I'm old enough to learn to knit and she'll start by teaching me to knit a pair of woollen stockings for myself.

It all looks very complicated to me. Groysie says I should be knitting a scarf which would be much easier. Annitante insists on a pair of stockings. She casts on the stitches and knits a couple of rows for me. I'm just knitting plain and eventually get the hang of it. I'm very pleased with myself when I see the stocking grow.

After school one day I decide to get on with my knitting. Groysie doesn't knit, so she can't help me.

When Annitante gets home from work, she looks at what I'm doing and gets cross with me. She says I've turned the knitting round and now I have several rows of pearl stitches, which will look like a band.

She takes the knitting away from me and is about to pull out the needles and undo my mistake. Groysie tells her to stop and that it doesn't matter, because no one will see the stocking under my long dress.

Annitante maintains that I should do the job right, but Groysie counters that and says that she expects far too much from a seven year old.

I carry on knitting. Annitante helps me with the heel and toes and then I knit the second stocking, getting help to finish that. I'm very proud of my achievement.

Chapter Nine

Granddad has found a job closer to home. He must apply for permission to move and gets it. He's working as a labourer in a very big engineering factory, which was privately owned before the war, but now belongs to the state. He only works the day shift, which starts at six in the morning, so he's home by four o'clock every day.

Annitante still works as a domestic help in the big villa and is usually home by six in the evening.

Tummy works as a carpenter's apprentice in a furniture factory, so he doesn't work shifts yet. We're all at home in the evening and have our meal together. Afterwards, Granddad always reads from the Bible and then discusses the passage with us all.

That done, we all kneel, and prayers begin.

Granddad always prays a long time. He always has so much to say to God. Groysie keeps her prayer short, as do Annitante and Tummy.

This ritual every evening takes forever, and I get very fidgety. I'm excused from saying prayers after the meal; I only have to say mine before going to bed.

Granddad says a prayer before and after every meal. They're short, just giving thanks for the food. It's only the evening prayers that go on endlessly.

Annitante is learning to play the mandolin and Tummy the guitar. They both sing in the Baptist church choir and want to play in the band as well.

Some days I walk home with Ernst from school. He can speak Saxon too, but he speaks the Hermannstadt dialect, which is somehow more refined than the Stolzenburg dialect. Over time I learn to speak this local dialect and can switch from one to the other. He says his mother has also spent five years in the Russian labour camps.

I ask him if she beats him along with his brothers and sister.

He looks at me as if I'm mad and tells me she never ever beats them.

Why should she, he asks me.

I tell him I don't know, but my mother beat me and my brother all the time and for nothing.

He says his mother is very kind and loves them all very much. After walking for a while not saying anything to each other, he tells me that his family will move to Austria one day.

I tell him my father's in England, but I don't ever want to go there and that I just want to stay with my Groysie.

School is in two shifts. One week it's in the morning, 7.30 to 13.20. The next week it's 13.30 to 19.30 in the evening. The school is small and can't accommodate all the classes.

As the nights are drawing in it's dark when we go home, so Ernst and I always walk home together.

We have to pass an old military cemetery. The cemetery walls have crumbled and never been repaired. All the graves and gravestones are overgrown with ivy, periwinkle, creepers and shrubs.

At night it's spooky. We both walk past very quietly and listen for any sounds coming from the cemetery. We always promise each other not to run. But it's never very long before one of us loses their nerve and bolts, with the other one following close behind.

When we're well past the cemetery and we think we're out of danger we have to stop, catch our breath and then we laugh like crazy until our bellies ache.

Groysie says we're silly. The cemetery is the same at night as in the day. She tells me that all we can hear are squirrels and other little animals making rustling noises in the undergrowth.

The days are getting shorter and colder and Christmas is not far away.

My German has improved immensely, and I have caught up with the rest of the class. We've mastered the whole ABC and are reading simple books.

I haven't made one friend at school. Nobody wants to play with me during break. I'm very much the outsider.

All the kids in my class have always lived in this neighbourhood. Their parents know each other and mix in the same social circles. They all belong to wealthy pre-war families, although they've all lost everything too. This was once a very well to do part of the city with huge houses and villas.

The city people all think themselves better than those from the villages and look down on them.

The boys in my class don't bother me at all, but most of the girls are nasty little creatures.

They call me peasant and gypsy and tell me my clothes are ugly and dirty. They say my Groysie is an old witch and that upsets me more than anything.

When I try to defend myself, they mimic, laugh and make fun of me. Some of the girls grab my pig tails and pull them or pinch and kick me. I try to keep out of their way.

One or two of the little girls also pick on Ernst because he's the other poor kid in the class. He's a lonely boy and tends to keep to himself. He says he wants to be my friend but not at school, as the other boys will call him a sissy if he's friendly with a girl.

One morning when I get to school, a bunch of girls from my class gather around me. They're all shouting, we know you're a gypsy, because only gypsies live in shacks.

I'm mortified and don't know what to say. I'm ashamed of where I live and have never told anybody. I think Ernst must have said something and, on the way, home I ask him about it. He says he hasn't told anybody anything. Then he says there's a path at the top of the hill above where I live, and people often walk along there. One of the kids must have seen me, he says.

One morning at school the teacher asks the class if they know what day it is. All the kids shout in unison St Nicholas.

One by one the teacher asks each child to stand up and tell the class what they got from St. Nicholas. Every child has received a little gift and sweets.

I've never heard of St. Nicholas and we certainly have never celebrated it in our family. When it's my turn, I stand up but don't say anything. One horrible little girl in the next row pipes up, why would he leave you anything, you're a gypsy.

The teacher rebukes the girl and I burst into tears, feeling sorry for myself.

That evening when Annitante comes home from work, she tells me to clean my shoes especially well this evening. St. Nicholas probably missed them because they weren't shiny enough.

I tell her my shoes will never be shiny because they're hairy.

She suggests I brush them well.

The following morning, lo and behold, there are a few sweets, wrapped in cellophane paper in one of my shoes. I'm absolutely delighted and can't wait to tell the kids at school that St Nicholas did leave me some sweets and I'm not a gypsy.

When I was quite a bit older and knew there was no St. Nicholas, Annitante told me what had happened.

Sabine, the youngest of the four children in the family she worked for, was in my class, though Annitante didn't know at the time. Sabine had come home from school that day and told her mother about the little girl in her class who hadn't got a present from St. Nicholas.

Her mother had asked Sabine the childs name and she's replied Renges, which was my surname.

Sabine's Mother knew straight away who I was.

She gave Annitante some sweets and told her to put them in my shoes that evening.

Chapter Ten

All the Christmases as a child were white with lots of snow. It was our first Christmas in the city. Granddad brought a small fir tree home a few days before. That year Christmas Eve was on a Sunday and we were all at home. We all went to church in the morning. In the afternoon Tummy and I made paper chains and decorated the tree. Annitante was given a few white candles and clip on candle holders by her employer and we put them on the tree too.

We didn't have any fancy glass ornaments like Heide had on her tree, but when we lit the candles before our evening meal, the tree looked very beautiful. It would have been really special had there been wrapped presents under our tree like under Heide's. I never ever received a present, be it Christmas, birthdays or any other time.

After we ate, we all went to the Christmas Eve Service at the Baptist meeting place.

The next day was Monday and Christmas Day, but everybody went to work, and kids went to school. Christmas and any other religious holiday was not celebrated by the communist regime. The school holidays, which was called winter holiday, started January first, which was a national holiday. It was 1951.

The winters were severe with mountains of snow. They lasted three to four months. Some mornings we'd wake up to a metre of snow, which was nearly halfway up our door. Granddad or Tummy cleared the snow from in front of the door, but didn't have time until much later in the day to clear the path through the neighbour's garden to the road.

I was usually the first to leave the house to go and stand in line for milk. The snow was often up to my waist and even higher at times, then I had to really struggle to get to the road. There, people had already walked, and it was much easier.

Standing for milk in those subzero temperatures that early in the morning was just horrible and by the time Groysie came at seven o'clock I couldn't feel my feet, they were like blocks of ice.

My shoes were not made to withstand the extreme cold and standing still for an hour didn't help. My clothes were equally unsuitable for the very cold weather and I used to get cold through and through. When I got to school and started thawing out, my feet were always very painful.

The queueing for all the other essentials continued daily. Groysie and I stood for hours sometimes. We'd walk on the spot and stamp our feet, but that didn't keep the freezing at bay. I often cried and Groysie then sent me home, but I knew she was just as cold and didn't like leaving her on her own.

During the winter months, the kids from the whole neighbourhood came with their wooden sleighs and rode them down the hill above and around our little shack. I didn't have a sledge and was happy to stay inside when I could. Another reason for not wanting to go out was that the kids from my class would see me come out of our house and then they'd give me a rough time.

We weren't the only ones who froze outside in the winter months. The mice and rats burrowed holes into our mud walls throughout the winter and came in every night looking for warmth and food.

Granddad was filling holes in the walls with stones almost on a daily basis, but those little creatures just kept on digging new ones. Granddad couldn't put poison down, it was much too dangerous, so he made several mouse traps and placed them under the beds. Every morning we woke up to several squashed mice in the traps. Granddad had placed a brick on the top of each trap, so there was no chance for the rodent to escape. The mice were such prolific breeders and they just kept on coming.

We had fewer rats, but they were sly and slippery and we couldn't catch any. Granddad said they were more dangerous than mice. They carried disease and could also bite.

One evening Granddad said the only way to rid ourselves of the rats was to kill them. We knew the hole where they came in, it was much bigger than a mouse hole. He made three wooden clubs to use as weapons.

The night of the rat hunt, Granddad left a few crumbs of polenta on a plate at the other end of the room from where the rat hole was. As soon as they heard the rat, Tummy jumped out of bed and plugged the hole with a round piece of wood. Groysie quickly lit both paraffin lamps. I woke up and wondered what the heck was going on. Annitante, Tummy and Granddad were all at the ready with their clubs.

They were standing on the floor shouting and making a noise with their clubs. Tummy said he'd seen two rats.

I was sitting on the top of the bed I shared with Annitante, knees pulled in tight, hoping the rats wouldn't run my way.

The rodents were terrified. They darted around like lightning, squealing with fear, changing direction in a split second. The adults were swinging and lashing out with their weapons, but these creatures were much too fast and jumping on everything, the beds, table and chairs.

Granddad said to just keep the attack up and keep them running, sooner or later they would tire and then they'd get them. The rats had so much energy, it took quite a while before they grew tired and slowed down. They were now being caught with a glancing blow here and there, until they were dragging themselves on the floor and then one of the adults went in for the kill.

I sat on the bed and felt quite sorry for these two creatures. It wasn't their fault being rats. In my childish way I thought they only wanted some food and warmth.

Granddad picked both rats up by their long tails and threw them out into the snow. The next morning crows were having a feast.

Every winter the mice and rats kept coming. The mouse traps were a fixture in our room and the rat hunts were ongoing.

We had precious little food as it was and couldn't afford to share it with the rodents. Groysie had to rethink where to keep the food, because they'd chewed their way through the wood in the back of the dresser and were getting into the maize meal and any other foodstuff.

Granddad brought home a metal box with a lid from work, so now all our food was kept in there and the mice and rats couldn't get to it. This did not deter them, they kept on coming all winter long.

One day I asked Heide if they had mice and rats in the house. She just looked at me as though I was crazy and said WHAT? I repeated my question. She went yuck, of course we don't. I was going to tell her that we had mice and rats, but I changed my mind. I felt very ashamed, as though it was my fault.

I asked Groysie why Heide didn't have rodents in her house. She said that their house was built with thick concrete and brick walls and that neither mice nor rats could chew their way through the walls. Our little shack was only built from bits of wood and clay and very easy for these creatures to burrow their way through.

I asked Ernst if they had mice and rats as they lived in a similar place to ours. He told me they did and said they were a big problem. He'd never told anybody else though and said I shouldn't either.

Queueing up for food all through the winter was very hard. We'd had so much snow. The tram lines were cleared of snow regularly, so the trams could keep running. This was the only transport in the city. The trams didn't go everywhere, so people had to do a lot of walking.

The sidewalks were cleared by the public and the banks of snow on the edge of the paths were so high that one couldn't see the other side of the street.

The streets were never cleared of snow. The few cars on the road, used only by communist bosses and military officers, where laid up for the winter. Instead they rode around in horse drawn sleighs.

During March the snow started to melt. Now we had to put up with mud almost up to our ankles. None of the roads where we lived were paved and nor were the sidewalks. Horse drawn carts churned up the road dreadfully and they became like a quagmire. The paths were not much better.

Every evening I had to scrape the mud off my shoes and spend a long time cleaning them. Groysie said it was important to have clean shoes, it said a lot about a person. I didn't ask for an explanation but thought having ugly clothes like I had also said a lot about me. Kids at school didn't want to know me and it was because I was different and didn't belong. So dirty shoes shouldn't make much difference. But Groysie made me clean them every night anyway.

The mud only lasted for a few weeks while the snow melted. The warmer weather dried the roads and pathways and baked them to a solid mass. Then we only had to contend with the never ending dust.

One Sunday that spring Groysie said I didn't have to go to Sunday school. Instead she was taking me to visit Mitzitante, whom I'd seen a little over a year ago when Annitante came and got me from my mother.

I was very excited to see this lovely old aunt again. We rode part way on the tram, then walked the rest of the way to her house.

Mitzitante was surprised, but very happy to see us. Her room was very big with lovely old furniture. There were upholstered sofas and chairs and they felt good to sit in. At one end of the room was a beautifully painted screen, which divided the living space from her bedroom. Behind the screen stood a double bed, a wide wardrobe and a dressing table. Her Singer sewing machine stood the other end of the room, next to a table and some shelving. The room was so big, our little place would have fitted at least four times into it.

There were beautiful hand embroidered garments, hanging on coat hangers on a rail. She told me they were silk and satin underclothes and night wear. Her clients were the new wealthy communists, who were the only people who could afford luxury clothes like these.

When I had visited with Annitante the first time, there had been a small room that served as a kitchen. The door to that room was now closed off as it had been taken away from her. The kitchen range, dresser, table and chairs were now standing along the wall as you walked in on the right.

At the end a double door led to another room, which belonged to her sister Grete, who became Gretchentane to me, but as yet we hadn't met.

I thought the place was very posh. Mitzitante had electric lights and several table lamps in her room. I'd never seen an electric table lamp. Her kitchen range burnt gas, which was just amazing to me. Mitzitante turned a tap on the front of the range and held a lit match to a burner and she had an instant flame which heated the top of the range. It was all quite magical.

There were three flush toilets in the courtyard, to one of which Mitzitante had a key and had to share with two or three of the other families. The courtyard was big and there were quite a few families living there. She also had to fetch her water from a tap in the yard, which she said was inconvenient as she wished she had it in her apartment. I thought she was very lucky to have all the things she had.

Everything in the room is very interesting to me and I'm wandering around looking at framed pictures and ornaments. Then I spot a funny looking black thing on a small table. I ask Mitzitante what it is. She tells me it's a telephone. I've never ever seen one. She tells me you can speak to anybody in the world on this telephone. I find that incredible and amazing.

She makes linden blossom tea for us all and gives me some bread and jam. Groysie and Mitzitante chat whilst I eat. I then look at a fashion magazine, which I find fascinating. I tell Mitzitante that in the pictures my father has sent to us, he looks just like the men in this book. Very elegant and smart.

Mitzitante says, my father always loved good clothes and dressed very elegantly and smartly and looked like the men in the magazine. He's a tailor after all she said and can make all these lovely clothes.

At the end of the visit Mitzitante tells me she's at home most of the time working and I'm to go and visit her as often as I'd like.

Chapter Eleven

I haven't seen Heide much during the winter months. I have been to her house a few times and played with her. I love going there. They have so much room and lots of nice things. Heide had scarlet fever and was ill for quite a long time.

Now that spring is here Selma's family come out most weekends to their garden. Quite often when Selma is at school in the morning, she comes out with a couple of her older siblings in the afternoon. It's good to have the little gang together again and we play in the surrounding fields and meadows.

Heide and Selma, never have to stand in line for food. They have parents and older siblings who do that. I know that Selma's family is more privileged than most, because her father is a communist party member. The food they bring out to their cabin is food that most people never see. She has salami, liver sausage and cheese in her sandwiches made from the nice bread I've seen a few other kids at school eat. They also bring out long sticks of bread, which I have never seen. They have all kinds of things that are never in the shops.

Heide and I often stand and watch them eat and wish we could have some, but they never offer us anything. I suppose with 12 kids to feed, they keep it all for themselves.

There's a deep wide gully which runs through the hills nearby to the main road that goes out to villages in the foothills of the Cibin Mountains. Dense thorn bushes grow in the gully. When the snow begins to melt the place is covered in snow drops. When the snow's completely gone and it gets a little warmer the gully is carpeted in violets and their wonderful perfume permeates the whole area.

This is one of our favourite places in spring. When Groysie lets me out for an hour or so, Heide and I wander off to the gully and lie among the violets and luxuriate in their wonderful scent. We always pick big bunches of violets and take them home.

Easter is a holiday we can always enjoy together as a family, as it is always on a Sunday. Groysie has managed to get 10 eggs and I help colour them in the water from boiled onion skins. The eggs end up a mottled golden brown and Groysie lets me rub them with a little oil to make them shiny.

Spring holiday from school is after Easter. Annitante tells me I have been invited to play with Sabine, the girl in my class where Annitante works. My aunt comes home at midday and takes me to the place where the Mansch family lives.

Sabine's Mother is a pretty, blonde, elegant looking lady. She was born and grew up in Germany.

The villa they live in is very big, much like all the other villas in this exclusive part of the city. They live in the whole villa. Sabine's father is an important man in one of the big factories in Hermannstadt. He's also a member of the communist party, which is required for a job like his.

Annitante has a key and she opens the doors. As I walk into the big marble hall, I'm speechless. There are several doors leading off the hall. A marble staircase winds up to the next floor and another one goes down from the hall.

Annitante and I walk down the staircase to a very big kitchen. Beautiful white cupboards are built along the walls. A huge kitchen range, fired by gas, stands along one wall. Another tall chest like thing stands along another wall. Annitante says that's a refrigerator, where the food is kept cool, so it won't go off.

There are taps on the walls from where they get the water. Under the taps are big square, porcelain bowls, which are filled with hot water from one of the taps and where Annitante washes the dishes. Wow! That is unbelievable. I've never seen anything like it. Then you just pull a plug out and all the water runs away. I think it's all quite magical.

Sabine and I are given a glass of milk and a piece of cake. I don't remember the last time I had a piece of cake. It must have been when I was about three and Granddad and Groysie still had their house and land.

I eat very slowly and savour every morsel. Sabine is impatient and wants to play, so leaves some of her cake. Annitante sees me looking at the leftovers on Sabine's plate and tells me I can eat it.

Sabine and I then go upstairs to the hallway and follow the next set of stairs up to the next floor. We go into a room which Sabine says is her room. To me it's like a fairy tale, beyond description.

The walls are pastel colours with flowers on them. I ask Sabine who painted all the flowers on the wall. Oh silly, she says, that's wall paper and the flowers are printed on. I don't want to look even sillier and ask if somebody stood there and printed them all on, so I keep quiet.

Her bed is covered in an equally soft coloured bedspread and when I sit on the edge it's lovely, soft and springy. She has a wardrobe all to herself, which holds only her pretty little dresses and coats. The furniture in the room is all painted white. A small table and chair stand along one wall, where Sabine says she does her homework. Above the table there are shelves with lots of brightly coloured books.

The windows are framed in lovely drapes. There are paintings on the walls and beautiful rugs on the parquet floor.

There's a big rocking horse in the centre of the room and a big box full of all kinds of toys I could not have dreamt of. Several dolls sit on her bed.

I don't know what to play with first, there's so many toys to choose from. I tell Sabine that I don't have any toys or dolls or books and that we live in a very small house that only has one room. I don't think she believes me and says she wants to come and see my house. I tell her that we wouldn't have anything to play with if she came to my house, but she says she still wants to see it.

When I need to go to the toilet, Sabine takes me into a room next door. I'm all agog. I've never seen an indoor toilet or bathroom in all my life. It must be so nice to live in a house like this.

Sabine tells me about her 2 brothers and sister, who are older than her and both have their own rooms too. It's all a bit too much for me to take in.

We both go downstairs again and into the garden. The villa stands in big grounds with lots of shrubs, trees and flower beds. A man is out there cutting the grass with a kind of thing he's pushing along, that's something else that's new to me.

Sabine takes me to a corner of the garden that has two swings and we play on them for a while.

Late in the afternoon, Annitante comes in the garden and tells me it's time to go home. I don't want to leave and wish I could live there.

On the way home, I ask Annitante how many rooms the villa has. She says there are 6 bedrooms and four bathrooms and another toilet on the same floor as the kitchen. There's the kitchen and dining room and a large living room and library. I'm adding up the rooms as she naming them. 10 rooms! That's unbelievable.

There's also a big cellar she tells me, where the washing is done in a kind of machine. It's beyond my childish comprehension that only six people live in this massive place. I tell Annitante that it isn't fair that some people have so much, and others have nothing. She agrees with me.

My aunt drops me off at home but tells Groysie she has to go back and work late, as the family is having a guest for dinner and she has to be there to serve and clear up afterwards. When Annitante works late, she eats her evening meal there. I ask her why she doesn't bring some of the nice food home for us. She tells me she's not allowed and if she were caught, she'd lose her job.

For days after, I go on about Sabine's toys and the grandeur of the villa, so much so that I think Groysie gets sick of hearing about it.

A few days later Sabine's mother brings her to our house. I'm glad she doesn't come inside as I feel ashamed of where I live.

When Frau Mansch has gone Sabine wants to go into our shack. I think she's quite fascinated to see how we live. There's no comfort or luxury here. I ask her not to tell the other children at school about where I live, because they would be even more horrible to me than they already are. She crosses her heart and promises faithfully she won't tell.

I take Sabine to see Heide. All three of us go to the gully and pick some wild flowers of which there are all sorts now. All the violets have finished blooming. We take the flowers back to Heide's house and give them to her mother. There's always lots to do at Heide's house. She has toys and we play.

Later in the afternoon Groysie and I walk Sabine home. I think she liked playing outside and meeting Heide. I hope she keeps her promise and doesn't tell those nasty girls at school about where I live.

Now that spring is here, there's a lot of work in the garden and I have to help. Then there's all the queueing up for food and my homework, so very little time is left for play. Groysie must get fed up with my nagging to be let out to play. The work is hard and endless, and I just want to be out and enjoying myself with the other kids.

Heide and Selma never have to go and queue for food or help around the house. They're considered too young to help and have older brothers and sisters, who do. All their time is their own and they can play to their hearts' content.

Granddad comes home with all kinds of stuff that he finds in the bins at work. He tells Groysie they chuck all sorts of useful things away. He brings home anything he might think he'll find useful. Bits of wood, pieces of corrugated metal, empty drums, bits of leather and string, rusty nails and screws and several other things. There's a whole array of stuff in a heap behind the shack.

Granddad's dug a big hole into the hill. Tummy's also brought some bigger pieces of wood home from work that were thrown away. He now uses Granddad's bike and straps the wood to it.

Granddad's managed to cover the hole he made with pieces of wood and some corrugated bits of tin. He's found a couple of strong thick posts to hold the roof up from inside and then piled thick earth on the roof to keep the heat out during the summer and the cold out in the winter. He's fashioned a door with bits of wood and this will be our cellar to keep potatoes and root vegetables in sand over the long winter months when it's impossible to buy anything in the shops.

Our garden is on the rising hill and when I help Groysie I can see the other kids play in the meadow below. I beg and plead with her to let me play just for a little while. When she does sometimes relent, she tells me to make sure I'm back before Annitante gets home, or we'll both be in trouble. Groysie is very kind and soft and has to answer to my aunt who is very strict and says I need to help. If it wasn't for her, I think I'd be allowed out much more. If at times I get too carried away with play and come home after my aunt, Groysie always comes down on my side and makes excuses for me. She tells Annitante to remember I'm not even eight years old yet and should have time for play. It's hard for Groysie, she just wants to keep the peace and not have to argue.

One day after school Groysie tells me I have to go to the villa where Annitante works. The monthly rent for the shack is due and my aunt has to go to the town hall and pay it, but she has forgotten to take the money with her.

I have a tiny woven straw purse on a long shoulder strap. The purse is open at the top with a toggle and loop holding the two halves together.

Groysie puts the money into my little bag and tells me to go straight to the villa and not dawdle on the way. She tells me Annitante must have the money and take it to the town hall before it shuts.

I start out with good intentions but after a while become distracted. I stop and investigate the lovely gardens of the villas on the way. I look at birds and listen to their songs. I watch squirrels chasing each other through the trees. I pick flowers on a grassy bank and walk along without any care swinging my little bag by the shoulder strap round and round in circles.

As I get closer to my destination I stop and just check my bag. To my utter horror there's nothing inside. Oh my, what am I going to do? I'm in a panic and start to cry. I turn around and retrace my steps. Groysie said it was the rent for the whole month. Would we get kicked out if we didn't pay it? I was so frightened I didn't know what to do. I walked back and forth, crying my eyes out and hardly being able to see through my tears as I'm looking for the money, which I never found.

My family worked so hard just to make ends meet and now I'd lost all this money. What to do now, carry on to the villa or go back home. I hadn't had any physical punishment since I left my mother. I was pretty sure this would earn me a good thrashing and I knew I deserved it.

I decide to carry on to the villa. I ring the front door bell and Frau Mansch answers the door. I ask for my aunt. Frau Mansch says Annitante couldn't wait any longer and has already gone to the town hall, with money she borrowed from her for the rent.

I walk home very slowly, delaying the trouble I will surely be in. When I get there, my Granddad's sister from the village is visiting.

Groysie looks at me and asks why I've been crying. It takes me forever to tell her that I've lost the money. I can see she's lost for words. "Oh, my child, what are we going to do Now?" She says.

I tell her it's OK, Frau Mansch has lent Annitante the money. But Utachen, we will have to pay it back to Frau Mansch. Groysie always calls me by my diminutive name or my child, even when she's upset or cross.

My great aunt is very kind. She tells Groysie that I shouldn't have been given that kind of responsibility at such a young age. Groysie admits that it hadn't been a very good idea to send me with all that money. She called me over and wiped my face with her apron as I'd started crying again and gave me a reassuring hug. We'll manage somehow, she said.

I was still worried. What would Annitante say. She would surely be very cross with me, which she was. Granddad said what was done was done and all the shouting in the world would not put it right. So, I got away without a hiding, which was more than what I deserved. In future I'd take more care if something was entrusted to me.

Chapter Twelve

My first school year is coming to an end. I can read, do simple sums and speak pretty good German. I'm still an outsider at school, most kids just ignore me. It's just a handful of girls in my class that make my life miserable, call me names and are generally mean to me.

Groysie tells me that I have to go to Kerz and spend the summer with my brother and mother. I haven't seen Christian for nearly one and a half years. I tell Groysie I don't want to go because I'm scared of my mother. She says maybe my mother has changed and she wants me to see my brother once a year so we don't become estranged. I told Groysie I'd do anything so that I wouldn't have to go to Kerz. I would work harder and not play with the other kids and I'd eat less. Groysie says the summer will go by very quickly and I'll be back in no time at all.

The morning I'm to go, Groysie packs my few bits into a small cloth bag. I only possess two sets of clothes. I wear my school clothes, which are the only good clothes I have, the other ones are tatty and worn.

Groysie has to wash my good clothes every other day and dry them overnight. This is another reason I get a lot of flak from some of the kids because I wear the same clothes all the time.

Groysie and I go by tram to the railway station, where she buys me a return ticket. She puts one half in my hand and tells me to show it to the conductor on the train and the other half she puts in the bottom of my bag and tells me not to lose it. I know I've learnt my lesson and will certainly carry the bag carefully and not swing it all over the place.

I'm very upset and cry when Groysie tells me she's not going with me. She says she would happily take me, but can't afford it. I ask her how will I know when I get to the stop in Kerz.

Groysie gets on the train with me and finds a woman who goes further than Kerz. She asks the woman if she'd be kind enough to make sure I get off in Kerz. The woman says she'd be very happy to help and will make sure I get off at the right stop.

Groysie tells me I'm nearly eight years old and a big girl and to stay with the woman who will look after me. I'm so upset and crying buckets already. I hug Groysie and don't want to let go. The whistle goes, and she has to leave the train.

I watch Groysie through floods of tears standing on the platform. I'm completely beside myself with anguish. The train slowly pulls away and she's gone.

The woman who's care I've been left in starts talking to me. I tell her through sobs why I'm going to Kerz and that I don't want to go, because my mother beats me all the time.

She tells me things are never as bad as one imagines. I don't say anything but know differently.

After numerous stops, we're finally in Kerz.

The woman helps me off the train as it's such a long way down to the ground. There's no raised platform here like at the station in the city.

As the train pulls away, I'm the only person who's got off. I stand and watch the train as it snakes along the track and disappears in the distance.

I stand near the empty track for ages. I feel totally forlorn and don't want to be here. I know I can't stand here forever and slowly start to walk along the dusty track towards the village.

There's been no contact between my mother and grandparents since Annitante came and got me. Nobody knows I'm coming. I'm worried and anxious about what my mother will say and do. I hope she'll say she doesn't want me and send me straight back to my grandparents. Then I think of Christian and am eager to see him again.

The dirt road goes through the Romanian part of the village first and eventually leads to the Saxon part.

It's a weekday and most of the villagers are working in the fields. It's quiet and very hot and the walk seems to take forever.

Occasionally a horse or oxen drawn cart trundles by and leaves a big cloud of dust behind. When I get to the Saxon part of the village, everything becomes more familiar. The lane where mother lives is right at the other end of the village. I turn into the lane which is completely deserted.

Very fearful, with my heart in my mouth and butterflies in my tummy I slowly walk on. All the dreadful memories are flooding back of the two horrendous years spent with my mother after she returned from the labour camps. The never ending beatings and emotional torture dished out by her, feel as if they happened yesterday. Her determination to break my happy and carefree nature and turn me into a shaking, quivering and frightened wreck are still so vivid in my mind.

Well, she certainly had succeeded. It had taken a lot of patience and hard work on my grandparents', aunt's and Tummy's part to regain my trust and for the happy and sunny disposition to return to me. Although my nightmares hadn't stopped.

I stood in front of the door to the yard, scared to open it and go in. When I picked up the courage and opened the door, there in the yard was Christian. He was playing with a very young toddler, still very wobbly on his legs. It was a little boy and he didn't have a stitch of clothing on.

I just stood and looked at them both. My brother just gawped at me and didn't say anything. He was barefoot and had a very old worn pair of shorts on. His head was completely shorn, and his lovely hair was all gone.

I asked who the little boy was. He told me it was his brother. But somehow that just didn't make sense to me. I told him he couldn't be his brother, because our father was in England.

Christian then said that mother had married again and had this little boy, so he was our brother.

Even at that age I was always full of questions. So, Christian told me that mother had married a Romanian man called Viorel and the baby was named after his father. He said I call him uncle and you have to call him uncle too.

I asked where mother and uncle were. He told me mother was working on the collective farm and uncle was in the army doing his national service. Christian had always been the quiet one and it was hard to get him to talk. I wanted to ask him all kinds of things, but he didn't want to talk. I almost felt as though he was angry with me. Maybe he was, for me going away and leaving him behind. He had changed so much. We used to be so close and now he didn't even want to talk to me. I felt very upset.

Christian just got on with some chores. He was only nine and a half and doing all kinds of things around the yard. I tried to play with little Viorel, but he gave me distrustful looks and toddled off behind my brother wherever he went.

It was hours before my mother came home from the fields, hot and tired, carrying a hoe over one shoulder and a wicker covered water bottle in her hand.

Her first words to me were, I heard from villagers that you were here. What's up, can't they feed you anymore?

There was no attempt on her part to give me a hug or a kiss and I just stood there, frightened and intimidated by her presence.

Haven't they taught you any manners and how to behave towards people, mother said. I could feel tears welling up in my eyes and my knees began to shake. I was determined not to cry and let her see how afraid I was.

Oh well, we'll have to see about teaching you some manners. I quickly said hello and said it was nice to see her. Oh, you can talk she said and I'm quite sure you're not pleased at all to see me.

By this time the baby had made his way over to mother and she picked him up. Mother hugged and kissed Viorel and made a big fuss of him.

The hurt went so deep seeing mother lavish such affections on her little boy. I'd always yearned for kindness, affection and love from her, but had never received it.

Things had changed in just a few hours. Being with Groysie I was happy and content. Now I was already becoming fearful, anxious and unsure of myself. I was already treading on egg shells, scared to offend or do something wrong and then having my mother's wrath rain down on me.

Mother didn't ask about my grandparent or school or anything else. She just wasn't interested. Christian just stood and watched without saying a word and then followed her into the house.

So here I was not even 8 years old and an outsider once again. All I wanted was to be part of the family and belong. I really missed my Groysie and wanted to be with her.

Mother worked on the land and was gone from early morning till the evening. Christian, me and the baby were left at home. We were given a lot of chores to do and were not allowed outside the yard.

There were a big flock of geese and chickens to be fed. We cooked potatoes in a large cauldron over an open fire in the yard to make the pig feed. They only had one pig, which was kept in a small pig sty in one corner at the back of the yard.

Christian got very impatient with me for not knowing how to do any of the jobs. I told him I wasn't used to doing these kind of jobs like him. That didn't make any difference, he shouted and bossed me around all the time, telling me I was useless and stupid.

What had happened to my brother? We'd always been so close and affectionate to one another. Everything had changed. He'd been indoctrinated by my mother and was treating me the same as she was.

When I tried talking about our Grandparents, he told me to shut up that he didn't want to know anything about them. He was still very angry with them for taking me away and not him.

When I was at my wits end, not knowing how to do things, I'd burst into tears. Christian never took pity on me, but derided, mocked me and threaten to hit me if I didn't do what he said.

I didn't know how I'd survive the long summer without a friend to stand by me and someone to talk to.

Every Saturday we have to sweep the whole yard and in front of the house, apart from all the other chores we have to do. We each take a bucket of water and drizzle it with our hands all across the ground, then it won't be too dusty when we sweep.

Christian fills the buckets from the well right to the top. It's much too heavy for me to carry and I just drag it along. The work is so hard, I ache all over.

Sunday morning, we only have to make the pig feed for the day, feed the geese, chickens and pig and then we can do what we want.

Mother dresses the baby and herself in their Sunday best and goes to her Romanian family for the day. We're just left for the day and told to be home by early evening.

When I'm finished with my chores, I wash my face, hands and feet and put my best clothes on and my boots. They're my winter ankle boots. They're not quite as big as they were when I first had them nearly a year ago. I don't have any socks or summer stockings, so I just wear the boots with bare feet.

Christian gets himself ready and I'm under the assumption that we'll go to church together. He tells me he doesn't want me tagging along behind him. He's meeting up with some other kids on the village green and I can do what the heck I like.

I feel very lonely, but at least I haven't got mother breathing down my neck. I walk to the Saxon church near the village green and hope I can find some girls there who'll play with me.

When I get to the church, people greet me and tell me it's good to see me. I remember some of the families and their children.

After the church service I decide to go and visit my mother's aunt. I know I'll get some food at midday there. The whole family is very pleased to see me and make a fuss of me. The old aunt immediately brings out some homemade bread, cuts a big slice and puts honey on it. Oh, it tastes so good.

The villagers get flour rations and have to bake their own bread, which is so much nicer than the black bread we get in the city.

The old aunt tells me that they haven't seen mother or Christian for a long time. She says since mother married the Romanian, she's cut herself off from her Saxon relatives and friends and has nothing to do with any of them.

I tell them that mother took baby Viorel and went to her mother-in-laws, and the rest of her Romanian family, for the day and we were left on our own. They all think it's terrible the way my mother has changed and how she treats Christian and me.

They ask about my Grandparents. I tell them we live in Hermannstadt now in a tiny little house, but we're altogether.

We all have our midday meal together. I ask for more bread and honey instead of the vegetable stew. Aunt is very happy to give it to me.

When I leave mid afternoon, the old aunt tells me not to tell mother where I've been. She would be cross and forbid me to visit again.

It's still a while before I have to be home. I walk down to the village green, where kids are playing tag and other games and I join in. I'm glad my brother's not there. I know he'd tell me to go away.

When I get back home I see some children playing in the lane. One little girl not much younger than me is playing with a naked doll. As I get closer I recognise it as my own doll.

Her beautiful clothes are gone. Her long hair is gone. It's sparse and matted. Her body and face are grimy and where one of her lovely blue eyes was is just a gaping hole.

With a big lump in my throat and near to tears, I go over and snatch the doll from the girl. She starts to shout and holler. I tell her it's mine, as I hold the bedraggled doll close to my chest.

The girl screams that it's her doll and tries to grab it from me, but I hold on tight. The next moment my mother is there, like an apparition from hell and yanks the doll from me and gives her back to the screaming child.

Completely distraught, with tears running down my face, I stammer, but it's my doll, look what they've done to her.

Mother grabs me by the arm and drags me into the yard and shuts the door.

She turns like a viper hissing at me. You're too old to play with dolls and besides, you'll have no time to play as there's plenty here for you to do.

It's the only toy I ever had, and you never let me play with her, I dare to tell my mother. I can see the anger rising in her and I'm afraid.

Don't you ever answer me back, she screams at me as she grabs the top of my arm and pulls me towards the cellar. She pushes me down the concrete steps to the cellar door and I end up in a heap at the bottom.

Still ranting and raving she opens the cellar door and drags me to the second door, pushes it open and literally throws me into the dark and musty inner cellar, then shuts and bolts the door.

I can hear the outer door shut and I'm left there. It's pitch black and I can't see a thing. I'm terrified. I shuffle backwards on my bottom until I can feel the damp wall behind me. I'm sobbing my heart out, mostly for the loss of my doll. How could she do that to me and be so cruel and give the only precious thing I'd ever had to another child?

I hadn't even been back a week and had already encountered and tasted my mother's insane rage towards me. I couldn't bear to think how

I'd survive the rest of the summer. I was soon distracted by noises. I knew mice lived in the cellar. I was used to having mice and rats around all winter in our little shack. They still made me nervous though. They were so quick and darted all over the place. One scurried across my outstretched legs. I tucked my knees up to my face and covered my legs with my dress. I kept moving my arms, shooing the little creatures away.

It was a long time before I heard the outer door open. The bolt on the inner door was pulled back and my mother the jailer stood there.

One more word about the doll and you'll spend the whole night down here after you've tasted the whip and had a good leathering, she said.

My tormentor was back with a vengeance. I had to tread carefully and watch my every step.

She would show no mercy.

We've had our evening meal, she said and you're going to bed without. I'd lost my hunger anyway and wasn't bothered about food. Certain parts of my body were sore, and I could already see the bruising on my arms and legs, where mother had grabbed me and thrown me down the stairs.

I was happiest when my mother wasn't around. I learned quickly and worked very hard. I tried to please and keep my mouth shut, but even that didn't always work. Mother always found something not to her liking and would punish me. She didn't have any willow wands any more, only horse whips and broom sticks.

When washing the dishes one evening after our meal on the porch, I spilled some water. Mother flew into a rage, called me a clumsy idiot who couldn't do anything right. She grabbed the broom and lashed me across the back with the handle.

Another day when she came home from work driving a cart and horses, she found me sitting round the back of the pig sty daydreaming.

So, this is what you do all day, she screamed at me as the blows rained down with the horsewhip. I'll teach you to be lazy, you good for nothing Satan's spawn.

Very rarely was it just a tongue lashing. The beatings were numerous and I'd started wetting the bed again. The vile language she used was painful to my ears. She swore a lot in Romanian. The Romanian language has the most diabolic, abusive and hateful swearwords imaginable and she knew them all.

I noticed that summer that Christian hardly got any physical punishment. She mostly just shouted at him. She saved all the beating for me. I resembled my father and she hated him with all her might.

Some days Christian had to go to work with mother and I was left on my own with Viorel, who was now used to me.

On days like that I was worried sick in case my little brother got hurt. I was left with him as long as 12 hours at a time.

Viorel was heavy and I had to lift him and carry him a lot. If something happened and he got hurt, I'm sure my mother would have beaten me to death.

The beatings I got were mostly for very small things. I didn't understand most of the time why mother hit me. If I wet the bed or came home a little later than she said on a Sunday, I expected to be thrashed.

Mother always dished me up with very small portions. I was always hungry. I became very thin again, and my body was full of sores.

On my Sundays off, when I spent my time at church and around other Saxon people, everybody was kind to me and gave me pitying looks. But none of them could do anything, or help me in any way, as that would have made things even worse for me.

In August after the wheat was harvested, Christian went to work with mother for many days. She had to plough her quota of the stubble in the fields.

All week long we went barefoot. We were only allowed to wear shoes on Sunday. My boots were too hot so I never wore them on Sunday either. The soles of my feet got so hard that I could walk on anything and not be bothered.

The fields were still being ploughed with old fashioned ploughs, pulled by horses or oxen. Christian had to lead the horses or oxen as they wouldn't keep walking on their own. Mother guided and pushed the plough deep into the earth behind.

The stubble in the fields was razor sharp and Christian's feet became very lacerated. I used to feel very sorry for him.

The next morning, he had to get up and do it all over again. His feet were in a terrible state. By the end of ploughing the fields, he could hardly walk, and his wounds became infected.

When I first arrived, I shared a small bed with Christian. Because I wet the bed, mother makes me sleep on a bare wooden chest with just a small blanket thrown over me. I sleep in the nude as I don't have any night wear. She says if we had a barn, she'd make me sleep there with the animals.

At church one Sunday a Saxon woman tells me that school will start in a couple of weeks and no doubt I'll be going back to Hermannstadt soon. Mother hasn't mentioned anything.

I've survived the summer and am over the moon to be going back to my grandparents. The following Sunday morning I get up and pack my few bits into the cloth bag. My return ticket is still at the bottom of the bag.

When I'm ready to go I stand there awkwardly, wanting to say goodbye and perhaps get a hug.

All mother says is 'well you'd better get going or you'll miss the train.' No goodbye, hug or kiss. She just stands and holds the door open for me.

Christian's gone already and we haven't said goodbye to each other. I don't care anymore, I'm just so pleased to be going and getting away from here.

I've no idea what time the train is due, but I run nearly all the way to the train stop. I have to wait quite a long time before the train arrives.

I'm struggling to get up the steps into the carriage. A man also getting on the train helps me. He tells me I shouldn't be travelling on my own, I'm much too young. I don't reply to that and just thank him for helping me.

I find an empty seat near the window on one of the wooden slatted benches. I sit down with a big sigh and relax for the first time in two months.

As the train starts to pull away and leaves the village stop behind, my anxieties, worries and fears are also left behind.

Back in Hermannstadt I get the tram back to the other side of the city. Groysie has also left a coin in my bag which pays my fare. I'm so happy to be back with my family in the city.

I tell Groysie that my mother has got married and has a little boy called Viorel, whom she loves a lot and is very affectionate towards. I tell her that I've had loads of beatings and mother doesn't love me at all. I tell my grandmother that I can count on regular daily beatings more than on meals I get.

Groysie says she had hoped that mother would have been nicer and kinder.

It's only a few days before school starts. Groysie and I go to the bookshop in town that supplies all the school stuff. The bookshop has a list of what's needed for each year.

It's such a struggle for my Grandparents to find the money for books, exercise books, pencils and all the other things I need. I also get a nib and a pot of ink. We start writing with ink in the second year. I'm quite excited about that. Groysie says she had hoped that mother would have helped a little. My mother didn't even send as much as an egg from her chickens when I left.

I'm quite pleased to be going back to school, even though I know those horrible girls will be there waiting to bully me and call me names. After the summer with my mother, I think I can take anything, as long as nobody beats me.

Annitante has a new job. She works in a clothing factory as a machinist. She only works eight hours a day now, six days a week, but three shifts. Most factories work three shifts round the clock. Her previous job had been much longer hours and much harder. Now she gets more time and is a lot happier.

Life soon gets back to normal. On Sundays it's church in the morning and Sunday school in the afternoon. Getting up at 5.30 during the week and queueing for milk. School one week in the morning and afternoon the next. The rest of the time lining up for other foods and helping Groysie.

We have a new teacher now that we're in class 2. She tells us that we're getting a new pupil in the class. It's a girl called Annemarie Grimme and she's physically handicapped and we're all to treat her nicely.

A little later in the morning the new girl arrives with her mother. She's very small and fragile looking. Her back and chest are hunched. Her head looks like it just sits on top of her torso without a neck. Her arms and legs are long and skinny. Her face is delicate with big blue eyes, high cheekbones and a pointed chin. Her hair is in two plaits, hanging down her back. She has the look of a gnome about her.

The new girl doesn't seem shy at all. She stands there beaming from ear to ear in front of the class.

All the kids sit in pairs at the desks, except Ernst and me. We both sit at separate desks at the back of the class. The teacher tells Annemarie to sit next to me and tells her my name is Renges.

No one ever calls me Uta, it's always Renges.

Being called by my surname and not my given name was something that upset me throughout my school years. It was another way to alienate me and reinforce the fact that I did not belong. Most of the kids in the class were called by their first names, by the teachers and the other kids. Ernst was another kid called by his surname Filtch.

I got to know Annemarie very well and we became best friends. The other kids and the teacher called her mostly Grimme, so she didn't belong to the elite either. I was happy to have a friend and we became inseparable.

Annemarie had a gentle and sweet nature. Over the following weeks I learned all about her.

At the age of one and a half, she'd fallen out of her pram and broken her spine. This caused her upper body to become hunched and deformed. She spent most of her early childhood in and out of hospitals. She was ten years old while the rest of the class was only eight. She'd missed the first few years of school, but her mother and her family had taught her to read and write. She said she loved reading and had a lot of books at home.

Annemarie lived with her mother. Her parents were divorced, but she saw her father a lot and they had a good relationship. Her grandparents and extended family lived in the same street, so her and her mother had always had a lot of support.

However, the fact that Annemarie had physical disabilities made no difference to the nasty little girls in our class. Annemarie and I were named the weird pair. I was the gypsy or the peasant and Annemarie the hunchback. These kids seemed to get a lot of pleasure from tormenting us both in the playground, by pulling our plaits, pinching, kicking and being spiteful in any shape or form.

Annemarie wore a special corset made from hard leather and steel to support her upper body. This of course could not be seen as it was worn under her clothes. The first time I saw her corset, It reminded me of the armour knights wore in medieval times. It covered her upper body from the neck down to her waist.

Being two years older, Annemarie was able to defend herself verbally very well and always came out on top. However, when kids started to abuse her physically, which was always during play time or after school, she was helpless.

I always stood up for her and tried to protect her, but I was also a target and these horrible girls ganged up on us.

One day Annemarie goaded the bunch and dared them to hit her in the chest or back. One girl took a swing at her with her fist, but soon regretted doing so, as she cradled her hand and started to cry. After that the kids called Annemarie turtle as well and said she had a shell round her torso. None of this stopped our tormentors finding other ways of getting at us both.

The trees are turning all those wonderful shades of gold, yellow and red. The days are still lovely and warm but are getting shorter. It's been very busy harvesting the potatoes, root vegetables and dried ripe beans from the garden. I can't help with the digging, but I'm pretty good at picking stuff from the earth and putting it into baskets. We only get to keep half the harvest. The other half is picked up by a man with a horse and cart and taken away. The land is owned by the state and we're only allowed to keep half of what we grow.

Our share is stored in the dirt cellar Granddad built in the hillside and that will help a good deal to feed us during the winter months, when vegetables are almost impossible to get.

One day the postman brings a letter. These occasions are very rare, and the mail is always from my father in England. The letters have always been opened and some of the writing crossed out, so it's not legible.

The two parcels mother received when I was with her, were the only ones we ever got. Soon after, the communist regime stopped all parcels from the west.

The letter Groysie now holds in her hand is sealed and looks very different from the letters father sends.

She says it's not from your father, I wonder who could be writing to us.

Groysie rips the envelope open, pulls out the letter and reads it to herself. I look at her, waiting to hear what the letter says. She looks quite bewildered and shaky.

We're on our own at home. I begin to get worried as she's not said anything. Groysie looks very pale and sits down heavily on a chair.

"What is it Groysie?" I say. "Shall I go and get Frau Friedsam, are you ill?"

"No, my child, I've just had an enormous shock" she tells me, as the tears start to stream down her old and wrinkled face.

Impatiently I pull Groysie by the arm. "Tell me, you're frightening me, what is it?"

As Groysie dries her eyes with her apron and tries to compose herself, she pulls a chair next to her and says, sit down next to me Utachen.

After a deep breath Groysie says. "Do you remember me telling you about your uncle Hans, who was captured by the communists in 1939, right at the beginning of the war? That's twelve years ago you know." She points out with a far away and sad look on her face.

"He's alive and coming home," she almost whispers as the floodgates open and the tears stream down in torrents.

"So, why are you crying, aren't you happy?" I demand.

"Oh, you can't begin to imagine how happy I am," counters Groysie. "But these are tears of happiness, my child, you'll understand one day."

As each member of the family gets home that day, there are more tears and jubilation each time and I think to myself that adults can be very strange.

The following few days there's so much excitement in our little house. I've never seen everybody in our family so happy and joyful.

Groysie is out every day queueing up for extra food. Annitante brings home one of those long white sticks of bread. She's quite pleased with herself and tells Groysie that a friend at work has connections, whatever that means. The bread comes from the special bakery for the party members only.

The big day arrives. The elation and nervous tension is already building even before I go to school. Annitante has worked night shift and gets home at 6.30 in the morning. She usually goes to bed but says she's so worked up she won't be able to sleep.

Annitante's brought home 3 eggs and a little sugar in a brown paper bag, also from the person with special connections. I ask her why she can't get stuff from this person with special connections all the time. She maintains it's not easy and it also costs a lot of money, but we should think ourselves lucky to have these extra luxuries.

I don't want to go to school. I think Groysie would have let me stay at home, but Annitante insists on me going.

The morning just drags on and on at school. My mind is not on my work and I'm worried that Hans will arrive before me and I really want to be there when he comes.

As soon as school is finished at 1.30, I'm out of there like a shot. Normally I tend to dawdle on the way home and if I'm walking with Ernst, we get distracted and stop, mess about and chat.

There's no keeping me back today, I practically run all the way home. When I get there, Annitante and Groysie are busy doing last minute things. I'm happy that my uncle isn't there yet.

Groysie has made a nice vegetable soup. Annitante is cutting the stick of bread into thin rounds. She gives me the small crusty bits from each end. It tastes so good. I wish I could eat bread like this every day.

She tells Groysie that the slices of bread will be dipped into beaten egg, fried and then sprinkled with sugar. Oh, that sounds so yummy, I can hardly wait.

I want to know how she knows how to make this food. Annitante tells me when she worked at the Villa, she learned how to cook and bake lots of things. The family there had all kinds of food and very nice meals were prepared every day.

Granddad and Tummy always work the early shift and will be home about 3 o'clock. I'm so impatient and don't know what to do with myself. I ask Groysie which way Hansuncle will come.

"How do I know," she says.

I go out every few minutes and look up the hill or at our neighbours garden. Then I see a young man walking down the hill. I run in shouting, he's coming, he's coming. Groysie says, just hold your horses, it might not be him.

We all run outside. Groysie's squinting and says he's too far away for her to recognise. Annitante with her young eyes shouts it's Hans, it's Hans and starts running up the garden path. Groysie stands momentarily, nervously kneading her apron with her hands. She then grabs my hand and say come Utachen and we both follow Annitante. The man is now at the top of the garden starting down the path.

Annitante's shouting Hans, Hans, as she's flying up the path. Groysie lets go of my hand and follows close behind.

I stop and watch as both women throw themselves at the stranger. A stranger to me anyway.

There's a lot of hugging and kissing going on, then all three of them are walking down the path, Groysie and Annitante either side of Hansuncle, arms wrapped round each other. They're all crying.

They all stop as they get to me. Hansuncle kneels and gives me a big bear hug and tells me what a fine and lovely little girl I am.

We all go inside the house, where Hansuncle puts down the small canvas bag he's been carrying.

Groysie tells Hansuncle she's sorry that he's found us in such poor circumstances and living in this hovel.

Hansuncle beams from ear to hear and says he doesn't care as long as he's back with his family. Compared to where he's worked and lived in the last twelve years, this is paradise.

There's so much to talk about and catch up on, no one seems to know where to start. Groysie offers her son a glass of water and asks him to sit down, she sits down beside him and holds his hand, as though he's still a little boy. Annitante is busy preparing the rest of the food.

I've stood the whole time and not taken my eyes of this new uncle of mine. He's very thin and his clothes are hanging off him. He's about medium height with short sandy coloured hair. He has bright piercing blue eyes. When he smiles, which he's done ever since he arrived, his whole face lights up.

I decide right there and then that I like my new uncle a lot.

Not long after Hansuncle arrived Granddad and Tummy come home from work. Tummy's very shy. He was only six years old the last time he saw his brother and now is eighteen and towers above him. Granddad's very emotional and embraces his second eldest son with real passion.

After our meal, everybody is full of questions. I'm only eight but am completely engrossed in the stories Hansuncle relates. I'm fascinated and horrified at the same time at the tales he tells.

Hansuncle was captured by the reds in 1939, right at the beginning of the war and spent the whole twelve years in the salt mines of Siberia. He tells of the deprivation and hard labour in the mines.

He talked of the long arctic winters, with very little food, poor living conditions and lack of medicines. So many died he said. Throughout the war and for a while after, the thousands of prisoners that died were replaced by new ones. It was a never ending flow of captured people brought to slave and perish in the inhospitable, white wilderness of Siberia. A lot of the guys around him were much bigger and stronger than him and yet they succumbed and died.

They had no hope or faith Hansuncle said.

Escape was not an option. When they were moved from one mine to another, the prisoners were chained to each other. Even had they had a chance to get away, they were so far from civilisation, they would not have survived the subzero temperatures.

Hansuncle said they lived in small wooden huts and slept on wooden pallets covered in straw. Every prisoner had a woollen animal skin to keep him warm.

They only received clean clothes once a month and these were worn at night as well for extra warmth. The prisoners were riddled with lice.

During the freezing long winter months all kinds of small rodents found their way into the huts. The prisoners caught these creatures, killed and skinned them and supplemented their meagre rations. During the very short summers, Hansuncle said they caught anything that moved, worms, bugs and sometimes they even snared a wild hare. Without the extra food, nobody would have survived.

After years of incarceration, Hansuncle said he came to terms and accepted his lot. He never gave up hope though of perhaps seeing all his loved ones again one day.

Everybody just sat and listened to our hero, with just the occasional question or remark. Groysie and Annitante said very little throughout, they just sat with tears running down their cheeks, red eyed, sniffing and wiping at their faces.

I knew we were very poor and had a lot less than most, but I couldn't get my eight year old head around what life must have been like for all those men.

Over the following months and years, Hansuncle related many more stories about life in the Siberian salt mines.

When I was quite a lot older I often marvelled at my uncle's strength and endurance to get through such suffering, deprivation and hardship inflicted by their communist oppressors and jailers.

I'd seen so much hardship in my short life and experienced rejection, severe physical and emotional abuse at a very young age from my own mother. Even as a little child I prayed and hoped things would get better.

To have lived without hope as these men must have done at times and still come out of it reasonably sane, was a miracle to me.

Hansuncle said they had no calendar and the only way to keep track of time was by the short summers. They didn't know the war had been over for 6 years.

A couple of months before he was released, the Romanian prisoners that were left were transported to a camp in Romania. There was no other prisoner who'd been in the camps as long as him. Some of these guys were near to death, they couldn't walk anymore and all of them were just skin and bone. They all looked like old men, not like young guys in their twenties and thirties.

After a couple of months rehabilitation and gaining a little weight, they were finally released.

In my early teens, I loved sitting and listening to Hansuncle's experiences in Siberia. I asked him once if he was angry and resentful having lost those precious young years of his life in such a dreadful place. He was only twenty-three when he was captured and thirty-five when he was released.

He told me never to waste time on anger, regrets or jealousy. These emotions will eat away at your heart and soul and will embitter you.

He said one will always find people worse off than oneself. Never give up hope. Where there's life, there's always hope.

While he was in communist captivity he learnt a lot about people's nature and very often he said men were defeated by their own negative beliefs.

No matter what happened now he said, he didn't think anything could ever be as bad as Siberia had been. He seemed happy, smiled and laughed very readily and enjoyed the simple things in life. He didn't have anything at the age of thirty-five, but he had the most precious thing, life and his family.

We were now six in our little shack. Groysie had managed to get some hay and straw and filled another big bag, which was resting on Tummy's bed. When it got late that first evening, the straw and hay filled mattress was put on the floor and that became Hansuncles bed while he lived with us. He said it was sheer luxury.

Chapter Thirteen

Life settled down again after the excitement of Hansuncle's return from the gulags. He got a job in the same furniture factory where Tummy worked as an apprentice. Hansuncle was a fully qualified carpenter.

Hansuncle brought a small canvas shoulder bag when he came home. I was intrigued to see what was inside. All he had in it were some papers, a toothbrush and toothpaste and a small shaving mirror, a razor and a packet of razor blades. I'd never seen any of these items before.

Granddad shaved with a cut throat razor and looked at his reflection in the small glass panel in the door of our little dresser in the kitchen. We didn't possess a mirror in our house. The big mirror on the wall, when I was very little, had to be left when my grandparents had been kicked out of their house.

Toothbrushes and toothpaste were like gold dust, nowhere to be found, but I'm sure all the party people had them.

My biggest fascination, however, was with the little shaving mirror. I picked it up all the time and loved to look at my reflection. Groysie keeps telling me not to play with the mirror, but I just can't help myself and one day drop it. The mirror shatters into many pieces.

Groysie's very cross and slaps my bottom a couple of times. I'm quite upset about breaking the mirror and also about getting smacked. Groysie or anybody else in the family has never laid a finger on me, but I know deep down I deserved the spanking for breaking the mirror.

I'm worried about what Hansuncle will say. He's very nice about it and says he'll just have to look in the glass panel on the dresser the same as Granddad, when he shaves. Heide, my little know-all friend, tells me I'm going to have seven years bad luck for breaking the mirror. That's rich, I tell her, how much worse can it get?

There's a lot of excited talk going around at school. Kids are talking about a man who's come to town and walks on a rope right across the town square from one building to another.

A wire has been spanned from one building across the small square to another building in the centre of the city. A man walks across the wire and does all kinds of tricks every evening.

I pester Groysie for days to take me to see this man. It doesn't cost anything, just our tram fare into the city. Hansuncle says he'd love to take me and I'm elated about going, especially with my uncle.

We ride into town on the tram. The square is packed with people and kids of all ages. Soon after we arrive, a man appears high up on a balcony with a long pole, which he holds in the middle across his chest with both hands and proceeds to walk along the long wire right over to the building on the other side of the square.

My heart is in my mouth as I watch with fascination, hoping the man won't fall off.

The show gets more and more fraught as time goes on. He brings out a bicycle, which he rides and does all kinds of tricks on. Then he brings out a chair and performs balancing acts. The show is so exhilarating, but at the same time frightening, that I hide my face behind my uncle a lot of the time.

When the show is over, I'm so relieved that the man is still in one piece and hasn't fallen and killed himself.

I can't stop talking and telling Groysie, when I get home, about the incredible evening and all the extraordinary things the man did on the high wire.

Sundays never change. Church in the morning for everybody. Sunday school for me in the afternoon and church again for the adults in the evening. Groysie still stays at home with me in the evenings, she says it's a little too much to expect me to sit in church all day long.

Annitante, Hansuncle and Tummy all sing in the church choir. Annitante and Tummy now also play mandolin and guitar in the band. They both still practise a lot in their spare time and I wish I could learn to play an instrument.

Hansuncle has met a young woman he likes and they start seeing each other fairly regularly.

The long bible sessions and prayers still continue after the evening meal. When we're all home, they go on for ever and ever, as there's so much more to be thankful for, now that Hansuncle has come home. Groysie often nudges me and tells me to get into bed and I'm asleep before the praying is over.

Christmas comes and goes. It's very low key, everybody has to work and food is as scarce as ever. Groysie says she would have liked to make some shaped biscuits to hang on our little tree as she did before the war, but couldn't get eggs, sugar or margarine.

Queuing for food and milk is ongoing every day, but doesn't get any easier, especially now that the freezing winter weather is here.

It's New Years Day. The winter school holiday has started and all the workers have the day off.

Granddad tells me he has a surprise for me. His foreman has told him to bring me to work, where a New Years party will be held for all the workers' children. This is done every year and the kids get presents.

Granddad, Groysie and I set off in the afternoon and walk to the factory where Granddad works. It's a huge engineering firm and several thousand people work there. Granddad tells me before the war it was privately owned and all kinds of farming and industrial machinery was made there. Now the factory had been renamed 'Arsenal' and all kinds of machinery and trucks were made for the military.

The massive front gates were open and hoards of people and children were hurrying along to get inside.

We went into a massive hall decorated with balloons and coloured streamers. On one side, tables were laid with all kinds of food I'd never seen. I was reluctant to try it, but Groysie picked a few bits she thought I'd really like and put them on a piece of paper.

Granddad got me a glass of coloured water. We took a seat in one of the many rows in the big hall. The food was good and the water was sweet. I liked it all.

A whole corner of the room was stacked high with all kinds of imaginable toys. There were wooden sleighs, bicycles of all sizes, tricycles, scooters, different size skis and skates with boots on. Then there were all manner of stuffed toys and dolls. It was unbelievable and to think that one of these fabulous toys was going to be mine.

After everybody had settled and eaten, a man stood up on a big table at the end of the hall. He had a stack of papers in his hand from which he began to read out names. All the kids were sitting excitedly in anticipation of having their name called out.

One by one children of all ages went up on their own or with a parent to receive their precious gift.

This process went on a long time and the pile of toys was decreasing rapidly. A lot of the children had not received anything yet, when the last toy was handed out.

I was completely gutted, dejected and felt so deprived, I wanted to cry. But how could I with all these people around me. Why had we been brought here to watch all these spoilt and incredibly well dressed children be spoilt even further. It just wasn't fair.

On the way out of the hall, two men stood at the exit and handed each child without a present a packet of six small colour pencils from a box. I took it and we left.

I looked up at my Granddad's face, which was red with anger. He took the pencils from me and threw them against a wall. His fury was palpable.

We're treated as second class citizens, he said. As if that's not enough they have to bring us here, degrade us even further and shove our noses into shit. I had never heard my Granddad talk like this.

The pencils are nothing but crap. The lead is like chalk and doesn't even stand up to being sharpened let alone used. They can keep their parties, we'll never come again. And so, all three of us, holding hands walked home.

Granddad said he noticed there was not one Saxon kid amongst the several hundred children that received a present. They were all the brats of the communist managers, foremen and party people.

Why have everything on display like that, Groysie said, and then disappoint so many children.

After the winter holidays, the kids at school started talking about Fasching, the carnival season, and all the parties they were going to. Invitations were handed out by children to all their friends. They were all discussing the wonderful costumes they were going to wear. I haven't received one invitation. Annemarie hasn't either. She tells me maybe one year her mother will give her a party and then she'll invite me.

I go home and tell Groysie all about these upcoming Fasching Parties. I say it's not fair at all, nobody has invited me.

She says come and sit down my child. Then she proceeds to explain how these parties are not for us and I wouldn't be allowed to go anyway. The whole thing is very much against what we believe in and it's all devil worshipping.

Secretly I still wish I could go, it all sounds a lot of fun.

Chapter Fourteen

Thomas gets his call-up papers and has to do his two years in the army. Being Saxon, he has to contribute to his national service doing manual labour, such as working in the coal mine, road building or on the railway.

He's put to work on the railway, laying tracks and general maintenance. He's quite pleased about that. He says it's easier than working in the mines or building roads.

I'm going to miss him. He's always given me his time and we've played Ludo together. He also rides Granddad's old bike and sometimes he takes me out on the cross bar and we ride around for a little while.

I find Sundays so boring and would do anything to get out of going to church and Sunday school, but that rarely happens unless I'm not well.

I bug Heide quite a bit to go with me and once in a blue moon, when she's forgotten how boring the last time was, she goes along. Afterwards she tells me not to ever ask her again. Having to sit still for that long, listening to the Sunday school teacher, almost drives her crazy, while all our friends are playing outside or having all kinds of fun indoors.

Heide was extremely spoilt being so much younger than her sister and brother. She was more like an only child and got her own way all the time. Frau Hannich, her mother, said she'd been a surprise in more than one way.

Being two years younger than me, very petite for her age, always dressed like a doll and as cute as a button, all neighbours and friends adore her and make a fuss of her.

Heide could wrap her parents round her little finger and rarely did what she was told. She was very naughty and cheeky, answered back all the time, stuck her tongue out at people and pulled faces.

When it suited her, and she wanted something, she was as sweet as honey.

When her mother was at her wits end she'd turn and say to me, Uta, why can't she be like you, nice and sensible?

I just smiled and thought, I'd get beaten to a pulp if I ever even thought of behaving like Heide.

When Frau Hannich really got to the end of her tether and was on the verge of pulling out her hair, she just sent Heide to another room. I never ever saw her get smacked. She'd make her stay there and send me home.

Heide didn't care, but I felt as though I was being punished.

I could always tell when Heide was pushing her mother close to the edge and would beg her to stop and behave herself. Of course, she never did and then got house arrest. This never lasted very long. Heide said she caused havoc and made a mess. Her mother, even more frustrated, would soon tell her to get out the house and go play.

Then she'd be back at my place wanting me to go and play. Often, my playtime was over, and I had chores to do. Heide just went off in a huff, as she hadn't got her way and had no one to hang out with.

Despite everything, I liked Heide a lot. She was my best friend out of school. When I was with her we always had a lot of fun. We were allowed to play on the top floor of their house, which had never been finished. All the furniture removed from the rooms, that were now rented out by the communists, was stored on that floor. We arranged tables and chairs into rooms and played all sorts of games. It was like an Aladdin's cave, with lots of interesting things to look at and chests to rummage through. Heide was always boss, and I mostly went along with what she wanted.

The long winter months are so hard. I wear layers and layers of clothes, practically all the things I possess and still am never warm enough. When the snow starts to melt and spring's on its way, I'm very happy, at least for a while until the end of school.

I love school. I like writing, reading and am now fluent in German. I also have my friend Annemarie.

During the winter months Annemarie doesn't go out during break. She's extremely frail and her bones are brittle. Falling over or being pushed could easily cause a break. I'm always on my own during play time. The horrible girls in my class still hassle me, so I try to keep away from them.

Annemarie is always glad when spring comes and she's able to go outside during recess.

Our school is small and only accommodates the first four grades. It's situated amongst residential Villas on the corner of a road right next to a stream and a forest, which extends to the foothills of the Cibin Mountains one way and almost to the centre of the city in the other direction.

We don't have a playground, or any other facilities, only the classrooms. There's no traffic at all in that area and so the kids play in the roads around the school. We're also allowed to wander by the stream and a little into the woods, as long as we can hear the school bell ring.

One day in spring during the break, Annemarie and I wonder a little further than usual, following the brook, which flows deeper into the wood and disappears under shrubs and trees.

We're both looking for early spring flowers along the bank, when I spot something weird a little further down the stream.

Let's go and see what it is, I say to my friend. The undergrowth is quite dense, and we push our way through to the place where I've spotted the strange thing.

Annemarie and I look at each other horrified. There lying in the brook, held down by rocks and branches, is a tiny naked baby.

It's lying on its back. The skin is a horrible doughy, blue colour. Its tummy is bloated and looks more like a balloon. A long thick dark thing is coming out where its belly button should be and the eyes are wide open and bulging.

The poor little thing. How could anybody do this to such a helpless little mite? Tears are running down my face and I feel very upset.

Annemarie says it's a newborn baby. Her aunt had given birth recently to a little girl and it was very tiny like this. I'd never seen such a small baby before and his little scrotum and penis were all shrivelled and blue.

I tell Annemarie to stay where she is and I'll run and get help. As I near the school, I call to the children playing to get a teacher.

Within minutes, two teachers are following me along the creek with a load of kids running behind them.

When we reach the spot where Annemarie is waiting, and they take in the horrendous scene, they tell us all to leave and go straight back to our classrooms.

We all do as we're told and the nightmarish, horrible scene is told over and over by the kids, who have seen it. All we were ever told was that the police had been called and they were dealing with it.

My nightmares never went away, but after that experience in the wood, I couldn't go to sleep at night. Every time I closed my eyes, I saw that gruesome picture in front of me. When Annitante was on nights, Groysie had to sleep with me. We were all in the same room, but I had to have somebody in bed with me.

To this day that picture is imprinted in my mind and I've never been able to erase it.

Chapter Fifteen

Spring is so wonderful. Unfortunately, it's followed by summer and for me that evokes all kinds of terrible memories. I just don't want it to come, but I know it will.

All the other kids are very happy that school will soon end. They're all talking about trips into the mountains, to the sea or to the countryside with their families.

All I can look forward to is hard work and misery. I don't give up pleading with Groysie not to send me to Kerz. I want to stay with her for the summer. All the begging and beseeching doesn't help me. Groysie says it's not up to her and I must go. I know, if it were up to her, she wouldn't send me, but Annitante has the final word and that's the end of the matter.

Within a couple of days after school finishes for the summer, Groysie takes me to the railway station. She buys my return ticket and tells me to look after it well. She finds a woman on the train and asks her to keep an eye on me and make sure I get off at Kerz. Then, without hanging around until the train leaves and making the parting even more difficult, Groysie's gone. I sit on the train, feeling totally miserable and sorry for myself.

All the speculating and day dreaming of what could have been gets me nowhere. I have to face the fact that I'm spending the summer in Kerz at my mother's mercy, to do as she wants with me, go hungry and work like a slave.

I don't even realise I'm silently crying until the woman sitting opposite me asks why I'm upset.

I'm quite a talkative and open child and I pour all my troubles and fears out to this stranger. The woman is kind and sympathetic to my plight and hopes I'll be all right.

Once again, I find myself at the deserted train stop in Kerz. I stand forlorn and disheartened, watching the train disappear in the distance.

I'm in no hurry to get to my mother's house. I find a grassy verge at the side of the dirt road into the village and sit down.

I sit there grieving over my circumstance. I'll be nine this summer. I know now that it's sometime in July. Groysie told me, but she doesn't know the date. I could ask my mother, but why bother, it really makes no difference.

I mull over what my friends Annemarie and Heide will be doing. I know they'll both have a lot of fun with their families and get taken out on excursions.

Then I remember hearing all the kids at school talking about their forthcoming summer and all the things they'll do with their parents and siblings.

Being brought up by very poor elderly grandparents deprives me of all the things young parents do with their children. Groysie thinks it's a waste of time and energy to go traipsing in mountains and forests when that time can be used to do something useful and productive.

That's a typical farmer's point of view.

All they've done is work hard all their lives, bring up big families and they have never been anywhere. Granddad had fought in the first war in Europe, but Groysie had only ever been to Hermannstadt and to Kerz when my parents got married.

In all their lives they never had a holiday. It was only the city people who took vacations. Farmers couldn't go and leave all their livestock for days on end. They had to be there seven days a week, all the year round.

I loved my Groysie and Granddad so much and never wanted to leave them. Although at times in my daydreaming, I wondered what life would be like having caring parents and siblings and doing all kinds of exciting things.

Sitting on the edge of the road, engrossed in my thoughts, a Romanian woman comes by. She stops in front of me and says, "You're Maria's girl. Why are you sitting there? Haven't you got anything better to do?"

I tell her that I've just got off the train and will be on my way soon.

"The train came ages ago," she counters. "You better get going," and off she trots. What an old busybody I think but would never dream of saying so to an adult.

I amble along the deserted dirt roads of the village, in no hurry to reach my destination. There's not a cloud in the sky and the heat is so oppressive. I stop from time to time, looking up at the chimneys on the houses, where storks have built their nests. These birds fascinate me. We don't get them in Stolzenburg or Hermannstadt. They only make their nests near big rivers and swampy areas, where they can catch fish and frogs. They're such beautiful birds, but how can they possibly carry a new born baby, they're not that big? They intrigue me when they throw back their heads on those long necks and clap their long beaks together, making an incredible racket, which can be heard for miles around.

After being distracted for a while, reality hits me and, as I'm getting closer to the lane where mother lives, I become more anxious and fearful about the weeks ahead.

That thought, however, is soon gone and I think nobody will care if I'm there or not.

When eventually I turn the corner in the lane, I find it totally deserted. Not a soul in sight, just a few small flocks of geese pecking at the grass against the fence on one side of the road.

I walk through the street door into the yard, but it's all quiet and no one's around, just geese lying under the gnarled old apple tree, which hasn't produced fruit for years. The chickens are having fun scratching around in the yard and enjoying their dust baths.

I'm very thirsty. I draw some water up from the well in the metal bucket and quench my thirst, using a tin mug, left at the top of the well. The water is always so cold and tastes good. I watch the three rainbow trout far below in the water. People keep a few of these fish in every well. They eat the plants that grow from the stones at the waterline and any bugs or flies that fall in. The water is kept clean and clear by the fish.

I then go back into the lane again and sit on the wooden slatted bench in front of our neighbour's house. I'm so unhappy being here. I wish I could just walk back to the station, get on the next train to Hermannstadt and back to my Groysie.

After a long wait that seems like hours to me, my mother turns the corner at the top of the lane, carrying two hoes on one shoulder and her wicker covered water bottle in the other hand. Christian then appears, tagging along behind mother, pulling a little wooden cart with Viorel sitting in it.

I stay put on the bench, feeling unsure of myself and not knowing what to say. As they come closer, I get up, walk towards them and say hello. Then I ask if they've been working in the fields, which I realise is a stupid thing to say, as it's so obvious where they've been and it's the only thing they ever do apart from Sundays.

Mother gives me a look as if to say, are you really that stupid or what? Then says, What does it look like? We haven't been to a dance, that's for sure.

I'm immediately put in my place and think I must just shut up and not say anything. Christian follows mother into the yard and I tag along behind them all.

Mother goes straight to the well and draws up a full bucket of water. She hands the tin mug to Viorel first. He's about two now and walks very well. Then she gives Christian a drink and finally has some water herself. I stand and watch, but she doesn't offer me any water. It's a few hours since I last had a drink and ask if I can have some.

"You're old enough to get your own drink," she snaps and walks off into the house.

They've only been back a few minutes and I've managed to say the wrong thing each time I've spoken. Mother is very cold and prickly around me and I sense that my mere presence irritates her.

Christian stays in the yard with Viorel, who's running after the chickens and chasing them all over the yard.

Nothing has changed. I know I'm not welcome here and a huge dark cloud comes down on me.

Some changes have been made since last summer. The first room in the cellar is being used as a kitchen and dining room. The cooking range, table and chairs and the dresser from upstairs have been moved into the cellar. The room has only a small window and it's much cooler down here in the summer.

The floor is clay and feels cool on bare feet. A door leads into the inner cellar, which is like a dungeon as it has no windows, where I spent many hours, locked up for punishment on several occasions last year. Being so close to it makes me scared and nervous.

Immediately behind the door, as you enter, the first room, is a slightly raised wooden platform, which serves as a bed sometimes.

I stand around feeling very uncomfortable and out of place, not for long though, mother soon finds jobs for me to do.

She informs me that her husband is now back from the army and I'm to call him uncle. My brother says uncle is a shepherd at the collective farm and is away most of the time from early spring to late autumn. Shepherds work in pairs and mind large flocks of sheep up in the foothills. Apart from looking after the sheep, they milk them daily and make cheese. In the spring they shear the flock and the wool is brought down to the village. The women wash the wool, then spin it into yarn and weave it into cloth during the winter months. Mother spends a large chunk of the year on her own with the two boys.

Christian and I are kept very busy with all the chores and working on the land.

My brother is ten and a half now and really has to pull his weight and I have to follow suit. Sunday is still the only day off and after six days of hard slogging, I'm always very tired. We're up at 6 every morning. Mother has already been up an hour or two. She very rarely gets more than four or five hours sleep a night. It's always eleven or twelve o'clock before Christian and I go to bed, so we only get six or seven hours sleep.

When we get back from working in the fields, there's a whole host of chores to be done; feeding the pigs, geese and chickens, drawing up endless buckets of water from the well to water the animals, more preparing pig food for the next day by boiling potatoes in the big pot on the open fire in the yard and then mixing in other feed.

We have to look after Viorel, sweep the yard as the chickens and geese crap all over the place. All these jobs have to be done in daylight hours and then, when it gets dark, we have to wash our faces, hands and feet in cold water by the well. We only eat after all the outdoor jobs have been done.

When we sit down to our evening meal, which is always a meagre amount and still leaves me hungry afterwards, I'm almost comatose and have to be careful not to fall asleep in my food. Then Christian and I still have the dishes to wash. Viorel has been in bed a few hours when we finally hit the straw sack.

I share a small bed with my brother. Viorel sleeps with my mother, but when uncle is at home, the little boy sleeps with us. There's very little room in the bed, but Christian and I are so dog tired, that nothing would keep us awake.

When Sunday arrives I'm so relieved not to have to work all day. We still have to feed the animals in the morning, but that's it and we have the rest of the day to do as we want.

Nothing has changed apart from the fact that mother now dresses in the Romanian traditional costume, which is so different from what the Saxons wear. She then takes Viorel and they go to their Romanian relatives. When uncle is at home, all three of them go off for the day.

Mother has converted to the Romanian Orthodox religion. She's really embraced the whole Romanian way of life and has turned her back on her Saxon heritage, customs and way of life. She never ever sets foot in the Evangelical Lutheran Church anymore and has almost nothing to do with the Saxons. She doesn't look anything like the woman I first met in her modern city clothes. During the week she wears the long drab skirts in the style worn by the Romanian women. She always has a scarf tied round her head, even in the heat of the summer.

All this upsets me more than I can say. I feel a deep hurt and betrayal. Christian says he doesn't care, but I know he does.

Sundays my brother and I go our own way. He's as reticent as ever towards me. I go off to church in the morning and then just hang around, hoping somebody will invite me back home with them for something to eat. Mother's aunt has died since last year, so I don't go there anymore.

Even though everybody is kind, I feel very much like a charity case and don't like people feeling sorry for me. I'd give anything to have a loving family and be out doing things with them.

We're allowed to stay out a little later on Sundays. In the evening I go to the village barn dance with some of the girls. I stand around and watch everybody, including all the little kids having fun. Then it's home to feed the animals.

After having been in Kerz for a couple of weeks, uncle comes home early one evening. I've never met him before. He's quite tall with black hair and a bushy beard. He has a big heavy sheepskin cape, draped over his shoulder, which reaches almost to the ground. Christian says it's the traditional shepherd's cape, which keeps them warm through the cool nights in the hills. Uncle greets me in a friendly way, then picks up his little boy and makes a big fuss of him. He then heads straight down to the cellar and curls up on the wooden pallet behind the door. He drapes his cape around himself and sleeps there until the following morning.

I ask Christian why uncle sleeps in the cellar. He tells me mother won't allow him in her bed until he's cleaned up and shaved, but he's too tired for that now and just wants to sleep.

My brother says that shepherds don't wash properly for weeks and they smell like their sheep and sheepdogs. Come to think of it, uncle did smell quite strong. However, I've never heard anything like it and think it's very funny.

Sure enough, the next morning, uncle is already up, clean shaven, apart from a small moustache, washed and dressed in clean pants and shirt. He only stays about a week and then he's off again for several more weeks.

I only see him once more that summer. He's a quiet young man in his mid-twenties. Christian says he's five years younger than mother. Uncle never says much, but I can tell he's a kind man and so gentle with his little boy.

During the week he spends at home, uncle goes to the fields with us all and then returns to the hills and the sheep.

It's an extremely hot July day, like all the days at the height of the summer in Transylvania. Out on the dusty earth roads leading to the fields, the heat mirages shimmer in the distance and every creature, be it human or beast, desperately seeks shade from the scorching heat.

For an unknown reason to me, Christian and I are left at home that day with Viorel and several chores we have to do.

I'm in the yard sweeping up. I find the big heavy twig broom hard to wield. I don't know where Christian is with Viorel. Whenever we're left on our own, my brother issues orders to me and I have to carry them out.

As I'm getting on with cleaning the yard, I smell smoke.

I stop what I'm doing, look around me to see where the smoke is and where the smell's coming from.

The village houses are built close together with just the yards separating them. The barns are at the back of the yards and the gardens are beyond. The neighbours either side had barns. Ours had burnt down when my mother was a child and was never been rebuilt.

As I'm standing watching, I can see smoke rising beyond our neighbour's barn to the right. At first the smoke is wispy and thin, but soon it grows thicker and billows out of the thatched barn roof. I can tell it's the barn two doors away that's on fire. I drop the broom and run out through the street door into the lane.

There are already people everywhere. Some just standing around bewildered, others running about in all directions, like chickens without heads, panic stricken and shouting. I look around trying to find my brother, but he's nowhere to be seen.

I watch in horrified fascination as dark smoke clouds grow and boil out of the barn roof, spreading and engulfing the whole structure. It's so frightening how quickly the fire has taken hold and nothing much can be done to stop it from radiating in all directions.

Villagers are running with buckets of water, drawn from neighbouring wells. They can't even get close enough to throw the water on the fire. For all the good it does, one might just as well stand there and merely spit at the fire. It's a completely hopeless situation and there's no chance at all that the fire can be brought under control and the barn saved.

Ladders have been hoisted up to the roofs of the adjacent barns and people are now climbing up, throwing buckets of water onto these roofs, to wet them, in an attempt to stop the fire from spreading.

Eventually the antiquated fire wagon comes rumbling down the lane on its metal wheels, with men frantically pulling and pushing the thing. The long hoses are unravelled and lowered into the nearest well.

Two men are furiously pumping the old machine to draw the water into the hose. Another man is holding the hose and directing the water jets towards the burning building.

Now the barn next door to us is on fire. Everything is as dry as tinder and it only takes a spark to set light to another building.

The old fire wagon is useless. Every time a well runs dry, the hose has to be pulled up, taken to another well and lowered down. Precious time is wasted.

The thatched roof of the second barn is burning like crazy and the barn the other side of the first one has also caught fire. People are moving further down the lane as the heat is so intense and becoming unbearable.

Our next door neighbour, an elderly woman, who's been standing in the crowd, suddenly takes off and runs to her yard. People all around try to stop her, but she manages to get free and carries on running. People shout and holler at her, but she runs straight into the burning barn, soon to emerge with her cat in her arms. Just as she seems out of danger and everybody gives a sigh of relief, the stork nest that has been on the barn roof for years, comes tumbling down in a big fiery ball, straight on the top of the woman and engulfs her in flames.

I stand there petrified as screams and cries rise from the crowd. The man manning the hose immediately turns the water jet on the woman and soon the fire is out. The poor old thing is still clutching her beloved cat. Our neighbour's body is completely charred. Two men carry her to safety and people surround them trying to help. There's no hospital, or even a doctor in the village.

The old woman's body was somewhat protected by her long clothing. Her head, face, arms and hands were very badly burnt. The cat got away with minor burns, but her mistress died several weeks later from her injuries. Medical care in the wonderful communist paradise we live in, is nonexistent in the small villages, people have to go for miles by train to get treated.

For days people relate stories about other fires that burnt down whole streets in the past. Luckily there was no barn in our yard, otherwise the whole street and maybe even houses could have been burnt.

All the workers in the fields had seen the fire in the distance and were hurrying back. My mother suddenly appeared and stood beside me. She was agitated, puffing and panting from the exertion of running nearly all the way home from the land, having seen the smoke and flames in the distance and knowing it was in her part of the village.

She's not glad to see that I'm all right but grabs me by the shoulders and demands where Christian is with Viorel.

I tell her I don't know and haven't seen them for ages.

She frantically runs from person to person asking if they've see my brothers. When mother returns to where I'm standing, she's very angry and

I feel as though it's my fault and she's blaming me.

"Don't just stand there you stupid girl, go and look for them," she yells, running off in one direction and me going in another.

I wander down several village street asking everybody I come upon if they've seen Christian and Viorel.

Eventually a woman tells me she saw Christian pulling my brother in the little cart right the other end of the village, not far from the railway stop. Now I know they're safe, I make my way home.

Even as very young children, if there was any trouble or threat of any kind, my brother ran and hid. He was always afraid of the dark and looked to me to protect him. Even though I was younger than him and afraid, I always put on a brave face.

When the fire started, Christian was in the lane with Viorel, skiving from the chores and letting me do them all. At the first sign of the fire he took off and went right to the edge of the village. He figured if the whole village burnt down he'd be okay.

A couple of days after the fire, two little boys admitted to playing in the hay loft with matches and that's how the fire started.

Summer is really dragging on. I can't wait till the end of August and going back to Groysie.

I really hate being here.

Whenever I get the chance I go hide somewhere and retreat into my own little world of make believe. It never lasts for long. When my mother finds me, I'm in big trouble. It always ends up with a beating or being locked for hours in the dungeon.

The mere sight of me seems to provoke and irritate my mother. I just don't know what to do to make things better. I watch as she adores her little Viorel, plays and laughs with him and somehow she's even kinder to Christian when I'm around. I know she'd rather not have me staying and how I wish I wasn't. I live in this world where hardly anybody ever talks to me. I feel very lonely and cry a lot when no one can see me.

At meal times, I'm always the last one to get my food and am always given far less than anybody else. I never leave the table having had enough to eat. The meals always consist of vegetables, done in a variety of ways, with polenta, or bread, baked in the clay oven in the yard. Collecting the eggs from the chickens and geese is my job.

We never get to eat them though, I don't know what mother does with them all.

I've been thinking more and more about running away and going back to the city. It's still about three weeks before school starts.

I just can't take any more.

Sunday morning, mother goes off with Viorel. Christian and I are left to get on with our day. I wait until my brother has gone and then pack my few bits into my cloth bag and head out towards the railway.

The only trouble is I have to walk through the Romanian part of the village to get to the train stop. I'm worried in case I run into my mother, or somebody who will tell her that I've left.

I decide to walk right on the outskirts of the village along the streams that run down from the mountains to the River Alt. It's still morning and everybody is at church. Later, all the village kids and some adults will be at the creek, enjoying the water.

I can't hang around, as I don't want to be seen. It takes a long time to get through some of the very dense willow shrub along the rivulets. This stuff grows everywhere, and big boulders often block my way and I have to make detours.

Eventually I can see that I've left all the village houses behind. I make my way through maize fields which give me further protection from being spotted. I can hear a train in the distance and wonder if it's going to Hermannstadt. I know I'm too far away to make it through.

As I get to the road leading to the railway, the train passes by. To my dismay it is a passenger train.

When I reach the railway stop, I sit down and put my shoes on. I go up to the ticket hut and, luckily, the man is in there. He's only there about half an hour before a train arrives and then he goes back to his house just at the back of the hut.

I ask him what time the next train to Hermannstadt is. He tells me that I've just missed one and there won't be another one until three o'clock. It's not even midday yet, so I have a long wait.

If I stay at the railway stop, I could be seen. So, I cross the tracks and go into a maize field. The rows of plants are high and dense, and no one will spot me there. If I pop my head out from the maize field, I can see a long way in the direction from which the train will come. I go a few feet further into the field, lay my old clothes on the dry ground and decide to stay there and rest. I'm very tired and am thankful to be able to just sit or lie there for a while.

I've got no food or water and it'll be early evening by the time I get back to Groysie. I don't care though, I'm out of my mother's clutches. I know she won't find out that I'm gone, until this evening, when I don't go home. She'll see that my things are gone, and I know she won't care, or do anything about it.

The time goes slowly, as I watch several goods trains and a couple of passenger ones go by.

I've learned from early childhood that in the height of summer, when the sun is almost directly above you, you don't have a shadow. Now my shadow is moving away from my body, so I know it's early afternoon.

I pack my bits into my bag and go back across the railway tracks, just as the man is entering the little hut. I ask him how long it will be before the Hermannstadt train arrives. He tells me not long.

I decide to sit behind the ticket hut, while I'm waiting, in case other people arrive and see me.

While I sit hidden from view, a goods train passes coming from the direction of Hermannstadt. If my train is due soon, it's probably waiting at the next small town of Fogaras on the side tracks, so this train can pass. This is a main line going down to Bucharest, but there is only one railway track. Trains are always pulling over and letting other trains by. It is quite a slow business and makes the trips a lot longer.

Not long after the train has gone, I hear a whistle in the distance. My train's arriving. I get up and go stand near the track.

There is no one else waiting for the train. When it finally stops, I hurry to one of the ladders going up into the carriage. The bottom rung doesn't even reach my waist. I quickly put the strap from my bag over my head, then grab the railing on one side and the bottom step and pull myself up onto it. I make my way up the next two rungs as the train slowly starts to move. I can't reach the handle to open the door to the carriage.

The train is picking up speed. I'm stuck outside the door with no means of opening it. I move back down a step, grab the top rung with one arm and keep on holding the railing tightly with my other hand. The train is going very fast now, and the fields are flying by in a blur. I'm petrified. All I can think is that I'm being punished by God for running away and will die.

Suddenly the door opens, a strong hand grabs me by the arm and hauls me into the carriage. When I look up I see a man towering over me, looking very cross. I'm shaking from head to toe, while he's shaking his head from side to side.

"What the hell do you think you're doing child?" He demands.

"I'm going home to my Groysie in Hermannstadt," I tell him.

"Isn't anybody with you?" He demands.

I shake my head.

"What kind of a person would let a little kid like you go off, let them get on a train on their own and travel to another city?" He questions.

I didn't want to answer him and tell him I'd run away, so I just shrugged my shoulders and found a seat near the window.

The previous year when I'd left Kerz after the summer, it had been a weekday and there had been several people at the train stop. I'd had help from a fellow traveller to get on the train, but mother hadn't taken me then either and seen me safely onto the train the way Groysie did.

That horrible experience had frightened me to death. I'm still sitting and shaking like a leaf.

As we're nearing Hermannstadt, the last stop on the line, I'm beginning to worry about what Groysie will say when I tell her I've run away.

Getting off the train here is easy. The bottom rung of the step almost touches the concrete platform and I don't need any help.

It's late afternoon. I've not had anything to eat since about seven in the morning, only a piece of bread at that. I search the bottom of my bag for my fair money. Groysie always gives me the right amount of money to go home on the tram. I take out my few belongings. It's no use, the money's not there. Maybe I've lost it or maybe it was taken. I'm tired, famished and have a two hour walk ahead of me. I sit on a bench outside the railway station, wondering if I have any other option, but know full well I haven't.

The sooner I start walking the sooner I'll get home. I pick up my cloth bag up and start my long trek home.

It's early evening, as I walk through our neighbour's garden towards our little shack. Groysie's sitting on the wooden bench outside the house, a bowl on her lap, peeling potatoes. I walk quietly up to the gate, open it, then stand there crying.

Groysie looks up. She's surprised to see me. She puts her bowl down, stands up and starts to walk towards me. Like a flash, I rush over to her, throw my arms around her legs and bawl my eyes out.

My dear Groysie bends down, enfolds me in her tender embrace and we just remain like that for a while. Oh, it's so wonderful to be back in her arms. I don't even care anymore if she's cross with me.

Then she just takes me by the hand and says, "Come, sit with me and tell me all about it."

We sit down on the bench and I pour my heart out to her. I tell Groysie about all the beatings, being locked in the cellar and always being hungry. "I just couldn't stand another day" I say to her, "so I just ran away."

"Oh, my dear child, you look so thin and bedraggled. I just can't understand how a mother can treat her own child like that, it's completely beyond me."

Later when Annitante comes home, she's cross with me for running away. She tells me what I did was wrong. If something had happened to me, they wouldn't have known about it. My mother might be worried and start looking for me when she finds out I'm gone.

I tell Annitante my mother wouldn't care if I was dead. I was pretty sure she was pleased that I'd gone.

Annitante thinks that might be true, nevertheless I had to promise never to run away again.

Those two or so weeks at the end of the summer holiday turned out to be the best time I'd ever had. I felt so happy and carefree, playing with my friends for hours on end.

I still had to do some chores and queue for food, but having no school or homework, there was lots of time left to enjoy.

Selma, Heide and I often walked to the River Cibin, where we'd take off our clothes, just keeping on our underpants and mess around in the shallow water on the edge of the river. On the way back we'd stuff ourselves full with wild strawberries that grew in abundance in the meadows.

At other times, Selma's siblings, Ernst and Lenke, and a Hungarian girl, my age, who lived with her family in Heide's house, congregated and played all kinds of games together.

In that short time, I experienced the carefree summer days all the other kids were enjoying and really longed to have those kinds of holidays myself.

Very soon September is here again and the ritual of preparing and getting ready for school starts.

Hansuncle comes home one day and tells us all he's going to get married soon. It's no surprise to anybody. He's been seeing Nicki ever since he returned from Siberia.

The whole baptist community we belong to, go on an outing one Sunday in the autumn. Everybody's taking the tram to the very last stop into the foothills. Rugs are spread on the grassy meadows and picnic baskets are placed together and food is shared.

Hansuncle and Nicki announce their engagement to the congregation. It was a fabulous day. People went for little walks, lay around and relaxed. Others played games with the children and generally had lots of fun.

Groysie and Granddad didn't come. I went with Annitante, Hansuncle and Nickitante, as I now called her.

The following Sunday I saw my first baptism at our church. A huge, deep tin tub was placed in front of the pulpit and filled with tepid water.

The candidates for the baptism all sat on the front two benches of the meeting hall. Women on the left and men on the right. They were all dressed in snow white robes.

After the service, each person being baptised got up in turn and went and stood at the base of the tin tub. The preacher helped them into the oversized bath, said a prayer over them and with the help of another man, submerged the rigid person in the water.

By the time the last person was baptised and dunked in the water, I was close to having a panic attack. Every time a person was lowered into the tub, I held my breath. I was frightened of water and felt as though it was I being drowned.

The thought of having this done absolutely terrified me.

I miss Tummy so much. He's only been home on leave once in the last year and he has another year to serve. When I saw him, I thought he looked very handsome and grown-up in his army uniform. I'm full of questions and want to know a lot of things about the army. Tummy is a quiet chap and never says very much. He tells me I chatter enough for him too.

Hansuncle and Nickitante get married in the autumn. The pastor, from our church, performs the wedding ceremony, after which only immediate family celebrate the union over a very simple meal outside our little shack.

Hansuncle has rigged up some planks for a makeshift table, where all twelve of us can sit and enjoy the meal together. I don't think we would have all been able to fit inside the hut.

The newlyweds have rented a room in an old tenement building down town, where I often go and visit them.

Groysie and I are both in the garden. She's digging up potatoes and I'm picking them up and putting them in a basket. When the basket is full, we both carry it down and empty the potatoes into the cellar Granddad's dug into the hill. This is our winter stash. We go back up the garden and repeat this process over and over.

I hear shouting from the top of the hill. When I look up, I see Heide standing up there, waving her arms about and shouting something.

As Groysie and I stand there watching, Heide runs down the hill, but can hardly speak she's so out of breath.

"You've got to come with me, Uta," she says. "You know the house in the next street where those two nice looking Romanian girls live?" She tells me panting.

"Yes, what about them?" I say.

"Well, the older one of the two, who's about eighteen or nineteen," Heide gasps, "She's been murdered."

"Who told you that, Heide?" Groysie enquires.

"I've just walked past the house," she says. "There are several policemen and lots of people standing outside the house and a woman said that the older of the two girls has been butchered."

"Come, let's go and see what's going on," says Heide, impatiently as she grabs hold of my arm and pulls.

Groysie tells me I can go, but I see doubt on her face. She obviously thinks Heide is making the whole thing up.

We both run up the hill over the top and into the next street. I can see lots of people have gathered outside the house Heide's on about.

We mingle with the crowd. People are saying the murderer is still in the house.

After a while, two policemen appear at the front door, escorting a young man in handcuffs down the steps and garden path towards the road. Heide pushes her way through the crowd, with me following behind, right to the front.

The young guy being led by the police is covered in blood and looks terrified. He's bundled into the back of a police van. Two police men get in behind him, a third one shuts and locks the doors then the van drives away. Heide and I stand and listen to all the horrifying and macabre stories people were telling.

The whole episode unnerved me, and I wanted to go home. I told Groysie that it was true, the young woman had been murdered and people were relating all kinds of gruesome tales about the killing.

The story released in the paper was horrendous. The young man was an army cadet in the military officers' school nearby. He'd been going out with the young woman, who then ended their relationship. Not wanting to accept her rejection, he'd got into the house and murdered her with an axe in the bath.

I was really freaked out by this. For months afterwards, I walked home from school the long way round which took about ten minutes more, rather than walk past the house where the murder took place.

I was having the most awful, vivid nightmares afterwards. The blood drenched murderer, chasing me, coming towards me or waiting in dark places for me with the axe.

How I wished I'd never gone with Heide to that house.

During different times of the year, school kids are required to do jobs in the community.

In autumn every child, of nine and over, has to stay on after school for two hours to rake, sweep and clear up fallen leaves from all the public parks in the area where they live. In the spring, we have to gather linden blossoms from the trees and take them to school.

Each child has to bring in 1 kg of blossoms.

In May we get the May Beetle. It has a four year cycle. Every fourth year, these creatures are prolific, like swarms or locusts. They descend on every tree and shrub, strip the leaves and blossoms and leave all the branches bare.

So, every fourth year, all school children are told to go out and kill these bugs, rip off their hard outer wings, collect them and take them to school.

Granddad says it's not a very effective way to control these pests, but everybody does their bit.

At the end of our garden are a few very old apple and plum trees that never bear any fruit. On a cool spring morning, when the dew lies heavy on the trees and grass, Granddad and I go up the garden to get rid of some beetles.

They're so dense on the branches, they almost hang like grapes.

Granddad shakes all the branches vigorously. The May beetles come raining down in a brown mass. They're still in a dormant state and lie thick on the ground. Granddad and I stomp in our boots all over them, then sweep the bugs into a bucket. We do each tree in turn, then Granddad burns them on a fire in the garden.

It never seems to make any difference, every morning for a couple of weeks the trees are laden with these pests, but we carry on killing as many as we can.

Every four years the plague returns.

In the autumn the circus comes to town.

Each school is allocated a day, on which they can take their pupils. I've missed it every year since I started school. Groysie hasn't had the money for me to go. Each time the class has been, the children talk about the circus for days after.

I tell Hansuncle how much I'd like to go to the circus, but we have no money to pay.

He gives me the money.

I'm so thrilled that I'll finally get to go to the circus.

The day before the class is due to go, the teacher collects all the money from the kids. I can hardly sleep that night with excitement. The following morning at school, I just can't concentrate and keep my mind on my work. Before we go home the teacher reminds us all what time we'll meet up outside the school for our trip.

She tells us we'll be going into the city by tram and then walk down to the river bank, where the circus tent has been erected.

Annemarie, my friend, has already been to the circus with her mother, so she's not going with the school.

I walk home with Ernst and chatter excitedly about our forthcoming outing.

He's going too, which I'm pleased about.

I was impatient all afternoon and kept nagging Groysie about the time. Eventually she said it was time to go. I ran nearly all the way to school.

When I got there, Ernst was the only kid waiting outside.

We both thought we must be early. As time went by nobody else arrived. I'd been so thrilled to be going to the circus and now it looked like I'd lost my chance.

I thought our alarm clock, which was as old as the hills, must have been wrong again.

Groysie said it had been a wedding gift. She was always correcting it when the factory sirens went off. Their wailing hooters sounded every shift change.

Neither of us gave up hope and kept waiting. As time went by, we became more and more miserable and felt very sorry for ourselves.

A very well dressed man walked past us. He stopped and turned round. I recognised him as being the father of a girl in our class. She was one of the girls, always very nicely dressed and had white bread sandwiches with meat, cheese or salami in them.

I asked the man what the time was, then told him we'd missed our class and they'd all gone to the circus. He said he knew because he brought his little girl and had seen all the children onto the tram.

He stood and thought for a couple of moments, then told us to wait for him there; he'd be back in a very short time.

Ernst said the man would perhaps come back and take us on the tram to the circus.

I was worried because I had no money and nor did Ernst, as we'd already given it to the teacher.

Moments later a black car stops on the road next to us and the same man steps out. He comes round and opens the back door for Ernst and me to get in.

I'm absolutely tickled pink. This is even more fantastic than going to the circus. I can't believe my luck. I've never ever been in a car before.

Cars are very rarely seen. Only army officers are driven around in them. Their drivers always get out and open doors for the officers and their ladies.

Here I am now, sitting in the back seat. It's all so plush with soft leather seats. I think the man is so clever, turning that wheel and making the car go just where he wants. I want to wave at everybody and shout, look at me.

I'm sitting next to Ernst, smiling from ear to ear, enjoying and savouring every moment of this magical event.

I don't want the car ride to end.

After a long journey, the man stops the car along the river bank, just as my class is filing into the entrance of the big circus tent.

Ernst and I thank Mr. Widlarz, then run and join our class as they enter the circus.

I find the inside fascinating with all the bench seats arranged in a circle round the outside of the arena.

It was a wonderful evening. I loved the elephants, horses, monkeys and other animals. The acrobats performed incredible feats and the clowns were hilarious. But nothing was quite as unforgettable, glamorous or luxurious, as the car ride.

I couldn't wait to get home and tell Groysie about my wondrous adventure.

Annemarie's friendship meant so much to me.

I felt so sorry for her, watching her struggle in that crippled body. Certain kids in my class never stopped being mean and nasty. I couldn't understand how they could be so horrible to my friend.

On occasions, I'd tell Groysie the things that were done to both Annemarie and myself and the nasty spiteful things said to us.

If I had nicer clothes, perhaps these kids would like me better.

Groysie said outward appearances shouldn't matter. I should be accepted and liked for who I was. She said I was kind hearted and always ready to help others. If only these kids would take the time to get to know me better, she was sure they'd like me.

That was no help or consolation to me. All I wanted was to be part of things and accepted.

Despite everything though, I was a pretty happy child.

I had my two best friends Annemarie and Heide.

I started going to Annemarie's house after school sometimes, so we could do our homework together. She had a lovely family, who all cherished her and were always very kind.

One of my places to spend time was Heide's house. They had a very comfortable home. At the front they had 2 rooms and a kitchen. Each room was so big, our little shack could fit three or four times into each room.

I loved their living room, with the bookshelf full of interesting books, which we could look at and read, whilst sitting on beautiful upholstered sofas and easy chairs. Richly coloured oriental rugs covered the smooth parquet floors. Frau Hannich had the most wonderful bone china displayed in glass fronted cabinets and Mr Hannich had a fabulous rock and gem collection in another show case along the wall. There were many beautifully framed original oil paintings and water colours adorning the big expanse of walls.

I was never happier than sitting in this room, with a book to look at and enjoying all this luxury.

Unfortunately, my little friend, Heide, did not appreciate the wonderful home, she lived in.

After a while, she got bored with books and I was dragged away to play houses on the unfinished next floor, with all the excess furniture from their house.

They had a wonderful summer house in the garden, where we often played. It was built completely out of bamboo, with big glazed windows, letting in lots of light. The big double doors, leading into the summer house, were made of small glass panels.

The couches and easy chairs in this place were also woven from bamboo and covered with lots of chintzy cushions. There was a row of shelves with books here too and an occasional table.

Frau Hannich spent a lot of her summer days in here.

Heide's grandparents and maiden aunt lived in the two roomed granny flat at the back of the house.

Heide's Granddad, a very frail old man, had died that spring and her granny had died soon after.

That only left her aunt, whom Heide mostly referred to as her crazy aunt.

She'd also spent many years in the Russian labour camps, from where she returned mentally ill. She never married.

Her brother, Heide's father, looked after her.

Heide takes me into the flat one day, when her aunt's out. The place is a complete shambles. The small kitchen has dirty dishes, pots and pans on every available surface. The living room is every bit as bad, with stuff strewn all over the place.

I follow Heide through a door into the bedroom, where all hell breaks loose, the moment we walk in.

She quickly shuts the door behind me.

Chickens are flying and running all over the place in complete and utter panic.

Heide tells me to stand still. The chickens don't know me and are afraid. I'm standing there, mouth wide open, taking in this incredible scene. The place stinks to high heaven and feathers are flying everywhere.

After a while, the chickens settle down and roost on the bed head, chair backs and anywhere else they can find.

The bed is covered in a heap of old blankets, which also serves as nests for the hens to lay their eggs in. Everywhere is covered in chicken poo.

Unbelievable!

The smell makes me retch.

Heide finds a few eggs, gives me a couple to hold and to my relief, we get out. I don't know what to say. I feel very embarrassed.

Heide doesn't give a damn. All she says is, I told you she's crazy, but at least we get eggs.

I tell Groysie all about Heide's aunt.

She says people like that can't help it and we have to have compassion for them. I keep thinking about that flat and the incredible mess and then, the beautiful home Heide lives in.

Heide told me that her granny looked after her aunt when she was still alive, and the chickens had lived in a coup with a run in the backyard.

After her granny died, her aunt had brought all the chickens in the house. Frau and Herr Hannich had tried to persuade her aunt to leave the chickens outside, which she refused to do and so, they just left her to get on with it.

Whenever Heide's mother sent her to get eggs, I waited outside in the yard for her.

The days are getting shorter and winter is coming up fast.

I don't relish the cold weather and thick snow. When I get up in the mornings, to go and stand in the queue for milk, it's pitch black outside and eerie.

Everyday, Groysie reminds me not to slide on ice, as it will wear the soles of my shoes away.

The kids at school make slides outside on the roads, which serve as our play area. During each break they line up, take a run and slide a few feet. It's a lot of fun and all the kids enjoy it. I usually stand and watch, remembering what Groysie's said.

Sooner or later, I can't help myself and join the other kids in the revelry.

Another way of entertaining ourselves during break is having snowball fights. We divide into teams and declare war. It also helps to keep me warm in the extreme cold.

Annemarie struggles walking home, especially in the winter, when the snow lays thick on the ground.

I've started walking home with her and carry her satchel, part of the way. She's so frail. Her skinny legs look like they could just snap in half. It must be awful to have her chest encased in that armour. Her breathing is always such an effort for her. When I watch her trying to catch her breath, it makes me feel breathless. Despite it all, she's one of the happiest kids I know.

Before Christmas, Groysie and I stand in several queues for meat, but never get any.

So Christmas Eve is celebrated with a bean soup, made from dried beans from the garden. I like bean soup, it's my favourite. I hardly remember what meat tastes like, as we only get it a couple of times a year, if we're lucky.

As the new year comes closer, I ask Granddad if we're going to the kids' party at his factory. He tells me definitely not, we don't need to be humiliated any more than we already are. I tell him I might be lucky this year and get a present and he tells me pigs might fly.

During the two week winter holiday, I stay indoors with my Groysie. I sit, while she's doing mending, sewing, cleaning and cooking, listening to bible stories she so often tells me.

I so wish I had a book to read. The girls at school lend each other children's books. I'll have to ask Annemarie to lend me one of hers. I know she has some as I've seen them on their bookshelf.

All the kids in my class go skating, skiing and tobogganing during the holidays and through the winter. I would love to do all these things too, but I don't have skis, skates nor even a toboggan. I don't have warm enough clothes anyway and would freeze.

After the holidays, the kids all start to plan for Fasching, which is something I'm not allowed to participate in, even if I were asked.

Before long March arrives and, with it, spring and Easter.

Annitante has brought home some colour for colouring Easter eggs, from the person with the connections. Groysie says all Annitante needs to do now is get some eggs from the same person.

To my amazement, Annitante comes home with ten eggs, just before the holidays.

I'm so thrilled. Finally, we're going to have coloured eggs.

Groysie hard boils them, dissolves one colour, at a time, in a bowl of hot water, adds a little vinegar and we place in two or three eggs.

She lets me stir them with a wooden stick until the colour is very bright. When they're all done, Groysie gives me a rag, with a few drops of cooking oil, and I rub all the eggs and place them on a plate.

The eggs look like precious jewels in red, blue, green and yellow.

Chapter Sixteen

May 1st - Labour Day. The biggest celebration in the communist world. Every year a massive podium is erected in the main square of Hermannstadt.

All the factory, office and shop workers have to congregate and take their turn to march past the podium and salute all the overfed, miserable looking, communist pigs, sitting there. This takes the whole morning.

After lunch, it's the turn of all the school kids to march by and salute all these blood suckers.

It's a very long boring day. All four junior classes meet outside the school in the morning. We walk in orderly file into the centre of the town, where we have to wait our turn to march past the podium. Everybody is bored to tears, including the teachers. No one has any choice, it's obligatory for all workers and school kids to attend every year, or face disciplinary action.

When it's finally our turn, we march past the podium, where we all have to turn our heads towards the vultures on the deck and salute. Even at that young age, I find the whole process completely obnoxious. These creatures in their dark sombre clothes look down on us, as though they're ready to pounce and suck the blood and soul out of us, which I suppose they're already doing.

By mid afternoon, the enforced march is over, and most people head out into the open somewhere. Not far from where we live, is what's known as the Young Forest. Heide and I often go out there and stand around watching couples and families paddle about on the lake in hired little rowing boats.

The Hermannstadt Zoo is also out there in the forest. It's a very small zoo and the animals are kept in tiny cages, in neglected conditions. Kids, under a certain age, can go in free of charge.

I don't like going into the zoo. The poor animals tear at my heartstrings, as they're pacing to and fro in their inadequate prisons. Heide begs me to go in with her. Sometimes I relent, but not always.

The animals in the zoo are all indigenous. The wolves and foxes are mangy, decrepit, nervous creatures.

The only brown bear is housed in a small round cage in the centre of the zoo, with all the other cages surrounding it. None of the animals have any outdoor space, where they can move more freely and get away from all the prying eyes. They have to live out their miserable lives in these small prisons, like the rest of us with barely enough to eat.

The bear upsets me most of all. Sometimes he lays down and his hind legs reach the cage on one side and his front legs touch the other side. It's so cruel and I can't bear to watch him. I get very upset and wish I hadn't come. I go home and cry my eyes out, as I tell Groysie about the poor animals in the zoo.

Groysie tells me I'm very compassionate and have a big heart. She says I shouldn't go to the zoo, as I become quite disturbed by seeing the poor animals suffer.

Heide is so different from me. Nothing upsets her, and she can just shrug off the plight of those poor creatures. When I see an animal or human being distraught and suffering, I can physically feel their pain and always end up so upset, I mull over the situation for days.

I go to the bread shop to get our ration for the day. The bread is only sold here, not baked. There's a very long queue and the shop is still shut. The store is right on the main road into town, where the tram runs.

As I stand in line, waiting for the bread van to arrive and the shop to open, I see a lovely little dachshund running across the road to our side. At the same time, I can see a tram coming. I watch, horrified as everything plays out in slow motion. The little dog runs right in front of the tram. I cover my eyes. I can't watch. When the tram has gone, I open my eyes, the poor little thing is lying on the track, nearest to us, with it's hind legs cut off. I'm absolutely mortified. I'm crying and asking people around me to do something. Nobody seems to care, it's only a dog a woman nearby says.

I want to scream and shout at her that the little dog hurts just as much as anybody else. The wretched animal drags itself onto the sidewalk, leaving a trail of blood from its severed legs. Dozens of people are standing in the queue, just looking on.

The scene is just horrendous. I walk over and kneel down by the little dog. The hind part of his body is lying in a pool of blood. He doesn't cry, or make any noise, just looks up at me with big sad eyes. I can't control my sobbing and heaving chcst.

A woman tells me to come away, as I can't help the dog. I ignore her and start stroking the poor little mite's head, while he looks at me. The back part of his body is twitching and shaking, then he closes his eyes and lays his head down.

The same woman tells me the dog is dead, but I carry on stroking him until his body stops twitching and he lies completely still.

I've forgotten all about the bread and start to walk home in a complete daze, with tears streaming down my face.

Groysie is always there, with her tender loving care, hugging and comforting me. What would I do without her? I tell her all about the sweet little dachshund. I tell her how nobody else cared, but I stroked him and stayed with him until he died. She tells me that she's sure the little dog would have appreciated my kindness.

Groysie said I was too sensitive for my own good and would, no doubt, get hurt a lot because of it.

In April, the weather starts to get warm and I can run around barefoot again. I love going to the grassy bit at the top of our garden. There's no fence there and the grass continues up the hill. When it's hot, I sit under the trees and look across the valley below, watching the trains go by in the distance. I watch, as the birds rebuild nests, or feed their young and wonder where they went for the winter.

The other side of the valley, beyond the railway line and the Cibin River, is the Hermannstadt airport. It's only small and is mostly used by the Romanian army and air force.

I can sit for ages and watch the small aeroplanes take off and land. Sometimes they have manoeuvres and the small fighter planes fly so fast and low, they look like they almost touch the hill behind me. They make such a terrible noise. I find them quite frightening yet fascinating. I sit and daydream, imagining that I'm flying away to some distant place and having wonderful adventures.

More often than not, Groysie's voice enters my fantasy world and brings me back to reality.

One day that spring, Heide comes skipping down our garden path and asks if I can go into town with her. Groysie wants to know why. Heide tells her there's a big fancy coach parked outside the Roman Emperor Hotel with lots of people from the West and everybody's going to look at it.

"What's the point of going and gawping at these people?" Groysie asks.

"Well," Heide says, "They're rich people, very finely dressed and I just want to see what rich people look like."

Groysie laughs, "Oh go on then, go and see. They're just people, like us, except for their fine and smart clothes."

Neither of us had any money for the tram, so it took us about an hour to walk into town. When we got to the Roman Emperor Hotel, sure enough, there stood the most beautiful posh coach, the like we'd never seen before.

A big crowd was standing around the coach, gawping and admiring it and hoping they'd catch a glimpse of the visitors.

After hanging around and waiting for what seemed an eternity, Heide announced she'd had enough.

"Your Granny said they'd be no different from us, so let's go," Heide informs me.

"But we've come all this way," I tell her. "Let's wait a little bit longer."

Heide always does what she wants, there is simply no compromising. "I'm going," she says. "You stay if you want. I'm going to get an ice cream."

"How are you going to get an ice cream, without money?" I ask.

"You just wait and see and I'll show you how," she answers, as we make our way through the throng of people and start walking down the main street of the city.

There are several cafés on the main thoroughfare, which are mostly frequented by communist party members and military officers, with their fancy women in gaudy dresses and painted faces.

I have often walked past these cafés on a Sunday, on my way home from Sunday School and seen these people, eating, drinking and smoking and enjoying the things, no ordinary person could afford.

At the first café, I follow Heide inside. The smell of cakes and vanilla makes my mouth water.

Heide walks right up to an officer, sitting with his lady, and tells him she's lost her ice cream money and would he buy her an ice cream.

I stand there stunned. Did I hear right? The officer opens his wallet, takes out some coins and hands them to Heide. I stand there thinking, that was easy!

Heide thanks him, then goes to the counter and asks for two ice creams, pays for them and then hands me one.

I was coming up to ten and Heide was nearly eight. She was very small for her age, cute as anything and seemed to get away with all kinds of things. I wasn't complaining, as I was enjoying my rare treat.

When we finished eating our ice creams, Heide turned to me and asked if I'd like another one, as we approached another café.

"You can't do that again Heide," I said. "Don't you have any shame?"

"Why should I?" She replied, pulling a face. "These officers have loads of money. They're always in cafés with their floozies, eating, drinking and enjoying themselves. Why shouldn't they give us a few Bani?"

If you looked at it that way it seemed to make sense, but I was too embarrassed and remained outside.

After only three or four minutes, Heide came out of the café, grinning from ear to ear, with two more ice creams.

"I think you do this quite often Heide, don't you?" I say.

"Of course, I do," she tells me in a cocky way as though it's her right. How else am I going to get ice cream," she says, licking her scrumptious cone.

"Just one thing Uta, don't ever tell anybody, especially my mother. I'll be in so much trouble."

"You, in trouble, Heide? You must be joking. You don't know what trouble is!"

"Swear you won't tell," she demands.

I promise to keep her secret.

As we wind our way home, Heide says we'll have to come again when another coach from the West is here. She says perhaps a coach from England will come and who knows, my father might be on it.

I tell her I don't think that will ever happen, but I can dream and live in hope.

It's June and the school year is ending once again. Exams are all finished and the last few days at school are relaxed and easy.

Marga, one of the girls in my class, asks me to her house after school one day to play. She's one of the girls who doesn't bother me, but she isn't too friendly either.

I can't wait to get home and tell Groysie about the invite. I've lived in the city and been to that school for 3 years now but am still not accepted by the other kids. I think maybe things are changing and I can make some more friends.

I hope there won't be too many chores for me to do when I get home. Groysie is very happy for me and says I needn't do any tasks, just have my food and then go and play. I'm in such a happy mood and skip off to Marga's house, which is opposite the school. When I get there, one of the nasty girls in my class is already there.

Marga tells me the game they intend to play needs at least three people and that's why she's asked Elke along.

She tells me the game is called Offended Liver Sausage and explains how it's played. She and Elke will hide and I'll have to find them. I say, "But that's hide and seek."

"Oh! Its a little different," says Marga, "and you'll find out soon enough why."

The house stands in the middle of a big garden with shrubs, trees and a summer house. The only place, we can hide, is in the garden.

I have to stand in the back facing the house, with my hands covering my eyes, and count up to one hundred.

When I'm finished counting out loud, I start to look for the two girls. I cover every bit of the garden, I look behind every bush, behind the summer house, walk all the way around the house, but they're nowhere to be found. I start all over again and look thoroughly, but still no sign of Marga and Elke.

Maybe they've gone round the house and managed to avoid me, so I decide to stay in front of the entrance door and just wait.

After waiting a long time for the girls, it dawns on me that they may be playing a nasty prank on me and I go home, feeling dejected and downhearted.

Groysie only has to see my miserable face to know things haven't gone well. I tell her what happened, and the game was called Offended Liver Sausage. She pulls a sad face and says that, without a doubt, the two girls had planned it all, just to be mean and cruel. She told me not to be so gullible and trust so readily and to stick to the friends I had.

I was very hurt, but even more so the next day at school. All the kids in my class were laughing at me and calling me Offended Liver Sausage.

Annemarie said it was a very mean trick the two girls had played on me and I should just ignore the name calling and be more careful in future. She said she'd never heard of such a game. Marga and Elke had made it up to be spiteful and nasty.

The time for me to return to Kerz for the summer is getting near. I'm really worried about going. Will mother punish me for running away? I have a terrible foreboding about my trip and beg Groysie desperately not to make me go.

She can't take me to the train station. She says I'm nearly ten years old now and a getting to be a big girl. She hands me my cloth bag and money for the tram and train. She says I'm to buy a return ticket and look after it well and keep the change for my return fare on the tram.

I can tell Groysie is sad and it hurts her to force me to go to Kerz and see me so unhappy, but she has no choice, it's not up to her.

I love her so much and can't bear to be separated from this wonderful woman. I hug her so tightly and then turn and walk up the garden path and up to the top of the hill. I feel rejection and sadness and am determined not to look back, but when I reach the top of the hill, I relent and turn around.

Groysie's standing outside our shack. She's holding the corner of her apron close to her face. I know she's crying and using the apron to wipe away the tears.

I feel bad for giving her such a hard time about going to Kerz. I know, if it was up to her, she'd keep me with her always and we'd manage somehow.

I know she's very unhappy about my going and worries what might happen to me. I wave to her, then turn and walk out of sight.

It seems like I'm on auto pilot. I don't remember the tram journey to the station at all. I'm standing in line in front of the ticket office window, my thoughts far, far away.

A woman behind me gives me a nudge and tells me she hasn't got all day. Will I buy a ticket or let somebody else go?

I awake from my reverie, buy my return ticket, then go outside onto the platform to wait for my train. At least, I do have a return ticket and, if things should get unbearable, I can always run away again. But Annitante has told me running away is bad and made me promise not to do it again.

The train journey is boring and long. The train stops at every piddly little village on the way. Even though the trip is so monotonous and tedious, I don't want it to end, but soon enough the train stops in Kerz.

I always seem to be the only person getting off here. But then what person in their right mind would want to come to a hell hole like this?

I stand, as usual, and watch the train go. I'm in no hurry, in fact I don't want to get there at all. All the bad memories from past years flood my whole being. I'm dawdling and taking my time going through the village.

When I get to the place where you have to turn either right or left, I take the right road, which takes me the long way round to the lane and my mother's house. It doesn't matter how long it takes, it's never long enough for me and I have to get there in the end.

I pass a few villagers, who greet me, I return their greetings politely. Eventually, I turn the corner into the lane, which is empty.

I open the street door and walk into the yard. Little Viorel, who is now about three, comes running to see who it is. He stops dead in his tracks, looking at me suspiciously. I say hello, holding my arms out to him. He turns and runs behind the house. Christian appears with Viorel in tow.

Christian just stands looking at me. I say hello. He says hello back, then turns and walks back to the chopping block, where he carries on chopping fire wood. I'm pleased to see him, but I don't think he's bothered one way or another.

I try to make conversation. I ask where everybody is. My brother looks at me as if to say, are you stupid or something?

"Where do you think they are? Working of course. What else do people do?" He snaps. "We can't all sit around doing nothing, like the people in the city."

"People in the city work too," I tell him defensively. "It's different work, but everybody works."

I know everything he says is what he's heard from my mother. She has a very low opinion about city folk. They're all lazy good-for-nothings.

I sense real animosity towards me. I feel very sad, but also scared. No matter what I do or say, it's always going to be wrong and criticised.

Being completely ignored by Christian, I go and sit in the shade at the bottom of the stairs, leading up to the verandah. I mull over all kinds of negative thoughts that go through my head. I feel as if every summer is a punishment, for what, I don't know.

It's late afternoon, when mother gets back from the fields. She looks exhausted. She just looks at me.

"When did you arrive?" She asks.

"This afternoon," I respond.

"So you've been sitting here since then, doing nothing?"

I tell her I would have helped, but didn't know what to do.

"Your brother never needs to be told," mother snaps at me.

I don't say anything but think, he lives here and knows what has to be done. To distract her I ask where uncle is. She tells me he's in the hills with the sheep and won't be back for a couple of weeks.

"Come with me!" She orders. "I'll find you something to do, I can't bear idle hands."

I'm expected to know how to do all the different chores. I get very tense and anxious. I worry about making mistakes when doing things. If I ask her for help or explanation, mother gets cross and impatient and tells me I'm useless.

When I ask my brother to help me with anything, he's as short tempered as mother and says I don't know anything. Their dislike for me is very evident in everything I do and things that happen.

Every summer, when I get off the train, I hope and pray that mother's and Christian's feelings will have changed towards me. I like to envisage being welcomed, embraced and maybe even loved. Instead, things seem to get worse every year.

I feel unhappy, dejected and abandoned.

The summer ahead looks very bleak. Why can't I have a loving, affectionate mother, like other kids?

I've asked myself that question so many times, without ever finding the answer.

The long hard days, the endless toil are a shock to my system. It's always midnight by the time I fall into bed and then we're woken up at six in the morning and another endless day of misery and hardship begins. I'm always so dog tired, I could drop down anywhere and go to sleep.

Most days we work in the fields with mother.

We leave early in the morning. On the odd days when Viorel is not left with his Grandmother, we have to take him with us. He's now old enough to amuse himself around us. We hoe weeds in rows and rows of different crops as far as the eye can see.

There's no machines doing any of the work, it's all done by hand. There's no respite from the toil or the scorching sun. Our scant clothing doesn't protect us at all.

Hay is still made in the antiquated way of cutting the grass by scythe, then turning it over after it's dried one side, so the other side can dry. The hay then has to be raked together and built up into hay stacks.

At midday, we find a shady place under a tree or bush and stop for something to eat. Lunch is always the same. Pieces of pure fat smoked belly bacon with a lump of bread or polenta and some onions. I'm always so hungry, I'm grateful for anything.

After our food, we get about 15 minutes break. Mother usually lies down and has a short nap and that's all I long to do, but Viorel doesn't give Christian or me any peace and we have to play with him. After boisterous play, Viorel usually sleeps for a couple of hours in the afternoon, but we all have to work.

The work in the fields is never ending.

By the end of July, the flax and hemp is cut. This job is done by scythes as well. It's mostly men who do the cutting and just a few women, some of whom, including the teenagers, gather the flax or hemp.

Christian and I are always the youngest kids working. The tall plants are gathered into bundles of a certain size and tied together, with a few strands from the plant. The bundles are laid down into big heaps, where throughout the day, they get picked up in carts, drawn by oxen and taken to the banks of the River Alt.

This goes on for many days.

When all the flax and hemp is harvested and deposited at the river, another process begins.

The plants have to be submerged in water for about two weeks.

Christian and I carry the bundles to the water's edge and pass them to mother. She submerges the bundles, ties them together with string and fastens the string to wooden stakes which have been driven into the river bed.

When a whole section is finished, we carry big stones from the river bank and mother places them on top of the submerged bundles to ensure they stay under the water and don't float away.

The job gets done section by section. The work is back breaking and by far the hardest we have to do.

It goes on for several days.

Viorel is left with his Romanian grandmother during this time, as we can't have him running around by the water.

After a couple of weeks and regular checks to make sure everything is still held down, it's time to get the flax and hemp out.

The husks of the plants have rotted in the water. They're slimy and smell putrid when Christian and I carry them to the bank. We just pile them in heaps until every last bundle is out. The river bank is wide and pebbly.

Each bundle is taken individually, held with one hand at the top, splayed out with the other hand like a fan and placed like cones on the hot stones and pebbles. The river bank ends up being covered in hundreds of individual little tipis, just touching each other.

It takes a few days for the scorching sun and intense heat to dry the husks of the plant, which becomes very brittle.

The dry bundles are then loaded on the oxen drawn carts again and several loads delivered to every household. The next part of the work is done in the back yards.

Instead of taking it to the collective farm, it's easier for everybody to do part of the process in their own places.

The next part I've watched women do for several years and have always found it fascinating. Mother says I'm old enough to learn how to do it now.

Three funny looking long wooden contraptions, on four legs, are brought to the yard and placed in a row.

Two thick wooden planks run from one set of legs to the other, with a big gap left in between. A third plank with a handle on the end fits snugly between the two outer ones. A thick wooden peg holds all three planks and the top of the two wooden legs together. The middle plank can be moved up and down by a handle on the end, which makes it a little like a guillotine.

The lower part of the middle plank is shaped into a sharp edge. This is then lifted by the handle. With the other hand a bundle of the dried hemp or flax is placed across the lower planks. The blade that goes in between is then brought down repeatedly on the dried plants. Every chop the bundle is pulled across a little until the whole length has been hacked into small pieces. This is repeated several times, until the husks are very fine and small. The bundle is then whipped up and down against the wooden contraption, so the husks all fall out and just the plant fibres are left. The fibres are then wrapped around the hand and the other half of the bundle gets the same treatment.

When it's all done, the fibres are combed with a small wooden comb to get every last bit of hull out and the fibres look like a mane of blond hair, all smooth, soft and shiny. The bundle of fibres is then twisted and tied in such a way, so it won't become tangled.

I'm only just ten years old and find the whole process extremely difficult.

Sunday can never come too soon to get some rest. Christian and I still have our chores to do in the morning before we can go out. Mother does her own thing as always.

This summer mother's told me I have to wash my own clothes as I'm old enough. After I put on my Sunday dress, I wash my work clothes in a bowl of cold water with homemade soap by the well. I do my best and wash my little work dress and one pair of underpants the way I've seen Groysie do it. Then hang them on the garden fence.

Every couple of weeks I wash my Sunday dress and underpants, so they're nice and clean. The work we do is so dirty. My work dress and pants get so grubby and filthy after six days, that they can almost stand up by themselves.

In church I often sit on my own during the service. Afterwards I tag along with the other kids. We often go to the streams. Everybody just messes about in the shallow water in their underpants. I'm always so tired and lay down under willow shrubs and go to sleep. When I wake up sometimes the kids have gone and left me behind. I always catch up with them on the village green.

August is wheat, rye and barley harvest. Every able body has to work to get the crop in. Men do all the cutting by scythe and the women and kids bundle the grain up, which once again is taken by the only transport available, oxen and carts, to the collective farm. Here the bundles are fed into the combine harvester by men and women. At the other end the grain is collected in light brown sacks and stacked into piles.

Trucks come and go all day long. The sacks are loaded on to them and driven away. No doubt most of the harvest ends up in Soviet Russia, like everything else produced here. Romania is plundered and robbed of all its agricultural products, coal, minerals and oil. The general population is left to fight and scrap in endless queues over the little the soviet communists leave.

I dread the grain harvest as much as I hate the flax and hemp gathering.

Christian and I have to go with mother every day after we drop Viorel at his granny's. Working in the fields, bundling the crop is the worst possible job. The men cut the wheat close to the ground and leave razor sharp stubble behind. The women gather the wheat into bundles and the children carry and make big piles of them.

Some kids and adults wear boots. Mother has some, but Christian and I don't. Christian and I shuffle with our feet trying to flatten the stubble, so it won't cut us. Despite that our feet become lacerated and always bleed. The soles of our feet are tough from running barefoot all summer long, but not hard enough to stop the sharp stubble cutting us.

Every evening when we get home, Christian and I sit with our feet in cold water. It's very soothing. We don't have any creams or bandages and have to carry on walking on the dusty packed earth in bare feet. My feet are still full of sores when I go back to Hermannstadt at the end of August.

After the grain harvesting is over my mother has a family of four from Hermannstadt coming to stay with us for one week as paying guests.

This family come every year but it's the first time they're staying at our house.

Mother has been very busy and I've helped to clean and get the big front room in the house ready. For the first time I can remember, she's got flowers in vases in the room.

One of the jobs I'm given is scrubbing the wooden floor boards on the verandah and the wide concrete steps down to the door leading into the lane.

Christian has been busy doing jobs in the yard. Cutting wood, tidying up and sweeping the big back yard that's always covered in goose and chicken droppings.

First, I water all the geraniums in the troughs lining the tops of the low outer walls of the verandah. Then I go down to the well, draw a bucket of water and empty it into another bucket to scrub the floorboards with.

The bucket is so heavy for me and I struggle to get it up each step. I clip the bottom of the bucket on the very last step from the top, it goes over and the water spills all over the verandah floor.

Having heard the clattering of the bucket, my mother appears in the doorway of the house. She stands there looking furiously down at me. I'm already shivering and shaking with fear, nervously blabbering that it was an accident, I didn't mean to do it and would clear it up straight away.

I'm wearing my Sunday dress as the guest's arrival is imminent. I'm soaked from the waist down.

In a couple of strides my mother stands towering over me, screaming abuse and yelling that I'm the most clumsy and stupid creature she's ever known.

Mother then grabs the front of my dress, yanks me off my knees and hurls me down the twelve concrete stairs.

It all happens so quickly. I tumble down the steps, head over heels, banging every part of my body on the way down and land in a heap at the bottom. Mother is standing at the top of the stairs still hurling abuse at me.

She's in a real rage now and ranting at me nonstop to get up, go to the well and clean myself up before she comes down to me and gives me the hiding of my life.

Christian looks on concerned. He comes over to me to try and help me up. Mother yells at him to leave me be and go back to his work.

I can feel wet trickling down my face. When I touch it there's blood all over my hand. One of my knees is bleeding too. I hurt from head to toe.

Mother orders me to the back of the yard, as she doesn't want our guests to walk in on this scene.

My body and head are throbbing. Blood's running down my lower leg and face. My feet are so sore from the stubble cuts, I find walking quite painful. I gingerly get off the ground and then realise that my dress at the front is ripped open from top to bottom.

I drag myself to the well at the back of the yard, with tears quietly streaming down my face. What am I going to wear now? Why is life so cruel and brutal? Why is my mother so sadistic?

Christian comes over to me at the well. He stands looking at me not knowing what to say. At least he seems to have some compassion for me after all. I tell him to go away otherwise he'll be in trouble too if mother catches him with me.

With real difficulty and each movement so painful, I draw water from the well and put some into the enamel bowl. We don't have flannels and I use my hands to wash the blood off myself. I have a cut on my face, but a much bigger one on my knee, which won't stop bleeding. I sit on the trough next to the well and let the sun dry me off.

My mother appears after a while with a needle and a reel of cotton. She hands them to me and tells me to sew the front of my dress up.

The only other time I'd tried to sew was when Annitante tried to teach me cross stitch when I was about seven. When I went wrong with my stitches, she'd whack me across my knuckles with a wooden spoon. This didn't help, it just made me even more cack-handed, which then ended in tears. Groysie intervened and told Annitante to leave me be, that I was too young to learn all the intricate stitches. I lost all interest in sewing after that.

Mother goes and gets on with her chores. I take my dress off and sit on the wooden bench at the back of the house in my panties. I start stitching the dress as well as I can. It seems to take me forever. When I'm finished

I hold the dress up and examine my work. The stitches are big and crude. I've made a real mess of it. The material is all puckered and I can still see some holes. The two halves don't meet at the hem. The whole thing looks just dreadful and shabby. I've done the best I can and put the dress back on. I feel like a gypsy kid in a ragged old dress. Just as well the school kids can't see me.

When I see mother, I think she's going to berate me about my stitching, so before she says anything I say I couldn't do the job very well. She simply shrugs her shoulders and tells me she doesn't care, that I'm the one who has to wear it.

Later in the afternoon the family of four arrive on their big black motorbike. I recognise the father. His name is Oscar Schomody, he's Hungarian.

Every spring, the streets in the centre of Hermannstadt are cordoned off and they have the annual motor bike race. Heide and I went for the first time this year. We didn't have to pay. We just stood on one of the streets and watched the racers whiz by. Oscar Schomody is a well-known rider and wins lots of races.

His wife is a pretty blonde Saxon lady with red painted lips. Her little girl Traute, who's equally pretty with short blonde curly hair, about five or six years old is sitting on the pillion in between her mother's legs.

Their son, who's dark haired like his father, who's name I don't recall, is sitting on a soft pad on the petrol tank in front of his father. They're all dressed in leather pants, jackets, aviator hats and goggles.

At the back of the motor bike two suitcases are strapped to a luggage rack.

Herr Schomody gets of the bike first, kicks the stand down under the rear wheels, then lifts his children down and holds his wife's hand as she gets off.

Christian and I stand together to attention. Viorel is looking at the big motorbike as though it's a monster from out of space. I don't think he's ever seen one before.

Mother has told us to be of help whenever it's needed and be nice and polite to our guests. As if we'd even dream of doing anything else.

Christian looks all tidy in his Sunday clothes. Viorel who runs around naked all the time and is tanned all over from the sun, like a gypsy with a snotty nose and grubby all over, is now washed and nicely dressed.

I'm the only one who looks a dishevelled mess. Bruises have started to appear all over my body. There's a big bruise on my cheekbone Christian told me, with a nasty gash.

Frau Schomody takes one look at me. "Goodness child what happened to you?" She asks.

I stand there not saying anything. It's more than my life is worth telling what happened. My mother pipes up. "Oh, she's just the clumsiest child in the world, she's always falling and hurting herself."

Frau Schomody replies, "But that looks more than just a fall."

"She fell down the stairs the silly goose, she never looks where she's going," Mother counters.

The lady seems concerned and comes closer to look at my face. "You have to be more careful child," she gently says. "You're lucky you didn't break any bones."

I stand there dumb. How I wish I could tell the truth, but I know I can't.

The following week mother spends at home, cooking breakfast, lunch and dinner for our guests.

The Schomodys go to the streams and river swimming. They go for walks on the other side of the river and pick wild strawberries and mushrooms. A lot of the time they take it easy and relax.

The whole family is always beautifully dressed. The little girl is dressed, like a doll, in pretty colourful dresses and gorgeous sandals. The mother wears the most stylish sundresses and strappy sandals and lovely bathing suits. Oh, how I wish I had just one dress like that.

The children are very spoilt, especially the little girl. She cries and throws terrible tantrums when she doesn't get her own way. She always says no to her mum and dad and hits them. The parents indulge their little angel and let her do exactly as she likes. They think their little darling's antics are so cute and adorable and everybody else loves her too.

My mother has taken the parents' lead and gives Traute a lot of her time and indulges her too. She picks her up and tells her what a sweet little thing she is. She even takes the time to play little games with her.

It makes me very upset to see mother behaving this way towards Traute. She's never ever given us a minute of her time or treated us nicely.

Mother kills a goose and a couple of chickens during the week. I have to hold one of the struggling chickens on a block of wood while she holds its head and chops it off.

Christian normally does it, but he's not around. I'm very squeamish about the whole thing. I hate seeing anything killed or hurt. Just as mother is about to bring the hatchet down, I let go of the chicken. She's very angry and it takes us a long time to catch another one.

When we try a second time, I turn my head away. I can't watch. I find it all too gruesome and upsetting. When the head's cut off I release the chicken and it jumps and flutters all over the yard, spurting blood from the neck all over the place. Mother is none too pleased with me.

I have to help with some of the easy preparations of the food and then help to take it to the table. It always looks so appetising and smells delicious. I'm sure it must taste out of this world.

My mother, I'm told, is the best cook in the village, having apprenticed with a famous cook in Hermannstadt. Pity we never get to taste any of her cooking.

Not once while the family from the city was with us, did we get the same food they had. Mother always made me clear the table after a meal. I was so tempted to dip my fingers into the leftovers but was too scared mother would catch me. She had eyes in the back of her head, I was sure of that.

On a couple of occasions Frau Schomody asked me to go to the river or for a walk with them. Mother always told her she needed me to help with chores and look after Viorel. I think she was worried I might talk and tell about the cruelty and violence she subjected us to.

After a week our guests packed their things, tied their cases to the luggage rack, dressed in their leathers, got on their bike and waved goodbye to us all.

How I envied those kids and the lives they had. They had the most wonderful mother and father. That's all I ever wanted. I didn't even care so much about being poor. But to have parents who loved and adored you, must be the best thing in the world.

Only another week before the end of August and then thank goodness I can return to my Groysie and Granddad, who must be the best grandparents in the world and I am so lucky to have them. I can't wait. Thoughts of running away from Kerz have crossed my mind many times through the summer, but Groysie said it was wrong and I mustn't do it again. It's been very hard to keep my promise, but I didn't want to disappoint her.

Christian has been going to the German school in the village, but it only goes up to the fourth grade. The other Saxon kids go by train every day to the next small town where the German school goes up to the seventh grade. My brother says he'd love to go there too with all his friends, but mother is sending him to the Romanian school in the next village, which has seven grades. The village is a two hour walk each way and no trains or buses go there.

Christian will walk there with some Romanian kids every Sunday afternoon, sleep and eat in the boarding room and walk home on Saturday afternoon.

I ask him what will happen in the winter when deep snow covers everything. He says he doesn't know.

Christian opens up and says he'll be pleased to get away from mother and all the beatings, cruelty and hard work.

He then tells me he's deaf in one ear from a beating he had when he was only eight years old.

He goes on to tell me that it wasn't long after Annitante came and got me and had took me back to Groysie and Granddad. He tells me what a terrible time that was. How much he missed me and wanted to go as well. He said he just wanted to die.

I was so upset to hear him talk like this. I loved my brother so much and couldn't bear to see him hurting so dreadfully with no one to talk to.

He said mother had given him a can to go and fetch a litre of paraffin from the village shop, for the lamps. When he got back he tripped, on a step going up to the verandah and spilled a little paraffin.

Mother had grabbed the nearest thing to hand, which happened to be the yard broom, and repeatedly hit him round the head and back with the heavy handle.

The pain had been so severe, it felt like the whole side of his face and head is on fire. Blood oozed out of the ear. The pain was unbearable for days after and he cried a lot. Mother never took him to the doctor in the next town and just let him suffer. Eventually the pain went, and he became completely deaf in that ear.

As I sat and listened, I cried, and my heart went out to my poor brother. I told him I was pleased that he was getting away from my mother for a lot of the time too.

As on previous occasions I walked to the train stop on my own. I felt sad to leave Christian, but very happy to leave my mother.

My bruises from being thrown down the steps were gradually fading, but still visible. I told Groysie and Granddad what had happened. They were both shocked, but thankful that my injuries hadn't been worse.

The punishments I received from my mother every summer were numerous and most of the time I couldn't even understand the reason for getting them.

It was good to be back at school.

Annemarie and I were very pleased to see each other again. We'd not been together all summer.

Annemarie invited me to her house one afternoon soon after the beginning of school. She'd had a wonderful holiday at the Black Sea with her mother. Her father had taken her out quite a lot and brought her wonderful gifts from his travels in Western Europe. He was an engineer working for the Romanian government and travelled abroad a lot.

I've already seen some of the presents she's been given, including a box of twenty Faber Castel colouring pencils in the most beautiful and bright colours imaginable. They don't break when you use them, like the Romanian rubbish I have to use.

Her father has also bought her a fabulous German fountain pen. Most kids in my class have fountain pens. Their parents have had them since before the war. I have to use a nib and ink. How I'd love a pen like Annemarie's.

She's been kitted out with everything from Germany for school, stationary items like pencils, erasers, geometry sets, even exercise books with very fine paper, not the thick rough stuff available here.

Annemarie tells me she has a lot more things at home, which she can't wait to show me. When I get to her house in the afternoon, all her presents are laid out on the dining table. There are more school supplies with a dictionary and a whole set of Heidi books plus a whole range of new winter clothes and boots. It reminds me of the time father sent us stuff from England and I know how happy she feels.

The object that intrigues me most is a strange looking contraption. It's like a pair of goggles that fit snuggly round the eyes. A short arm extends out from the goggles, at the end of which is a slot.

Annemarie tells me to clip the goggles on my head. She then drops a slide into the slot and the scene in front of my eyes comes to life. She says what I see is in 3D, I haven't got the foggiest what it means, all I know is, the picture in front of my eyes looks so real as if I were there.

When she takes the slide out I beg her to let me look longer. Annemarie laughs and says there are lots of slides and wouldn't I like to see them all.

In all she has a box of fifty slides. I sit and look in awe and wonder at Niagara Falls, the Sky Scrapers in New York, The Grand Canyon, The Pyramids, Wildlife in Africa, The beautiful Islands in the Caribbean and Hawaii. Then there are lots of slides from the European Capitals, London, Paris, Rome, Madrid and a host of others. Pictures from famous mountains in the world.

It's like going on a world tour and experiencing everything live. I'm so overwhelmed by it all, I'm completely speechless. If I could have anything at all, this is what I'd want.

I go home and tell Groysie all about Annemarie's presents from Germany. I think she's very lucky to have such lovely things.

Groysie tells me she doesn't think Annemarie is lucky. She says all these material things she has, don't compensate for having to live her life in that crippled body and not be able to do all the things other children do. Groysie says she's sure if Annemarie had the choice, she'd rather be strong and healthy and forego all these worldly things. It gives me food for thought and I realise Groysie is right.

Annemarie is very kind and always lets me look at her special pictures whenever I go round. She also lets me use her colour pencils and some of her other stuff. After what Groysie said to me, I don't ever feel envious over the things she has.

That autumn, my class goes to see a film with Hans and Lotte Hass. The film is all about diving in the Red Sea and the wonderful underwater world. Some of the kids have already seen the film with their families and talk about it nonstop.

I'm not allowed to the cinema, but I am desperate to see this movie. I tell Groysie that everybody has to go as it's an educational film. The teacher told us we didn't have to go, it was only for those who wanted to go.

I feel bad for lying to Groysie.

Annitante says she'll write a note to my teacher, so I can be excused from going. I beg Groysie to let me go. I tell her it's a good film all about the beautiful fish and wonderful creatures under the sea.

Groysie says she can't see any harm in me seeing such a movie and gives me the money to take to school.

I'm over the moon and just hope Annitante doesn't find out that I lied.

The film is just wonderful, way beyond anything I could have imagined. I sit glued to the big screen, not even wanting to breathe, marvelling over the bright, vivid colours of the underwater life. It's the first time I've been to the cinema. Annemarie goes all the time and sees all kinds of films. I completely fall in love with the big screen and wish I could go sometimes too, but it's against our religion.

The incredible experience of watching that film remains imprinted in my mind forever.

Hansuncle and Nickitante have moved from their one roomed place in town. She's expecting a baby. They've found a small annexe, that has two rooms at the back of a house, right the other side of town from us.

It takes at least an hour and a half to get there. It's a tram ride all the way across the city and then a long walk. The tram fare is expensive, so I won't be able to visit very often any more. When they lived closer, I visited all the time.

The train track, down in the valley below us, runs right past the back garden, where my uncle now lives. Walking along the train track is a direct route and only takes about an hour to get there and doesn't cost anything.

The first time we try this new way, Groysie goes with me.

She shows me exactly where to walk and never to go on the tracks. After that I often visit my uncle and aunt on Saturday after school and stay with them overnight. The next morning, we all go to church and I go home with my grandparents.

Baby Renate is born on October 18th. She's a sweet little thing. Her parents absolutely adore her and have fallen madly in love with their little girl. Groysie tells me it's her birthday too, which I didn't know, as birthdays were never celebrated.

We've started having games at school once a week for an hour. Our playground is the street outside the school.

The teacher marks two halves on the road with chalk for dodge ball. I love playing games, especially dodge ball.

Two boys are usually the captains of the teams. I'm always one of the first kids to be picked for a team. I'm very agile and run well. Most of the time I manage to stay in the game till the end. This is the only time at school where I'm accepted and wanted on a team.

Poor Annemarie just stands on the side line watching and cheers us all on. She says she doesn't really mind watching.

It's the time of year again when Groysie and I have to make endless trips to the furniture factory where Hansuncle and Tummy work. We haul back cartfuls of sawdust in a little wooden cart which Hansuncle has made. The sawdust serves as fuel for the winter to heat our little hovel.

Granddad has rigged up a shed of sorts, near the house, from bits and pieces, to store the sawdust.

Every year Granddad seems to erect another little wooden hut to house something or other and the place is beginning to look like a shanty town.

Granddad has put up a rickety old fence round the shack. Somebody has given him a puppy, which is called Frunza, it means leaf in Romanian. The pup is tied to a chain. The chain runs along a wire that's stretched the length of the little fenced in yard.

Frunza is such a sweet little dog, always so pleased to see me. I go out and play with him whenever I can. He's never let off his chain and sleeps in a small wooden doghouse, Granddad has made. All he gets to eat is polenta and table scraps, but then we don't have more than that ourselves.

When Granddad brought the dog home, Groysie said, "What the heck do we need a dog for? It's only another mouth to feed."

Granddad told her the poor unfortunate little creature was going to be drowned and he would make a good guard dog.

"What?" Groysie laughed, "A guard dog? What on earth do we have that needs guarding?"

"Oh well," Granddad said. "I thought Uta would like the little dog."

And of course, I did, I was very happy to have Frunza.

One day, Annitante brought home a book called the Pilgrims Progress. For a while this book replaced the ritual of the bible reading and never ending prayers after our evening meal.

Religious literature was forbidden by the communist regime. They kind of ignored bibles, but any other religious books were strictly forbidden and yet people still manage to get hold of them. A friend from church lent my aunt the book.

Every evening, when Annitante's not at work, she reads the Pilgrims Progress to the whole family. I have to sit and listen while passages are read, then discussed and analysed. Everybody seems to have their own idea about what the author means. I get so bored I want to scream.

Another evening Annitante brings home a large poster and sticks it on one of the blank whitewashed walls. This is the only picture of any sort that adorns the walls of our shack. Annitante sits down with me and explains the meaning of the brightly coloured poster.

On the left hand of the poster, a wide road leads from the bottom to the top of the picture. Along both sides of the wide road are big elaborate buildings with signs written on the front. One says 'Dancehall,' another says 'Casino'. Further along there's 'Bar', 'Ladies of the Night' and 'Theatre' and so on.

I've no idea what these places are I tell Annitante. She says they are bad places, where people go and sin.

I ask what it is they do to make them sin.

Annitante tells me the people drink, gamble, dance, smoke, party and all kinds of other things God wouldn't like. Parading, along this long wide road are fancy dressed men and women doing all these sinful things.

Some are embracing and kissing, others are smoking and drinking. Women in frilly dresses pulled over their knees are dancing. They all look like they're having fun to me.

At the top of the road there's a big fierce fire burning. The word "HELL" is written in big letters over the fire, where a grotesque figure, with horns and cloven hooves, is sitting. He's wielding a whip over all the revellers in the road.

On the right side of the picture a narrow path meanders from the bottom to the top. There are no big buildings along the path, just a few very humble dwellings. There's just a handful of people with large sacks on their backs, bent over, with the weight of their heavy burdens.

Along the way, two or three narrow paths join the wide road with the narrow one. There's a couple of bedraggled figures, who have dropped their load by the way side on the narrow path and are making their way over to the wide road. They've been seduced by all the worldly things and have abandoned their faith.

There are also one or two figures in fancy clothes, walking from the wide road over to the narrow one. These people have repented and want to walk the narrow path for everlasting life with Jesus.

The narrow road leads to fluffy white clouds at the top of the poster. Angels are singing and playing harps. God, in beautiful robes, with a white beard, is sitting on his throne. His arms are held open wide and extended to receive the people with their heavy burdens from the narrow path.

This whole image is terrifying to me. Annitante says all the people on the wide road end up in hell and that's what happens if you go to these places and do the things people do there.

Annitante tells me I must always walk the narrow path and not indulge in the sinful things other people do.

I tell my aunt that all the kids at school, even Annemarie and Heide, they all go to parties and the cinema. She tells me they'll all go to hell.

This really upsets me, and I start crying.

Granddad's been listening and now tells me what Annitante says is true and I must listen to her. He also says if people were meant to smoke, God would have created us with chimneys on the top of our heads. He also maintains when people dance and twirl round and round, it's the devil who's driving them with his whip.

I believe everything Granddad tells me and promise I won't do these terrible things. I think about the times I've told lies, when I've wanted to do some of the things the other kids, do and wonder if God will strike me down, or if I'll go to hell.

I'm in grade four now, my last year at junior school. Next autumn all the kids in my class will go to the senior school in the city centre. It'll take an hour to get there and I'll be going by tram some of the way.

I've heard the adults talk about this. They're already worried about how they're going to manage the tram fares every week.

This year we start having Russian lessons. We still speak Saxon at home, but my German and Romanian are equally good. Romanian is taught in German school right from grade one and, of course, it's the first language in Romania. One has to speak it wherever one goes, work, shops, government places etc.

We've had four Romanian kids in our class from grade one; twin boys and two girls.

Some of the Romanian parents want their children to learn German, so they immerse them into a German school for the first four years, where they become fluent. When these kids reach senior school, they go into the Romanian educational system. Until college only Russian is taught as a foreign language.

Professor Tiachuk is our Russian teacher and has a reputation for being very strict. All our teachers in junior school have been strict and all the children have the highest respect for them.

Behaviour is the first subject on our end of school report each year and if you don't get top marks you have to repeat the year.

Everything we've heard about the Russian teacher is true. She's even worse than we all expected.

First, we have to learn a completely new alphabet, which proves to be pretty challenging for all the kids. When we mispronounce words, it really annoys the teacher. She shouts the words out and makes us repeat them over and over, making us put the intonation on the right syllable.

"I don't want you to speak like peasants from outer Mongolia," she shouts at the class. "I want all my students to speak with an educated and refined Russian accent."

There's one boy in our class, who's been kept behind from the previous class. He's quite a rebel, cheeks and answers the teachers back all the time. We've never experienced such behaviour from any other child towards a teacher and are all taken aback.

The boy slouches in his desk and says in a loud voice. "What difference does it make what kind of Russian we speak? I don't want to learn, let alone speak the stupid language. I certainly never want to go to Russia."

The teacher stands in front of the class, her face and neck flushed, bristling with rage. She stares at this kid for a moment or two. The attention of the whole class is on him. He carries on lounging in his seat as though he hasn't a care in the world. I think he's so brave to talk to the teacher like that.

Without a word, the teacher marches up to the boy, grabs him by the ear and yanks him on to his feet. He stands there defiantly staring in her face.

The teacher seems to be lost for words. We can all see she'd like nothing more than to hit him. That's not allowed. The old days of physical punishment in schools have gone. Beside herself with anger, she stomps back to her table and faces the class.

She spits her words to the whole class, saying that she can't make us learn Russian, but she can keep us in the fourth grade until we're fourteen years old and leave school. She says we have to make our choice and can defy her as much as we like, but that she'll win in the end.

We all sit as quiet as church mice, except for the belligerent kid who piped up that school's no bloody use to anybody anyway.

This boy was like that in all the lessons.

The teachers just didn't know what to do with him. He lived way out in the woods somewhere and said he was happiest when he was climbing trees. He was often absent from school. His parents obviously didn't care whether he went to school or not.

At the end of that school year when we went to the school in town he remained behind again. He eventually made it to grade five where he was at the age of fourteen when he left school. We all felt that way about learning Russian. We would have rather learnt English or French. Why would anybody want to learn the oppressor's language? Having no choice, we had to knuckle down and do it anyway.

Another lesson most kids hate is Social Studies, which we start in grade five in our new school.

Our headmaster, who's a real creep and no doubt a communist, otherwise he would not have the job, takes us for these lessons. He feeds us all a load of propaganda and tells us how lucky we are to live in this wonderful communist paradise. He often talks about the West; how poor people are, dying of starvation and oppressed by the upper classes. He tells us they live in workhouses and have to work round the clock.

The headmaster can be quite devious and throw in subtle crafty questions about our parents and what they talk about at home. He does it in such a way that makes him seem interested in us and our families.

I've had it drummed into me not to repeat what's said in our house. Thousands of people have been taken away by the Securitate (secret police). Very often, somebody, with a grudge against a work colleague or neighbour, has reported them, and told lies about things they are supposed to have said about the communist regime. There were so many political prisoners, who had to do hard labour or were imprisoned for months or even years.

After a Social Study class, I'd go home and tell my family what we were taught. Groysie said the stories our headmaster was telling us were true, but life had been like that two or three hundred years ago, but certainly not today.

My Grandparents often talked about life before the war. Everybody in Transylvania had a very good standard of living. It was the richest country in Europe and very prosperous before the war. Bucharest had been known as the Paris of the East. They had all kinds of minerals and oil. Some of the best farming land and vineyards were right where we lived. Big herds of livestock grazed in the valleys and the foothills of the Carpathian Mountains. People had plenty of everything and were free to come and go as they pleased.

Stalin was the most hated man and just one wrong word against him could get you years behind bars.

He was responsible for the death of millions, far more than Hitler ever killed. We were fed so much rubbish and the newspapers spouted nothing but propaganda about how Stalin had saved us from tyranny and oppression from the West.

I didn't know anybody who believed any of it.

Heide comes to my house one day and asks Groysie if I can go to the public bath with her. I've never been and pester Groysie until she lets me go.

Heide says we have a choice. We can go to the swimming pool or get a cubicle with a big bath tub and sit in the hot water for an hour. The swimming pool sounds enticing, but I can't swim and I don't have a swimming suit either. I'd have to go into the pool in my underpants. Sitting in a hot bath up to my neck sounds divine.

So we decide to go for the bath.

Heide's been to the public baths quite a bit with her mother and knows all the ropes. The Roman Baths are in the town centre. We pass it on the tram every time we go to church.

It's one of those old impressive looking buildings with pillars and arches, like the ones I've seen in books in Heide's house of the Roman times.

The big domed entrance hall with marble floors and pillars is quite majestic looking. I look around in awe.

Heide goes over to the cash desk and pays the lady behind it some money. She's given a big key, two towels and a small bar of soap. There are several doors leading to different parts of the building. Heide tells me there are steam rooms, cold and hot dipping pools, shower rooms and of course the big swimming pool.

"What an amazing place and people come here to do all these things?" I ask.

"Of course they do, silly," she says.

We take one of these doors which leads into a long corridor, which is a little steamy and warm. There are doors either side of the corridor with numbers on them.

Heide checks the number on the key and then opens the door with the corresponding number.

The cubicle is quite big with a massive white enamelled bathtub along one wall. Heide puts the plug in the bath then turns on both taps. Piping hot steaming water is gushing like a torrent out of one tap and cold water runs out just as fast out of the other tap. I watch with interest and amazement, as I've never seen so much hot water.

At my house, we have a small tin tub that hangs on a nail on the outside of our shack. Once a week, Groysie brings it in and sets it in the middle of the floor. She boils two big pots of water on the wood burning stove, then adds it to the cold water she's already poured into the tin tub, which still only brings the water about a quarter up the side.

Groysie then places two wooden chairs in front of the bath and drapes a blanket over the chair backs, to provide some privacy for the person in the tub.

Granddad always goes in first. He has to sit with his knees tucked up as there's no room to stretch his legs. I often wash his back for him. He doesn't stay in long as everybody has to have a turn.

Annitante always goes in next and if Tummy is there, he goes after her. Every time somebody else gets in, Groysie adds some more hot water. By the time it's my turn to get in the tub, the water is dirty and scummy. I sit and stretch my legs. Groysie washes my back and I do the rest. She doesn't go in the tub, she'd rather have a strip wash when no one else is in the house.

After undressing and hanging our clothes on hooks at the back of the door, we stand and watch the enormous tub fill up with all this steaming hot water. When it's about half full we both climb in.

The water is already up to our chests, but we let it run until it reaches our necks. The bath is so wide and long, we can lie side by side completely stretched out and sill not touch either end.

Wouldn't it be lovely if we could do this every week, I say to my friend.

What an indulgence. I go under the water, roll around and savour every moment. I've undone my plaits and washed my long hair with soap.

It feels so good. When the water cools off a little, one of us pulls out the plug to let some out and then we turn on the hot tap and more boiling water gushes out.

After what seems like a long time, a bell rings in our cubicle. Heide says we have to be out in ten minutes. I get out reluctantly, dry myself, get dressed and then we leave.

Groysie heard about the Roman Baths for weeks afterwards.

A couple of weeks later Heide's mother asked if I'd like to go to the cinema with Heide. I told her I wouldn't be allowed. Frau Hannich said she'd talk to Groysie. I told her it wouldn't make any difference, she wouldn't let me go, as going to the cinema was against our religious beliefs.

She asked if I'd like to go into town with them anyway, as she had some things to do in town and Heide was going with her.

All three of us went into town by tram. Heide said she was going to the cinema anyway, while her mother was doing her errands. Frau Hannich said I could go if I wanted. I was in a quandary now. Heide wanted me to go with her and suggested I just didn't mention to my grandmother that I'd been, which would not be lying. So, I agreed to go with Heide. Her mother said she'd be waiting for us outside the cinema when the film was finished.

As we were lining up to get our tickets, I kept looking around in case somebody who knew my grandparents or aunt saw me. When we finally got inside, the cinema was full. Heide grabbed me by the arm and lead me down to the first row, where there were still a few seats available.

We were right underneath the big screen. Sitting on the wooden seats with our heads bent right back was extremely uncomfortable.

It was an Indian film with Romanian subtitles. The story was about an orphan boy who'd studied hard and become a doctor. He'd fallen in love with a girl from a wealthy family, who forbade him to see their daughter. All the trials and tribulations of the clandestine love affair follow, then the boy finds his real family, who are also wealthy. That of course changes everything, they marry and live happily ever after.

I enjoyed the film, in particular all the beautiful colourful Indian costumes. I felt very sad for the young couple during the film and was pleased it had ended happily.

I had to be careful not to mention anything to Groysie. I'd have been in a lot of trouble and she wouldn't have trusted me anymore.

When I got back from Kerz at the end of the summer, a high fence had been built around some land on the crest of the hill above us. Heavy machinery had been brought in and there was constant noise coming from behind the fence. Big trucks laden with all kinds of building materials came and went all day long.

Two soldiers with rifles are posted day and night outside the big double gates. Heide as cheeky as ever asks one of the soldiers what they're doing. He tells her he doesn't know and to get lost.

All kinds of rumours and speculations go around. Pretty soon people say an atomic shelter is being built. Granddad says he's heard it from a reliable source and it all makes sense. The Military Officer School is just round the corner. In the event of an atomic attack from the West, all the top brass from the school can shelter there.

It takes over a year to build the shelter. When the fence eventually is taken down, it looks just like a park with grass and lots of young trees. In the far corner is a very small building with a door, which looks quite insignificant.

That summer in Kerz there had been a lot of rumours that Stalin was dead. Nobody really knew for sure if it was true or just wishful thinking.

The Soviets kept it under wraps for a long time before Stalin's death was finally announced in Romania. Everybody was delighted and wanted to celebrate. People had high hopes that with the death of this evil tyrant, the oppression of the masses would come to an end and the suffering would stop.

The Reds had overthrown the Romanov Tzarist regime and centuries of serfdom and misery to replace it with something equally as bad if not worse.

Unfortunately, nothing changed. Only other power crazy maniacs carried on where Lenin and Stalin had left off.

Food and clothing shortage was as bad as ever and the never ending queueing was relentless. Annitante said every garment made in the factory where she worked, was for export to the USSR.

I needed new winter boots, my old ones were far too small. Everyone else in the family wore their shoes for years. Granddad was always mending them with scraps of plastic or leather which he salvaged from the bins at work.

One week, when Annitante worked mornings, we went out every afternoon traipsing round all the shoe shops in the hope of finding a pair of boots for me. The story was always the same. No children's shoes, perhaps next week or not in your size, try again another day. After six days revisiting the same shoe shops over and over, I still had no winter boots.

The following week, Annitante couldn't take me, so Groysie went with me. Towards the end of the second week, there was a huge line up outside a shoe shop.

Groysie and I stood in the queue for at least a couple of hours. When our turn came, the sales woman said she only had one pair of children's boots left, but they were a size smaller than Groysie thought I needed.

The woman said they were lovely red boots and sold out very quickly.

Red shoes, what a dream! I recalled the beautiful red sandals and boots I had from England. I only had to look around to see that the Romanian shoes were a poor substitute for the shoes my father had sent. But beggars could not be choosers.

I was so fed up dragging around all the shops and the endless queuing and knew that Groysie was tired with all the walking too.

"Can I try the shoes on?' I asked my grandmother, "Maybe they've been marked with the wrong size."

The assistant said she'd be happy to bring the boots out and let me try them on. The red boots turned out to be the nicest shoes I'd seen apart from my English ones. I was quite excited and determined they would fit.

The woman undid the laces wide on each boot. I pushed my foot into one of them with some difficulty. I managed to get it in, but my toes were curled up and pressing against the end of the shoe. I tied the laces, then crammed my other foot into the other shoe. I stood up and looked down at the red boots. "They fit! They fit!" I told Groysie excitedly.

Back then we had no way of measuring feet. The assistant told me to walk up and down the shop.

My toes were cramped and already hurting. With a big convincing smile on my face I walked back and forth in the shop and told Groysie the shoes fitted very well. We paid and then went home, pleased the hunt for shoes was over.

Next day I wore my new boots to school. There were several other girls who wore the same shoes. I was the only kid though walking pigeon toed, trying to take the pressure of my toes, as my boots were crippling me, and my toes hurt like crazy. I couldn't wait to get home and get the things off my feet.

That evening when Annitante saw the shoes, she knew just by looking at them that they were too small. Groysie told her I'd insisted they fit. I said they did fit in the shop, but they must have shrunk, or my feet had grown since the day before.

Granddad laughed, but Annitante didn't think it very funny. She said there were plenty of people looking for kids shoes and it wouldn't be a problem selling them. However, that still left me without winter boots and all those days had been wasted running round the shops.

Groysie said before the war, the shops were laden with food and all kinds or merchandise. People had lots of choices. They went to tailors and cobblers who made clothes and shoes to measure. These were the best quality and lasted for years and years, like Groysie's winter boots that Mischuncle had made for her before the war. They were about fifteen years old, but still very good and just had to be re-soled every few years.

Now most people had to get what was available and be thankful for getting anything at all. Whenever I got a new piece of clothing it was bought several sizes too big and that way it would last longer. My clothes were too big for a year or so, then fit for a while, then ended up being too short and tight, with the sleeves halfway up my arms. Groysie would make a little joke about my clothes being too tight. I only had to spend the summer with my mother and my things would fit again as I always came back very skinny from there.

I didn't like Groysie saying things like that, it upset me. She'd say she didn't mean it and give me a big hug and everything was all right again.

Snow would fall in a couple of weeks and I still had no boots. Granddad had an idea. He took my old boots and cut the toes off them. He had some bits of leather from which he fashioned toes and sewed them on to the end of the shoes.

They look hideous I told Granddad. But at least they fit and don't cripple your feet, he answered.

I'm not going to school in those horrible things. I'm the laughing stock at school as it is, I said. The kids will be horrible, they'll have a field day and torment me more than ever.

I was very upset and didn't want to go to school. Some of the girls in my class didn't need a reason to be nasty and bully me. This would give them new ammunition to make my life hell.

My poor Granddad felt sorry for me. He lifted me on his lap and gave me a long hug. He said he wished he could give me all the nice things, a little girl should have. The main thing was, I had a pair of boots and they'd keep my feet warm until we could find some new ones.

So once again I was a spectacle and the butt of all jokes in my class, until the novelty wore off and kids found something else to ridicule and torment me with.

Before Christmas our teacher asked all the class to bring in family photographs. We were to write about each person, describing their personality, looks and what they did. I took several pictures my father had sent of himself from England. He looked well dressed, elegant and handsome in the photos. They'd all been taken by a professional photographer.

I took a couple of pictures of my parents on their wedding day and one that was taken of my mother, brother and myself when Christian and I went back to her after her return from Russia. In this picture we were all dressed like city people.

I didn't take any photos of my grandparents. Right from the very first day at school in Hermannstadt, kids had made fun of my grandparents.

They'd called them tramps, dirty peasants and other choice names.

Deep down I always felt ashamed and tried to avoid being seen with my grandparents. They were the most wonderful people in the world and where would I be without them? In spite of knowing all that and loving them so much, I'd do anything to save myself from the endless harassment and ridicule I had to put up with at school.

I was very proud to show kids my photographs. I thought my father looked far more handsome and elegant than any father on any other picture and my mother was as lovely as any other mother.

During the break the nasty girls followed me outside, giving me a hard timc. They called me a liar and thief. They said I had no mum or dad and had stolen those pictures and made the whole story up. They said I lived in a fantasy world, telling everybody my father was in England.

Annemarie defended me and told the kids to leave me alone. I was very upset. Why wouldn't these girls believe that I had a nice mum and dad?

Just you wait and see, I told them, my father will come back from England one day and take me back with him.

The nasty girls laughed and thought that was hilarious. You go on dreaming and living in your make believe world they taunted me.

On Sunday afternoon on my way to Sunday School, I always passed a beggar who sat under a bridge in town. He had no legs. His torso was placed on a ragged old blanket. He was extremely haggard looking and dirty.

I always felt very sorry for him and often asked Groysie to give me something to take for the beggar. She'd usually give me a small piece of bread, polenta or 10 bani. I told my Groysie that he wouldn't be able to buy anything with 10 bani. She said if everybody who passed him, gave him that much, he would end up with quite a decent amount of cash.

When I had nothing to give him, I'd make a detour, because I felt bad for not having anything for him.

The pauper was always very thankful for what I gave him and said God bless you my child. He made me feel as though I'd helped him a lot when I really hadn't.

I often wondered how he'd lost his legs, where he lived and if he had a family. It affected me deeply seeing homeless people, or ones with physical or mental disabilities. I always dwelt on things like that.

Groysie said it was good to have compassion for others, but I shouldn't let it get to me so much, because there was nothing we could do about it, beyond the little bit I did.

Chapter Seventeen

Granddad's health was rapidly failing. The rheumatism was getting worse all the time and the pain in his hands was unbearable. Groysie applied herbal compresses on them, which she made up herself. I don't know if they really helped, but the doctors in the hospital said they couldn't do anything for him.

There were no general practitioners. If you had something wrong with you, the hospital was the only place to go to. It was always so crowded, and one could spend the whole day waiting just to be seen by a doctor.

Even though he earned little as a labourer, he couldn't give up work. We were desperate for every bit of money that came into the house.

Granddad had already been told that he'd never be entitled to an old age pension as he hadn't accrued enough working years in the communist regime. The fact that the very same regime had taken everything from him and thrown him out of his home penniless, made no difference. Rules were rules.

Granddad was a broken man. He felt he was failing us all. He spent more and more time in hospital and was bringing home less and less money from work.

The burden to pay the bills and keep food on the table, became harder and heavier on Annitante by the day.

Winter school holidays come and go. I visit Mitzitante from time to time. She's a bit eccentric. I like her a lot, she's so nice and always full of joviality.

I tell her we're going to have a Fasching Party at school this year, but I'm not allowed to go.

"I'm so sorry," she tells me. "That religion your family follows is so strict, you can't do anything or have any fun. I tell you what," Mitzitante says. "You tell your grandparents you're visiting me and then go to the party from here. If I happen to see them, I'll say you spent the time with me."

I feel so bad about telling lies, I say to my aunt. I've told lies once or twice before and I worry about it.

"Well, I think it's wrong that they forbid you to do anything, but I tell you what," she says. "You come here before you go to the party, I'll make you a simple costume, into which you can change and then go to the party from here. Afterwards you come back here, change back into your own things, that way you won't have lied about having been with me."

I tell Mitzitante I'll think about it and let her know.

She tells me not to worry about being punished. If God wants to punish anybody, he'll punish her for coming up with the idea.

I feel very mixed up and guilty, even though I haven't done anything yet. Nevertheless, I take my aunt up on her offer.

On the afternoon of the party, my friend Annemarie is unwell and I'm there on my own. It's not a lot of fun, as kids exclude me from most of the games and I stand around just watching. I leave after a short time and go back to Mitzitante's place.

I tell her that my friend wasn't there and I think I've been punished for lying to Groysie.

"Nonsense child!" She says, "you just don't know how to have fun and enjoy yourself, because of all the restrictions that are placed on you."

One afternoon, after finishing my homework, I sit with Groysie, while she's doing some mending. Mitzitante comes up in the conversation. I ask why my aunt never got married. I'd seen a lot of photographs in an album and she was very beautiful when she was young. Groysie starts to relate to me what happened to Mitzitante when she was young and why she never married.

When Mitzitante was a girl she lived in Hermannstadt with her parents and two sisters, Hermiene and Grete. All three girls were nice looking, but Mitzitante was by far the most beautiful.

Hermannstadt was full of wealthy Saxon businessmen and merchants. Mitzi's family was ordinary, not rich, but not poor either.

Mitzi fell in love with the son of a very rich family and the young man was totally besotted with her.

When his family found out about the relationship, they forbade their son to carry on seeing Mitzi.

Mitzi and her lover carried on a clandestine relationship and she became pregnant. The boyfriend thought this would change his family's views on things and they'd be allowed to marry.

The boy's family, however, was more determined than ever to keep the two young people apart and arranged for their son to be sent abroad. Sadly, the young man took his life by hanging himself.

Mitzi's parents sent her to a relative in Budapest, where she had the baby and it was adopted.

I wanted to know if the baby had been a boy or girl, but Groysie didn't know.

Mitzitante never got over her loss and never married. She threw herself into her work to try and forget and ease her pain.

I told Groysie that sounded more like a fairy tale, but with a sad ending.

I wanted to know if Mitzitante ever had any other boyfriends. Groysie said that, to her knowledge, she'd never looked at another man.

When I visited my aunt afterwards, I looked at her through different eyes and wondered about her life. I wanted to ask her about her past, but never mustered up the courage.

I thought the story Groysie had told me was very romantic. It was a terrible shame it had ended in such a sad way.

My father has started writing more regularly.

Groysie helps me respond to his letters. It seems very strange to be writing to somebody you don't know and have never met.

Father has remarried recently. His new wife's name is Evy. She's Estonian and German speaking. Father has sent a photo of the two of them standing in front of their two storey, semi-detached house.

Groysie says I must address them both when I write and call her Mutti. I feel very happy about that, as I have no loyalty to my own mother and would love to have a new mother, who loves me and cares about me.

Evy is as tall as my father in the pictures. The faces on the photos are quite small and the features not that clear. She has short, blonde, curly hair, wears very smartly tailored clothes and very high heeled shoes. She's turned out perfectly, with a leather handbag on her arm and matching gloves.

My father's letters are not at all informative. They're usually very short and it seems like he's just doing his duty. He doesn't say what they do or what kind of life they lead. He never asks questions about any of us.

His letters are always opened and censored and often things are crossed out. I'm pretty sure the same is done to our letters to him.

After two years, Tummy has finished his national service. I'm so thrilled that he's home again. I've missed him so much.

He gets a job in the furniture factory, where he worked before the army, the same place as his brother, Hans.

Tummy says he wants to save up for a second hand bike. The old one of Granddad's gave up the ghost long ago. Walking to work takes a long time. Even if he goes by tram, he still has a long way to walk and of course the tram will cost money.

Bikes are very hard to come by, be they second hand or new. He tells me a chap at work has one for sale, but he's worried that he'll sell it before he has enough money to buy it.

It's Easter Sunday and the whole family is celebrating at our little house. Hansuncle, Nickitante and baby Renate are there too. I love it when we're altogether.

Time goes so quickly afterwards. It's the last term at school and soon we'll be starting preparations for the end of year exams.

After exams each year, all the parents are invited to the annual open day. They get a chance to discuss their children's progress with the teachers.

None of my family has ever been to an open day to find out from the teacher how I'm doing. I'm at an age where I'm wondering why not, as all other parents go.

I ask Groysie if she's not interested in what I do at school and how I'm getting on. She tells me that she is. "Then why don't you go and talk to the teacher?" I ask.

She says they know from my school report, if I do well or not. I protest that all the other kids' parents go.

"So, what can the teacher tell me?" Groysie asks, "that I don't know already from your report. If your mother and father were raising you, I'm sure they'd go and talk to the teacher. They're younger and have more energy, but I'm old and can do without all that extra traipsing about."

I shrug my shoulders and think that nobody really cares. The next moment I feel bad and know that's not true. I go over to my Groysie, give her a big hug and tell her it's all right if she's tired and doesn't want to go.

"You're such a good girl," she says. "I know you always do your best. You bring home very good school reports."

The summer holidays are here once again. My departure to Kerz is imminent. I'd be so happy if I didn't have to go.

The day before I'm due to leave, Granddad comes home from work in the morning. When Groysie sees him, she thinks he must be ill.

No, he says, he's all right. He then tells us that every summer the children of the communist party people at work are sent to a holiday camp in the foothills of the Cibin Mountains for 2 weeks.

Granddad's foreman has asked him if he wanted his granddaughter to go, as there were a few places left. I can see Granddad's very pleased.

"The only thing is," he says, "we have to be there in an hour, as the lorries with the children are leaving then."

I can hardly believe my luck. Now I don't have to go to Kerz, or at least not yet. Granddad asks if I want to go. He says I'll be one of the younger kids. I'm still only 10 but will be eleven in July and the kids, who are taken to this camp, range from 10 to 14 years old.

I'm lost for words, but over the moon about my good luck. Of course, I want to go, I tell Granddad.

It only takes a few minutes to gather my few bits and put them in a bag. After giving Groysie a big hug and a kiss, I'm on my way with Granddad.

When we arrive at the factory, three open backed lorries are standing in the big yard, already loaded with children.

Granddad lifts me onto the back of one of the lorries, where I find a space on one of the many wooded benches, placed in rows, and sit down. There are two or three adults in each truck, looking after the kids.

It's the first time I'm going somewhere new without anybody I know, but I don't care. I'm just so happy not to be going to Kerz.

When all the children are on board, the tail gates are put up and secured. All the parents stand around as the little convoy starts to pull away. All the kids are calling out goodbyes to their loved ones. Granddad is standing in the background with a huge smile, waving. I know he's very happy for me.

Once the trucks are out of the city, one of the adults suggests we sing a song and tells us what song. All the kids start to sing a Romanian song, which is unfamiliar to me. I can't join in but am happy to just listen. The kids are singing at the tops of their voices, which helps to drown out the noise the trucks make.

I look around me. I don't see any boys and all the kids look Romanian. Then I spot a couple of older girls, sitting together at the front of the lorry, who definitely look Saxon.

It's a beautiful sunny day, not a cloud in the sky. I enjoy the ride with the wind blowing in my face, as I'm watching the mountains get closer and closer.

Eventually the trucks stop outside a school in a small Romanian mountain village. Everyone is helped off the truck and told to go into the school yard. I don't see any boys. This must be a camp just for girls. We're divided into four groups and taken into the school building.

There are four classrooms. Each group goes into one of them. The room has narrow wooden pallets with thin mattresses lined up in rows against the walls. We're all told to go to a bed and put our belongings down.

A lot of the older girls know each other. They must have been to the camp before and made friends.

There are three other Saxon girls in my dorm. One of them is the same age as me. It's her first time too. Her name is Kati. A Romanian girl agrees to swap places, so we can be next to each other. The other two Saxon girls are fourteen and know each other from school, but this is their first trip too.

We all get along well. The two older girls tell us they'll keep an eye on us and make sure we're okay. Blankets and pillows are handed out and we all make our beds. When everybody's done, we're told to go to the canteen, which is across the road from the school.

The canteen stands in a big yard, which is partly fenced off, where dozens of chickens scratch and peck in the dirt. In the corner of the yard is a small enclosure with a couple of pigs. One of the older Romanian girls says laughing. "There's our dinner on legs for the next two weeks."

I tell Kati, the girl I've palled up with, that I think the Romanian girl must be joking. I can't imagine having chicken or meat every day for dinner, when we're lucky to get it twice a year. I'll be eating more meat than I've eaten in my whole life, since the communists took over.

I was soon to find out that the Romanian kid was right. We had chicken or pork every evening for our main meal, with salad and potatoes, cooked in a variety of different ways. The food was just the best I'd ever had, the portions very generous.

At breakfast time we had milk, home baked bread and jam. Lunch was always outdoors, on an outing somewhere into the mountains. Each child got a packed lunch of sandwiches, packed with cheese, ham, salami or liver sausage and a piece of fruit. There were lots of fresh springs, from where we drank water.

The forests in the foothills were covered in blueberries and raspberries, which we picked every day and brought back to the village to eat after our dinner. I'd never eaten such good food and so much of it.

Every child was weighed on the day of arrival, then again on the last day. I'd gained nearly 4 kg during the two weeks. When Groysie saw me, she said the extra flesh on my bones suited me.

Out of the 100 children in the camp, there were only 8 Saxon girls and a handful of Hungarians. Everybody got on well, but everybody tended to stick to their own kind. As we all spoke Romanian, there were no language barriers.

The washing facilities were primitive, but adequate. The wooden washhouse stood in the corner of the playground, with several wooden troughs for water. We washed in cold water pulled up from the well nearby, which was carried into the washhouse.

Most of the kids lived in nice houses with indoor plumbing, so they moaned and groaned about having to wash outside in cold water. It didn't bother me, as this was all I knew.

The toilets were in the other corner from the washhouse in a wooden shed. They were not individual stalls. Just one long wooden seat with ten holes cut at intervals, stretched the length along one wall of the shed. So, you had to sit side by side with a whole bunch of other girls doing your business.

Underneath the toilet shed was a humongous cesspit, which stank to high heaven. Big fat maggots and worms, as thick and big as a thumb, crawled in the quagmire down below. Some of these vile things managed to crawl out and slither along the seats and floor. They were just gross, and I hated going in there. If possible, I would hold out, if I could, until we went out into the mountains, then go somewhere behind a bush, which most kids preferred to do as well.

After our evening meals, games were arranged, and everybody took part. It was so much fun and I'd never enjoyed myself so much.

Everybody had to be in bed by 9 o'clock. Lights went out at 9.30. All the youth leaders gathered in the canteen to relax and socialise.

The dorms became quite lively after lights out. Some of the older girls climbed out of the windows to go and find local boys to have fun with. They had to be very careful. If caught, they were in a lot of trouble. These girls said they never did anything bad, but just liked the excitement and having fun.

The younger girls all remained in their beds and told scary tales.

On the last evening at the camp, a show was put on by all the kids. A handful of girls took it upon themselves to organise it. They approached everybody and asked if they could sing, dance, or perform in any other kind of way.

The eight Saxon girls all got together. One of the older girls took charge of our little group. She taught us all a dance routine, which we performed. We also sang a couple of German songs, which turned out to be beautiful.

The Hungarian girls did similar stuff to us. The Romanian kids did most of the entertaining, as there were so many of them. We all had a great evening.

The next day after a cooked midday meal, everybody packed their things. We folded all our bedding and left it neatly at the end of our beds.

Three trucks arrived early afternoon to take us back to the city. It had been a fabulous holiday, one I'd never forget. Back at the factory yard, the girls were embracing and saying their farewells. Most of them knew they'd go back again the next year. I lived in hope of returning to the camp in the mountains again, but it was my first and last time.

Granddad said it was only the kids of the privileged few, who were selected for these special treats, the same as at the New Year's Party.

Nevertheless, It had been wonderful for those two weeks. I'd lived and experienced the way a very small elite minority lived in our communist Utopia.

Chapter Eighteen

After getting back from the summer camp, I secretly hoped that I wouldn't be sent to Kerz, but, with another eight weeks of school holidays left, I had to go. Being there two weeks less than other years was some consolation. I was beginning to feel quite grown up, as I was now coming up to eleven.

When I arrived at my mother's house, I was greeted with the usual enthusiasm by her, "Oh! So you're back again." She said this as I entered the yard, where she was standing with a seven or eight month old baby in her arms. I asked who the baby was, to which she replied, he's your brother, Hani. He was beautiful. Fair skinned, blond and blue eyed, so different from his brother Viorel, who was dark skinned with brown eyes and black hair. Hani took after the Saxon side of the family, whilst Viorel was just like his father.

Nothing had changed. Mother was as mean and hardhearted as ever. Never a kind word or any affection for Christian and me. She lavished it all on her two little boys, which really showed and was very hard to take.

Now there was even more work than ever with the new baby. Christian and I were late to bed and early to rise, with endless days of chores and backbreaking work in the fields. The days were unbearably hot. The dirt roads to the fields were baked by the sun. Walking in bare feet burnt and was very painful. At the beginning of my time there it was always difficult, but after a while the soles of my feet hardened, which made walking on the hot dirt roads easier.

It was like being a hired hand, working from morning till night. Hardly anybody ever spoke to me except to give orders or criticise the work, I'd done. I was used to it and didn't expect anything else.

Christian didn't have any time for me either. He worked very hard all day, doing a man's job in the fields and at home.

Oh, how I struggled with the long hours and hard physical work expected of me daily. I was so miserable and unhappy.

When mother went off with her husband and two boys on Sunday, Christian and I were left to roam the streets. I hung out with whoever accepted me, but never really feeling I belonged.

The weeks dragged on endlessly. I couldn't wait for the end of August and going back to Hermannstadt.

The last Sunday that summer in Kerz, I was just about ready to go to church. My brother had already gone, and my mother had also left with her brood.

I walked through the door into the lane and almost bumped into my Granddad and Annitante.

I stood dumbstruck for a moment, not believing my eyes, then just threw myself at my Granddad, hugging and kissing him. I was beside myself with happiness to see them both. I wouldn't take my eyes off Granddad in case he was an apparition and would disappear any moment.

They told me they'd come to visit our neighbour, Gretetante. She was also a member of the Baptist Church and Granddad had known her for many years.

Granddad asked where Christian and the rest of the family were. I told him my brother was somewhere in the village with other kids. My mother, uncle and their two little boys were with their Romanian family, where they spent every Sunday. Granddad was quite disgusted with my mother for leaving us on our own and excluding us this way.

Granddad then told me to go and look for Christian, whom he hadn't seen for about six years, while he and Annitante went next door and visited our neighbour.

I found Christian on the village green in front of the church, playing with a bunch of boys. When he saw me, he told me to get lost and not follow him around. I told him Granddad and Annitante were at Gretetante's next door and wanted to see him.

He told me to go, he would follow. Was he ashamed to be with me? I felt very sad that he didn't even want to walk with me.

All four of us had a wonderful day with Gretetante.

We had a midday meal together, cooked by our host and then went for a walk to the River Alt, where we sat in the shade of big willow trees, watching young people swim and enjoy themselves.

When it was time for Granddad and Annitante to leave, I wanted to go with them. Annitante was reluctant to let me go back with them, but

Granddad said I could, as there was only a week left before I went back anyway. I quickly went to my mother's house, collected my few bits and walked back to the railway stop with Granddad and my aunt. Christian came to see us all off.

As we walked through the Romanian part of the village, I spotted my mother standing outside a house with a group of women. She had Hani in her arms.

The moment she saw our little group approach, she disappeared into the house. Christian said she wanted nothing to do with my father's family and that was the reason she went inside.

Granddad said it was very sad that she carried this hatred for them. They'd always been good to her and treated her like a daughter.

When we said our goodbyes to Christian at the railway stop, he got extremely upset. He told Granddad he wanted to go with us too, but of course he couldn't. We were all upset to see my brother in floods of tears. It made me realise how unhappy Christian was and I felt very bad about it.

I thought myself very lucky to live with my grandparents and only spend the summer holidays in Kerz, with my mother.

As the train pulled away, I watched Christian through the window. He was small for his age. He stood there wiping away the tears, a lonely and forlorn looking figure. My heart ached for him.

Back in Hermannstadt, I had another week before school began. It was great being able to catch up with my friends.

It was my first year at the senior school, which was in the city centre. I was excited about going by tram every day.

I loved Hermannstadt, particularly the old walled inner city. This medieval citadel was about 800 years old. The Saxon people built it. Thick high walls had surrounded the whole city at one time, but parts had been destroyed or crumbled with age. A large part of the wall was still standing close to my school, with the Harteneck Towers built into the wall at a few hundred metres intervals. In the days of the Ottoman Empire, each tower was manned by a trade: carpenters, tailors, butchers, etc. Each one of these trades was responsible for the upkeep of their tower and keeping it stocked with ammunition.

Outside the wall, the deep long moat was still visible, but now it was covered in grass and not water, as it once was.

I loved walking along by the wall and imagining the battles that had raged here in the middle ages. From here, my ancestors fired arrows from the towers and walls, and poured pitch down onto the Turkish invaders, mostly keeping them at bay until the next attack.

Hermannstadt is full of old churches of all denominations, cloisters and monasteries. There are several squares with big buildings and old houses built around them. All kinds of narrow and quaint alleys connect different parts of the city centre, which makes the place very interesting and exciting to explore.

This was now my daily stomping ground, which gave me a strange but special feeling.

My days still started with queuing for milk, then at 6.30, I had to leave and get the tram into the city. School started at 7.30.

It was an old building in a road called Little Earth. The small enclosed courtyard, was just big enough to accommodate the students, whilst they stood around during the break. There was no room to let off steam or play games. The school was a two storey building. The rooms on the ground floor were accommodation for the headmaster and his family and the caretaker and his wife. The second floor had six classrooms.

Saxon children from different parts of the city came to this senior school. There were three classes for each year. Year 5,6 and 7 were housed here. The classes had been mixed up, so that there were kids from different schools in each class. I was happy, as Annemarie and I were still together in the same class.

As there were only six classrooms and 12 classes to accommodate, we went to school in two shifts, alternating on a weekly basis - mornings were from 7.30 to 1.30; and afternoons were from 1.30 to 7.30 in the evening.

The Romanian kids had all the big schools. Some had been built since the war. They had big playgrounds, an assembly hall and gymnasiums. All the kids went to school in the mornings. They didn't have the shift system the Saxon kids had to put up with.

We had no playground, gym or hall. Once a week we got an hour in the local recreation centre, which was a 20 minute walk each way from our school.

The teacher walked us there in an orderly and quiet fashion. The hour would be spent in the gym, during the winter months, or on the track and field, during the warmer weather, then we'd all walk back to school.

Some kids hated sport and moaned and whinged about it. I just loved it and couldn't get enough.

Starting the day, by riding the tram into town, was great. The whole class from the previous year went by this mode of transport to school.

Each tram consisted of two cars. The front one was completely closed in. The second car had an open platform each end, like a small balcony.

All the school kids liked these open spaces and we squeezed into them and ended up like sardines in a can.

Even on the coldest winter mornings and evenings, we'd all be bunched together at the ends of the second carriage, blocking the exits. Adults would become frustrated and infuriated with us, fighting their way through the mass of kids trying to get on or off.

Like any kids let loose, we made plenty of noise. The conductor often came out and told us to be quieter, which worked for a while, then mayhem would break out again.

The only thing that kept us reasonably quiet was when people threatened to report us to our school. We didn't behave badly, we were just loud and noisy at times.

For my friend, Annemarie, the change of schools was hard. She struggled with the longer days and the extra travelling. We had a lot more books and school stuff to carry. Lugging her heavy satchel around proved too much for her.

She had a twenty minute walk to the tram. Her mother, or grandmother, came with her every day, carrying her school bag for her. I met them there and then carried her school stuff the rest of the way. Despite being two years older than the rest of the class, she was tiny for her age, but she was feisty, considering all her problems.

Annemarie refused to ride inside the carriage in the warm. She'd rather freeze outside on the platform with the rest of the kids.

Since starting the new school, I've seen very little of Heide. After the extra homework we get, which takes me at least a couple hours to do every day and then helping with chores and queuing for food, there's no time left for anything else.

Chapter Nineteen

Granddad's health has deteriorated even more. He gets pain in his chest now, from time to time. Groysie says she wished he could stop work, then his health might improve.

One afternoon, as I'm doing my homework, a man comes to see my Grandmother. He informs her that Granddad's in hospital, very sick.

Groysie and I immediately set off to go and see him. The hospital is in town, close to my school.

We find Granddad in bed, with wires running from a machine, attached to different parts of his body. He looks very pale and poorly. I ask Groysie if he's going to die. She reassures me that he won't, but I'm very frightened. The doctor tells my Grandmother that Granddad has had a heart attack and they're doing everything they can for him. He will remain in hospital for a few weeks.

I don't know how long Granddad is in hospital for, but it seems a very long time. On school days, I visit him every day. The hospital is only a five minute walk from my school. When school is in the mornings, I go after school, but, when it's in the afternoon, I go before school. School finishes at 7.30 in the evening and that's too late to visit.

I love my Granddad so much. I can't bear to think of life without him. Every time I turn up to see him, his face lights up. He's very tired and old. He doesn't talk much. I more than make up for his lack of conversation by chattering nonstop, while I sit holding his hand and stroking it.

After what seemed like an eternity to me, my Grandfather comes home from hospital. He's become frail and is walking with the aid of a stick.

He's at home for several more weeks before he returns to work. I love having both my Grandparents at home everyday.

We're well into autumn now. The landscape all around is beautiful. The parks, forests and distant foothills are aflame with reds, oranges and yellows. The mountain peaks are already covered in snow.

Annitante has been engaged to a young man, called Misch, from Stolzenburg, the village where my Grandparents come from. He visits most Sundays. Annitante and Misch go to church together and do things with the other young people from the Baptist community.

I don't know what's got into my aunt. She's been acting peculiarly of late. She's been going out in the evenings and coming home late. She's 29 years old and can do what she wants, but her behaviour is very much out of character. She's never gone anywhere on her own before.

Pretty soon Granddad wants to know where she goes and who with. Annitante says she just goes out with some of the girls from work, but doesn't tell him where.

There's a lot of tension and unease at home. Very often there are arguments between Annitante and my Grandparents. They try to keep it low key when I'm around. But I can feel the strain everybody's under. I just can't figure out what's going on. I've never ever heard my Grandparents argue amongst each other and I wonder what the cause of the quarrel between them and their daughter is.

Prayers after the evening meal are strange too. I don't know why Granddad is praying and harping on about forgiveness for my aunt. He never says what she should be forgiven for. All I think is it must be something very bad to keep going on about it.

I haven't seen Misch, Annitante's fiancé, for a while. Then, one Sunday afternoon, there's another big upset at our place. Misch arrives and seems very agitated.

To my delight, Groysie says I can go play with Heide. I don't need to be told twice and happily skip through the neighbours' garden to join my friends at play.

The gang is out in the meadow, playing dodge ball. They're all surprised to see me, especially as it's Sunday and I'm rarely let out to play.

I love playing dodge ball and throw myself whole heartedly into the game. There's a whole bunch of us there and we have a lot of fun.

As the light starts to fade, everybody starts to drift away and go home.

I'm walking home with Heide. She wants to know where I've been and why I've not been round for weeks.

I tell her about Granddad's heart attack and him being in hospital for a long time. I tell my friend that things are bad at home because there are lots of arguments between my Grandparents and aunt and that I have no idea why, but wish I knew what's going on.

"You don't know why?" Heide says surprised.

"No, I don't," I reply.

"Your aunt is having a baby!" She informs me.

"What? Don't be silly, Heide, she's not married," I reply somewhat angrily. Heide laughs.

"You don't have to be married to have a baby, silly!"

I feel cross with my friend, insinuating that Annitante is having a baby, when I'm pretty sure only married people have them.

"You're, you're lying." I stammer

"Oh well, have it your way," Heide says, "but you can ask anybody, the whole neighbourhood knows about it. Haven't you noticed how fat your aunt has got round the middle?"

Now, come to think of it, Annitante has been wearing baggier tops and she does look fatter.

Heide tells me she's heard her mother and sister talk about it and that's how she knows. I leave Heide outside her house and walk home.

I see my aunt in a completely different light now and can't imagine her getting up to no good with Misch. Only bad girls do things like that and besides, it's against our religion. I can understand why all the arguing has been going on for a while now. I've always been told that having sex or a baby outside of marriage will bring shame on the family.

Just as I'm about to enter our hut, Annitante's fiancé is leaving. He looks upset and angry.

Annitante's sitting on a chair, crying buckets. She's beside herself with grief and remorse. My Grandparents are standing like stone statues, looking forlorn.

I feel very awkward. I don't know what to say or do. Groysie tells me to do some homework.

"I've already done it," I protest.

"Well, do some more then!" Groysie insists.

I feel angry, but don't know why. Even Heide, who's only 9, knows more than I do. She made me feel really stupid and ignorant earlier on. Her family is much more open with her and tell her things, which nobody in my family would dream of doing with me.

During the weeks that follow, Annitante doesn't go anywhere except work. She doesn't even go to church. She's stopped going out with her girl friends in the evening and just sits at home. Her fiancé has stopped coming round all together.

When next I see Heide, I tell her that Annitante and Misch should have got married and that would have made everything okay.

Then Heide drops another bombshell.

"My mum says", Heide informs me, "the baby is not Misch's and that's why they've split up."

"So, whose baby is it then?" I demand.

"How the heck do I know?" Heide replies. "My sister, Inge, told my mother that your aunt went on holiday with two girlfriends in the spring. They went to a mountain chalet. My mum then said if that was the case it all fitted and the picture became clear."

I'm more confused than ever now.

"What do you mean?" I ask my friend, feeling cross and frustrated. She's younger than me and yet she has all the answers. Am I stupid or what?

Heide continues, "My sister told my mum that the baby is due sometime in January, which means your aunt went and got pregnant in the spring, when she was on holiday."

Oh, I want to cry. I'm just fed up with it all and wish everything was back to normal in our house. Nobody talks to each other much any more and the atmosphere is horrible. All everybody seems to do is pray for forgiveness for Annitante.

When she's not at work, Annitante sits and knits or sews baby clothes. Nobody is happy or joyful about the forthcoming birth of the baby.

When Hansuncle and Nickitante were expecting their little girl, they never stopped talking about it. Everybody was overjoyed and thrilled about the upcoming event. The birth of my aunt's baby was never mentioned, as though that would keep it from happening. I felt very sorry for Annitante.

During the last few weeks of her pregnancy, some of the young women from the church started to visit our house on Sunday afternoons. They all sat quietly and chatted to my aunt and then prayed together.

Annitante seemed very lonely and sad. Granddad told her she'd ruined her life and would pay for her sins for the rest of her days. She would have a constant reminder of what she's done.

It all went over my head and I didn't know what to make of what Granddad was saying. When Christmas came, Annitante stayed at home, repenting and praying for forgiveness, while the rest of the family went to church.

Soon after Christmas I got very sick. I was throwing up all the time and couldn't keep any food down. I had such terrible pain in my head and didn't know what to do with myself. It was during the winter school holiday. Groysie tried to make me better with herbal remedies, but nothing helped.

After a week, my Grandmother took me to the hospital and was told I had a bad sinus infection. For many weeks after I went to the hospital twice a week for some kind of electrical treatment to my head, until I got better.

One early morning in January, Annitante started to moan and groan in bed beside me. Groysie heard her. She got my aunt up, they dressed quickly and left to walk to the tram. The maternity hospital was in the city centre. Groysie was worried and hoped they'd get there in time.

Groysie came home in the afternoon. I was already home from school. She told me my aunt had given birth to a baby girl and they were both well.

I didn't know why, but I felt very sad and started to cry. Groysie asked why I was crying. I told her that I felt very sorry for the little baby, because she had no father and I hoped her mummy would be good to her and love her. I said I hoped my aunt wouldn't take her unhappiness out on her baby, the way my mother was doing to Christian and me.

Groysie reassured me that we would all love the baby and she was sure her mother would love her very much. She said it wasn't the baby's fault that she was born outside of marriage and didn't have a father. That made me feel much happier.

I couldn't wait for Annitante to come home with the new baby. She called her Marianne and she was such a good little baby. She hardly ever cried. It was almost as though she knew she was here under sufferance, had to be good and not upset anybody.

All her friends from church called round to see the new baby. I thought it was strange how my aunt glowed with pride and showed off her little one. During her pregnancy she was so remorseful, withdrawn and ashamed.

After her short maternity leave, Annitante went back to her three shift job in the clothing factory. She took Marianne to the crèche at work, which was open twenty-four hours a day, whatever shift she was on. Groysie was getting too old to look after a newborn baby. I became extremely fond of my baby cousin and loved her like a little sister.

Everybody in the family loved the baby girl. She was a happy little thing. I could see right from the beginning that my aunt truly loved Marianne and I was sure she'd always be very good to her, which settled my negative thoughts and made me feel happier about my cousin's future.

The spring after Marianne was born, I started sleepwalking. I only did it around the full moon. I'd wake up being walked back into the house by Groysie, after wondering about outside.

At evening prayer after our meal, Granddad would pray for me. He saw my sleepwalking as being possessed by the devil and would pray to banish this evil from me.

I became frightened and disturbed by Granddad's prayers and wondered what sin I had committed to be punished like this. I hoped that the prayers would drive this terrible affliction out of me.

I couldn't help thinking back to when mother had ranted and raved at Christian and me and called us Satan's spawns. I was so frightened and wondered what was going to happen to me.

I told Heide's mother about my sleepwalking. How Granddad was praying to drive evil spirits out of me.

She was horrified at what I'd told her. She sat me down and explained that quite a few children sleepwalked when they got to puberty. That was when they started to turn from children into adults. There was absolutely nothing wrong with it. However, what my Granddad was saying and instilling such fear into me, was completely wrong. She told me not to believe a word of it, it was a load of religious nonsense.

The sleepwalking went on until I was about 13 years old. My Grandfather continued praying for my soul and banishing Satan from me.

I tried to think of what Frau Hannich had told me, but it still freaked me out, hearing these special prayers that were meant just for me. At times I did wonder if I was possessed by something evil. It always made me very anxious and frightened to go to sleep, especially when it was a full moon.

Apart from having baby Marianne in our midst, life went on in pretty much the same way. Shortage of food and the never ending line ups were all part of everyday life.

I liked my new school, but Annemarie was still my only friend. I was not accepted by the kids who'd come from other schools. I knew that they only had to look at me, see my poor attire and reject me. To them I was just a poor kid, a peasant or a gypsy. I thought I might as well accept it, as this was all I'd ever be to these city kids.

The trams, which are the only public transport in the city run on single tracks. At regular intervals the track divides into two, where the trams from opposite directions wait and pass each other. It is at these interchanges, where passengers get on and off. The double track then goes back into one, until the next interchange.

A lot of adults jump on and off the running boards of the second carriages whilst the tram is in motion. Some older kids do it too. Very often they end up on their back sides or faces splayed out on the road. Groysie keeps telling me I must never try it, as it's very dangerous.

As usual, a whole load of school kids are packed onto the open platforms at each end of the second tram carriage, riding to school.

Our tram leaves the interchange and starts picking up speed. Kids at both ends of the carriage, closest to the road are yelling at a girl, who's just missed the tram, to jump on. I can't see a thing from where I am. I don't know if she's jumped on or not.

I'm on the platform at the end of the carriage. Seconds later, we see the girl lying on the road next to the track, with one leg severed and lying in between the two rail tracks.

Kids all around me scream and shout. I feel so sick and am trying very hard not to throw up. Pretty soon my breakfast ends up all over the back of another kid. Other children are being sick and complete hysteria breaks loose.

The conductor comes out to tell us all to be quiet, but then sees the horrendous scene receding into the distance.

People are running from all directions to help the girl on the track. All the kids are shouting at the conductor to stop the tram. He tells us that there's nothing we can do and the best thing is to go to school, as we'd only be in the way.

Somehow we all manage to get to school. All the children, who witnessed the terrible accident, are so traumatised and wander around in a haze, reliving the nightmare over and over.

Our teacher gives us all a long lecture about jumping on and off trams before we go home. We're also told that the girl has survived and is recovering from her amputation in hospital.

Granddad is busy making something at the end of our little shack. He's got an assortment of different sized planks and bits of corrugated tin sheets. He's building a lean-to against the end wall.

When I ask him what he's doing, he tells me that somebody at work has promised him a young nanny goat and he's building a small stable for the goat to live in. He says next spring the goat will have a kid and then we'll have milk, so I won't have to get up at 5 every morning to go and stand in line anymore.

I'm pleased about that, but that's still a year away and, in the meantime, the relentless morning queuing still goes on.

The following week, Granddad comes home with a very young goat in tow. She's black and white and her name is Balutza.

At first, I'm excited and eager to take Balutza out on a piece of rope tied round her neck. She loves eating the shrubs in the hedgerows and around the fields. Sadly the novelty of taking her out wears off and it becomes a chore, for which I'm usually responsible. When I complain to Groysie, she asks if I would rather queue up for milk every morning. I tell her that I will have to do that anyway until Balutza has a kid and then we'll get milk.

Groysie gives me a look and I know that's the end of the discussion and answering back is not acceptable.

There's hardly ever any time for play now with Heide and the gang. If I'm not taking the goat out to feed, I'm having to go and line up for food, or helping Groysie in the garden. Sometimes, when I go out with Balutza, I see all the kids playing in the fields. I tie the goat on a bush and join in the games.

One afternoon, when I go to get the goat, she's nowhere to be seen. The rope is still attached to the bush, but it has been chewed through.

I panic. I don't know which way to go. She could be anywhere. Living right on the edge of the city, we're not far from woodland and forests. There's lots of open ground all around us.

I'm dreading the worst. What if she's headed for the woods. I know there are plenty of wolves around, as we hear them at night. Poor old Lisi comes to mind and being killed by the wolf.

I ask my friends, who are still playing ball games, to help me look for Balutza. We all spread in different directions and start looking for the stupid animal.

I'm very cross with the goat, but very worried and frightened. I'll be in a lot of trouble if something happens to her.

After what seemed like an eternity, Ernst, the boy in my class, comes walking from his house, pulling Balutza behind him on the short piece of string left round her neck. He found her in their garden eating his mother's vegetables.

I was so relieved and thankful, I wanted to throw my arms around him and hug him, but of course I didn't, I just thanked him and told him I hoped his mother wouldn't be angry about the vegetables.

After that I never left Balutza tied up. I stayed with her all the time, which was very boring, especially as I could see the other kids play.

She was growing fast, getting big and strong. She pulled me wherever she wanted to go. Her strength and stubborn streak were very hard for me to handle. I often ended up in tears when I couldn't control her. When she decided to run, she would just pull me along behind her. Frustrated and angry, I'd pick up a stick and smack her with it, to bring her under control.

Granddad's health deteriorated week by week. He was having more and more time off work. He was forced to retire at 65. Without a pension, or any other sort of income, he was entirely dependent on Annitante and Tummy. There were six of us in the little household. My aunt's and uncle's meagre wage had to stretch a long way.

Granddad got very depressed over our situation. It was hard for him to accept all the losses after the war and being put in this position at his time of life. There were a lot of sombre moments, when serious discussions took place amongst the adults, on what could be done to survive. Things were pretty desperate.

There was talk about sending me back to my mother for good. I refused to believe that this would happen. Deep down I knew it could, but was unwilling to accept it.

The evening prayers were never ending. Granddad prayed passionately, asking God to help us. I was very concerned about my grandfather. I could see he was in great despair and didn't know what to do to make things better.

Within days of being let go from his job, Granddad had another heart attack and we thought we'd lose him. He was in hospital for many weeks, but did come home eventually. He spent a lot of his time in a deck chair he'd made years ago, sitting under the cherry tree he'd planted next to our little house, which was now quite big and providing dense shade in the summer.

My first year at the school in town was drawing to an end. It had been a busy year in many respects. We got a lot more homework, which I often did in the evenings. The days were spent lining up for food and all the other chores. The light from the paraffin lamp was poor, so my eyes got very tired.

Hansuncle and Nickitante had moved into a little one roomed house similar to ours, which had a garden. They were only a 20 minute walk from where we lived. They were in the next street from my friend Annemarie, close to the forest, that led into the foot hills. Renate, their little girl, was 20 months old now.

The week before school finished, Nickitante asked Groysie if I could go and live with them during the school holidays and look after Renate, while she went to work.

I was very happy about it and begged Groysie to let me go. I told her it would be so much better than going to Kerz. After Groysie discussed it with Annitante, it was agreed that I would go and live with my uncle and aunt for the summer.

I couldn't believe my good luck at not having to go to my mother.

Everybody worked 6 days a week. My aunt got a job in a factory, where they make wooden boxes for transporting fruit and vegetables. They both worked the morning shift only. They left the house at 5 in the morning and returned at 3 in the afternoon. Sometimes they had to work overtime and then they were gone for 12 hours. It was a long day for me being left on my own with a toddler.

Every morning before they left, Nickitante gave me a long list of instructions for jobs I had to do while she was gone.

Renate was a very lively little girl, who demanded a lot of my attention. She was a tiny thing, very cute and absolutely doted on by her parents.

We had no indoor plumbing. There was no well in the yard and every drop of water had to be carried in buckets from a standpipe on the main road about 200 metres away, which was a long way, especially carrying full buckets of water.

I had to fetch water several times a day. Nickitante insisted I carry two buckets to even the load. If I didn't fill them, she berated me, telling me

I was big and strong enough to fill them up. By the time I got back to the house, my arms felt like they were twice as long and had come out of their shoulder sockets.

A big chunk of my time, in the course of a day, was looking after Renate and feeding her. I had to make the beds, wash up, sweep the floor and yard and chop wood for the fire. In the afternoon, I had to make a vegetable soup, or potato goulash for our evening meal. Every Monday morning, I had to soak all the bedding and all our clothes in a solution of soda crystals in a metal bath. This always meant fetching loads of water.

On Tuesday, I had to heat metal buckets full of water on the wood burning stove and then wash all the laundry, by hand. Loads more water had to be carried. Rubbing the washing in the solution of soda crystals, wore all the skin off the back of my fingers and made them bleed. This made my hands very sore and painful. They didn't completely heal until it was time to do it again.

When I complained about my sore fingers, Nickitante just told me it was all part of the learning process. She'd done it from the age of 9. I told her hard work wasn't new to me either, as I'd done it since I was much younger than 9.

On most occasions when my aunt came home from work, she'd criticise and find fault with what I had done.

The beds weren't made to her liking. She'd strip the lot, make me stand and watch how she made it, then strip it again. Then standing and giving me instructions, I'd have to remake the bed, exactly as she wanted. She was a slave driver and wanted perfection. The only difference from being here, or in Kerz ,was I didn't get beaten, which was a bonus for me.

She was always looking for things to find fault with. I hadn't swept well enough, or hadn't beaten the handwoven runners well enough, or hadn't put enough of certain vegetables in the soup or salt. On and on it went. She made me feel very depressed and useless.

One day, when I was chopping wood, I didn't see Renate stand directly behind me. As I swung the hatchet, I caught her a glancing blow on the forehead. Luckily, it was the back of the axe that caught her and cut her forehead.

Poor little mite was lying on the floor screaming, with blood pouring from the cut. I was panic stricken and didn't know what to do. I ran across the street for help. The neighbour came over and took control of the situation. She said I was lucky Renate hadn't been closer, as I could easily have killed her.

That's all I needed to hear. I was already terrified out of my wits and just wanted to leg it out of there, back to my grandmother.

The neighbour cleaned Renate up and stopped the bleeding. Then she bandaged her head. I asked her to stay with us until my aunt got home from work. I was so frightened of the trouble I was going to be in.

To my surprise, things turned out very differently, when my aunt got home. Instead of me being in trouble, the neighbour gave my aunt a lecture on leaving a toddler with a kid, barely 12 years old, all day long. On top of which the woman told my aunt she'd watched me, day in, day out, working nonstop, doing chores way beyond my age, working my fingers to the bone. She told my aunt she ought to be ashamed of herself for treating me, like a slave.

Nickitante was very defensive and told the woman I was old enough and responsible enough to be left with a young child.

I'd been only 8 and Christian, 9, when we were left with our one year old half brother, all day long. Maybe we'd been lucky nothing bad had ever happened.

That evening I got a real dressing down by my aunt. She told me to be more careful in future. It didn't stop her, however, from making me do all those chores.

Towards the end of the summer holiday, I was in the back yard washing clothes. My fingers were rubbed raw and bleeding.

I heard the gate open. When I looked up, Groysie was standing there. I hadn't seen my grandmother all summer. On Sundays, my aunt and uncle went to church and always left me at home, with Renate.

I threw my wet arms around my grandmother and started to cry. I'd missed her so much. I was sobbing my heart out. She led me to the garden bench, where we both sat down.

"Now, now my child, what's the matter, why all the tears?" Groysie said kindly, holding me close to her chest. I still couldn't talk. She held me at arms length, holding my hands in hers, just looking at me. I winced. My hands hurt. She looked down and saw the state they were in.

"How long have you been doing the washing?" She asked.

"Ever since the beginning of summer" I told her.

"Your aunt is treating you every bit as badly as your mother," Groysie said angrily. "I would never have agreed to you coming had I known she was going to treat you like this."

"You were supposed to look after Renate, not do all the household chores for her." My grandmother was very annoyed.

"Oh! She's going to get a piece of my mind," Groysie promised. "She's used you like a slave, my child."

My grandmother said she had to go for bread, but would be back when my aunt was home from work.

Late that afternoon, my grandmother came back, ready to wage war. I could always tell when she was angry, which was not very often.

I'd never heard Groysie speak like she did to my aunt or anybody else for that matter. Nickitante tried to defend her actions towards me and said that hard work had never hurt anybody.

Groysie was so disgusted with my aunt's behaviour and retort. She told me to get my things and we left. My grandmother was cool towards my aunt for quite a long time after. There were only a few days left before school started. Groysie let me go and play with my friends quite a bit. She'd actually seen with her own eyes the abuse my aunt had put me through. I could always tell when she was sorry for me.

While I'd been staying with my uncle and aunt, they'd asked me if I'd like to go and live with my father in England. I was horrified at the thought and told them never. I didn't know him and would never leave Groysie.

After all the hard work during the summer, it was a relief to go back to school and get back to my regular routine.

Annitante confronted Nickitante and asked her what she intended to give me for looking after her little girl and doing all her work.

Nickitante thought taking me off my grandparents hands for the summer was enough payment. She had given me food and a roof over my head, which she thought was enough.

An argument erupts. Annitante tells her sister-in-law what she thinks of her and how disgusted she is with her behaviour.

A few days later Nickitante turns up with a very gaudy piece of material, which she hands me, as though it was the crown jewels.

After my aunt has left, Annitante says the material is more suitable for a gypsy, not a young girl like me. I tell her that now the kids at school will have even more reason to call me gypsy.

Groysie says we shouldn't complain, it's better than nothing. Annitante maintains that my aunt had bought the horrible piece of material on purpose, because she'd been shamed into giving me something.

Chapter Twenty

Early that autumn, Granddad writes to my father in England, explaining the hopeless situation we're all in. He tells him that I need a home and he should make every effort on his part to get me out of Romania to live with him.

Granddad then gets in touch with a retired lawyer, he knows, to help us file papers and apply for my immigration to England.

We know lots of Transylvanian Saxons, who have applied to leave Romania and go to Germany, but nobody's allowed out, even for holidays, let alone for good.

Heide's brother is 18. He's one of the top skiers in the Romanian international team. When they compete in an Iron Curtain country, he and other Saxon skiers are always on the team. However, when they go to competitions in the West, all the Saxon members of the team are left behind. Given half a chance, they would all defect, so they're not trusted.

Groysie talks to me about going to live with my father, but I don't want to hear about it. I get very upset and tell her that I'll never leave her and will only go if she goes with me.

Groysie tells me that she's too old for such changes and belongs here with my grandfather. They won't live forever and I belong with my father, who will take good care of me and give me a good education. I'd also have a new mother, whom, she hoped, would be good and kind.

Both my aunts tried very hard to convince me of the wonderful life I'd have with my father and new mother. I'd have my own bedroom, beautifully decorated, and lots of lovely clothes.

I would have everything, my heart desired, and I'd have food, I couldn't even imagine in my wildest dreams.

In spite of everybody painting such fantastic pictures of my new life in England, making it all sound like something from a fairy tale, I would not be convinced. I remained adamant that I would never leave my Groysie.

On my first day back at school, Ernst and I get called out to the front of the class by the teacher. He announces to the whole class that we will receive monthly bursaries of 25 Lei each. This is the equivalent of four loaves of bread.

I receive the bursary because I'm considered an orphan, as I live with my grandparents. Ernst is given the measly help because his mother is raising 4 children on her own.

Each month the teacher calls Filtch and Renges to the front of the class. I'm still addressed by my surname by teachers and pupils. I find it hurtful and discriminating. The majority of kids are called by their Christian names.

The teacher then presents us with the pathetic 25 Leis. The kids make fun of us and we have to endure further derision and ridicule.

I tell Groysie how humiliated I am every time this happens and how mean the kids are to both Ernst and me.

Groysie feels sorry for me. "We can't refuse the money," she says. "We need every bit of help we can get."

There are several class outings from school this autumn. One is to a glass factory. We have to bring money for the bus fare. I can't go, no money for the bus.

Then there's a day outing to the Red Tower Pass. This is where the River Alt cuts through the Carpathian Mountains and flows through from Transylvania into Valachia, where it joins the Danube on the border of Romania with Bulgaria. The class will visit an ancient monastery. The whole area is full of history, which we have learnt. This is where the Roman Legions built roads through the mountains, during the times, when the Roman Empire was all powerful.

I would just love to go. That history fascinates me, but I can't. No money for the train fare.

The class gets taken to the Hermannstadt National Theatre to see Mother Courage and her Children. This happens to be free. I can't go. It's a sin.

Life just doesn't seem to be fair, or any fun. If it's not money, then it's religion that stands in the way.

One evening in the autumn, after school, all the kids are packed on the tram going home. It's already dark and about 8 o'clock.

Suddenly the tram comes to a halt in between interchanges. The conductor tells everybody to get off and get the tram a little further along the line. This only happens when a tram has broken down or there's been an accident.

Tram accidents happen quite often. We never see car accidents, because there are hardly any cars on the roads.

As we all walk along the road to get to the other tram, there's a crowd of people gathered around the tram lines in between the two stationery trains.

The street lighting is pretty poor. The kids are all curious and we push our way through the crowd to see what's going on.

A man's torso is lying between the tracks. The head is completely cut off, lying this side of the tracks. The legs are cut off above the knees the other side of the tracks.

It's such a gruesome scene. All the body parts are lying in pools of blood.

All the kids are standing, looking on, with morbid fascination. The head's not far from where I'm standing, but face down.

A woman in the crowd is very traumatised and ranting about witnessing the whole thing. This guy had been walking just in front of her on the side walk, swaying from side to side, obviously very drunk. Suddenly, he just turned, walked towards the tram lines, tripped and fell head long across the tracks in front of an oncoming train. The driver never had a chance to even brake, let alone stop.

A man is taking charge of the situation and tells everybody to leave. He yells at the kids to go home. We shouldn't be there looking at this horrible scene. Too late now, we've seen it all and the ghoulish picture is imprinted in our minds.

We all hang around at a distance for a while longer and then get on the waiting tram and go home. Horrible nightmares haunt me for weeks afterwards.

The next day we found out, the man who got killed, lived in the next street from us. I knew him by sight. He was only about 30 and had a wife and a 3 year old son.

The funeral was on a Sunday. I asked Groysie if I could see Heide in the morning. She told me I could see her for a little while before church, but I wasn't to go to the house of the widow.

The Romanian Orthodox tradition was to have the body, lying in an open casket, at the house. Family, friends and neighbours went and paid their last respects on the day of the funeral.

I told Heide how all the school kids had been at the scene of the accident, just after it had happened. I described the horrible details to her and told her I couldn't get that awful picture out of my mind.

Heide said we should go and pay our respects. I told her I didn't want to look at the man again. She said the undertakers make the dead look very good. He'd be all dressed and I wouldn't even know he'd been in an accident. She said I should go, I could then have a different picture of him in my mind. I told Heide not to tell Groysie that we'd been, as she'd forbidden me to go to the house.

When we entered the widow's house, the coffin was standing in the middle of the room. The young wife was sitting nearby with her little boy on her lap, crying nonstop.

There was a stream of people filing through the house and past the coffin. As Heide had said, the man looked just as though he was asleep. No sign of the accident. His shirt came right up to his chin and a lovely bow tie held everything together. He looked like the man I'd known. Seeing the young woman, with her little boy, did upset me though. Heide and I both said our condolences to the widow and left.

I was glad I'd gone. I now had a different picture in my mind, but it didn't stop me from having bad dreams.

Marianne will be one year old in January. For the past two or three months, Annitante has left her at home, when she's been on the night shift, from ten in the evening till six in the morning.

It's so much easier to leave her at home to sleep with me. My aunt is home by 6.30 and the baby's still asleep.

The poor little mite is so good natured. When Annitante works the morning shift, starting at 6, she gets Marianne up at 5 o'clock, feeds her, dresses her, then bundles her in blankets and takes her to the crèche. There's never a peep out of the baby. It takes half an hour to get to work. In the winter my aunt pulls her in a sledge, Granddad's made, and when there's no snow, she uses an old second-hand pram.

When Annitante is on the two to ten shift, she has to get Marianne from the crèche, when she's already asleep and bring her home.

When I'm at school in the morning, I go to the factory at six in the evening, fetch Marianne from the crèche, feed her and put her to bed at home.

When I'm at school in the afternoon, the tram passes my aunt's factory about 8 in the evening. I get off there, pick my cousin up and take her home with me.

If she's still up, when I get to the crèche, Marianne jumps up and down with joy in her cot when she sees me, stretching out her little chubby arms to be picked up. She's just the loveliest, happiest little thing and I love her to bits.

Annitante is very grateful that I do this. It makes life so much easier for her. It's also much better for Marianne. Dragging her out, in all weathers, all hours of the night, seems so wrong.

Soon after her first birthday, Marianne gets scarlet fever. She's admitted to the isolation unit at the children's hospital in town, which is in the next street from my school. I pop in every day to see her. At the beginning she's very sick and sleeps most of the time. I would so much like to go in and stroke her cute little face, I have to stand at the glass window and just look at her.

When she starts to get better, she gets very excited when she sees me, with a big smile on her face. She reaches out her little arms, wanting to be picked up. I have to remain behind the glass window. I wave and pull funny faces at her, which makes her laugh. I feel so bad for her. She's so little and doesn't understand and when I leave, Marianne gets upset and cries, desperately stretching her podgy little arms towards me. It upsets me and I end up crying too.

After what seems like a long time, Marianne is fully recovered. Annitante and I go to pick her up and bring her home. She's so pleased to see everybody again. It's delightful to have her around. She brings us all so much joy and happiness.

One evening, towards the end of winter, I picked Marianne up from the factory crèche. It was about 8 o'clock and dark. I had to cross the main road, where the tram ran. I always picked a spot, where I could see a long way in both directions. The snow had begun to melt and there were black oily puddles around the tram lines.

Because there was no snow on the track, it was harder to pull the sledge across. My worst nightmare happened. The sleigh got caught on the track and tipped over. Marianne fell face first into the black sludge. I desperately looked up and down the railway track, expecting a ghost train to appear out of nowhere. What a relief, not a train in sight. I quickly dragged the sledge onto the sidewalk, then picked Marianne up, she was covered from head to toe in black greasy muck. Her little face was covered in grime. I put her back in her sleigh and wrapped her up in the blanket.

Poor little thing. She was in shock and looked completely bewildered. Then after getting her breath back, a very loud cry erupted from her. I knelt down by her, wiped her face with the blanket and then tried to comfort her, by cuddling and kissing her. As I was doing all this, a tram went by. I was so relieved that Marianne wasn't hurt and nothing worse had happened. After having seen several accidents on the tram lines, I was always extra careful when crossing. Being anywhere near the tram always made me feel terribly nervous.

When I got home and explained what had happened, Groysie was very kind and understanding. She said it could have happened to anybody.

The end of the school year is nearing. I'll be going to Kerz this summer. I haven't seen Christian for nearly two years. I'll be thirteen in July. I've seen lots of changes in my body over the last year. I won't be able to run around in underpants anymore, as my breasts have started to develop. We don't have biology at school only zoology, where we learn about animal development and how they procreate. Neither of my aunts or Groysie has said anything to me about these changes I'm going through. I've got no idea how they'll affect me.

One thing's good though, my sleepwalking has stopped. What a relief. All the praying to banish Satan from me must have helped.

Every week, when we have PE at the recreational centre, some of the girls are excused from joining in. I know it's something to do with a thing they call periods. Nobody talks about it and I've got no idea what it is.

I ask Heide, one day, if girls in her class miss PE. She tells me there's only one girl, who has a period. Well, they are two years younger than me. I ask Heide if she knows what a period is.

She certainly knows more than I do. She tells me her sister and mother have periods. Most girls get them when they reach their teens.

"You'll be getting yours pretty soon," she says.

"You still haven't told me what it is." I say.

"Well, I'm not a hundred percent sure," Heide says. "I know you bleed every month from where you pee and have to put rags in your underpants to stop the blood from running down your legs."

I tell her that's gross and I think she's making it all up.

"No, it's true and if you don't believe me ask my mother," Heide replies.

Heide asks me if I've ever seen blood in our outhouse

"Come to think of it, I have from time to time."

She tells me my aunt has periods. All women do, she says, but she thinks Groysie is too old to still have them.

I tell her I hope I'll never get anything so awful. She just laughs and says, "of course you will." That's the end of the conversation about periods for quite a long time.

A new boy has come to our neighbourhood this spring. He's living with an older couple, called Kessler, who have no children. His name is Yuri. He's 16, blond and very good looking. He's joined the gang in the meadow several times. He's sporty too.

Selma says her older sister Hilde, who's 15 likes, Yuri and has her eye on him. When we're all out playing in the fields, we can see them making eyes at each other.

Yuri is by far the best looking boy around and we all like him.

Selma, Heide and I often find an excuse to go round to the Kesslers' house, just to get a glimpse of Yuri.

I think he likes the attention he gets from all the girls. He's very polite to us all, but we're only kids and he's not at all interested in us younger ones.

Mr. Kessler drives a wagon and horses. He delivers all kinds of goods for the state and Yuri helps him.

I feel a little put out. My friends will be spending the whole summer here, getting a chance to see Yuri. I have to go to Kerz. As much as I hate going, it's no use kicking against it. I have to go anyway. After last summer's fiasco with my aunt, Groysie says she'd rather I went to Kerz and besides, she thought it would be good to see Christian again.

My two little brothers have grown so much. Hani is nearly 3 and Viorel is 6. Christian is now 14 and has finished school, but he's still no taller than me.

My brother tells me he'll start a tailoring apprenticeship in September in Hermannstadt. The master tailor, he'll learn the trade from, is a good friend of my father's. They'd both done their apprenticeship together in Hermannstadt, all those years ago.

Christian seemed very pleased with the prospect of living in Hermannstadt and away from mother.

The summer dragged on for ever. Nothing had changed. We worked hard six days a week. A lot more was expected of us and the chores became bigger and harder. Mother still did her own thing on Sundays with her family. Each year she looked more and more like a Romanian woman, in her traditional Romanian costume.

Christian went off with his Saxon friends, who were all boys and I tried to fit in as well as I could with the local Saxon girls.

The Saxon families were always pleased to see me. Everybody seemed quite happy, in spite of the drudgery and hard work all week long.

Sunday was special for everybody. People had their families and friends around them. They enjoyed their simple lives and took it easy for the day.

I often wondered how life would have been had my father come home after the war, like all the other men. I was pretty sure we would all have been happy together as a family. It made me sad to think about it, so I didn't dwell too much on my thoughts.

In the early evenings on Sunday, there was always the village dance to go to. It was usually held in somebody's barn or in the Saxon school hall.

A lot of the young couples dressed in Saxon national dress, which was very beautiful and I loved seeing it. Even the kids and young teenagers wore traditional costume. These clothes were handmade and beautifully embroidered. So much work went into making them. They were handed down through the generations.

My mother had also had a very beautiful Saxon costume, which would have been handed down to her by her mother. She got married in it. I never ever saw it. She must have got rid of it. But it was something that was rightfully mine and she should have given it to me.

All the couples and even the kids at the village dances were very good dancers. Children started to dance when they weren't much older than toddlers.

I couldn't dance. I had always been told it was a sin. So I was quite content to stand and watch.

Mother's attitude towards me hadn't changed at all. She was still as mean as ever, verbally abusive and lashing out physically without good reason. I felt it was simply my presence that infuriated her and made her see red.

The never ending long hot summer did pass. With great relief I made my way back to the railway stop one Sunday morning at the end of August. I'd survived all the abuse and nastiness another summer holiday. It felt good to be going back to Hermannstadt and my Grandparents.

One day, not long after school started, Christian turned up at our little abode. He only had a small bag with him, in which he carried a change of clothes. He told us he was starting his apprenticeship in a couple of days and asked Groysie if he could spend a few days with us until he found lodgings closer to work.

We were all very pleased to see him, especially Groysie, who was over the moon. She hadn't seen my brother since he was 6 years old and here he was 8 years later, almost a young man. She told him he could stay as long as he wanted. There was always room for him, no matter how small our little shack was. So he shared Tummy's bed, in which they slept head to toe.

Christian was with us for a while, but then he found a room in town, which he shared with another apprentice. He did visit often. It was good to get my brother back again after so many years. We got on well now that he was away from my mother's influence. We became good friends.

Chapter Twenty One

My last year at elementary school had begun. All the kids were talking enthusiastically about what they were going to do when they left. Most of them were planning on going to high school, if they passed their final exams. Some of them were even looking beyond that, going on to university.

I had my own dreams, but never talked about them. I didn't know what would happen after this year. There had been talk of sending me back to my mother. Things were pretty dire financially at home. I tried not to think about it, it upset me too much.

Our maths teacher, from the previous two years, was now also our form teacher in our last year. She was the fairest teacher, out of all the teachers, I'd known. She didn't show favouritism to any student. She treated everybody equally. I liked and respected her a lot for that. Her name was Professor Pletosu. She was Saxon, married to a Romanian.

The previous year, our form teacher had been Professor Pankraz. He was our German and history teacher and also took us for our weekly politics class. During our politics lesson, he'd enter the classroom and ask what we wanted to do.

What he was supposed to do, was teach and convince us students how wonderful communism was and what terrible and repressed lives people in the western world lived.

Instead, he told us about his student years at university in Leipzig. He talked at length about pre-war life in Transylvania and Germany. The stories about his youth and life in general during the twenties and thirties were enthralling. We all sat listening, without a peep out of anybody.

He was taking a real chance in relating how wonderful things were before the war. Somehow he didn't care.

That autumn of 1956, there was a lot of talk about an uprising in Hungary. From the end of our garden, on the hill, we had a good view of all the trains in the valley below. Night and day, long trains went from east to west, carrying tanks and soldiers.

The newspapers were denying all rumours that there was trouble in Hungary. We were fed a lot of propaganda about the West planning an attack on the communist countries. The troops were being stationed on all the borders to protect us from the invaders.

Nobody seemed to believe anything the papers said.

After church one Sunday, Granddad said, one of the elders had told him he had a radio and managed to tune into a German station, where he'd heard all about the Hungarian uprising. However, the communist regime managed to intersect and disrupt most radio transmissions from the West, but sometimes snippets were gleaned by the people. If anybody was caught or reported to have listened to a Western station, they would be put away for years.

There was great hope amongst the people that the unrest would spread to the other Iron Curtain countries and communism would be overthrown.

Eventually talk of the revolution in Hungary died down. People said hundreds of Hungarians had been killed in vain. Nobody dared to stand up to, or voice an opinion against the oppressive communist rule.

Christian often visited on Sundays. It was always good to see him. We managed to rekindle the closeness we had, as very young children. He opened up about his life with mother and the cruelty and hardship, he'd endured at her hands. When I was there for the summer, he said I became her whipping boy, which eased his plight.

He felt the same way as I did: unloved and unwanted. He talked about how differently she treated her two little boys, how she loved and cherished them both.

My brother was so happy to live in Hermannstadt and hoped, after his apprenticeship, he could find work and make a life for himself away from mother.

On one of his visits, Christian told me he'd bumped into Frau Schomody. She was the lady who spent some time with her husband and two children, at mother's house one summer, as paying guests.

How could I forget all the wonderful food mother had cooked for these people? She lavished endless attention on them all, catering to their every whim, especially the spoilt little girl. She treated the family like royalty and had Christian and I running around like little slaves.

Frau Schomody had invited Christian to their home. He said he had accepted her invitation and gone to the house. They lived in a lovely part of the old city. The big villa stood in beautiful grounds, which they didn't have to share with other families. Christian said he'd never seen such a big beautiful place before.

Herr Schomody was a bigwig in the chocolate factory in town. I told my brother I didn't even know there was such a factory. If there was, no one ever saw as much as a square of chocolate anywhere in the shops.

Christian then told me that these people had a pigsty at the end of the garden, hidden away behind shrubs. He'd gone with the son to feed the animals.

He said he couldn't believe what they were feeding the pigs.

"Potatoes and maize, or course," I blurted out, which is what we did in Kerz.

"Chocolate!" My brother said. "They melt it down with some water and milk and that's what they give to the pigs. They're so big and fat, you wouldn't believe it."

I said to Christian Id never ever seen chocolate in the shops, where were they getting it from.

Christian said, the Schomody kid had told him all the chocolate is exported to Russia. But Herr Schomody brings broken chocolate home, which they feed the animals.

"Wow!" I said, "did you eat some?" I couldn't believe it when my brother said no. "Why not?" I asked. Christian said he was too shy.

"So, you just stood and watched as the pigs were being fed all that chocolate?" I said in amazement. "If that had been me, I would have asked for some."

Christian said we'd both have to go and visit, but we never did.

At the beginning of the winter term, which started mid January after our school holidays, two girls from our year where chosen to go to the gymnastics club in town. I was lucky to be one of the girls. Brigitte, the other girl, and I were the most athletic in our year. The club was in the afternoon. We could only go alternate weeks, when we were at school in the morning.

I was very happy to do this extra activity. I'd never been involved in anything outside of school and loved any kind of sport, or games. I was also spared queuing for food on that afternoon.

The gym was big with every imaginable apparatus. The day we went was just for girls. We were divided into several groups. All the kids were roughly the same age. Brigitte and I were the only two Saxon girls there. A lot of the girls had been doing gymnastics from an early age, so they were very good.

At the end of the term, our time at the club was finished. I'd loved every minute of it and was sorry it all finished.

However, that spring term, I got the chance to go to the local art school for the day. Again two girls from my year were chosen for this and I happened to be one of them. I was thrilled. I loved anything to do with art.

Throughout school, we never had music lessons, or art lessons, as such. The only time we got to draw and colour was during our botany, zoology and geography lessons. It was on the basis of these drawings that I was chosen to go to the art school for the day. The other girl, I went with, was Ilse. It was a wonderful day. We had the opportunity to use oil and water colours. It was so much fun. I would have loved to have gone to a school like that all the time.

Chapter Twenty Two

It was coming up to two years since my Grandparents had applied for me to go to England. We hadn't heard anything in that time from the government. My family had pretty well given up hope that I would ever get permission to leave. I wasn't upset about it at all, as I didn't want to go in the first place and leave my Groysie.

Towards the end of that school year, I kept badgering my Grandmother to let me have my hair cut short. She refused to hear about it. Why would I want to have my beautiful long hair cut and end up looking like a boy? All the girls went to barbers and had very similar hair cuts to boys.

I was fed up with the long plaits down to the back of my knees and wanted to be like the other girls. I'd never had short hair.

Not a day went by without me nagging Groysie about having it cut. I became obsessed with the idea and just wouldn't let it be.

My hair was a thick dark chestnut brown. Very often, when I stood in line for food, women around me remarked about my gorgeous, shiny long hair and how they wished they had hair like it. They'd comment on my green eyes, which they said complemented my hair perfectly.

I thought having short hair would save a lot of work every morning. Groysie combed it, then plaited the long braids, which took about fifteen minutes. For some reason, I thought having short hair would make me fit in better with my peers.

After the never ending nagging, Groysie finally gave in. She gave me the money to go to the barber and have my hair cut.

I was overjoyed. After school, the next day, I went to a barber in town. There were several men, boys and girls sitting, all waiting to have haircuts.

When it was my turn, I sat in the special chair in front of a big mirror. It seemed weird seeing all of my upper body and face in the mirror. I never had the chance of looking at my reflection, so it was a little alien. I quite liked what I saw though. My green eyes really stood out above my high cheekbones. I examined my features, which were fine and regular and my lips were full and pink.

Standing behind my chair, looking at me in the mirror, the barber asked how much I wanted cut off. I told him I wanted the typical hair cut all the girls had. Longer at the top, but graduated and cut short into the neck.

He stood holding my plaits in his hands. He asked several times if I was sure.

"Most women would give their eye teeth to have hair like this," he said. I insisted I wanted it cut. The barber said he would like to buy the plaits. I told him my grandmother had told me specifically to bring them home.

The barber held one of my plaits in his left hand close to the nape of my neck. Before he cut, he asked again if I was absolutely sure.

It was my hair. I wanted it chopped off. I was getting a bit fed up with this man's reluctance to cut it.

"Yes! Just do it!" I told him.

The barber cut the first braid and laid it on the shelf below the mirror in front of me. I looked at it. It was beautifully braided by Groysie and lay there thick and shiny. Then he cut the second plait, close to the hairline, and laid that, next to the first one.

I looked at myself in the mirror. My hair hung very straight halfway down my neck. It looked awful. I could feel the tears welling up. All my life I'd had long hair. The reflection in the mirror was not at all pleasing.

The barber noticed that I was near to tears. He reassured me my hair would look a lot better once he'd styled it.

So I sat watching, as he snipped away and put some shape and style into my short hair. But my hair was dead straight without a hint of a wave or curl. When it was finished, I was not pleased with the end result and thought I looked ugly.

The barber put my two plaits into a brown paper bag. I paid and left to go home. All the way home on the tram I felt self-conscious. I was sure everybody was looking at me, thinking how horrible I looked. I buried my face in my arms and cried my eyes out.

When I got off the tram, to walk the rest of the way home, I was determined to stop crying and put on a brave face. I would tell Groysie I loved my new hair style.

When I walked into our little shack, I just burst into tears and told Groysie I wished I'd listened to her and that I hated the way my hair looked.

She never said I told you so. She simply smiled and said, one good thing about hair was that it grows and if I didn't like it, I could let it grow again. My Grandmother always seemed to have some words of wisdom. They always made me feel better.

It didn't help when people, who knew me, kept asking why I'd cut my lovely hair. It certainly didn't make any difference to the way the other kids treated me, which in my naive opinion, I'd hoped it would.

At school, we are in the full swing of preparing for our final exams. The results of these exams are all important for getting into high school, where I hope to go as well.

One Sunday evening, with the whole family present, Granddad says he has to tell me something very important. Discussion about what to do with me when school was finished, had been going on for weeks in my absence.

Everybody had hoped beyond hope that a miracle would happen and I'd get permission to go to England. As this was not the case, the decision had been made to send me back to my mother after my graduation.

The words hit me like a bombshell. I was completely dumbstruck, but then the tears started to flow silently down my face.

Groysie embraced me, held me tight and stroked my head. Granddad said life was very difficult, but had become even more so in the last couple of years since he'd stopped work. He was a very sick man and spent a lot of time in hospital. Getting no old age pension and having to rely for their living on Annitante and Tummy, it had become harder and harder to make ends meet.

Granddad said they'd always done the best they could, but now it was my mother's turn to take responsibility for me.

I was devastated. I told them my mother didn't give a damn about me and life in Kerz would be completely unbearable.

"What was the point of studying and doing the exams to graduate from elementary school, to end up working my fingers to the bone on the land?" I said.

Granddad told me that all education and everything we learn is of value and we must always make the most of all our chances.

I reasoned that I'd be happy to leave school and just get a job, as long as I could stay with them.

Granddad looked very sad. He maintained that he and Groysie had become too old and tired to carry on being responsible for me.

I knew I'd lost the argument and had to accept their decision, no matter how many suggestions or ideas I came up with.

Secretly, I never gave up hope. My mind was working overtime to figure out a way to convince them all to let me stay with them.

I thought if I worked very hard and got good grades in my exams, the family would think it a waste to send me back to Kerz and let me stay.

I told Heide and her mother, as well as Annemarie and her mother, about my dilemma. They were all very sympathetic to my plight. They'd all hoped and prayed that permission would have been granted for me to go to my father in England. Heide's mother, who was always very kind, told me not to give up hope.

In spite of all the turmoil going on in my life, I studied hard for my exams and ended up with very good grades.

The week after open day at school, Professor Pletosu asked me to remain behind after the last class. I had no idea why she wanted to see me. As far as I knew, I hadn't done anything. I'd done well in my exams, so I knew it wasn't about that.

When all the kids had left, my professor closed the classroom door and asked me to sit at a desk. She brought a chair and sat opposite me.

She asked why nobody from my family had come to the open day to discuss what was happening about my education.

I told her my Grandfather was very sick and Groysie didn't feel comfortable talking to clever people, like teachers. I told her my family was very happy with the grades I'd got and didn't think it necessary to discuss it.

Because of the good grades I got, Professor Pletosu assumed I'd go on to high school. I said I'd like nothing more. Unfortunately, I was being sent back to my mother, who lived in the village of Kerz, to work on the land.

The look on her face told me that she was shocked by what I'd told her. She said it would be such a shame and a terrible waste, as I'd achieved such good grades.

We chatted for a while and I explained my situation.

Then she told me she'd like to come and see my grandparents and try to persuade them to keep me in the city and let me carry on with school.

I told her my family had made their decision. I didn't think talking to them would help and change their plans. I didn't want her to come and see the poverty we lived in.

I didn't mention the talk I had with my teacher to Granddad and Groysie. I just hoped she would forget about it and not come.

Granddad was lying in his deck chair under the cherry tree by the shack. He often sat in his chair in the shade resting and taking short naps.

I loved sitting outside with Granddad, doing my homework. He enjoyed listening to my idle chatter about my day at school. Groysie was always busy doing something in the house, or working in the vegetable garden nearby. Granddad was unable to help anymore, as he was always in pain and short of breath.

Groysie looked up from what she was doing in the garden and announced that a stranger was coming down our garden path.

I looked up and, sure enough, Professor Pletosu was striding down the narrow dirt path. "It's my professor from school," I said sheepishly to my grandparents. "I meant to tell you she was coming to see you, but forgot." I didn't say that I'd hoped she wouldn't come, as I was too ashamed of where we lived. At that moment I would have given anything to have become invisible.

Instead, I stood up and started walking towards the teacher. She'd just passed the little outhouse, which smelled very bad in the warm weather. I'm sure she must have noticed the stench, but showed no sign of being offended by it.

The teacher introduced herself to my grandparents. She said it had been rather difficult to find us. I thought not difficult enough. There was no street sign for our road or number for the house. She'd been lucky to come across a neighbour, who knew us and gave her directions how to get here.

Groysie offered to bring a chair out the house, but Professor Pletosu said she'd be fine on the wooden bench along the wall.

I brought a chair out for Groysie to sit on and then joined my teacher on the bench. She went straight into explaining the reason why she had come.

She told my grandparents that I was a very bright child and had finished school with very good grades. The teacher then said that she'd had a chat with me at school and learnt that I was to be sent to work on the land. She considered this to be a terrible shame and a waste of a bright young life.

Both my grandparents sat quietly and listened to all the professor had to say. When she had finished, Granddad sat up in his deck chair. I could see just doing that was quite an effort for him. He looked so old and sick.

He sat for a brief moment, trying to control the pain, which was evident on his face. He then proceeded, in a calm and even voice, to explain the situation we were in. The family had lengthy discussions trying to find a way to keep me with them. In the end it just wasn't possible. It had been a very hard decision, for all the family, to send me back to my mother.

Professor Pletosu said she fully understood. Nevertheless, she felt sad to see a young life wasted.

Graduation was only a couple of weeks away. All the girls at school were talking about the new dresses and shoes, they'd wear for the occasion.

Annemarie asked me if I had a new dress. I told her I hadn't. A couple of days later she invited me to her house. When I got there, her mother was at home, sewing a very pretty pale green dress for Annemarie.

Frau Grimme was pleased to see me. She was usually at work, when I went round. Annemarie's grandparents lived very close, but she was happy left on her own. She was 16 and very sensible and mature for her age.

Frau Grimme showed me a picture of the dress, she was making. It looked beautiful. The bodice was fitted, and it had a round neck and short sleeves. The skirt was gathered and very full. A wide sash adorned the waist and tied into a big bow at the back.

What Frau Grimme did next rather puzzled me. She picked up her tape measure and proceeded to take my measurements. I stood still and didn't know what to make of it. She explained how grateful she was for me being such a good friend to Annemarie, that she could never thank me enough for all the help and support, I'd given her daughter, throughout our school years, so that making me a dress, was the least she could do as a way to say thank you.

Annemarie had wanted us both to have exactly the same dress. I was thrilled to get such a beautiful garment and thanked Frau Grimme over and over for her kindness. I couldn't wait to get home and tell Groysie the good news.

On the day of our graduation, Annemarie and I went to school together, proudly wearing our identical dresses. Frau Grimme told us both how beautiful we looked.

I couldn't believe that I looked every bit as good as all the other girls in my new dress. For the first time ever, I didn't feel shabby and intimidated. Some of those nasty girls couldn't resist making jibes. "Oh, look at the odd couple, they're not so odd, they're matching today!" But I didn't care. At least, I wouldn't have to put up with them any more. The graduation took place in the big hall of a Romanian school. All the students sat in the first few rows at the front.

When my name was called to receive my school leaving certificate, I felt very proud. The room was filled with parents and families, but none was mine.

Annemarie's mother and Professor Pletosu both congratulated me, gave me a hug and wished me well.

For a very short time, I felt happy. Then a big black cloud engulfed me, as I realised this was the end of an era. I had only days left, before my life would change drastically.

I stood and watched the excited chatter and laughter of all the other students. They were all going on to parties to celebrate with family and friends.

I said goodbye to some of the professors, Annemarie and her mother and left the happy event, feeling utterly deflated and very sad.

Over the next few days, before finally leaving Hermannstadt, and my grandparents for good, I never truly gave up hope that, maybe, some miracle would happen and I wouldn't be sent to Kerz.

Everyday, when I was alone with Groysie, I'd bring up the subject of being sent to Kerz. Drowning in my own tears and sorrow, I'd plead and beg her, not to make me go back to my mother.

I told my grandmother I'd be better off dead than live the life that was awaiting me in Kerz. It upset her terribly to hear me talk like this. It troubled her, even more, that she couldn't do anything about it. She made me promise over and over that I wouldn't do anything silly. I told her I wouldn't, but wasn't sure I could keep my promise.

The day of my departure arrived much too soon. Everything, I owned, was in a cotton bag. I'd said goodbye to Tummy, early in the morning, before he left for work. I was going to miss him so much.

Marianne was now two and a half. This little girl had become very dear to me. I'd been there doing things and caring for her the whole of her young life. Now it was all coming to an abrupt end.

Marianne looked a little puzzled and asked why I was crying. I just held her in my arms, hugged and kissed her and told her I just felt very sad.

I embraced my aunt and said goodbye, then watched, as she pushed Marianne, in the old pushchair through the neighbour's garden, on her way to work.

When I went back in the house, Groysie was sitting at the table looking sad. I told her I'd meant to tell my aunt and Tummy, how much I appreciated everything they'd done for me, but I'd been too upset to talk. I asked Groysie to pass my message on to them both, which she assured me she'd do.

Later that morning, in very low spirits and with a breaking heart, I tore myself away from the two most important people in my life. I loved them so much. They meant everything to me.

Groysie had to stay at home with Granddad. He was very sick again and confined to bed.

I stood and looked down at my Granddad, with tears running down my face. There was so much I wanted to say to him, but I couldn't speak. As I embraced him, I wondered if I would see him again. He'd lost a lot of weight. His face looked haggard and worn out. Then I turned and walked out of the shack with Groysie.

At the gate to our neighbour's garden, I fell into my grandmother's arms and didn't want to let go. I was taller than her now. We clung to each other crying. She then gently pushed me away and told me to go and asked that God would take care of me.

I walked through Frau Friedsam's garden. Before I rounded the house, I looked back. Groysie was still standing at the gate, wiping tears away with her apron. I waved one last time, then turned and entered my black world.

I was so steeped in misery, I don't remember the ride on the tram to the railway station. I'd done the trip so often, that I was sure I could have done it blindfolded.

All the other times, I'd had a return ticket. This time my ticket was one way only and I suddenly felt abandoned and absolutely terrified.

When I'd said goodbye to Heide and her family, her mother told me she would pray, that I'd get permission to go to England.

Sitting on the train going to Kerz, all kinds of foreboding thoughts crossed my mind. One thing was for sure, I had to stop feeling sorry for myself, put on a brave face and just get on with it. My mother would certainly not have any sympathy or pity for me.

Then a thought struck me. "What if my mother didn't want me there all the time and sent me packing? Surely my grandparents couldn't turn me away."

Groysie had assured me that now I was almost fourteen years old, I'd be an asset to any family. Mother would be happy for an extra pair of hands, especially as Christian wasn't in Kerz anymore.

I told Groysie I would only be valuable to mother as a slave, not as her child, as she didn't consider me part of the family.

When I got off the train in Kerz, I went and sat on the bench by the little hut. As we'd approached the stop at my village, the urge to stay on the train had been so strong. But what would I do and where could I go? The thought was too horrendous to even consider and even more frightening than living with my mother.

I picked up my bag and started walking towards the dirt road that led to the village. I hated this place and thought it was the most Godforsaken place on earth.

I passed a number of villagers. They always made the same remarks.

"Oh, you've come home Uta, to see your mother and brothers"

"How you've grown Uta,"

"You're a young lady now."

I wouldn't say anything in response, just greet them politely. They all meant well.

As always, mother wasn't surprised or pleased to see me. When I told her I was there for good, her response was "So, they've had enough of you, have they?"

That remark cut very deep, I knew it wasn't true, but nevertheless, it hurt so much.

"You told me last summer you wouldn't be coming back any more, you'd be going to England," mother said in a mocking way. I still kept quiet.

"So your father doesn't want you either? eh?" She goaded.

"Well, let me tell you this. He never did, otherwise he would have come back years ago."

I just stood and looked at my mother. I wished I could tell her how deeply her words hurt me. That would have pleased her, no doubt, so it was better to say nothing.

"Well, there's plenty to do here and I can always do with the extra help."

Chapter Twenty Three

And so my life in Kerz began. Never ending work on the land and chores round the house from six in the morning till midnight. By Saturday night, I was always completely exhausted. Sunday, the slave got the day off.

Viorel and Hani were now seven and four years old. Uncle was hardly ever there. His job, as a shepherd, took him into the hills from spring to autumn. It certainly was an easier job than working on the land. The shepherds sat around all day, minding the sheep and the sheepdogs did all the rounding up. In the evenings they had to milk the sheep and then make cheese, but the days were spent relaxing in the meadows on the foothills.

On Sundays, mother took herself off, with her boys, to her Romanian relatives, leaving me to wander around the village, finding my own amusement.

I wore my beautiful graduation dress and went to church every Sunday morning. The first Sunday, I noticed we had a new vicar.

At the end of the service, the vicar stood outside the church door and bade every parishioner farewell, as they filed past him. When it was my turn, he asked if I was new to the village, as he hadn't seen me before.

I told him I lived with my mother in the Little Lane. He then asked who she was and if she was at church.

I said she went to the Romanian Orthodox Church with her husband and my two half brothers.

He wanted to know why I didn't go with them, to which I replied that they'd never asked me. I told him that they spent all day with their Romanian family.

The vicar seemed rather puzzled and asked what I did for my midday meal. I told him I didn't get a meal on Sunday.

He then said, "Well, my child, you can't go hungry all day. My wife has made a soup. I have two small children and you're very welcome to join us."

I felt shy and embarrassed. I assured him I'd be all right, but he insisted that I go with him. When all the parishioners had gone, the vicar closed the church doors and then we walked over to the vicarage, adjacent to the church.

I met the vicar's wife and his little boy and girl. They were around the same age as Viorel and Hani. His wife was a pretty young woman, dressed in city clothes. We all sat down and ate vegetable soup with bread. Afterwards, we sat in the garden, chatting and playing with the two children.

They were a very kind family and I often had my Sunday meal with them. Sometimes other families asked me to eat with them. I was always glad to accept. I think there was a kind of unspoken rule, that somebody always asked me to join them for Sunday lunch. I felt embarrassed, but was grateful not to have to go hungry all day long. In the afternoons I joined the other girls from the village in whatever they were doing. In the evening, we all went to the village barn dance.

One of the young men in the small village band, that played at the dances, also sang Old Saxon and German folk songs very beautifully. One song in particular always brought tears to my eyes. It affected me very much. It made me sad and left me feeling deep sorrow.

The German words of the song.
Waldeslust, Waldeslust,
O wie einsam schlagt die brust,
Meine Mutter liebt mich nicht,
Meinen Vater ken ich nicht,
Sterber mocht ich nicht,
Bin noch zu jung.

English translation.
Forest joy, Forest joy,
Oh! How lonely my heart beats,
My mother loves me not,
And my father I know not,
I don't wish to die,
I'm much too young.

I always felt as if these words were written for me. I would just go outside until the song was over. But the sadness always lingered for a long time.

One Sunday, after lunch with the vicar and his family, he asked if I knew the history about the church and monastery in Kerz. He said all the old ruins around the church and rectory, had once been a Cistercian

Monastery. I confessed my ignorance and said I would love to hear more about it, as history had been one of my favourite subjects at school.

Several Sunday afternoons I spent time with the vicar, walking through the church and around the ruins, learning the fascinating history of this ancient and first Cistercian Monastery in Eastern Europe.

Village of Kerz, the River Alt and the Carpathian Mountains in the background.

Christian Renges (Brother), Lorenz Renges (Grandfather), Thomas Renges (Tummy),
Anna Renges (Grandmother, my Groysie) and Me, Ursula Ute Renges

Lorenz, conscripted into the German Army

Lorenz and fellow soldiers, during the war

Lorenz, on far right, early on in WW2

After the war - one of many smartly dressed photos of Lorenz sent back to Romania to his family

After war, Another photo of Lorenz, sent to family.....having fun with friends on the English east coast

Mitzitante

Lorenz back row centre - Christmas in English prisoner of war camp, Near Ely, Cambridgeshire...1944/45

Ursula age 14 with Lorenz - first Christmas in Whittlesey, England 1957

Hans, Gitys husband, Mutti, Ursula, aged 15, and Vati

Ursula, aged 16, Mutti, Hans and Gity

Gity, Ursula, aged 17, Mutti and Vati

Ursula, age 17, in Skegness on the seafront

Chapter Twenty Four

Cistercian Monastery - Kerz, Transylvania.

The first documentation of the Cistercian Monastery in Kerz dates back to 1216. In 1241, the Tatar invaders destroyed most of the church and buildings, surrounding it. The work became more intense after the invasion and the church and buildings were rebuilt.

At the beginning, the monastery demanded strict discipline and the monks' mission was to spread Christianity. They taught the local people to cultivate the land and vineyards.

In the war against the Turks (1421-1432), the walls of the monastery were damaged and, in the course of time, discipline also began to get lax.

King Corvin closed the monastery in 1474 and donated its possessions to the Catholic church in Hermannstadt.

In the 16th century, the greatest part of the church and the monastery fell into ruins. However, the main part of the church has survived hundreds of years.

The western wall of the monastery is two floors high and is still visible today.

The Western wall of the church is still standing, as well as the tower, which was built in 1495. Some of the outside walls are also standing.

The main nave of the church has no roof. This area is a graveyard for soldiers of the 1st and 2nd World Wars. It is said that an ancient king is also buried there.

In the 1550s, the Saxons, who lived here and were Evangelical Christians, took the church over and it is still in use by the Saxons today.

Its interior conveys the same simplicity and coldness of the early days, when the monks occupied it. The architecture of the buildings remains the same, so the atmosphere of the Cistercian Abbey is still alive.

The Cistercian Order originates in France. It is an enclosed Roman Catholic order of monks, which was created by a breakaway group of 21 Cluniac monks, who, in 1098 left the abbey of Molesme in Burgundy, along with their abbot.

Their motivation was to live in strict observance of the rules of Saint Benedict. The Cluniacs were an off shoot of the Benedictines.

In 1098, the breakaway group acquired a marshland plot, south of Dijon, called Citeaux (latin for Cistercium), hence the name Cistercian.

The monks from Molesme petitioned Pope Urban II for the return of the abbot, who was instructed to go back to his position in Molesme, where he spent the rest of his life. Some of the monks remained in Citeaux and elected a new abbot.

They stopped wearing the Benedictine garments and chose to wear white wool robes. They became known as the white or dirty monks.

The abbot of the day, forged an alliance with the Dukes of Burgundy and worked out deals with them to be gifted farmland, vineyards and rocks from quarries, to build a church and monastery.

All monks were from noble families. To keep them in their accustomed lifestyle, they recruited lay brothers to do the work on the land and work in trades.

By the year 1111, this economic mode proved to be very successful. Groups of 12 monks were sent out to find land and build other churches and monasteries. They also built nunneries.

Cistercian monks played leading rolls in the Crusades, in both, military and spiritual aspects.

The Knights Templar were literally warrior Cistercian Monks, who took normal monastic vows and, who were also licensed to kill.

Cistercian Abbeys generally followed a standard design. They all had a common layout.

These abbeys were often constructed away from populated areas, in remote valleys near rivers or streams. Cistercian monks played a big part in developing the water wheel.

Statues or pictures were not allowed in or even near the churches. The windows were generally clear glass. They used water as a source of power, from the nearby rivers or streams.

The churches were always built on the north side of the land, with monasteries and cloisters to the south. Buildings were made of smooth pale stone with plain columns, pillars, arches and windows. Plastering was kept extremely simple or no plastering at all.

The Cistercian Order spread very quickly to the whole of Europe, the one in Kerz being the first in Transylvania. It also spread all over the

British Isles.

It is suggested that the early name of the abbey in Kerz may have been 'Our Lady of the Candles'.

The German word for candle is Kerze and hence, the name, Kerz for the village.

I began looking forward to Sundays. It felt like I was part of the vicar's family and had a certain feeling of belonging. The children liked having me around and I played with them.

Mother never talked to me. She was not interested or asked how I spent Sundays. I never told her where I went or what I did. She never showed me any affection or warmth. I was more than happy to keep my distance, as I was still very afraid of her. Her taunting and mocking ways towards me never stopped.

Befriending the vicar and his family was a godsend. The rectory became my refuge for a few hours most Sundays. The summer would have been unbearably miserable and lonelier, than I could have imagined, without them. I told them the way things were at home and all my concerns. They were sympathetic to my plight. The vicar said, if things ever got too bad, I could always find refuge with them.

I could talk to the vicar and his wife in a genuine open way, which I'd never done with any other adult. They always listened, but were never judgemental.

I would so dearly have loved to have such a relationship with my mother, but knew that would never be. I would have loved to have known more about her childhood and parents. I wanted to ask questions about her time in the Russian labour camp, but she was completely unapproachable.

When I watched mother with her two little boys, saw the way she doted on them and showered them with affection, I felt deep pain. I was envious of the closeness they enjoyed. I'd never ever sat on her lap, been embraced, or hugged and kissed, like my little brothers and that hurt me very much.

I was afraid of the future. I didn't know how I'd endure the long weeks of loneliness, cooped up in the winter months, with no one to talk to. No doubt, mother would teach me all the things women did, like spinning, weaving, embroidering, sewing and a host of other skills, required for life in a village.

Autumn proved to be every bit as hard and labour intensive, as the summer. The work was never ending. Harvesting went on for weeks. Every able bodied man, woman and child had to pitch in to bring the harvest in at the collective farm. We worked from dawn till dusk.

The poor horses and oxen got no rest either. They were pulling fully laden wagons all day long. I always felt sorry, watching them straining on their yokes or harnesses, dragging their heavy loads and often up hill.

The work didn't end after getting home from the fields. All the chores at home still had to be done: getting the pig feed ready, then feeding them, milking the two cows mother had at home in the new barn the collective farm had built, then taking the milk to the collective farm. Geese and chickens all had to be taken care of too. My job was to wash the boys from head to toe, by the well, before they went to bed. By the time we ate late at night, I always felt too tired to eat. However, I aways ate whatever little portions my mother served up. By midnight, I was so exhausted, I could just about manage to crawl into bed with my two little brothers, who'd been asleep for hours. I'd go out like a light.

There was not even time for occasional daydreaming, in which I could sometimes indulge, during the long summer days. It was my only way of escaping from reality. I often hid away somewhere for 10 minutes, or so, after going to the outhouse at the back of the garden. There I could sit quietly and let my mind wander into a world of make believe. It would never last for long, as my mother would notice my absence and her screaming for me, would bring me back to reality.

It was late one mid October evening, Viorel and Hani had been asleep for hours. Mother had gone to take the milk to the collective farm. Uncle was still in the hills with the sheep. Soon the animals would be driven down to the village and stabled for the winter. I like sitting on a low wooden stool, soaking my feet in a bowl of cold water. After working and walking barefoot all day, it was sheer heaven to be sitting, doing nothing for a while, and refreshing my sore and aching feet. Leaning against the wall with my back, I'd often drop off to sleep, only to be woken by my mother's cutting voice, when she got home.

It was on such an evening that I was woken up by a knock on the door. I was wondering who could be calling so late at night, as I was saying come in.

The door opened wide and Nickitante stood there as large as life. At first, I thought I must be dreaming.

Then she spoke, "Hello Uta, aren't you going to ask me in?"

I was so taken aback by her literal apparition in the doorway, it took me a moment or two to come to my senses and answer my aunt.

"Of course! Of course!" I Said. "Do come in and how are you?" I dried my feet quickly and took the bowl into the back yard and threw the water out.

When I came back into the house, my aunt was standing in the middle of the room looking at my two brothers asleep in the bed.

"So what brings you here and so late at night?" I asked.

"You'll never guess," she beams.

"I have the most wonderful news."

"You've come to take me back to Hermannstadt?" I blurted out.

"Oh! Much better than that. You've got your papers to go to England," she says, with real joy in her voice.

At first I was overcome with happiness to be getting out of this hell hole. But then a sadness came over me. It would mean leaving Transylvania and never seeing my grandparents and family again.

I threw my arms around my aunt and sobbed my heart out.

"Uta, I thought this would be the happiest moment of your life, so why the tears?" Nickitante said puzzled.

"I don't know. It is an overwhelming relief and joy, but tinged with the sadness of leaving all the people I love so much behind. I wish we could all go to England," I tell my aunt.

I'm full of questions and want to know how everybody is back at home.

She tells me Granddad's been in hospital quite a lot, but the rest of the family is well. Renate and Marianne were asking about me a lot and wanted to know when I was coming home. They'd all missed me. I told Nickitante that I'd missed them all and couldn't wait to see everybody again.

I'd been in Kerz for nearly four months and what miserable, godforsaken months they'd been. Every Sunday I had hoped Christian might come for the day, but he never came and I couldn't blame him. Nobody ever wrote either. It was not something my family did. When I first got to Kerz, I asked my mother if I could get some writing paper and a stamp to write to my grandparents. She screeched at me, did I think she was made of money. Why would she pay for such senseless rubbish as writing paper and stamps. I never asked her for anything again.

I sat chatting to my aunt while we were waiting for my mother to come home. She told me there was one more hurdle to overcome, before I was free to go to England. My mother had to sign papers, agreeing to let me go, as she was my next of kin and legal guardian. Nickitante was worried that my mother might refuse, especially as I was now that much older and a big help to her. She also thought my mother might refuse out of sheer spite and hatred towards my father and me.

Nickitante said she'd purposely caught the last train to Kerz that evening, so my mother wouldn't have too much time to think about things. We were to catch the 6 o'clock train the next morning to Fogaras, the county town, to finalise my papers, get my passport and, most of all, for mother to sign for my release.

My mother came home shortly before midnight. Nickitante told her the news and explained what had to be done. Mother had no objection and we all went to bed.

My aunt woke me up at five the next morning. I'd already put my few belongings in the bag, the night before, and was ready to go. Mother had already taken the boys to her mother-in-law.

That morning, the walk to the train station was never ending. My heart was beating fast. I was very anxious and worried that my mother would change her mind and not sign the relevant papers. Nickitante was chatting about everything just to keep mother's mind off what was happening.

We were still a fair way from the train stop, when we heard the shrill whistle of the train in the distance. Nickitante grabbed mother under one arm and told me to get hold of her the other side and we all started to run, practically dragging my mother along between the two of us. Puffing and panting, we reached the train stop, just as the huge locomotive came to a halt.

We all climbed up the steep ladder, which was now much easier for me, than a few years ago. We sat down on the slatted wooden benches, catching our breath and recovering from the mad dash, we had to make.

I sat quietly, but very anxious, looking out the window at the landscape flying by. The train stopped at every village on the way. Each time the train slowed down, I wondered if mother might jump up and get off, having changed her mind to go along with Nickitante's plan.

Thankfully, mother was still with us, when we got off in Fogaras. However, she could still change her mind, nothing was certain until she'd actually signed the necessary papers. We walked to the town hall in the centre of Fogaras, but the offices were still closed, so we sat on wooden benches in the hallway.

It was another long, anxious wait and my nerves were getting pretty frayed. I looked at my aunt and knew she also felt the strain.

It wasn't as simple as I'd imagined. My aunt had all the necessary papers. She also had some small photographs, taken of me when I still had my plaits. We had to go to several different departments.

The first thing we got was my birth certificate. I'd never seen it before. While we were waiting to be seen in another department, I had a chance to look at this document. I read every line. It was like looking at somebody else's identity.

My name on the birth certificate read Ursula Ute, not Ute, as I'd been called all these years. How could this be. I didn't even know my first name was Ursula. I looked at the names of the parents: Lorenz and Maria Renges, nee Roth.

I looked at my mother, questioning the name. She became quite defensive.

"An aunt of yours registered your name in the Ursuline Cloister in Hermannstadt after you were born. I wanted just Ute," my mother said. "Your aunt registered you Ursula Ute. I was not very happy," mother said in a sour voice.

"I like Ursula better than Ute," I told mother, but she didn't reply.

Then I saw my date of birth July 29th, 1943. I felt that I finally had my own identity. Groysie had always told me that my birthday was in July. She didn't know the date. On my school leaving certificate, my date of birth said 29th November. My grandmother said that was incorrect. I was definitely born in the summer. Finally knowing these details, made me feel good.

As I was sitting there, I felt as though I'd been given a new identity for starting a new life, with my father, in England.

My mother didn't hesitate for a moment, before she signed and gave her consent for me to leave the country. It was such a huge relief to me and my aunt. I couldn't wait to get away and never see my mother again.

By midday, all the paperwork was finished and I held a dark red passport in my hand, with my picture and all my details inside. The majority of people in Romania would have killed to have such a document. Nickitante said I must be the luckiest girl in Romania.

Mother wanted to go in a shop and buy a tape measure, then we all walked back to the train station. We didn't have to wait too long for a train to Hermannstadt, which also stopped in Kerz.

After we sat down, mother got her tape measure out. She told me that she wanted to make me a dress from a skirt she no longer wore. She then proceeded to take my measurements.

The visa in my passport was only valid for one month, from the date the document was issued. It meant that I had to leave Romania and enter England within that month. Just before mother got off at the stop in Kerz, she said she'd like me to go back before I left for England, so she could give me the dress, she was going to make for me. I reluctantly said I would. My mother left with just a goodbye, without even a quick hug for me, or my aunt.

After she had gone, I told Nickitante that I didn't want to go back to Kerz at all. My mother had never given me anything in all those years. I was adamant that I wanted nothing from her now.

My aunt said I should go and say goodbye to all the people who had been kind to me while I was in Kerz. At the same time, I could see my mother and little brothers for the last time.

It was an enormous relief to be away from my mother again. I was much more relaxed and sat chatting to my aunt. I couldn't wait to get back to Hermannstadt to see my grandparents and the rest of the family. I was trying not to think about having to leave them all again so soon and for good. But for now I was happy and living in the moment, enjoying my freedom and escape from mother's clutches.

My reunion with my family and friends was bitter sweet. I told Groysie that I was worried about going to England. I didn't know my father and what if his wife turned out to be a real evil stepmother.

Groysie kept telling me that everything would be fine and I'd have a good and wonderful new life.

I was also concerned that I didn't speak English and deep down, I felt fearful, but anything had to be better than living with mother.

The next time Christian visited us, which apparently he did frequently, I told him the news, that I was finally going to England. He said he was very pleased for me and then started to cry. He told me he wanted nothing more than to go to England too. He wanted to know why the application to go hadn't been made for both of us. I couldn't give him an answer .

I felt so bad for my brother. It was very unfair that I had all the luck. I was getting away from this miserable, oppressive communist regime and all the people I loved had to stay behind and endure the never ending suffering.

I told Christian that I would talk to our father and ask him to apply for permission to get him to England too. He seemed somewhat placated by my suggestion and we never spoke about it again.

The little time left was very busy. Annitante and I spent endless hours, traipsing round shoe shops. My shoes were too small and I needed new ones. After a lot of searching, we finally found a light grey pair. They were three sizes too big, but they just had to do, as we were running out of time. Annitante said we could stuff some paper into the toes, then they would fit.

Hansuncle made a small wooden case. He screwed a leather strap to the top, which served as a handle. He then stained the plywood dark brown. I'd never seen a travel case before, let alone owned one. I was very pleased with my gift from Hansuncle.

I visited Mitzitante, once more, to tell her my news and say goodbye. She'd been very good to me over the years and I'd become very fond of her. She was over the moon that I was going to my father and told me I would become a beautiful young English lady.

Mitzitante introduced me to a friend of hers, who had a brother in London, England. The brother worked at Buckingham Palace for the Royal Family. The friend asked if I would take a small gift to her brother from her and her mother, as nothing was allowed to be sent by post to the west. He had been a prisoner of war and had also remained in England. He was a single man at the time, but had married an English woman.

I told her I'd be very happy to do that.

She gave me a jar of homemade rose hip jam, which was her brother's favourite, an embroidered leather Saxon belt and a letter.

The lady also offered me an old handbag of hers, which was worn and scuffed. She suggested I apply several coats of brown shoe polish to the bag and polish it well between applications. The bag would look like new again. I didn't have a handbag and was more than happy to accept the present.

I did what I'd been told and the handbag turned out quite well, I thought.

I went back to Kerz one Sunday just for the day. I called in at my mother's mother-in-law to let her know I was there and I'd pop round the house a little later.

I then went to see the vicar and his family. They were absolutely delighted with my good fortune. The vicar said he'd wondered where I'd been the past few Sundays, as he hadn't seen me. I thanked them for all the wonderful times I'd spent at their house and what a difference it had made to my life, while I was in Kerz .

We said our goodbyes. They wished me all the best and a wonderful life in England. When I got to my mother's house, she was there with uncle and the boys. We all had some lunch together, then mother brought out the dress, she'd made for me. I tried it on and it fitted very well. Mother said I looked nice. It struck me that was the first compliment, mother had ever paid me and the first time she said something nice to me.

I was wearing my pale green graduation dress. The new dress was a much darker green, with a slight shimmer to it. It was fitted into the waist, with a tie sash and a white Peter Pan collar. Mother said the green of the dress really brought the green out in my eyes.

I didn't stay long. I was anxious to get away. I thanked her for the dress, gave Viorel and Hani a hug and said goodbye to uncle. I didn't know him well, as he'd hardly ever been around.

Mother and the boys walked to the street door with me. I embraced her awkwardly. I could feel the tension in her body as well. It was the only time I can remember having mother's arms around me. It felt weird and unnatural. Then I turned and walked down the lane. She never wished me well, or said anything else, except goodbye.

At the end of the lane, before I turned the corner, I looked back to wave, but the lane was empty.

I felt happy, although my happiness was tinged with a certain amount of sadness. I had expected her to still be standing there with the boys, giving me a last wave. Who knew, if we'd ever see each other again? I was her only daughter, after all and all I'd ever wanted was a good and loving mother. I walked to the train stop, lost in thought about how things had been, trying to understand and come to terms with everything, but, of course, I couldn't make sense of anything.

I was glad when the train finally arrived. I said a silent goodbye to the village, where I'd been born, where life had been so abysmal and the place held such dreadful memories for me. I just wanted to forget everything that ever happened there and promised myself I would never return. However, the evil ghosts I left behind on that day, were to haunt me for the rest of my life.

Chapter Twenty Five

The week before I left for England, was hectic, to say the least. I visited friends and family to say goodbye. Everybody was so happy for me. They all said I was the luckiest girl alive getting out of this communist hell hole.

Heide's mother, in particular, was overjoyed. She'd often taken me under her wing. Frau Hannich was kindness itself. She was a tiny woman, full of energy and a wonderful mother to her three children. Heide's father was lovely. He was a jolly man, always kidding around. He always had a big smile on his face and a twinkle in his eye. I came to love both of Heide's parents.

Frau Hannich embraced me very warmly and held me for a long time. She said she was so thrilled that I was finally going to my father, where I would have a wonderful life and all the opportunities I deserved. She told me I'd finally have parents, who'd care for me and love me.

Heide's sister, Inge, who was now twenty, told me she'd like to take me to see a very good German film, that was showing, as a farewell gift. I told her I wouldn't be allowed to go. She said we'd go to a café in town and have an ice cream first. I was to tell Groysie that's where we were going and afterwards, we'd go and see the film.

For the second time in my life, I went to see a film, which was forbidden. It was a musical and a love story, set on the Mediterranean Sea in Italy. I was enchanted and lost in the romantic world on the screen. I fell madly in love with the lead actor, Vico Torriani. His leading lady was gorgeous and I was jealous of her. The songs in the film were beautifully sung by both leads and very catchy. I still remember and sing some of them to myself today.

Walking home afterwards, Inge said I'd see lots of good films in England. She told me everybody, who knew me, wished they were in my shoes, leaving the communist hell we lived in. I was the only person, Inge knew, who'd managed to get out.

That last week flew by. The day of my departure was suddenly there. It was Thursday the 14th November, 1957.

Both my grandparents, Annitante, Marianne, Nickitante and Renate accompanied me to the railway station. Both Hansuncle and Tummy had to go to work in the morning and we'd already said our goodbyes. Christian had been round the previous evening. It had been so difficult to part from him. I promised him again that once in England, I'd do my best to get father to get him out too.

At the railway station, we met Herr Teutsch, the pastor from the Baptist church, who was accompanying me to Bucharest, from where I was to fly. He knew people everywhere connected to the church. We were to spend the night with friends of his in Bucharest. The next morning he was taking me to the airport and seeing me off.

Herr Teutsch was a well travelled man and that's why Granddad had asked him to take me to Bucharest. He would have liked to go with me, but he was far too sick. Even coming to the railway station was a huge effort for him.

With all my family standing on the platform, my departure was getting closer all the time. I was becoming more and more anxious. All kinds of thoughts were racing through my mind. I couldn't help but fret about what unknown world I was going into. I couldn't speak a word of English. There were so many, what ifs? I didn't dare to voice my deepest fears to my family. I just kept telling myself that anything was better than being with my mother.

One by one, I embraced my family. Little Renate first, who was now four years old, then her mother, Nickitante.

I was already crying, but the tears were streaming down my face like a waterfall now. All those beloved faces were swimming in front of me.

My cousin Marianne was nearly three now. I hugged her so tightly and didn't want to let go. I loved that little girl so much. When I embraced Annitante I wanted to say so much, but couldn't speak for sobbing my heart out.

Granddad stood, propping himself up on his walking stick. He wasn't feeling well at all, but had insisted on coming to the station. When I embraced him, it felt like my heart was going to break. He was the dearest man to me. He'd gone through so much in his lifetime: two world wars, fighting in the first one, then the Second World War and all the hardship that had brought. He had lost one son, then another son and his daughter suffered under the Russian gulags for years, and a son who did not return. Then, after the war, everything was taken away and Granddad was left homeless and penniless and had to live in poverty for the rest of his days.

Granddad didn't want to let me go, tears were running down his face. He was just a physically and emotionally broken old man.

When he spoke, he told me how happy he was that, at last, I would be taken care of by my own father. He would now have peace of mind and could end his last days, knowing I would be all right. He said his time was coming to an end and we wouldn't see each other again until I joined him with the Lord. He wished me everything wonderful in life and told me to remain true to my faith. I was crying buckets now.

Then it was time to say goodbye to Groysie. I saw her careworn beloved face through my watery vision. Her eyes were red from crying. My Grandfather's words about not seeing each other again, had come as a bitter blow to me. Now I was wondering if I would see any of my family again. These had been the only people in my whole life, who had ever loved me and truly cared for me. Why was life so cruel?

I hugged my Groysie so hard. I didn't ever want to let her go. Then the shrill whistle blew and all passengers had to board the train.

Groysie had to prise my clinging arms from around her neck. Herr Teutsch led me to the train and helped me up the steps. He then handed me my little wooden case and got on himself.

I hurried into the carriage and stood at the window, looking out at the pathetic little group of people standing on the platform, supporting each other, looking at me with tear stained faces. At that moment, I felt as though my world was coming to an end.

The train started to pull slowly away. I pressed my wet face to the window and watched, as I was leaving everyone, who had ever been dear to me behind and recede into the distance.

I'd never felt so wretched and miserable in all my life and this was supposed to be a happy occasion.

I sat near the window, opposite Herr Teutsch. He just looked kindly at me, without a word, and left me to my sorrow and grieving. I buried my face in my arms and sobbed uncontrollably, until I was too exhausted and fell asleep.

When I woke up, I felt sad and empty. Herr Teutsch was still sitting opposite me, reading. He looked up and smiled, without saying anything, as though he was waiting for me to speak first.

I mentioned to him that I felt sad, that I hadn't been able to say all the things I'd wanted to my Grandparents and family at the station. I'd been far too upset to talk.

He suggested when I got to England, I could write a letter to them all and tell them everything I meant to say on the platform. I thought that was a very good idea and it made me feel a lot better. Herr Teutsch brought out a paper bag, with sandwiches, his wife had made for us both. We both sat quietly eating.

The journey took about four hours. We arrived in Bucharest in the late afternoon. The train had taken us through some of the most beautiful scenery through the Carpathian Mountains, but I'd been so steeped in misery, that it had all left me unimpressed.

Herr Teutsch got a taxi outside the station in Bucharest, which did excite me somewhat. It was only the second time I'd been in a car. I felt much calmer now and enjoyed the ride.

Hermannstadt had overwhelmed me, as a small child. Bucharest, on the other hand, was something else. I sat looking out of the taxi window in wonderment at all the beautiful buildings, parks and tree lined boulevards. There were a lot more cars here too and lots of people going about their business.

The taxi took us to an old part of the city. We passed many grand villas, that stood in their own ample grounds, behind walls and wrought iron fences and gates. These villas were even more beautiful and impressive than the ones that surrounded our garden shack in Hermannstadt.

Herr Teutsch told me, this had been the most prestigious part of Bucharest before the war, where all the wealthiest people had lived and owned the properties. Now everything belonged to the state. Each villa had a number of families living in one or two rooms.

The taxi stopped in front of a very impressive place. Herr Teutsch paid the driver and we walked through a huge open wrought iron double gate, along a flagstone driveway to the massive villa.

On the wall to the side of the high double front doors, was a long line of doorbells, with a different name against each.

Herr Teutsch pressed one of the many buttons. We didn't hear the bell ring in the house, but moments later an older woman opened the door.

The woman greeted Herr Teutsch effusively and embraced him. She then turned to me, shook my hand and welcomed me. We both followed the lady into a very large marble floored entrance hall. A long curving staircase, the like I'd never seen before in a house, wound along one wall up to the next floor onto a galleried landing.

We were taken across the hall to one of the many big double doors. The lady opened it and bade us to enter and take off our coats. We were in a big room with several very high windows, overlooking the garden. The parquet floor was covered in lovely rugs. The room was beautifully furnished, with wonderful paintings hanging on the high walls. The windows were adorned with magnificent heavy drapes. I'd never seen a room as lavish as this before.

A door, which stood, open led to a smaller room, which was the kitchen and dining room. Our hostess asked us to sit down. She then went to the kitchen to make tea and refreshments.

When the lady was gone, I asked Herr Teutsch, who these people were and if they were rich. He told me they'd come from a very wealthy business family before the war. The villa had been theirs, but had been taken away after the war and now belonged to the state. These had been the only two rooms they'd been allowed to occupy.

Like everybody else, they were paying rent to the government for living here. That's how the system operated.

The man of the house was a lawyer. Before the war he'd owned a large law practice and had also been a judge. Now he just did a mundane office job. Herr Teutsch said it was a travesty to see such a clever man reduced to this.

Our hostess came in, carrying a tray with a pretty china teapot and cups and saucers. It was a bit different from our tin mugs at Groysie's. She poured out the tea and put a thin slice of something yellow in each cup. I was a little reluctant to drink the tea. Herr Teutsch noticed my reservation and explained that it was a lemon slice, which made the tea taste good. That was the first time I'd been given real tea. At home, we only had herbal tea, which Groysie made from dried peppermint from our garden and linden blossom tea, which we picked from the trees and dried.

I asked how many people lived in the villa. I was told nine other families. "It must be a huge villa," I mused.

"Yes, it's huge," the lady told me. Before the war she'd had servants doing all the cleaning, cooking and gardening.

It was beyond my comprehension, living in such a place and having people doing everything for you.

The lady of the house took me back into the large entrance hall to show me where the bathroom and toilet were. A door nearby, led into a large tiled bathroom, with a tub, so big, a whole family could have fitted in. It was very different from the small tin tub, hanging on the wall, outside our little shack back in Hermannstadt.

I was then shown the toilet in a much smaller separate room next door. I was told this bathroom and toilet were shared with two other families. The other two bathrooms and lavatories were shared by the other families.

I thought it was all very grand and would have been more than happy to have shared such a luxurious house.

I washed my face and hands in cold water. It felt good to get rid of the dirty grubby feeling, after all the crying, but I couldn't get rid of the deep bleak sadness, I felt inside. I tried to get my head around the thought of going away so far and possibly never seeing all those dear people, I loved so much. I had to fight really hard not to start crying again and become engulfed in total despair. I quickly washed my face in cold water once more and returned to the apartment.

The lady of the house was preparing the evening meal. Her husband would soon be home from work.

Herr Teutsch was engrossed in a newspaper and I was left to ponder over my own thoughts, which wasn't good. My eyes kept welling up with tears. It was difficult for me to keep them from flowing over.

When our host came home from work, we all sat down to the evening meal, made entirely of vegetables. Meat was every bit as difficult to come by in Bucharest, as it was anywhere else in the country and was considered a luxury.

After the meal, the lady made up a bed on a divan in one corner of the room. She placed a beautiful oriental silk screen around it and said that's where I would sleep. I was very tired after the day's travelling and emotionally exhausted. I said good night to everybody, undressed behind the screen and slipped under the cosy covers. It felt so soft and luxurious. I'd never slept in a bed like it. I was used to sleeping on a straw mattress, which was very hard. This felt like I was floating on a cloud. It was wonderful. I fell asleep very quickly to the sound of soft talking voices of the adults beyond the screen.

Morning came much too soon. The lady of the house was standing next to my bed and in a gentle voice told me it was time to get up. She put a dressing gown on my bed and said I could have a bath before breakfast, if I wished.

I couldn't think of anything nicer. A bath in that massive tub, what a delight. As I stood up, I could feel something running down my leg. As I looked down I could see a thin line of blood running down the inside of my thigh. To my horror, I'd started my period early. I looked at the bed. To my great relief there was no sign of any blood on the sheet. I quickly put on my underpants, then, using the large man's hanky, I had in my handbag, folded it and placed it into my panties. I put on the dressing gown and went to the bathroom.

I was a late developer, as far as my periods went. They'd only started a few months ago, shortly before the end of school. Most of the girls in my class had got them a year of two before me. I had not been prepared for this change by any of the women in my family.

Luckily, Heide had told me a little about it. So when it happened, I went to see her mother, who explained everything to me. She also gave me some small cloths, which she showed me how to fold and place inside my panties.

Heide's mother told me before the war women bought special pads or cotton wool for this purpose. She hadn't seen any such pads since the war and cotton wool was like gold dust.

Heide's mother told me that I must soak the rags and wash and dry them at the end of the day. That's how I learned how to look after myself and keep clean every month.

I felt very embarrassed about the whole procedure though. I'd try to do it so nobody saw me, by taking the washing bowl to the back of the shack, washing the pieces of material out and hanging them on the fence behind the house. No one came near and respected my privacy.

In Kerz I did the same. My mother never ever mentioned anything about my periods or tried to explain why women had them.

In the bathroom, I let a lot of hot water run into the tub. When I got in, it came right up to my neck. I was suddenly back with Heide at the public baths. I lay for a long time luxuriating in the warmth of the water.

When I got out the bath, I dried myself carefully. I didn't want to get blood on the towel. What was I going to do. This curse, as all the girls referred to it, would be with me for the next few days. I'd just have to clench the muscles down below and go to the toilet very often. The hanky I'd used was already stained. I just refolded it and put it back into my undies. I wished I'd remembered about my periods. With all the upheaval and excitement, I'd completely forgotten. I put the dressing gown back on and went next door to the toilet. There to my utter relief was a big roll of toilet paper.

At home we didn't have toilet paper. Groysie cut up newspaper Granddad brought home, into squares, threaded them onto string and hung the bits of paper on a nail in the outhouse. In Kerz we didn't even have that luxury. Every time you went to the loo, you had to hunt for large leaves from shrubs and plants. Luckily, I was never there in the winter to find out what they did then, when snow lay thick on the ground. Maybe they washed their bottoms with snow.

I folded a whole lot of toilet paper up and put it in the dressing gown pocket. It wasn't absorbent like cloth, but it would have to do.

Back in the room, I put the folded toilet paper into my handbag and got dressed behind the screen. I then folded all the bedding and left it neatly on the divan.

The man of the house had already left for work. The table in the kitchen was laid for breakfast. Herr Teutsch, the lady and I had breakfast together of bread, jam and tea. Soon after a taxi was waiting for us in the street to take the church minister and myself to the airport.

I said goodbye to the lady and thanked her for her kindness and hospitality. Herr Teutsch was coming back to stay another night.

The trip to the airport was much further than the one we'd made the evening before from the railway station, which was in the city centre.

The taxi drove out of the city and well into the country before we reached the airport. Herr Teutsch paid the taxi driver. Carrying my little wooden case, he then lead me through the entrance doors into the airport building. We walked into a large hall with counters along one wall. We went to one of the counters, where I had to show my passport. I didn't have a ticket. My father had arranged everything from England and paid for my flight. My case was taken and a number of different labels were stuck on it. The woman on the desk saw my confused look. She reassured me everything was fine and that I'd get my case when I got to England. A young woman then came to take me to a waiting room, from where I would be escorted onto the plane.

Herr Teutsch shook my hand warmly. He wished me a safe trip and a happy life with my father. I thanked him for being so kind and bringing me to Bucharest. Then I followed my escort to a door leading into a waiting room.

The waiting room had rows and rows of seats. I was shown to the front row and asked to sit down. Another person would come and take me to the plane when it was time.

Through the huge glass window, I saw a massive plane standing close to the building. People were busy loading all kinds of things into the hold.

The name " S A B I N A " was written in very large letter on the side of the aircraft. Later I was told it was the The Belgian National Airline.

I sat watching the workers outside going about their business. I marvelled at how such a gigantic thing could get off the ground and stay up in the air for hours on end. It was an absolute mystery to me. The only planes I'd ever seen were the fighter planes the other side of the valley in Hermannstadt. They were tiny compared to the great big monster standing outside the window here. I had also seen planes very high up in the sky, but they'd looked no bigger than a heron or a stork.

As I sat and mused over things beyond my understanding, a lovely young woman in a very smart uniform walked over to me.

She addressed me by my full name and in German told me she was the air hostess from 'Sabina' and would I follow her. My heart skipped a beat. Was this really happening to me?

I picked up my handbag and followed her through big glass doors onto the tarmac out to where the plane stood. She then started to climb the long steps up to the open door or the aircraft. As I followed up behind her, I couldn't help but admire her shapely long legs in the smart high heeled shoes. She was wearing some kind of very fine stockings with a dark line all the way down her legs. I could see right through them. I wondered what they were made of, as I'd never seen anything like it before.

This young woman looked beautiful. The clothes she wore fitted like a glove. I couldn't help but compare my own drab and shabby attire with hers. My coat was old and worn. The sleeves were halfway up my forearms. The dark green dress mother had made for me was hanging way below the hem of the coat. I was wearing scratchy thick woollen stockings held up with elastic above the knees. I was shuffling along in my ugly grey shoes which were far too big, trying to keep them on my feet.

As I got to the top of the stairs and looked up, an extremely handsome young man greeted me and held out his hand. He was wearing the same uniform as the air hostess, only with trousers of course. I shook his hand and he led me through into the plane.

I was at an age where I started noticing the opposite sex. I knew a good looking guy when I saw one. This chap was as handsome as any I'd seen in fashion magazines at Mitzitante's. Or the wonderful looking actors in the two films I'd seen. He was tall and dark haired. His beautiful wide smile revealed sparkling white teeth and made me feel as though my legs might buckle under me.

I felt the warmth rising from my neck up to my hairline and was sure I must be bright red in the face. I felt very embarrassed and intimidated in my rough shabby clothes. The young man welcomed me onto the flight. He said he hoped I would enjoy the trip and if there was anything at all, I wanted or required, I was only to ask. Wow! I thought, what more could I want. I was speechless. Nobody had ever said anything like that to me before.

I was then shown to a seat a couple of rows from the front of the plane. Before I sat down, I stood and looked down the length of the aircraft. I couldn't believe how many rows of seats there were. Two either side of the long passage, running all the way to the very end of the cabin.

The air host helped me off with my coat, which I was glad to discard. He placed it into a space way above my head and closed it with a door that pulled down. I found everything fascinating. After I sat down, belts from both sides of my seat were brought round my waist and clipped together in front.

As I sat there, a very odd thought struck me. I was the only person apart from the air host and hostess on the plane. All the other seats were empty. I'd been the only one waiting in the waiting room. We were obviously waiting for other passengers to join us. After a few more minutes, the door onto the plane was closed and locks secured by the air host. The long steps were wheeled away from the aircraft and the plane began to slowly move.

The air hostess came over to my seat and said we were taxiing to the end of the runway and then we would take off. She asked me to stay strapped into my seat until she told me, then I could get up and move around once we were airborne.

By now I felt pretty nervous. There was no way I wanted to get up and move around. I sat in the seat next to the window, from where I watched with great interest, everything going on outside.

The plane started to slowly move backwards. The two air stewards sat down in two seats facing me at the end of the cabin and strapped themselves in. I was somewhat worried by now. Everybody was fastened into their seats. Now I was wondering why?

The aircraft came to a stop at the end of the runway. I looked over to where the air host and hostess where sitting. They both looked very relaxed chatting to each other.

The air hostess looked over at me. She must have seen the look of concern on my face. She gave me a big smile and said everything was fine and we'd take off in a couple of minutes.

Somewhat reassured, I turned and looked out of the window with anticipation, having no idea what to expect.

The plane started to move and very quickly picked up a lot of speed. As I watched the ground flash by, we suddenly started to lift off the ground and rise like a huge prehistoric bird into the sky. It gave me the weirdest feeling. I wasn't quite sure if I liked it or not.

The landscape below opened up and I could see a long way. The buildings, houses and trees grew smaller and smaller. The roads and rivers meandered through a patchwork of fields and meadows. Everything down below looked like a miniature world. There were no clouds and I could see forever. I could even follow the curve of the horizon, which seemed incredible.

I was mesmerised and enchanted by the toy world that lay far below and all my fear and anxiety settled down.

The plane had risen into the sky at a very steep angle, but now had levelled out and was flying straight.

Both the air hosts unbuckled their belts and got up. The stewardess came over to me and told me I was to keep my belt on at all times, unless I needed to go to the toilet. She then told me there was one washroom at the front and two more at the rear of the cabin. It had been a few hours since this morning when we'd left the house. I was getting a little worried about how my paper pad was holding out.

I got up, took my little bag and went to the toilet at the front of the plane.

The inside of the little room was just amazing. It was spotlessly clean with mirrors on one wall. There was a small toilet, a tiny sink to wash in and there were several bottles of lotions and potions. As I didn't know what any of them were for, I opened the door and called the air hostess. I asked what the stuff in the bottles was for. She pointed to each container in turn. One was liquid soap, another one hand lotion and the third was eau de toilette.

Then she pointed to a slit in the wall beside the hand basin where paper was hanging out and told me they were paper hand towels.

What luxury! I'd never seen anything of the kind. I thanked the young woman, then closed and locked the door. I stood and marvelled about everything for a while, then sampled the stuff in all the bottles. Who'd ever heard of liquid soap? Nobody in my family had creams and perfumes. Everything smelled wonderful.

First I used the toilet. When I flushed it, I got such a fright. The noise was immense and for a moment I thought I'd get sucked down into the small hole. Then I washed my hands and face and down below, then used folded paper towels to line my panties. I put cream on my hands and face, which was a first and then sprayed myself liberally with eau de toilette. This was sheer indulgence and I loved it. Then I went back to my seat.

The handsome young man came over to me to make sure I was buckled in. He told me I smelled beautifully, in fact I made the whole plane smell marvellous.

Looking back, both air hosts must have been amused at me smothering myself in perfume and smelling the whole plane out.

I told the air hostess that I was curious why I was the only passenger on board. She told me the only passengers they ever had from Romania were communist party people, or important business men. However, today I was the only passenger and I had the whole plane to myself, until we got to Budapest.

The stewardess then undid a clip on the back of the seat in front of me and, like magic, a small table came down parallel to my lap. The host then placed a tray, with all kinds of food and drink, on the little table.

I sat and looked in wonderment at the feast set before me. The hostess sat down next to me and explained what all the different foods were. I'd never seen such an array of goodies, let alone know what most of them were.

There were several small white china dishes. I was told they where different vegetable salads and one was a fruit salad. This was all very new to me. There were slices of different meats on a small plate and some cheeses on another one. A tiny bread loaf nestled in an indentation of the tray. Butter was in the tiniest dish, I'd ever seen. A tasty looking piece of cake was in, yet another dish. A small wrapped bar, which had chocolate written on it, was amongst all this wonderful food. Suddenly, I remembered the chocolate father had sent in the two parcels all those years ago. I picked the little bar up, unwrapped it and the smell of the chocolate took me right back to that little girl and the first time she'd tasted such delights. Then I ate the yummy contents.

There was a glass of orange coloured liquid on the tray, as well. I asked what it was and was told it was orange juice. The stewardess said it was made from oranges and tasted very good. "What was an orange?" I asked. She got up and went behind the curtain at the front of the cabin. Seconds later, she returned with what looked like an orange ball in her hand. She handed me the ball and told me to dig my fingernail into the skin and smell it. As I did so, a wonderful aroma, which I couldn't describe assaulted my nostrils. She said it was a tropical fruit that could be eaten or made into juice. She said to keep the orange and she'd help me peel it later.

I was eager now to taste the juice. I picked up the glass. The juice was so good, I drank it all down in one go. The air hostess laughed. She then peeled the orange, as I watched with fascination, and set each individual segment down on my tray.

There were so many wonderful things, all at once. I didn't know where to start first. The hostess suggested I start on the savoury things first and have the fruit and cake at the end. She also refilled my glass of juice.

I ate every single morsel on the tray. It was the most tasty and delicious food I'd ever had. I'd never eaten so much and was full to the gills. The air hostess took my tray and asked if I wanted anything else. I told her I was full to burst and couldn't possibly eat another thing.

After a little while, the steward came and sat beside me, which made me feel quite giddy to have this handsome young man so near. We chatted for a while. I told him I was going to England to live with my father. He said England was a wonderful country and I would love it there.

He had a deck of playing cards and asked if I'd like to play. I told him I'd never played cards. He showed me a simple game and we played until we started to descend into Budapest. Both air hosts sat down again and strapped themselves in for the landing.

In the Hungarian capital, we all had to get off the plane, go to the airport building and wait there for a while.

When we re-boarded the aircraft, two male passengers got on with us. They both sat together further back in the cabin.

Now that I knew what the take-off was like, I felt much more at ease. The planes descent and landing into Budapest had worried me. I'd been looking out the window with knots and butterflies in my tummy, watching as buildings, roads and fields grew bigger and raced towards us. I'd felt pretty scared. The landing itself hadn't been bad, just a bump and we were racing along the ground again. Then the terrifying noise from the engines breaking, to bring the aircraft to a halt had really freaked me out. I thought something terrible had happened and we'd all perish there and then. The air host explained that the noise was normal and there was nothing to worry about.

My whole day was evolving into new experiences all the time. I hardly had time to take one in before another one presented itself.

Taxiing to the runway for the second time for take-off, the air host announced the safety procedures in French, then what I assumed must be English and then German, while the hostess demonstrated all the safety measures in case of an emergency. German was the only language I understood. Our next landing would be Cologne, where we remained on board.

No sooner had we landed and taxied up to the terminal building, the door was opened, steps pushed against it and people started boarding.

I sat and observed with interest and fascination, as all the men, women and children passed by my seat at the front of the cabin.

Everybody was immaculately dressed and very elegant. Most men and women wore hats and gloves. The women looked like real ladies to me. They all had high heeled shoes on and stockings like the air hostess. I wondered if I would ever possess such beautiful clothes and shoes.

As the ladies passed my seat I could smell a lot of different perfumes. I admired their red painted lips and fingernails.

Even all the children were smartly and stylishly dressed and all wore white ankle or knee length socks.

I felt like a pauper by comparison. I just wanted to melt away and not be seen in my shabby clothes. I remained in my seat the whole time, until we got to Brussels, which was our next destination.

When everybody had boarded, the door was shut and locked again. The plane seemed pretty full. I wondered how we were going to take off with so many people on board. My fears were soon alleviated, as once again the plane was soaring into the never ending blue sky, now tinged with a little yellow and orange on the horizon.

To my delight, food and drink were served again. I just couldn't get enough of it. Throughout this leg of the flight both hosts were kept very busy. Shortly before we landed in Brussels, the host came to me and asked that I remain in my seat after we'd landed, until all the other passengers got off.

At last, when everybody had disembarked, the two hosts and I got off. They escorted me into the airport building, which was gigantic compared to the one in Bucharest or Budapest. We entered a massive hall from where doors and corridors led in all directions. There were hoards of people everywhere. Some were sitting, others were waiting or hurrying every which way.

I was taken to an office by my escorts and introduced to a man, who was to take me and put me on my next and last flight to London, England. I said goodbye to my two air hosts and watched as they walked out the office in their smart uniforms, the pair of them looking very handsome and not at all tired from their long day.

Not long after arriving in Brussels, the man whose care I was left in, took me to another big waiting room full of people. He told me he would stay with me until I boarded the BEA flight to London. He said it was an English airline, which would take me to my final destination. When I got there he said, I was to sit in the waiting room until somebody came for me.

The time was well into the evening now and it was completely dark outside. The long day and all the excitement of it had made me very tired.

When it was time to board a young attractive air hostess in a different but equally smart uniform came and collected me. She escorted me to the plane where we both boarded. She told me she'd been assigned the job to look after me until we arrived at Heathrow Airport, London.

By the time everybody had boarded and the plane was very full, I was very sleepy. The next thing I remember was the stewardess checking my safety belt and informing me that we would soon be landing at Heathrow.

I'd lost all track of time. I asked what the time was and was told it was 10 o'clock. The young lady said it was midnight in Romania. No wonder I was so tired. I'd been travelling all day.

I was completely exhausted. All the day's events had been incredible and dreamlike. It had been like some unbelievable fairy tale. Then I thought of my family thousands of miles away in Hermannstadt and the tears started welling up in my eyes.

It was the 15th November, 1957. A day I would never ever forget. A day when my life changed completely. I was so lucky, which I fully understood. But at that late hour and at a very low ebb, I felt very sad, abandoned and completely bereft, not knowing where my future was going and what kind of life was waiting for me. The flight from Bucharest to London, with three stops on route had taken 10 hours. That same flight today takes two and a half hours and is direct.

After we landed, the air hostess accompanied me into the terminal to collect my case. I'd never seen a luggage carousel before and thought it was a very clever idea.

As I was waiting for my case, I watched all the smart leather suitcases go round on the moving belt and wondered what other people would make of my little wooden box. When my case appeared, which was easy to spot amongst all the smart leather luggage, I grabbed and lifted it up with ease. There was only a change of clothes inside and the presents from my aunt's friend to her brother in London.

The stewardess then took me through customs and finally to a large waiting room. She asked who was meeting me. I told her my father, but I didn't know him, only from photographs. She asked if I'd be all right, as she had to leave. I assured her I would be fine. My escort took me to a seat by some very big doors and told me to wait there for my father. She said to watch the doors, as he would be coming through them. Then she left.

The time was 11 on the massive clock on the wall in the arrivals lounge. An hour had already passed since we landed. I was very tired and not too interested in what was going on around me. I sat and just looked at the entrance doors.

Where was my father? Why wasn't he here waiting for me? As time went by and it was getting later and later, I began to fret.

What if he had decided he didn't want me, or maybe something had happened to him? What would I do? I didn't speak a word of English and didn't have a penny to my name. I was thousands of miles from home with nowhere to go. The more I thought about it, the scarier it all became.

While I sat there, I'd seen loads of people come and go. They'd been meeting family and friends. Lots of hugging and kissing and happy reunions. All I could think about was where was my father and when would he come.

At midnight there was still no sign of him. There were just a handful of travellers left in this massive hall and soon they were gone too, leaving me all alone.

A while after midnight, men and women entered the hall with brooms, mops and dusters and some kind of machine that sucked the dirt up in its path, as it was pushed along. I didn't know what it was, but found it interesting to watch.

One of the cleaning ladies walked over to me. She talked to me in what I assumed must be English. I didn't understand a word and all I could do was shrug my shoulders and shake my head.

She left me sitting there, walked to a corridor and disappeared. Minutes later she came back, accompanied by a man. They both walked straight over to me. The man proceeded to speak to me in the same unknown language. I took my passport out of my handbag, which had the piece of paper, with my fathers details. I handed this to the man. The woman left and went back to her cleaning.

The man beckoned for me to follow him. I picked up my case and went with him. He took me to an office and pointed to a chair for me to sit on. He then spent quite a while making phone calls. After a while, another man came to the office. He exchanged a few words with the man already there, then turned to me. He spoke to me in a couple of other languages, which I didn't understand, before he tried German. At last! What a huge relief! Somebody could finally talk to me in my own tongue.

He asked all kinds of questions. When he seemed satisfied with what he wanted to know, he told me they would try to get in touch with my father.

After a while, I was told my father wasn't listed in the telephone book, which meant nothing to me. The man then said they'd spoken to the police, where my father lived. A policeman had been sent on his bike to my father's house to talk to him and see why he wasn't at the airport to meet me.

The man, who spoke German, left the office. The time seemed to drag on, as I was sitting there, unable to speak to the chap, left in the office. In spite of being dead tired, my mind was working overtime, envisaging all kinds of terrible scenarios. Everything was doomed and nothing good would ever happen to me.

The whole day now seemed surreal. The wonderful fairy tale had turned into a terrible nightmare, from which I would soon wake up.

I kept looking at the wall clock, which now said 2 o'clock at night. Shortly after the phone rang. The man picked it up and had quite a lengthy conversation with the person the other end, then hung up. He made another phone call. The man, who'd spoken German to me, returned and explained, that my father had instructed them to put me in a taxi and send me to his house in Whittlesey. I was escorted out of the airport building, where a taxi was waiting to take me to my father.

The driver put my little case in the boot, then opened the door for me to sit next to him at the front. This was exciting. The other three times I'd been in a car, I'd sat in the back seat. This was great, I could see much more from the front seat.

The trip to Whittlesey was very long. We drove all night. There were no motorways or dual carriageways in England in those days. The road went through lots of towns and villages to reach our destination.

Being nighttime and very dark, I couldn't see anything of the countryside. However, the towns and villages, we passed through, were well lit and the styles of the buildings and houses looked very different from the ones in Transylvania, but very interesting.

The taxi driver didn't speak any German. From time to time he made a gesture, by tipping his head to one side and lying it on his palm, then pointing to the back seat.

It was obvious what he meant. Each time I just shook my head.

I was far too excited to sleep. In spite of not being able to see any scenery, I loved the drive and going through the towns and villages. There was hardly any other traffic on the roads.

At the start of the trip, the driver had spoken to me several times. Of course, I hadn't understood a word. Then he'd repeat what he'd said, but much slower. I'd still shrug my shoulders.

Why do people think if they speak slowly and loudly to you in a foreign language, you'll understand? It's still all double Dutch, no matter what. Eventually, he gave up trying to talk to me and we drove, in silence, the rest of the way.

When we got to Whittlesey, the driver pulled up in front of a building with a blue lamp hanging over the door with 'POLICE' written on the lamp. He gestured for me to remain in the car, while he went inside.

I figured it was the police station, as the word police was not that different from the word Polizei in German.

When the driver returned, a policeman in uniform was with him. The police man pointed back in the direction where we'd come from. The taxi driver got back in the car and after a short drive he stopped in front of my father's house, which I recognised from photographs he'd sent.

I felt very nervous. Butterflies in my stomach were whirling up a storm. I was suddenly extremely tired. My legs where like lead and I felt sick.

The driver came to my side of the car, opened the door and I got out. He took my wooden case from the boot. As we went through the gate into the garden, the front door of the house opened.

My heart was in my mouth and I thought my knees would buckle right under me. I looked at the man standing in the doorway of the house, who was my father.

As we walked closer, my father came two or three steps towards me and embraced me awkwardly. It felt very strange to have a man's arms around me, whom I only knew from a photograph.

He led me and the driver into a small hallway, where my stepmother was waiting in her dressing gown with a cigarette in her hand.

I thought she looked very different from the pictures I'd seen of her. She appeared much older than her thirty two years. She had short curly flaxen blonde hair, which later I found out was dyed. Her face was gaunt and she looked very thin. She reached out her hand, which I shook. There was no warmth in our first meeting and I assumed she must be nervous too.

I wasn't sure how to address this new mother. Groysie and my aunts had told me to call her Mutti, German for mother.

Both the driver and I were shown into the living room and asked to sit down. We were asked if we wanted tea. My stepmother went out to the kitchen to make it.

I sat and admired the lovely room which was to be my new home. It looked very comfortable and luxurious. The windows each end of the room were framed by nice curtains. The floor was covered in a thick red and green patterned carpet. The green upholstered sofa and armchairs were very comfortable. We never had furniture like this. All I'd ever sat on were wooden chairs or benches.

The dining table and chairs with upholstered seats looked very nice and so did the sideboard. In fact everything in the room looked new and pristine.

A fire was burning and crackling in a strange open fireplace. It looked warm and welcoming. I had never seen anything like it.

While I sat taking in my new surroundings, my father and the taxi driver chatted. My stepmother came back in the room after a short time, carrying a tray with china cups and saucers, a china tea pot and a couple of other china vessels. I thought the pretty china had been brought out for the special occasion. I found out later that everybody used china every day.

She then poured tea in the cups and asked if I liked milk and sugar. I wasn't used to drinking proper tea, so I just said yes to everything.

When I tried the tea, I really liked the sweetness, but wasn't sure about the milk. I'd never had milk in tea, but I soon learned to like and enjoy the way the English drank it.

After the taxi driver finished his tea, he said goodbye to us all and left.

I asked to go to the toilet. To my horror, I discovered I'd bled through onto my dress and wondered if I'd stained the upholstery on the chair I'd sat on.

I felt very embarrassed and didn't know how to approach my stepmother about the subject. I'd never discussed it with any of the women in my family. How could I talk to a complete stranger about it?

As I came out of the toilet, my father's wife was standing in the hallway to tell me the bathroom was right next to the toilet. I went in to wash my hands. She followed me and stood in the doorway.

Did you know you've got your period, girl, she said. I told her I knew. It had been very difficult coping with it on the trip.

She left me in the bathroom and I heard her go upstairs. She came back with a package and a kind of elastic belt with loops and hooks. She explained what it was. My stepmother took a slim, long pad with loops each end out of the box. She showed me how the pad attached to the belt after putting it round my waist. She told me to get undressed and have a good wash in the sink. She left again, soon to return with clean underwear and some of her own clothes for me to wear.

She was slightly taller than me. I was very thin too, so her things fitted me reasonably well. Everything was new to me. I enjoyed washing myself with the soft flannel and beautiful smelling soap. The towel was soft and fluffy and felt very good on my skin.

The towels I was used to were thin and just small strips of cotton. I'd never used a washcloth, had always washed with my hands.

When I finished washing I put the elastic belt round my waist and attached the loops of the pad to the front and back of the belt. It felt very comfortable and secure. My stepmother had told me that I must change the pads several times a day, wrap the used ones in toilet paper and leave them in the bin under the wash basin, later to be burnt in the kitchen wood stove, which heated the water in the house.

Then I examined the clothes my stepmother had left me. There was a straight dark green skirt and a soft red long sleeved jumper. The materials they were made of were of a quality I'd not had before. There were a pair of white panties and a matching vest and a full length petticoat, all trimmed with lace. Everything was so delicate and beautiful, I couldn't believe it. There was a bra also trimmed with lace. Wow, I never thought I'd get to wear such a thing, it was something I'd only dreamt of. Some of the girls in my class had them and how I envied these garments. I was pretty well developed and Annemarie had told me I really should be wearing a bra. These sort of garments like all others were very hard to come by in Romania.

I put all the clothes on and looked at myself in the big bathroom mirror. I thought I looked very nice. If only the girls in my class could see me now!

Then there was a strange belt, which I had no idea what to do with. I called my stepmother. She told me it was a suspender belt to hold up my stockings. I had to take my skirt off again. She fastened the hooks round the back. The belt sat on my hips as though it had been specially made for me. It fitted perfectly. Then she handed me a pair of fine see through stockings, just like the ones I'd admired on the air hostess and all the other elegant women. I was shown how to put them on so as not to ladder them and then attach them to the belt at the front and the back. Everything felt very good and comfortable. Here I was now, just a day later wearing such fine stockings. They were like gossamer and felt soft to the touch and skin.

No more elastic bands to hold up my thick, ugly, scratchy stockings, which I had to haul up from time to time, as the elastic bands gradually slid down over my knees. My stockings then ending up all wrinkled round my ankles. What a site I must have been to all the other travellers.

I couldn't believe the transformation I'd gone through and what a difference these lovely clothes had made. I kept looking at myself in the mirror. Perhaps the jumper and skirt were just a tad too big, but not much.

I'd hardly ever had clothes that fitted. At first they would be way too big, then they'd fit for a little while and then get too small for me. But I had to wear them however they fitted.

When I finally emerged from the bathroom, feeling fresh and clean and quite grown up in these clothes, I heard voices from the door opposite. I knocked and walked in. It was the kitchen. At the table sat a man somewhat younger than my father, who was forty three, eating breakfast.

My father introduced me to the young man, who's name was Colin. He was their lodger. Father explained that Colin would be staying with them until May the following year when he would get married and emigrate to New Zealand.

Over the next few month as I got to know Colin better, I found him to be very nice and polite. He was a motor mechanic and worked in a local garage. He was twenty eight years old. Closer to my stepmother's age than my father's.

When Mutti asked me what I wanted for breakfast, I said a cup of tea and some bread would be great.

Colin had a plateful of food, which was unfamiliar to me. I noticed the wonderful white loaf of bread on the table and thought that would be wonderful.

Vati, which is what I called my father, laughed and said they could do better than just bread. He asked Mutti to cook breakfast for me too.

The kitchen table was covered in a lovely white tablecloth, embroidered with colourful flowers. There were three more places set with china plates and cutlery. A big white china teapot stood in the middle of the table with matching milk jug and sugar bowl nearby. There was a dish with a large piece of butter and two jars of jam on the table.

While my father and stepmother were chatting to Colin, no doubt explaining what had happened during the night, I sat quietly looking around me, taking it all in.

Everything in the kitchen was very unfamiliar. Mutti was cooking eggs in a pan on a gas stove, which lit up just at the turn of a knob. At eye level there was some kind of meat being cooked, under something called a grill. I'd never seen anything like it. Slices of bread were also toasted under the grill.

In one corner of the kitchen was another kind of stove, which father said heated the water in the big water tank for the hot water in the house. Then there was the kitchen sink with the draining board on one wall under a window and a food pantry in another corner of the kitchen.

The kitchen alone in the house was nearly as big as out little shack in Hermannstadt. I couldn't help but think of my family back there and how little they had, just struggling to survive. Here there was so much.

When my breakfast was set in front of me, I sat and looked at it for a while. Vati said eat it before it gets cold. I'd never imagined eating all this food for any meal, let alone breakfast.

Father explained that this was the traditional English breakfast of bacon and eggs. Very often he said people would add sausages, tomatoes, mushrooms and baked beans to it. I was so astonished by what he said, but did not voice my opinion.

I was wondering if I should have some bread as well. There was a whole loaf there, but I thought that would be greedy. My father picked up on my reluctance and generously buttered a piece of bread for me. The bacon and eggs, with the soft buttered bread tasted like sheer heaven. It was so good. I drank tea with milk and sugar, which I was already beginning to like.

When I finished eating, father said I must try some toast with jam or marmalade. I told him I'd eaten more than I'd ever eaten for breakfast before. He said it didn't matter and I could eat as much as I wished.

A funny little rack with toast in the slots was put on the table by Mutti. I'd never had toast and didn't know how to go about it. Vati told me to butter the toast first, then put jam or marmalade on top. I told him I didn't wish to be greedy. Back home I'd be lucky to get a piece of black bread for breakfast. He said not to think about that and enjoy all the nice things that were here.

How could I not think about the hardship back in Transylvania? But for now at least I was happy to enjoy the wonderful food in front of me. I ate two pieces of toast, one with butter and jam and the other one with butter and marmalade. They were both really delicious. When I spread the toast thinly, father said to put more on, as there was plenty from where that came from. I asked if they had to queue very long every day for their food. Vati said no one lined up for food here. Everybody bought what they wanted, when they wanted. I was flabbergasted. I couldn't envisage never having to queue up for food any more.

When Colin finished his breakfast, he left us sitting at the table and went to work. The three of us sat for quite a while longer. Vati was full of questions about everybody back home.

Mutti only had tea and toast for breakfast. Then she sat and smoked several cigarettes, one after another. Vati said he seldom smoked. Just occasionally in company after a meal. He remarked that Mutti smoked like a chimney, which made me want to laugh and brought to mind what my Granddad said, that if we were meant to smoke, God would have made us with chimneys on our heads. I didn't say that though.

Mutti didn't take kindly to my father's comment and replied in a short and sharp voice that she earned her own money, could do what she wanted with it and anyway, smoking was her only pleasure.

On that very first morning I sensed discord in my stepmother's reaction. I wondered how she could say that smoking was her only pleasure, when she lived in such a lovely house, with all these beautiful things around her and most of all the fantastic food they had. I knew from pictures that she also possessed beautiful clothes and shoes.

We were still at the breakfast table, when there was a knock at the kitchen door. Until then I hadn't realised that there were two doors to the house. The front door led into the hallway and the backdoor to the kitchen.

Mutti opened the door. A young woman with a very large covered wicker basket stood outside. My stepmother asked her in and she placed her basket on a kitchen chair, then removed the cover. There to my utter delight were loaves of bread of different shapes and sizes and all kinds of cakes, buns and other baked goods.

My father told me this was the baker's lady. Every day, except Sundays, this young woman and a colleague drove a horse drawn wagon loaded with all kinds of baked goods through the area they were allotted by the bakers and deliver whatever people wanted to their doors. There were several of these teams that covered the whole town. On Saturday mornings, these women would be paid for goods left throughout the week before.

Mutti asked if I would like to choose something special from the basket. I had no clue what anything was and asked her to pick. The baker's girl was paid by Mutti, then left to get on with the rest of her round.

I'd been absolutely amazed to learn that people didn't queue for anything. But this was incredible. Food was being delivered to their kitchens.

Soon there came another knock on the door. This time it was the milkman. He carried a square wire basket stacked full with bottles of milk and other containers which were new to me. The bottles had different coloured shiny tops. Some were silver, some red and other golden. Then there were other containers in the wire basket, which Mutti said were different types of cream. I didn't even know what cream was, so that was explained to me.

The milkman placed three bottles of milk and a container of cream on the kitchen table. Mutti paid him too and asked him to leave an extra pint of milk every day, now that I was here. When more milk than the regular order was needed, a note was left for the milkman under an empty milk bottle at the back door and the extra milk would be left during the week. I was beginning to wonder if my parents had to go out to buy anything. My father told me afterwards that both the baker and milkman were very interested in how I got out of Romania and they had both wished me well and hoped I'd like living in England.

How could I not like it here? Everything so far had been like a magical fairy tale, with everything so plentiful.

Father said he's taken the day off work, but he had some jobs to do. He asked if I'd like to go into town and do the rest of the shopping with Mutti.

Mutti left the kitchen to get washed and dressed. I sat and mused over all the incredible new things I'd experienced since leaving Bucharest.

When my stepmother returned to the kitchen, she was dressed to the nines. She was wearing a beautifully tailored suit. The straight skirt came just below the knees and a very smart jacket. A matching hat crowned her blond, curly head. She wore very high heeled shoes. Her fine stockinged legs were very thin. Her leather tan gloves and handbag, matched her shoes. When I admired her accessories, she told me she'd bought them in Berlin on her last visit to her mother and sister. She certainly looked very elegant.

I got my coat from the hall and put it on. I stood, feeling shabby and dowdy in my rough coat, that was far too small. I wondered if Mutti still wanted me to accompany her, as she might be ashamed of me.

I watched as my stepmother powdered her face and applied lipstick in the kitchen. This made her look a little more attractive, although she was not at all good looking, by any stretch of the imagination. How amazing what stylish clothes, face powder and lipstick could achieve. There was hope for me yet. I'd always considered myself quite ugly and plain.

When we stepped out of the house, it was a bright, crisp, sunny November morning. The front garden was part lawn, with shrubs along the fence, dividing the garden from the neighbour's. Chrysanthemums, in an array of colours, were still blooming. As we walked to the gate, I could see the garden was very well kept.

I looked around at the houses and saw how very different they were from what I was used to. They were all brick built. None had been rendered or painted. The bricks were left in their natural state. I remarked about this to Mutti and asked why the houses were all unfinished. She told me this was how they were built here.

All the streets had concrete paths and the roads were paved with asphalt, unlike all the muddy roads and pavements, where I'd lived. I thought how wonderful it was not to get mud all over my shoes anymore and not having to scrape and clean them all the time. In the next street, we stopped in front of a big thatch roofed house. We walked through a gate in a tall evergreen hedge.

In the garden to the left of the house stood a wooden building. When we went in, I realised it was a grocery shop. At the front, was a wooden counter and, on either side, on the walls, running all the way to the back of the store, wooden shelves, went up to the ceiling. They were stacked full with all kinds of tins and packets.

I'd never seen so much food in a shop and such variety. The shelves in the shops at home were always empty. When food came into the shops, no one bothered to put it on shelves, because it was never there long enough and just handed straight from the containers, to the customers.

Mutti took a list out of her handbag and handed it to the man behind the counter, who'd greeted her very politely by her surname, Mrs. Renges.

The shopkeeper scanned the list and ticked every item off. He wrote down a number against each item and added them up. He then took a thick book from a shelf nearby, opened it to a page, which had Mrs. Renges written in big letters across the top. I looked on with interest.

The grocer added a number from the book beneath the one he'd written on the paper and added them both together. Mutti paid and we left.

I was puzzled. When back on the street, I asked Mutti why she'd paid the man and yet we'd come away empty handed.

She explained how it worked. If she needed anything during the week from the shop, either she or Vati would come by and pick things up. Rather than fiddling with small amounts of money every time, the items would go on her tab. On Saturday, when the shops were only open till noon, Mutti simply gave the grocer her list, which he tallied up, added the items from the previous week and she'd pay it all in one go. The groceries, on her list, were then delivered to the house in the afternoon.

This was getting more incredible all the time! Everything was delivered to the house, one never had to carry anything.

When I write home and tell them all about the way things are here, no one will ever believe me.

We were getting closer to the town centre. Whittlesey was a market town with about twelve thousand inhabitants. The streets were busy with cars and bikes on the roads and lots of women, on foot, doing all their weekend shopping, before closing time at 12 o'clock.

Our next stop was a shoe shop. As soon as I entered the store, the smell took me right back to the first parcel, we'd received from my father, with the shoes. My shoes had smelled the same as this shop. Mutti said it was the smell of leather. I've always loved that smell.

A woman greeted us and showed us to a couple of chairs. The shop was big and all the walls were shelved out. Every available space on the shelves had boxes stacked high. The shopkeeper chatted to Mutti for a bit and then got some kind of weird contraption, with which, she measured my feet. Then she, went through a door into the back of the shop and returned, with several boxes, stacked high in her arms and placed them on the floor next to my chair.

The lady took one box at a time, took the lid off and handed me one shoe. When I put the shoe on, it fitted like a glove. The leather was so soft and didn't hurt my foot like my own shoes. I tried on the other shoe and walked up and down the carpet in the shop. Then I sat down, I told Mutti the shoes were very comfortable and fitted perfectly and how much I would like to have them.

My stepmother said I should try all the other pairs the woman had brought out, as I might like another pair better. I tried on another three or four pairs. All the shoes were so beautiful and comfortable. I liked them all. Choosing a pair was a big dilemma now. I was quite confused. In Transylvania, I'd have been over the moon with any of these shoes, even after spending hours or days looking and queueing for them.

After long deliberation, I chose a lovely pair of light brown slip on shoes. They were very soft leather and fitted perfectly. I felt as though I was walking on air.

Mutti asked if I wanted to keep my old pair. I was more than happy to throw them into a basket, the shopkeeper pointed to, and never see them again.

The next stop was the green grocer. There was such a wide variety of vegetables and fruit, laid out perfectly on display counters around the walls and centre of the shop, the like I'd never seen before. Mutti left a list there too, paid, then we left. Everything, she ordered, would be delivered later.

Our last stop was the butcher. I couldn't believe how many different cuts of meat were displayed on a counter behind glass. There were all kinds of raw meats and chicken. Then, there were roasted meats, of all sorts, cut into thin slices, like the ones I'd had on the plane. There were sausages and pies. There was so much food! We were the only customers in the shop. Mutti handed her list one of the butchers. He then weighed all the different meats, written on the paper, wrapped everything in paper and wrote her name on it and set the parcels to one side. He added up everything we bought and Mutti paid. She also ordered some meat to be delivered a couple of times during the week, for which she'd pay the following Saturday. The butcher's boy would deliver our order in the afternoon, on his bike, with the big square basket at the front.

After the whole morning shopping, we returned home, not having to carry a thing. How wonderful was that!

Just before we got back, we stopped to visit Mrs. Rose. She'd been my parents' landlady, before they bought their house. They'd both lodged with her.

Mrs Rose was a very short plump elderly lady. I would visit her a lot over the following months. She had a television. I'd never seen one before and was absolutely fascinated by the box. I had no idea how it worked, but loved watching it anyway, although I didn't understand a single word at first. Mrs. Rose was always very kind and generous and always made me very welcome. The fact that we couldn't converse at the beginning didn't really matter. She liked to spoil me and give me things I'd never had before. I loved the cakes, biscuits and wonderful Cadbury's drinking chocolate, made with milk, that she gave me every time I visited.

When Mutti and I got home that Saturday after shopping, I was overcome by tiredness. All the travel and continuous excitement over the past couple of days had pumped so much adrenalin into my system, which had kept me on a permanent high. Now I suddenly crashed.

Mutti made ham sandwiches and tea. Vati joined us for lunch. I was so worn out, I sat and ate without saying a word. My father gave me a very strange looking fruit. He called it a banana. They only grew in the tropics, he said. He told me they were really good and he thought I would like it.

I looked at this funny fruit and took a big bite out of it, before anybody could stop me. I pulled a face and said it didn't taste nice at all. Mutti said I had to peel it first, but my father thought it was so funny, he couldn't stop laughing.

Bananas became one of my favourite fruits and I could eat a whole hand in one go.

I told Vati in amazement about the shopping that morning and never once having to queue for anything. I said it would be great if my relatives could come for visits, to see how wonderful everything was here.

Father said it would perhaps not be as good an idea as I thought for people to visit from back home. After seeing what life was like here, they would become extremely dissatisfied with their lot in Romania and never find happiness or peace again.

I thought it was an odd thing for him to say. I wondered if he'd felt like that about coming home to us, after the war, and, therefore, decided to remain in England.

Had mother been right about all the things she'd said? Had my father been very selfish and abandoned us all for a better life? Vati saying that, kind of left a sour taste in my mouth and I felt upset. How could he say such a thing, when I wanted to share our good fortune with all my family?

I didn't say anything and just told them I needed to sleep, as I was dog tired. My father said he would come upstairs and show me everything, as I had only crept into bed in the dark, after arriving in the early hours after my flight to England. Narrow, steep carpeted stairs led from the hallway to a small landing. On the landing, a door led to the left and two doors to the right.

The first door on the right was half open. From what I could see, the room looked very small. I discovered much later that this room in most average English homes is referred to as the box room. They were usually 6 x 7 feet or 7 x 8 feet big. This one was most definitely the 6 x 7.

A wooden table stood against the back wall with bales of cloth, a pile of folded paper patterns and other tools of the tailoring trade, like scissors, tape measures, boxes of cotton reels and pins, etc. The floor covering was lino and in a very messy state. All kinds of off cuts, cotton, buttons and other stuff from my father's work, littered the floor. On the left wall underneath a window, up against the table, stood an old Singer treadle sewing machine. The door did not open fully, because the sewing machine was in the way. On the right against the wall stood a very low narrow bed. The three pieces of furniture completely filled the room, with very little space in between. A wooden chair stood in front of the sewing machine, which my father said I could use to put my clothes on.

Vati explained that the bed was temporary and collapsible, and I would use it for 6 months, when Colin would be getting married and would move out, his room would become my bedroom. Once Colin left, I would have his room as my own.

My father left me in the tiny box room, I lay down with all my clothes on, I felt so very tired. The bed was comfortable enough and certainly miles better than the straw mattress, I'd been used to. In spite of it all, a real sense of disappointment washed over me.

My aunts, back home, had painted such wonderful pictures of a beautiful bedroom, with lovely furniture, bedding and all sorts of other things. I'd envisaged something, that I'd seen in the villa, where Annitante had worked. Here I now was. It was more like Cinderella sleeping amongst the cinders.

Then I felt bad for having such ungrateful thoughts. Six months would pass and then I'd have my own bedroom. With that thought, I closed my eyes and fell asleep.

When I woke up, it took me a moment or two to realise where I was. It was still light outside and I could hear voices from downstairs. Minutes later when I walked into the kitchen, Mutti was standing by the stove cooking. Vati was sitting at the kitchen table, chatting to her.

My father said it was only the three of us for dinner. Colin spent Saturday evening and all day Sunday, with his fiancée and her family, in Peterborough.

All the different emotions of the last few days and then very little sleep, had left me completely exhausted. I didn't even remember what we had for dinner that evening because I was so tired. As soon as the meal was over, I asked if I could have a wash and go to bed.

After a warm bath, wearing one of Mutti's nightdresses, I was very glad to slip in between the sheets of my narrow little bed. I was dead to the world, as soon as my head hit the pillow, and slept until 10 o'clock the following morning, which was Sunday. I'd slept for 15 hours and felt so much better for it.

On Sunday afternoon, we went to visit friends of my parents, Margaret and Fred. They lived in Whittlesey too. Vati didn't have a car, so we walked to their house, which was only ten minutes away.

We'd been invited for afternoon tea, which I assumed would just be a cup of tea. In England, it seemed, everything revolved around tea, which I liked and found interesting. To my amazement, tea turned out to be a feast! I discovered that the feast of tea in England, took place around four or five o'clock.

The table was beautifully laid, with a pretty tablecloth and china. A huge platter, with a variety of small sandwiches, stood in the middle of the table. The traditional china teapot, milk jug and sugar bowl were set down near by. A large bowl of mixed tinned fruit and cream and a selection of home made cakes completed the rest of the spread.

Fred and Margaret didn't have any children. She was English and he was Saxon, from Transylvania. Fred had been a prisoner of war too. My father and he had met in the POW camp, near Ely, in East Anglia. They'd become good friends. I liked them both a lot, right from the beginning.

Margaret didn't work. She enjoyed being at home and looking after her husband. Their house was immaculate and spotlessly clean.

Fred worked in a flower nursery in town. The flowers were sent all over England. Some he delivered himself. He said he'd be making a trip to Hunstanton on Sea. If I liked, he could take me with him. I told him I'd love to go, as I'd never been to the sea.

Fred and Margaret asked us to stay for the evening. About 8 o'clock, Fred announced that he was going to get fish and chips and asked if I would like to go with him. I had no idea what fish and chips was. Fred and I walked to the corner of their street, where he showed me the fish and chips shop. At every turn, it seemed like a new adventure lay in front of me. I wasn't complaining. It was all just too wonderful.

Before we even entered the shop, I smelt a nice aroma. When we went in, the smell of the fish and chips was overwhelming, but so good. A woman, behind a counter, was serving a couple of other people. She greeted Fred by name.

A little further back in the shop, a man with his back to us, was busy fishing food out of huge containers with a big slotted spoon. He was placing what looked like large pieces of fried fish onto a shelf at eye level.

I was intrigued, never having seen food prepared in this way. Fred explained that fish and chips was an old English tradition. The fish was dipped in batter and then fried. The chips were cut potato sticks, also deep fried.

I watched the shopkeeper's deft movements, as she slit the end of a greaseproof paper bag, placed a big piece of fish into it and then piled a mound of chips on top. She then put the bag onto a sheet of newspaper and wrapped it all up. She repeated this four more times, then put all five packages into a brown paper bag and handed it to Fred. He paid and thanked the woman, then we left.

Back at the house, Margaret had warmed plates in the oven. We all sat round the table again and were each given a hot plate with a huge piece of fish and loads of chips.

Fred said that a lot of people ate fish and chips straight from the paper, which, they claimed, tasted better than eaten from a plate.

I copied what everyone else did and put salt, vinegar and pepper on my food. Then I took, what I was told, were pickled onions from a dish, and put them on my plate too. Everything so far had tasted too wonderful for words and I was ready to try anything.

I'd only eaten fish two or three times in my whole life. My brother, Christian, caught small salmon trout in the River Alt, in Kerz. A lot of kids fished there, but not with a fishing rod. They'd get in the shallow water, on the edge of the river, feel around in the muddy edge amongst the vegetation with their hands, where the fish often hung out. The fish liked being tickled. The kids then grabbed them and threw them out onto the grass river bank, where the poor things thrashed about until they suffocated. A pliable willow twig with all leaves removed was then used to thread through the fish gills and out of their mouths. It was quite a site to see a long willow switch, with small fish hanging from it.

My brother knew how to gut and descale the fish. I loved playing with the little airbags, that came out, when he cleaned the fish. They were then dipped in maize flour and fried. Christian could do all this. It made for a very tasty meal. Mother always had too many things for my brother to do, so catching fish was very low on her agenda. Oh! How I enjoyed my first fish and chips in Whittlesey and many more after that! The meal was finished with, yet another, cup of tea and then my parents and I walked home.

On Monday morning, my father had already gone to work, when I got up. When I walked into the kitchen, Mutti was sitting at the table, wearing her dressing gown. The whole kitchen was enveloped in a cloud of smoke. She was writing a letter. I'd realised, over the past couple of days, that Evy was not a very friendly person. In fact, she came across, as cool and standoffish. When we were on our own, she hardly spoke, which made me feel very uncomfortable.

I greeted her, and, out of politeness, I asked to whom she was writing. Without looking up at me or stopping to write, she curtly announced that the letter was to her mother and twin sister in Berlin.

I tried to make conversation. She made it pretty clear that she didn't wish to talk, by responding in terse monosyllabic words.

I stood around awkwardly for a while, not knowing what to do.

After what seemed an embarrassingly long time, Evy stopped writing and showed me how to make toast. She said I could help myself to butter and jam, which was already on the table.

Everything was strange and new to me. I didn't want to do anything wrong, so I stood and watched as the toast browned. I took it to the table and helped myself to butter and jam and poured a cup of tea from the tea pot.

To break the awkward silence, I asked how long ago my father had left for work. She didn't seem to welcome my idle chatter, so I just sat quietly and ate my breakfast.

It was only four days since I'd left Hermannstadt and my family. At times it seemed much longer. I missed them all so terribly. The pain and loss cut very deeply into my whole being. I thought about them constantly. When my father wasn't around, I felt very lonely and wondered how my life would turn out.

I was determined to make every effort to help with anything that needed doing. I'd go to any length to please my stepmother and get her to like me. Over the past couple of days, I'd noticed a reticence in her. I hadn't seen any kind of affection or warmth from Evy towards my father either. When she wanted him to do something, she never asked, but gave orders, which my father immediately carried out without question. He seemed on edge around his wife and I wondered if I was there under sufferance on her part.

I finished eating and took my things to the sink, where a pile of other breakfast dishes were waiting to be washed up.

I started running hot water into the bowl in the sink to wash up.

"What are you doing Girl?" My stepmother snapped.

"I'm going to wash the dishes," I replied.

"Leave them," she barked, in a coarse voice.

"I'd like to do it and help," I said feebly.

Mutti just grunted and got back to writing her letter.

I washed and stacked the dishes on the draining board, then took a tea towel and started drying them.

"Leave that," she ordered, as she stubbed out her cigarette in the overflowing ashtray. "It will dry by itself."

Timidly, I said, if I dried and put the dishes away, then it wouldn't need doing later. So she just let me get on with it.

Back home, we only had crockery and cutlery for one meal. Everything had to be washed up each time we ate, so it was ready for our next meal. Our home was very sparsely furnished, without ornaments or any kind of clutter, so it was always tidy.

The last couple of days Evy had left dishes in the sink all day long and washed them in the evening. I'd dried them and stacked them all on the kitchen table, where they remained.

I left Mutti in the kitchen, writing and smoking. At times, she lit a new cigarette from the old stub.

I was fascinated the way she took a long drag from her cigarette, then let a dense cloud of smoke out of her mouth. The smoke just drifted over her top lip and disappeared up her nostrils. Then she inhaled deeply and blow out a long stream of smoke through her pursed lips and nostrils.

She smoked Senior Service Cigarettes, which had no filter. The first and middle finger on each hand were stained a browny yellow. Her nostrils and the part between her upper lip and nose were also nicotine stained. I'd seen this on men in Romania and gypsies, who chain smoked, but never on a woman. I thought it looked awful and very unladylike.

I washed and cleaned my teeth. I enjoyed the luxury of a bathroom and really liked cleaning my teeth, which was a new experience for me. I'd never owned a toothbrush back home. They were like gold dust and never seen on sale in the shops.

I'd used Hansuncle's toothbrush, on a few sly occasions, without toothpaste. He'd been given it, when he was released from the Siberian labour camps.

I was lucky to have nice, white straight teeth. But then we never had sugar of any kind, which obviously was the reason for having good teeth.

I went upstairs and made my bed. The floor and table were in a mess, with all kinds of things, from my father's trade, lying everywhere.

I thought of going downstairs and asking Mutti for a broom to sweep up, but changed my mind, as I didn't want to get my head bitten off.

I got dressed in one of my summer dresses from home. It was chilly out, but, with my coat, I'd be warm enough.

I went downstairs again and, when Mutti looked up, as I entered the kitchen, she said, "You can't wear those clothes, we're going into Peterborough. Go back and change into the clothes, I gave you."

I did, as she said, and put the clothes on, I'd worn for the past couple of days. Then I sat on my narrow bed and let my thoughts meander all over the place. In the meantime, Mutti had gone to the bathroom, then come upstairs and dressed and gone down again. When she called up to me, "Girl come on, we're going into town." I got up and went downstairs. I don't remember her having called me by name once, since I arrived. I hated being called girl, I had a name, why didn't she use it?

Mutti was very smartly dressed, in completely different clothes from before. She obviously had quite a lot of different outfits.

Her golden curls were covered with a stylish hat. She was wearing long brown tailored trousers and a twinset in a soft cream wool, with small pearl buttons all down the front. All the clothes, she'd worn, were beautiful and I longed to wear such lovely things. Her brown leather handbag and gloves matched her very high heeled shoes. She did look smart. Her face was powdered, which diminished the nicotine stains on her nostrils and above her upper lip. Her lips were bright red.

I started to put my old coat on. She quickly said, "No! No! I can't take you into town in that." She handed me one of her jackets from the coat rack in the hall, which was slightly big on me, but a hundred times better than my coat.

Mutti put on a beige trench coat and we left the house.

After a short walk, we got to the main road, where after a few minutes a bus came and took us to Peterborough.

I was awed by the big double decker bus. We went upstairs and sat right in the front seat over the driver's cabin. It seemed as though there was no driver and the bus went all by itself. I got a very good view all around from up there, but thought the landscape very flat and boring.

Mutti had chosen the top deck, because smoking was allowed up there, but not downstairs. The ride into Peterborough took about half an hour and she smoked a couple of cigarettes on the way.

My stepmother told me Vati had given her money to buy me clothes and some material for a winter coat, which he would make for me. I was very excited at the prospect of having new clothes.

The bus went to a car park, near the centre of the city, where everybody got off. Peterborough was a city with a very beautiful cathedral. It was a lot bigger than Whittlesey, where my parents lived. We walked along Bridge Street, one of the main roads in the centre. The street was lined with wonderful shops, displaying all their stylish goods behind massive glass windows. I walked along open mouthed, admiring fabulous dresses and coats on mannequins. All the shoe shops displayed umpteen different types of shoes in their windows. It was all just incredible. There were windows that had wonderful looking cakes and bread on display. I hadn't seen anything like it. There was just so much stuff everywhere and so much to take in.

The roads were busy with cars, motorbikes and bicycles. The pavements had people rushing in all directions, going about their business.

The first shop, we went to ,was Marks and Spencer. It was so big, I couldn't even see all the way to the back of the store.

Down the centre, were large display counters, stacked high, with all kinds of clothes.

I found the shop and the experience totally overwhelming. Where did one start to look for things, with so much stuff on offer? There were just a few people, dotted about, looking at things and buying. Sales staff, of all ages, in smart uniforms, were serving customers, or tidying up garments that had been looked at and just left.

"Why wasn't the shop full of people standing in queues?" I asked Mutti. She said that there was no need. There was plenty to go round and people could buy things, whenever they wanted.

I'd been so conditioned to think that everything, one bought, could only be got by standing in line for hours.

I stood and just looked around me. Everybody was well dressed and looked prosperous. I thought of all the terrible things we'd been taught at school about the west. How oppressed people were and starving. Why did the communists do this? What did they think they would gain by it? Some people may have been gullible enough and believed all the crap they were fed, but most of them had known what life was like before the war, had travelled abroad and knew it was totally untrue.

Mutti took me down an aisle to the ladies' section. The choice, for each item, we were buying, was endless. I found it hard to make up my mind, so my stepmother advised me on what to get.

All the underwear came in different pastel colours. Everything was so soft and delicate, trimmed with matching lace. Mutti bought two of everything in white: bras, vests, underpants, knee length socks and nylon stockings.

It was like all the birthdays and Christmases, of my whole childhood, rolled into one.

I watched the sales lady fold everything neatly, then put it all into a paper carrier bag, with the M&S logo on it. She handed me the bag with a friendly smile on her face.

Even that was a pleasure, as everybody in Romania, serving in shops, was always surly and unfriendly. Mutti paid and we carried on further down the shop.

We came to rows upon rows of dresses, skirts, trousers, blouses and tops, all on coat hangers, hanging on rails. Then there were more rails with coats and jackets in all kinds of styles and colours. It really was never ending. My brain became addled with so much around, I couldn't think straight. Each item, I looked at, was more beautiful than the one before. How did one decide what to buy?

I tried on a whole variety of things in one of the cubicles, in the dressing room. I felt very confused, but did decide on a delicate white blouse, with puff sleeves and a red, slightly gathered needle cord skirt. I stood and admired myself in the full length mirror and wished the kids in Romania could see me now.

The second item, I chose, was a blue knitted straight jersey dress, with a belt of the same material. It was the smallest size in the ladies section and fitted me like a glove. Looking at myself in the mirror, I felt very grown up and elegant.

There was still more to buy. I got two white lace trimmed petticoats to wear under my dress and skirt. This was a new garment, that most people back home didn't wear, as they were never sold in shops. Mitzitante used to make them from silk and satin, embellished with beautiful embroidery round the top and hem. But those garments were only for the rich communist women.

Mutti bought a soft warm scarf with matching gloves, which I wore straight away. A box of six, delicate white hankies, with my initial embroidered in one corner, and a small light brown handbag were added to all our purchases and then we left the shop.

I was in seventh heaven. Never before had I owned so many beautiful things, let alone all at once. When I walked out of that shop, carrying the bags with all my new things, I felt like the luckiest person alive.

After a little while, my thoughts returned to my poor brother and the rest of the family back home, having nothing and living in poverty. It certainly dampened the pleasure I was feeling and I wished I could share my good fortune with them all.

Mutti and I then walked along Bridge Street into Westgate and the Town Square. From here, I saw the front view of the magnificent Peterborough Cathedral. I'd never seen such an old and impressive building before. I was promised to be taken to see the inside of the cathedral another time.

Our next stop was a tailor's shop in Westgate. My father did some tailoring for the manager there. Every Saturday afternoon, Vati came into Peterborough, to deliver the work he'd done the week before and pick up other jobs to be done the following week.

My father only did his tailoring in the evenings and weekends, as he had a full time job in an engineering firm, near Whittlesey. He hadn't been into town on Saturday because of my arrival. My stepmother was delivering and picking up work for him today.

On entering the tailor's shop, a dark haired slim man, about my father's age, in his early forties, greeted us. He was smoking a cigarette. Everybody seemed to smoke. Women and men, walking along the streets, were all puffing away.

The man embraced Evy and kissed her on the cheek. He then turned to me, shook my hand and said something I didn't understand. Mutti said he'd asked how I was and if I liked England. She then replied to the man in English, which I didn't understand either. We were led through the shop, which was fitted with floor to ceiling shelving on both sides. Every space on the shelves had bales of cloth in a huge variety of colours.

Just off the centre and along one side, stood a beautifully polished long old table. On it were a number of items: a yard stick, measuring tapes, scissors, paper pads and a number of other items. At the end of the table was a very ornate till.

Everywhere I went and everything I saw, was new to me and intriguing. I found all the people and way of life very interesting. I thought everybody must be rich. A lot of people had cars, which at the time were all black.

The man took Evy and me into a fairly large room at the back of the shop. In the centre stood a table and chairs. On the table, sat a tray with a teapot, cups and saucers, milk jug and sugar bowl.

The man walked over to a stove, that stood against one wall, picked up a kettle, went over to the sink and filled it with water. He put it back on the stove and turned on the gas. While the kettle was coming to the boil, he gestured for us to sit in the easy chairs. While busying himself making tea, he amiably chatted to Evy.

From the moment we'd walked into the shop, I'd sensed a change in my stepmother. Her whole demeanour towards the man became flirtatious. She giggled at everything the man said and blushed a lot. I'd not seen Mutti act like this or be so friendly before. Everytime he was close enough, she touched his arm, or hand, as she spoke to him. It made me feel uncomfortable and embarrassed.

The man offered Evy a cigarette. When he lit it for her, she put her hand on his. We were there for about half an hour. They both drank tea and smoked, while I tucked into the biscuits, which I could eat nonstop.

The man and my stepmother chattered all the time, with her laughing at everything he said. There was a real rapport between them. I wondered what they were talking about, not understanding a word, they were safe to talk about anything.

Evy obviously liked this man a lot, it was evident in the way she spoke to him and her body language. I'd never seen her act like this towards my father.

After finishing our tea, we all went back into the shop. Mutti asked what colour coat I'd like. I told her blue.

Back home you were lucky to get a coat, let alone choose a colour or style.

The man brought bale after bale of different shades of blue cloth to the table in the shop. The materials were all so different. Some were smooth, others had mottled bits interwoven. Then there were some with all kinds of patterns. They were all fabulous materials and the choice was endless.

The man then rolled out the cloth, I'd chosen, and measured the required amount and cut it. He folded the piece of material neatly, wrapped it in brown paper, then tied it with string and handed the parcel to me with a big smile, which one seemed to get everywhere.

Evy paid. The man embraced and kissed her cheek and shook my hand. Then we left. Mutti carried one of my bags, whilst I had the other one and the brown paper parcel. We walked back towards the Cathedral, turned into Bridge Street and on to the bus station. A bus for Whittlesey was standing waiting to leave. The service was very good. Every twenty minutes, a bus left the station for Whittlesey, some of them went onto March, the next town.

That evening, when Vati got home from work, I was so full of what we'd done all day and chatted to him nonstop. I displayed everything I got on the furniture and chairs in the living room. He seemed pleased that I liked everything. I must have thanked him a hundred times during that evening for all my new clothes.

He wanted to see me in my new dress, skirt and blouse. I proudly tried them all on and turned this way and that, so he could see me from all angles. He told me I looked very grown up and smart.

Everyday, coming home from work, Vati stopped at the little corner shop on the main road and bought me a big bar of Cadbury's chocolate. Every evening, I ate every last morsel of the chocolate. Whenever I offered my parents a piece, they always declined. This went on for several months, until I had my fill.

Mutti had the rest of the week off. I'd rather have had my father at home with me, he was much more fun to be with and we could chat endlessly. Mutti never asked questions about home or seemed interested in me. She did what she considered her duty and no more. I tried very hard to be helpful in all ways, but she was often churlish and declined my offers.

At the end of that first week, I sat on my bed and wrote a long letter home. I said all the things I'd so much wanted to tell them all when we parted and how much I missed them all. I wrote a little about all the amazing things I'd experienced, but played everything down, as I didn't want to tell them just how wonderful everything in England was, knowing they had nothing.

I told them how much I liked the English people and how friendly and generous everybody was.

Chapter Twenty Six

The following Sunday, we were all invited for afternoon tea at Uschi and Bruno Geschwend's. These were German friends of my parents. Bruno had also been in the POW camp with my father.

They both worked on a farm outside Whittlesey and lived in a nissen hut, on the farm. Bruno worked on the land, whilst Uschi cleaned the farmhouse and did all the washing and ironing for the farmer's wife. They had a little girl, called Brigitte, who was about 4 or 5 years old.

The farm was a good half an hour's walk from Whittlesey, along a country road, right near the River Nene. As soon as we crossed the bridge over the river, a beautiful big farmhouse came into view, set in lovely, well kept gardens.

The nissen hut stood closer to the river, also surrounded by a pretty little garden. I thought the building itself, looked very interesting with its domed, corrugated roof, going down to the ground each side.

We were greeted by the whole family at the front door. Uschi was a small raven haired woman in her early thirties and very attractive. Bruno was quite a well built man and looked a lot older than his wife. They were both very friendly. Brigitte, their little girl, was cross-eyed and seemed shy.

I loved their home from the minute I walked in. It was quaint, cosy and tidy. An open fire was burning in the hearth, which was very welcoming. I loved the fireplaces and open fires in all the English houses. Most of them burnt coal and they gave out a lot of heat.

I felt very much at home, especially as I could converse with both Uschi and Bruno.

We all had a wonderful afternoon together. I played with Brigitte. She had some lovely toys, with which I really enjoyed playing, even at my age. As I'd never had any toys, everything was new to me. In the late afternoon, we all sat down to a traditional Sunday tea, very much like the one we'd had the previous Sunday, when we visited Fred and Margaret. We ate cold meats, cheeses, salads, cakes and drank tea. It was delicious.

It was dark by the time we left.

Uschi told me she only worked in the mornings at the farmhouse and was at home every afternoon. She said I was welcome and could visit any time I wanted, when my parents were at work.

There were no street lights on the country road to Whittlesey. Vati had brought a torch along, which lit up the road on our way home.

The next morning, both Mutti and Vati left the house at 6.45 to go to work. They both worked eight hours a day plus an hour for lunch, getting back about 5.30 in the evening. That evening, after I'd been on my own all day, Vati brought home a newspaper, in which he showed me a small article. Of course I couldn't read it. He told me it was about me and how I'd come to England at the age of 14 to live with my father and how he hadn't seen me since I was three months old. He said a friend of his had put the article in the paper. I looked at the article and, sure enough, my name was written there. It felt strange.

The days at home, on my own, seemed long. I did what I could in the house. Mutti was very untidy. She never ever made their bed, so I'd make the beds, wash the dishes, sweep the kitchen floor and dust furniture. I was happy to have something to do. If I tidied up too much, Mutti got cross and told me to leave things where she put them. So I stopped doing any clearing up. I hated seeing all the mess and things being left lying about. The place would have looked so much better,if it was tidy.

I enjoyed listening to their German records, which they'd brought back from Berlin, on their beautiful modern record player, which was housed in a cabinet, that came up to my waist.

I went for short walks and familiarised myself with the neighbourhood. Whittlesey was on the edge of the fens. It was flat, as far as the eye could see. I'd been brought up with the Carpathian Mountains, all around me and beautiful forests and hills. The scenery around Whittlesey was dull and uninteresting. There were so many other good things about the place, which more than made up for the lack of hills and mountains.

I often popped round to see Mrs. Rose, who was always pleased to see me and made a fuss of me. She always had homemade cake in a tin and assorted biscuits in a biscuit barrel. It was always drinking chocolate for me and tea for her. We'd sit companionably, eating cake or biscuits and drinking our hot drinks.

The only problem was the language barrier, but that didn't seem to matter too much. She'd still chatter away in English and I'd shrug my shoulders. Then she'd just laugh, as she realised, I hadn't understood a word!

She was a very kind, gentle little woman. I towered above her. She would always give me a big hug before I went home.

On some days, when I didn't call round, she'd pop by and see that everything was all right.

Quite often, in the evenings, I'd go round to watch her TV. I loved the variety shows in particular, with all the singing and dancing, for which I didn't need to understand English. I would watch anything though, as I was fascinated by the magic on the box.

One evening after work, Vati wrote a letter to the man in London, for whom I'd brought presents from his mother and sister.

We both sat at the kitchen table together. I wrote to my family back in Transylvania, keeping them up to date with what I was doing and life in England. I kept telling them how wonderful, generous and friendly the English were.

I would have loved to have sent parcels to them. But the communist regime in Romania had stopped parcels from the West years ago. It was just so unfair that we had so much of everything here, yet my family and all the people I loved back home, were struggling to make ends meet and survive from day to day.

I still hadn't received a letter from home. I so wished they'd write. I was worried, as I knew my Granddad's health was poor and declining all the time. I was eager for news and just wanted to hear from them.

Fred came round, one evening, and asked my father if I could go to Hunstanton with him, for his weekly flower delivery. I was very thrilled to be going to the sea.

The next morning, a while after my parents left for work, Fred turned up in the delivery van. I really liked Fred. He was a warm and friendly chap and always seemed happy. I had noticed, during visits to them, or them to us, that he adored his wife and she was very loving towards him in return. Theirs was so different to the relationship between Mutti and Vati.

We chatted nonstop all the way to Hunstanton. Fred was full of questions about home and what life was like in Transylvania. He'd also been married during the war and had a son the same age as me, from his first marriage. He had tried for years to get him out, but his application had been rejected several times. He said he would keep on trying, although it was a pretty hopeless situation. His son lived with his mother. The fact that he was a boy made it much harder to leave. The communists kept all males, they were needed for national service and were considered more valuable than women. The fact that I was being brought up by old Grandparents may also have helped in my case.

I really enjoyed the long ride through East Anglia to the coast. Fred pointed out all kinds of things to me and explained what they were.

When we got to Sandringham, he told me the Queen had a beautiful castle here. She had several castles all over England and Scotland.

I told Fred about the man, who worked at Buckingham Palace in London, and how I hoped I could visit him. He said that would be a wonderful opportunity for me to visit London. The city was incredibly old and full of history. I told him we were just waiting for a reply to Vati's letter and then, hopefully, I would go.

As we drove over the crest of a hill, I got my first glimpse of the sea in the distance. At first I didn't know it was the sea. It was just a big expanse of grey water.

I'd always imagined the sea to be blue, the way it had been in the film I saw with Inge, Heide's sister, back in Romania. That had been in Southern Italy on the Med, where the beaches had been golden sand with lots of palm trees waving in the breeze. Little boats, with colourful sails, bobbed on the aquamarine waters. I got a dreamy, warm feeling inside, just thinking about he film.

As we drove into the town, people on pavements, were holding down hats and grabbing onto scarves, as they were battling strong winds. It was December now and pretty cold. In Hunstanton it was even colder and damper than inland. I could see the sea and the strong relentless North Sea wind was whipping up the water into big waves.

Fred parked the van in front of a flower shop in town. I remained in the vehicle, while he unloaded buckets full of flowers and took them into the shop. The bitterly cold wind was coming through the open back doors. I was wearing my new blue winter coat, that Vati had made, which kept me very warm.

When Fred was finished with the delivery, he drove to the seafront and parked the van in a small car park overlooking the sea, where we had a good view.

The sea looked even rougher here. Huge waves were crashing onto the rocks along the shore. People were hurrying about, wrapped in thick winter coats and holding onto hats, so they wouldn't be blown away.

We sat and ate the sandwiches, Fred's wife, Margaret, had made for us. Then we drank tea from a Thermos flask.

I told Fred how disappointed I was about the sea being grey. I told him about the film I'd seen about Southern Italy. He said the Med was a very different sea, mostly calm, blue and warm. Whereas the North Sea, especially during the winter months, was grey, turbulent and extremely cold.

The trip to Hunstanton and back took best part of the day. All the roads we drove on were mostly narrow country roads. I'd had a wonderful day. Just being in a car and driving made me very happy.

We received a letter from London. The man and his wife wanted me to go and stay with them for a few days. All my father had to do was put me on a train at a prearranged time and they would meet me at Kings Cross Station.

I really wanted to go and visit these people, but Mutti and Vati decided against it. They didn't want me to travel on my own and neither of them had the time to take me to London.

Vati made a parcel of the things I was to deliver and sent it with a letter.

I was terribly disappointed, not being allowed to go. I'd travelled on trains on my own since I was eight years old. I'd come all the way from Romania to England on my own and hadn't come to any harm and that was without speaking English. Now I'd picked up a few words and was sure I'd get by.

Fred had told me London was one of the biggest and most beautiful cities in the world. People from all parts of the globe came to visit this incredible place. One could spend weeks in London and still not see everything.

We had a letter back from London, thanking my father for sending the parcel. The couple expressed their disappointment that I was not going to visit them. We never heard from them again.

The week before Christmas, my parents were due to go to London on a coach trip to see 'My Fair Lady' on stage. The tickets had been booked before my arrival.

It was decided that I would take Evy's place and go with my father.

Early the following Saturday morning, Vati and I went, by bus, to Peterborough, from where the coach left for London.

I was delighted to spend the whole day with my father.

The coach took the same road, as I had travelled on the night I arrived in England. This time, however, it was daytime and there was lots to see.

The coach stopped about halfway between Peterborough and London in a place called Baldock. Everybody got off the bus and bought food and drinks in a café. After the short break, we all got back on the coach and continued on to London.

Passing through the North London Suburbs was amazing. We went through endless tree lined roads, with big houses either side, set in lovely gardens. There were lots of open spaces, which Vati said were parks. He told me London was a huge city and it would take a while to get to the centre, where we were going.

Eventually, we came to downtown London and the West End. I didn't know where to look. The buildings were all incredible. I'd never seen so much activity. Everywhere, I looked, there were red double decker buses. I watched as they went round corners and wondered how they managed to stay upright. There was so much to marvel at. When I spotted a black man, I was speechless. I'd only ever seen them in books. There was none in Romania or in Peterborough.

Watching the crowds on the pavements, I saw people of all colours, races and cultures. Some wore strange clothes in vivid, gorgeous colours, I'd not seen before. My father told me, London was a cosmopolitan city, where traditional costumes from different countries of the world were worn. Wow! London certainly was the most interesting place, I'd seen.

The coach finally stopped outside a café, in The Strand. The driver told everybody they had several hours to go shopping or sightseeing. We all had to meet up at this café, at 5 o'clock in the afternoon.

Vati wasn't familiar with London. He didn't know his way around the city. He seemed nervous and out of his comfort zone.

Apart from all the red double decker buses, the roads were full of all kinds of motor vehicles. One particular type, of which there were so many, was a black, funny, square looking car.

Vati pointed to a red sign on the front of each of these cars, which said TAXI. This was the famous London Cab.

We stood at the kerb, Vati stretched out his arm and almost immediately one of these Taxis came to a stop alongside us.

My father spoke to the driver and then we got in the cab. He'd asked him to take us on a sightseeing tour.

The London Cab was very different from any other vehicle I'd been in. The driver sat on his own in an area just big enough for him, with a sliding glass window between him and the passengers.

The cab was very comfortable with a lot of leg room. There were fold up seats, opposite where we sat, where there was room for two more people, who would have sat facing us.

We saw the Houses of Parliament, Big Ben and Westminster Abbey. We drove through all those famous London streets, with shops second to none. Oxford Street, Regents Street, Piccadilly and Trafalgar Squares. The shop fronts were just beyond belief. I would have loved to have stopped and gone into them.

We drove through Hyde Park and crossed the bridge over the Serpentine. Then we drove past Harrods in Knightsbridge, past the Victoria and Albert Museum and the Natural History Museum. The buildings were completely awe inspiring. I wondered what these buildings must they be like inside?

The taxi drove across some very interesting looking bridges over the Thames and finally, into the City of London. Many famous buildings were pointed out to us. We stopped briefly at Tower Hill and took in the amazing sight of the Tower of London and Tower Bridge. We drove past St. Paul's Cathedral. The driver pointed out where the Great Fire of London had started.

By the time our tour was over, I was completely overwhelmed by everything I'd seen. It had been such an astounding, intoxicating experience. I felt as if I was drowning in all the information I'd received and tried to take in.

I could never have dreamt then, that just a few years later, this amazing city would become my home for 46 years and that I'd work by the Tower of London and regularly go to West End shows and clubs. I would eat in wonderful restaurants in Knightsbridge and Soho and shop in all the famous stores.

I loved every moment, I lived there, and never tired of this magnificent, energetic, vibrant, sprawling metropolis.

My father asked the cab driver to take us back to the Savoy, which was the name of the café, where we were all to meet up.

The cab pulled up in a semicircular drive in front of a huge impressive building. A man, in a beautiful uniform, opened the taxi door. As I got out, he held my arm.

I was treated with such respect and courtesy, as though I was somebody special. Vati paid the taxi driver, who then drove off.

The man, in the uniform, held open the door, to the impressive building, for us to enter. My father spoke to him, whereupon the doorman pointed away from the hotel down the street.

We'd been dropped off at one of the most famous London Hotels, The Savoy, where the very rich and famous, from all over the world, stayed.

Vati said we wanted the Savoy Café, which was a little way down the road. When we got there, it was very different from the place we'd just come from.

Just a few people from our bus group were there. It was still early. Vati chatted to a couple of people and then we found a table and sat down. This was a new experience for me. I'd never eaten in a café, or restaurant before.

I was very hungry and enjoyed the meal. I remember having chips. I had ice cream for desert, which was a big treat.

After the meal, we sat drinking tea. Vati had bought a newspaper and was reading it. I was more than happy to sit quietly, watching people around me and reliving the fantastic day and all the incredible things, I'd seen. It had been a very special day.

At 6.30, the bus driver arrived and informed us that it was time to leave for the theatre. Everyone was going on foot as it was just 5 minutes away.

Vati told me London had many theatres, where famous actors and actresses performed on the big stages.

I was ecstatic about seeing famous actors and actresses, live on stage.

The inside of the theatre was huge and quite magical. The seats were all upholstered in plush red velvet, which flipped back into a vertical position, when not in use. I'd never seen seats like it.

Our seats were downstairs, not too far back from the massive stage. I looked around me in wonder. Behind and above us, were two balconies, spanning all the way across the theatre, one above the other. The railings of the balconies were ornate and painted gold. Either side of the theatre, high up, were several rows of equally ornate gold painted boxes, where just a handful of people sat in each. Fancy, elaborate chandeliers and wall lights lit the auditorium.

Vati and I sat watching people arrive. Most of the ladies were dressed in evening gowns, made up to the nines, bedecked in jewellery. They were escorted by men, in black dinner jackets or suits. My father looked as good as any of them in his smart tailored suit. I thought he looked stylish and handsome and was proud to be with him.

Just in front and below the stage was the orchestra pit, where the musicians were getting ready for the performance. As the lights dimmed, the orchestra started to play.

A hush went over the entire theatre. I sat, with bated breath, not knowing what to expect. Then the heavy, plush, red velvet curtains began to part and draw aside. The safety curtain lifted all the way up and out of sight and the show began.

I couldn't understand a word that was being said or sung, but sat completely spellbound by the stage settings, the music and the dancing and, most of all by the actors and their costumes.

Vati had explained to me by reading from the programme, he bought, what the show was all about. He couldn't give me a running commentary, as there was complete silence in the audience.

We sat close enough to the stage to see all the features and every facial expression of the actors. The magical fairy tale was playing out right in front of me. I loved the singing and dancing.

At half time, when the curtains came down, Vati and I went to the bar and drank orange juice. I couldn't wait for the second half of the show to begin and found it was even more enchanting and magical than the first half. In spite of not understanding the language, I was enthralled by the wonder and beauty of the show and was very sorry when it ended.

The audience, clapped, whistled, hooted and cheered at the end. The actors came back on stage one by one and took their bows. The cast returned onto stage several times. The audience was ecstatic and the atmosphere electric. I'd never ever heard so much noise, clapping and cheering.

The curtains came down for the last time and people started to file out of the theatre. Vati asked how I'd liked the show. I couldn't find words to express how I felt. All I knew was I wanted to see more of this kind of thing.

The coach was waiting close to the theatre on The Strand. When everybody was on board and accounted for, the driver pulled away and our journey back to Peterborough started.

I was very tired, after such an exciting day, and slept most of the way back to Peterborough, with my head leaning against Vati's shoulder.

We arrived in Peterborough in the early hours of the morning. A couple, in our group, who were from Whittlesey, had left their car in the car park and gave us a lift home.

I hummed tunes from my Fair Lady for weeks after going to see it. I just couldn't get the spectacular show out of my mind.

Chapter Twenty Seven

As Christmas was drawing closer, everybody was busy shopping and preparing for the holidays.

The shops had been decorated and were selling all kinds of exotic foods, clothing and gift items for several weeks. Everything, I saw and experienced, was way beyond my wildest dreams.

Big Christmas trees had been erected in the market places in Peterborough and Whittlesey and decorated with multicoloured electric lights. Most houses, one walked by, had a decorated Christmas tree in the window. Everywhere looked very festive.

Vati brought a small pine tree home, which I was allowed to decorate with baubles and candles, Mutti and I bought.

My thoughts were often with my family back home. I wondered what kind of Christmas they would have. Would they manage to get a bit of meat or the ingredients to bake a few biscuits?

I knew, no matter what, the family members, who didn't work evenings or nights, would get together, go to church and celebrate Christ's birth. Christmas was all about that, not about eating, drinking and presents.

The shops, here in England, were laden and groaning with the weight of all the food and goods. Back home, I knew the shops would be, as empty as they were the rest of the year.

My first Christmas in England was amazing. At the same time, it was tinged with sadness for my family in Transylvania, and my not being able to share my good fortune with the people, I loved most.

Christmas Eve was very busy. Vati worked in the morning. Mutti and I did all the food shopping. She said she didn't like cooking or baking, so she bought cakes from the baker and biscuits in the shop.

Vati spent the afternoon in Peterborough, taking his tailoring back to the shop and doing last minute shopping.

A parcel was delivered that morning. It was from my stepmother's family in Berlin. She opened it up and put all the beautifully wrapped gifts under the Christmas tree, where others had already been placed. I wondered if any of them were mine? It would be a first and I felt eager for the time to come, when we opened these presents.

Since Mutti and Vati got married in 1952, they spent every Christmas Eve with Bruno and Uschi at their place on the farm. They all kept this tradition going, as it was the way it was done in Germany and in Europe, in general.

Early evening on Christmas Eve, the three of us set off for the long walk to the farm by the River Nene. We walked briskly to keep warm, as it was pretty cold. I was wearing my new coat, Vati had made, and some of the lovely clothes, we'd bought, when I first arrived. Both my parents were smartly dressed. Mutti wore her beaver lamb coat and Vati a heavy winter coat.

Uschi and Bruno's nissen hut was festively decorated, smelling of wonderful baked things. A big fire was blazing in the fireplace. Their home all looked very cosy and welcoming.

We all sat round the fire, chatting for a while and drinking sherry. It was something the English drank before a meal. I was given a small glass. The sweet drink was good, it warmed up my insides, after our long walk and gave me a wonderful feeling of wellbeing. The meal turned out to be very special. A big golden roasted and stuffed capon was placed on the table. A number of side dishes, which were unfamiliar to me, were brought in from the kitchen. It was a mixture of English and German traditional Christmas fare. Everybody feasted, until they were overfull.

After the fabulous meal, Uschi, Mutti and I cleared the table and washed up. Then everybody sat round the fire. I was amazed that the eating continued. Mince pies were brought out and a variety of chocolates in beautiful boxes. Liqueurs in tiny glasses were handed round. There was so much food and, somehow, I managed to keep eating.

Later in the evening, Uschi handed out the wrapped presents, from under the tree. I was delighted to be handed a beautifully wrapped gift, tied with pretty ribbon. I sat and admired the wrapping and the bow on my present.

Vati sat next to me on the sofa. He nudged me gently and said, "Aren't you going to open your gift?" I told him it seemed a shame to spoil the lovely wrapping.

I took the paper off very carefully, so as not to tear it and folded it up to keep with the pretty ribbon. Inside was a flat box, which contained three very fine white handkerchiefs, trimmed with lace and a fancy 'U' embroidered in one corner.

It was the first Christmas present, I'd ever been given. I felt overwhelmed and could feel tears stinging my eyes, but managed to suppress them. I thanked Uschi and Bruno for being so kind to me.

Brigitte got a beautiful big doll. She had several other dolls already.

I related the story about the doll, my father had sent, when I was five years old. I told them how mother wouldn't allow me to play with it and, when going back to Groysie, when I was six, she wouldn't let me take it.

I told them how devastated I'd been when I found a neighbour's child, playing with the naked, damaged and hairless doll, on my return to Kerz for the summer, when I was eight.

Vati said jokingly, that he would buy me another doll, but thought I was really too old now. Little did he know, that I would really have loved to have had a wonderful doll like that, even at my age.

Everybody got nice presents. The men got shirts, ties and slippers. Uschi and Mutti received fragrant soaps, nylons and perfume.

How I would have loved to have spent an evening like this with my family back home and given them all wonderful gifts, like we'd all received.

It was well after midnight, when we walked back across the Wash to Whittlesey and home.

I was on a real high and still excited about the evening. On the way home we sang German Christmas Carols.

Vati explained to me, that in England, the big celebration took place on Christmas Day. Children, of all ages, hung up stockings on Christmas Eve before going to bed. Father Christmas then came down the chimney at night and filled the stockings up with presents.

I said that it must be wonderful to be a child growing up in England.

When we got home, I was still wide awake. Vati said we should sit down and have a night cap and open our presents from under the tree.

Mutti made drinking chocolate for us all. Vati stoked the coals in the fireplace, which were still glowing red, and got a fire going.

From Germany, I got a lovely delicate woollen scarf, that went well with my blue winter coat, Vati had made.

My parents had bought me a red twin set of wonderfully soft lambswool and a pair of fleecy lined red slippers, trimmed with white fur round the top. I was lost for words and couldn't thank Mutti and Vati enough.

Colin, the lodger, was spending Christmas with his fiancée and her family, so we had the house all to ourselves.

I went to bed very happily that evening, with wonderful thoughts in my mind. For the first time, I didn't have any nightmares. Hopefully, they would become less and less.

My mother was always the centre character in my night terrors. She always tried to get to me in some ghoulish form or another. I could never get away from her, no matter where I ran to or tried to hide. Many nights I'd be woken by my father shaking me gently, from my screams and shouts. I always ended up in tears, shaking and completely exhausted. I dreaded going to bed at night and being tormented by the memories of my mother, even though she was thousands of miles away.

Christmas morning, after breakfast, we all got ready to go out again. There were no buses running that day.

My parents were very friendly with the owner of the tailor shop in Peterborough and his wife. They saw them socially quite often. Ray, the shop owner had a car. All four of them would drive from pub to pub and drink. They called it pub crawling. There was no law against drinking and driving.

Mutti said she loved brandy and could drink as many as ten in an evening. Vati was never much of a drinker and just smoked the occasional cigarette. Mutti and Ray however, smoked like chimneys and drank like fish.

About 10 o'clock on Christmas morning, Ray picked us up in his car and drove us to his house in Peterborough, where we were all spending the day, with his wife and three children.

They lived in a big house, with gardens all around. The rooms were much bigger than the rooms in our house. It was decorated with streamers and balloons. A big Christmas tree, stood in a corner of the living room. It was beautifully decorated and reached all the way up to the high ceiling.

Their little girl was four or five years old, dressed in a beautiful dark green velvet dress, like something out of a child's picture book. She was a pretty child with fair ringlets down to her shoulders.

Her twin brothers, about a year old, were also dressed immaculately in their festive outfits, crawling around the floor.

As soon as we got there, the adults started drinking. The little girl and I drank orange juice, mixed with lemonade. This was a new drink for me, which I really liked. I was having one new experience after another. At times, I felt quite overwhelmed.

Everybody congregated round the Christmas tree and was handed one or more presents.

This time, I received a pair of nylon stockings. I'd learnt enough English so I could thank Ray and his wife for my present.

I still didn't understand enough to follow conversations, as most of my time had been spent with my parents and their German speaking friends.

At the beginning of January, after the Christmas school holidays, I was going to start school and then my father said my English should improve quickly.

Ray's wife had been busy for several days before Christmas, preparing for the festivities.

What a feast we were presented with. The table was so heavily laden with food, it almost groaned. The place settings were in rich festive colours and each place had a red or green tube-like decoration on it.

Vati told me they were Christmas crackers, which had little gifts, funny hats and jokes in them. It was another English Christmas custom.

I couldn't get over all the many traditions the English seemed to have. I loved them all and never got tired of new ones.

The food was scrumptious. I'd never had turkey before. I was amazed at the size of the bird. I thought it would feed dozens of people. All the different dishes, that went with the dinner, were so tasty.

We had Christmas pudding and custard laced with rum. I really thought I'd died and gone to heaven!

We drank wine with the meal and I was allowed a glass, as well.

Stuffed to the gills for the second day in a row, we all relaxed for a while and watched the children play.

The twins were put to bed for a couple of hours, whilst the rest of us had lots of fun playing games, which I didn't know, but was very happy to partake in.

I could never, in a million years, have imagined life could be so wonderful.

At teatime, we all sat down to another incredible meal. There were meats and salads I'd not eaten before. We had trifle, Christmas cake and mince pies, served with tea. The kids all got ice cream.

I was eating everything coming my way. My father encouraged me. He loved seeing me eat. I think I was making up for all the years I'd gone hungry.

About 8 o'clock in the evening, Ray drove us home. What an unforgettable day it had been. When we arrived home, the three of us sat for a while, relaxing and listening to German records.

The next day was Boxing Day and another holiday. Fred and Margaret had asked us for Afternoon Tea. It turned out to be another special meal with all sorts of traditional English goodies.

After the meal, we all sat around the fire, cracking nuts and eating chocolates. I found it very hard to comprehend how much food everybody had consumed.

I received yet another present from Fred and Margaret. In fact, I got two: a box of chocolates with a picture of an old English thatched cottage on the lid, and another box of hankies. They were every bit as lovely as the first box, with lace trim and violets embroidered in one corner.

The following morning, Mrs. Rose popped by. My parents had already gone to work. She brought me a Christmas gift, as well, it was a lovely rose scented hand lotion. Wasn't I just the luckiest girl in the world? I had received all these presents, from people, I barely knew.

My parents weren't church goers, only weddings and funerals, they said. I was pleased not having to spend all day Sunday in church any more. I'd been to the pictures a couple of times and to the theatre in London. Mutti and Vati drank and smoked. These were all things that were considered terrible sins.

Back in Transylvania, before the war, Vati had belonged to the Baptist Church. He'd obviously followed that strict religious path, because my Grandfather expected his children to do so.

Uncle Misch had left the Baptist Church, when he got married and joined the Lutheran Evangelical Church, to which his wife belonged.

As a young child, I didn't understand why uncle Misch and my grandfather never saw each other. It was only, as I got older, that I could see why the rift had occurred.

Granddad demanded that all his children submit to and observe the very strict faith of the Baptist Church.

By remaining in England, my father had escaped the demands of his father and was able to live his life, as he wanted.

I felt that way too, although I still believed in God and was convinced he made it possible for me to come to England.

My upbringing had been extremely repressed. I was told that most things people did were a sin. I couldn't do things other kids did.

However, the last couple of years with my Grandparents, I'd started to question our way of life and the strictness of our religion.

Everyone around me was doing all kinds of things considered sinful by Granddad, but nothing bad ever seemed to happen to them. They all had a great time and enjoyed life to the full.

Yet, my family abided by every rule in the bible and we were poorer than everybody else.

Granddad had been sick for years. Annitante had an illegitimate child. We lived in a shack. Why wasn't God helping us?

When I told Groysie what I thought, not daring to voice these opinions to my Granddad, for fear of him being disappointed in me, she told me that following the narrow and righteous path, was a hard cross to bear. However, we had to do it to gain everlasting life with God in Heaven.

I was glad that I would never disappoint them now. They would never have to know that I wasn't following the rigid, strict religious rules, they'd brought me up with.

The New Year arrived and soon I'd start school. My father had been to see the headteacher and enrolled me to attend the local senior school.

The evening before my first day at school, Vati told me he'd arranged for Janice, the twelve year old girl next door, to walk to school with me.

I felt extremely uneasy and apprehensive. I would have liked Vati to take me the first day, but I didn't say anything.

My parents had left for work early and I was sitting in the kitchen, waiting for Janice.

All kinds of thoughts went through my mind. What if the kids didn't like me and were nasty to me? My school experiences back home had been mostly bad ones.

I couldn't speak English, so how would I defend myself? Oh well, as long as I didn't get beaten up by the other kids, I could cope with anything else.

At 8.30, Janice knocked on the back door and I followed her through the front garden into the street.

I wondered why she wasn't carrying a school bag with all her books and things, but had no way of asking.

We did the 20 minute walk in complete silence. School started at 9 o'clock and we were there in good time.

I'd not seen the school before and was amazed at how big it was. The modern two storey brick building was of a pleasing design with massive windows. The front gardens were landscaped with lawns, trees and shrubs. A wide paved driveway lead to very big double doors at the front of the building. Children were coming from all directions, filing in through the entrance.

'Sir Harry Smith Secondary Modern School' was written in big letters on the wall above the entrance.

This meant nothing to me. It was much later that I learnt, that this school was for children, who'd failed exams to go to Grammar School, from where a high number of students went onto University and professional jobs.

The kids in this school only stayed to the age of 15 and then went on to manual work, apprenticeships, jobs in shops and factories. They were obviously not the brightest, nor the most ambitious children.

Janice and I walked into the huge foyer of the school, from where long corridors led into various parts of the building. A very wide staircase rose to the next floor.

There were lots of kids, milling about, ranging from 12 to 16 years in age. Everybody looked at me. Several kids spoke to Janice, but all she said to each of them was just hello.

We walked across the foyer to one of the corridors and stopped at the second door on the right. Janice knocked on the door and waited until she got a reply to enter.

The room was spacious, with a big desk in front of a window. An older man was sitting behind the desk, facing us.

The man immediately rose, walked round the desk and reached out to shake my hand. He said something, which I didn't understand.

While he spoke to Janice, I glanced around the room. There were several upholstered easy chairs on one side, positioned around a coffee table. On the opposite side, a bookcase, stacked full of books, stood next to a door, leading into a smaller office, where a young woman was sitting at a desk, busy at a typewriter.

I gathered the man must be Mr. Burgess, the headmaster, to whom my father said, Janice was to take me.

The headmaster addressed me once more, but all I could do was shrug my shoulders. Janice beckoned for me to follow her and we left the room.

We walked back to the entrance hall and up the wide staircase. All the kids seemed to be going in the same direction along one of the corridors. I thought it was odd that they were all walking the same way.

The next morning, it all became clear to me. Each morning, before classes, assembly was held in the big hall. Every child had to attend and the teachers too.

The staff all sat at a very long table on the stage. All the students sat on rows of chairs in the hall.

This is where all kinds of announcements were made. Here kids were reprimanded for serious misconduct or received commendations for various achievements and given prizes.

The National Anthem was sung each morning and prayers were said by one of the teachers, before the school day began.

Janice took me into a classroom on the second floor. A male teacher was sitting at a table, looking through papers.

He was obviously expecting us. He came over and greeted me by name. His name was Mr. Bryant, the form teacher of this class.

The headmaster had also addressed me by the name Ursula, which I was not used to, as I'd always been called Uta or Ut, by my mother. My father called me Ute, but the English pronunciation was horrible. It sounded like hooter to me. My stepmother seemed to prefer calling me Girl, as though I didn't even have a name.

This morning, both the headmaster and my form teacher, had called me Ursula, my first given name, which I really liked. From then on, I introduced myself, as Ursula, and became known by that name, outside of my family.

The classroom was very big and bright, with several large windows. There were three long rows of double desks all the way to the back of the class. Shelving was fitted all around the walls of the classroom, with all kinds of school stuff, stacked on them.

Mr Bryant showed me to the middle desk in the front row, where I sat down. Janice said cheerio and left my classroom to go to her own.

The teacher brought a German dictionary to my desk and a piece of paper, on which he'd written in disjointed German, that he didn't speak the language and nor did any other teacher in the school. The dictionary was for me to use and make myself understood. Oh my goodness, this was going to be very interesting. I thought maybe one or two of the teachers would speak, at least, a little German.

Kids soon started filing into the classroom and sitting at all the other desks.

Mr Bryant gestured for me to stand up. He spoke to the class, which I didn't understand, only my name.

The teacher then asked a plump blonde girl, with glasses, to come and sit next to me. Her name was Anne. She became my escort, whenever we left our classroom to go elsewhere in the school, for lessons, sport or into the playground for recess.

The days that followed were surreal. Every child in the school took an interest in me. They were all nice and wanted to be my friend.

All the boys seemed to like me. Some were nice and friendly, others, I could tell, were teasing me. It was all harmless though and I didn't mind.

I was caught once or twice, by being asked to repeat something, that was said to me, which I did. To me, it was all about learning the language. The kids would all fall about laughing.

I soon cottoned on that I was being asked to say something naughty and so stopped repeating things, which then brought the teasing to an end.

Everything at school was new and incredible to me. Everything we needed and used, was provided by the state, down to every last pencil, eraser and pen.

Back home, my Grandparents had to pay for everything for school. Yet, we'd been indoctrinated, by the communist regime, that people, in the west, were so poor. We were told stories from the Dickensian era about England. My family always said that we were told nothing but lies.

For days to come, I discovered wonderful things about my new school. The playground was massive, surrounded by huge grass playing fields. We had an enormous gymnasium, with every apparatus imaginable.

There was the big hall, that seated every child in the school for assembly and all kinds of other functions the school had.

The lab for chemistry was unbelievable and the art room was inspirational.

The sewing room with 12 sewing machines and all the equipment, needed for our lessons, was large and bright.

For the boys, there was a big workshop, where they did carpentry and metal work. They did that, while the girls had sewing lessons and domestic science.

The domestic science room was enormous and had every sort of equipment, that any chef would have been delighted with.

We had special teachers for all these subjects.

I thought, "Oh! My heart bleeds for these poor English kids, who've got nothing." This was the school for the dropouts, more or less, kids, who had little, or no, ambition.

I couldn't help thinking of my school back in Transylvania. We only had four classrooms in an ancient building. The courtyard was so small, that everybody had to stand around and couldn't move, like sardines in a can.

There was only one toilet in the yard for the whole school, which was dilapidated and stank to high heaven. We had to go to school in two shifts, because there wasn't room for all the Saxon kids.

The Romanian kids had bigger and nicer schools. Some were brand new with all mod cons.

The Saxon children and people in general had to make do with much less. The discrimination had all started after the war when the communists took over. We became second class citizens. The Saxons had colonised and built Transylvania into a great and prosperous country, but now they were slowly being pushed out.

My first day at school in England was too amazing for words. I sat at my desk and listened to the teacher talking. I liked the sound of his voice and the English language. He'd given me a whole list of words to look up in the dictionary. I wrote each word down with the German word next to it. I wrote pages and pages of words. I found a lot of them were similar to the German or Saxon equivalent, which made picking up English much easier for me.

I noticed from day one, that some of the kids in the class were noisy, disruptive and didn't listen to the teacher. When Mr. Bryant raised his voice and chastised the offending student, which was always a boy, he'd just stand smirking at the teacher.

The kids here didn't seem to have the same respect for the teachers, as we did back home.

There was one boy in particular, who did exactly as he pleased. The teacher was always sending him to see Mr. Burgess.

This boy sat in the last row in class. One day he brought a newspaper to school and proceeded opening the paper and reading it during class. The teacher told him to put it away, which the student just ignored.

The kid was smoking a cigarette behind the paper. All this behaviour was completely beyond my comprehension.

Mr. Bryant started walking towards the back of the class. The boy lit the corner of the paper with his cigarette, which went up in flames. He then threw the burning paper on the floor and walked out of the room laughing, whilst the teacher was stamping on the flames to put them out.

I went home most days telling Vati and Mutti about what this boy got up to and how totally unbelievable I found it all.

My father said he was the kind of kid, who'd never amount to anything and would most likely end up in prison. I never knew what became of him as an adult.

During the first break every morning, I'd go to the foyer with Anne, where crates of milk were stacked by the door to the playground.

The small glass bottles contained one third of a pint of milk. Each child in the school was entitled to one bottle.

A lot of kids didn't want the milk. In the second break, kids could help themselves to more milk. Most days I had two bottles of milk. I loved it and had not been able to drink it like this, back in Transylvania. What little milk we got, had to be divided between all six of us and was mostly used in the preparation of food.

Most kids stayed for school dinners. The dining hall was massive, with long wooden tables and benches.

All tables sat 10 people, including a teacher and prefect, at each end, on chairs.

There were several dinner ladies in white hats and coats, who cooked the meals, from scratch, in the adjoining kitchen.

I thought I'd died and gone to paradise. The food was fantastic and I loved it all. Every Friday, we had fish and chips, with peas.

We were given a variety of wonderful dishes like: shepherds' pie, toad in the hole (sausages baked in Yorkshire pudding batter), wonderful stews and roasts, sometimes pork chops. The meals were always served with mashed or roast potatoes, except for Friday, when we had chips.

The vegetables were all locally grown: cauliflower, carrots, brussel sprouts, broccoli, cabbage, beans and more. Everything was cooked fresh daily. The same meal was served up to all the kids, as well as the teachers.

Trays of food were brought to each table, where the teacher dished it up and the prefect took it to each child. What more could you wish for? This was like manna from heaven, for only one shilling a day.

After the main meal, there was always pudding, otherwise, known as dessert. There were fruit pies or crumbles, different types of sponge puddings: chocolate, spotted dick, jam or syrup. The desserts were served with lashings of creamy yellow custard from big jugs. I'd never eaten so much good food and often ended up having seconds.

A lot of the kids pushed their food around on their plates and complained about it. It was the done thing not to like school dinners. I just loved it all and couldn't see what other kids were complaining about.

The dinners at school were a damn sight better than anything Mutti cooked. I thought they were pretty wonderful. My stepmother made it clear she hated cooking and didn't make much effort to make the food tasty.

It didn't take long before I picked up a fair amount of English. I loved school. Everything, we did, was a lot of fun: the cookery and sewing classes, the games and gymnastics and the art projects. The kids in this school were way behind with maths, science and other subjects, that I'd done in Romania. There was nothing new for me to learn. I was able to concentrate on learning the language and enjoying all the new things available to me.

During the winter months, we only had gym, once a week, in Romania. The whole class had to walk to the gymnasium, which was a fair distance from the school.

During spring and autumn, we did athletics on the track next to the gym, still having to walk there and back. I'd never learned to play games.

At my new school, all the girls played field hockey during the winter months. At first I thought it was crazy going out in all weathers, dressed in a scanty gym slip and socks, chasing a ball, with these curved sticks. It was all new to me, but I loved every minute out on the field.

It didn't snow much in England. Even if it did, it usually melted the same day and didn't stop games being played outside.

During the warmer weather, we played netball, another game I had to learn, and get to know all the rules.

The boys played football in the winter and cricket during the spring and fall.

We all did gymnastics twice a week. Sport seemed to be an important part of the school day.

I couldn't understand why kids didn't like school and constantly moaned about it. I loved every moment and would happily have gone on Saturday, as well. But, in England, kids only went five days a week.

We never got any homework and didn't have to carry heavy satchels, crippling our backs. To me, it felt like the camp, I'd once been to one summer in Romania.

During February, we got a week's school holidays, called half term.

During this break, I visited Mrs. Rose and was pleased that I could converse with her.

A couple of afternoons, that week, I walked to the farm and spent the afternoon with Uschi and Brigitte.

Uschi was very kind and I could talk to her about anything, which I couldn't do with Mutti.

When I first arrived in England, I'd found my stepmother to be cold and distant most of the time. I'd hoped, over time, things would change. I so wanted to have a close relationship with her, as I'd never had one with my own mother. But three months on, Mutti was as offhand, indifferent and detached, as ever. There had been no way to crack that defensive shell of hers, in spite of doing my best and trying very hard to please her.

She had this harsh way of talking and making everything she said into an order. She did this with Vati too. She would just bark out the orders and he'd obey, like a slave.

“Lorenz, get me this or that,”

“Lorenz, light the fire!”

“Lorenz, I told you to do something or other!”

And so it went, with my father jumping to fulfil every wish of hers. There was never a please or thank you.

At least, she addressed him by his name. When my stepmother spoke to me, it was always “Girl do this” or "Girl I want” on it went.

I was like my father, always ready to do her bidding and jump to it. Throughout my childhood it had been the only way to survive, especially in Kerz. You never waited to be asked a second time, or all hell would break loose.

When I came home, after school, I did lots of things I wasn't even asked to do. I wanted to help and please, especially Mutti. I imagined it would please her, and therefore, our relationship would improve, but it seemed to have just the reverse effect.

Mutti was a very untidy and messy person. Me going around trying to help by tidying and cleaning up, seemed to infuriate her.

She'd get cross and tell me to leave things where they were. She didn't need a fourteen year old to show her how to run her home.

I told her all I wanted to do was help and make things easier for her, as she worked all day.

She told me she didn't need my help.

I felt rejected and unsure of what to do and how to act. I couldn't talk to my father about it. When he was around, my stepmother ignored me most of the time. I didn't want to say anything negative about her, as that would perhaps cause trouble between them. I carried on doing what was expected from me, but didn't take the initiative to do other things.

I told Uschi how things were at home and nothing I did seemed to please my stepmother.

Uschi said Evy was a hard nut. She'd always been like that from the first time she met her. She had no compassion or sympathy for others.

I wanted to know more about Mutti's background and started asking Uschi questions.

Uschi had met Evy in 1949 in a mental hospital in Yorkshire, where they both worked in the kitchens. They'd both been sent from Germany, on work permits, to England.

Uschi's boyfriend had also been captured by the British and spent some time in a POW camp in East Anglia, where he met my father.

After the war ended, and the prisoners were released from the camps, Bruno had also decided to remain in England. He'd worked on the same farm, near Ely, with my father, Fred and a number of other Saxon and German ex-prisoners.

Bruno had found out that Uschi was working in England too and they had become reunited.

Uschi started visiting Bruno on the farm. She suggested Evy go with her and that's how she met my father.

Uschi married Bruno and they moved to the farm near Whittlesey. My father also moved to Whittlesey, lodged with Mrs. Rose and worked on a different farm with Fred.

In the meantime, Evy got a job on a farm in Yorkshire and also arranged for her twin sister to come to England and work on the same farm.

Evy carried on seeing my father, whenever they got time off.

Mutti's sister, Gity, worked as housekeeper in the farm house. Evy loved working outdoors, especially with animals.

Gity was deported back to Berlin after a few months. Uschi knew why, but didn't tell me. All she said was that Gity had committed an indiscretion towards the farmer's wife and was thrown out of the country and couldn't return.

Evy stayed on at the farm. She married my father in 1952 and moved to Whittlesey, where they both lodged with Mrs. Rose. Evy also worked on the farm with my father.

Evy was born in Estonia in 1925. Her father was Austrian and her mother was German. In 1939, when the communists entered Estonia, she fled with her father, mother and twin sister to Poland, which was occupied by the Germans.

Her father managed a large farm in Poland, where the twins had a good life, during their teenage years. They had all the labour that was needed on the farm. Their teenage years were spent riding horses, going to the theatre and concerts and generally leading a leisurely life.

Evy's father died of pneumonia during the latter part of the war. Her mother and the twins stayed on at the farm until the communists invaded Poland.

The three women retreated with the German army and eventually, ended up in Berlin. They moved into an apartment, with her aunt, just off the Kurfursten Dam. The aunt had been married to her mother's brother, who'd got killed by the Russians. They had a cousin, their age, named Gerti. All five women lived together.

As the war raged on, the apartment next door became available and Evy, her mum and sister moved into their own accommodation.

They lived right in the centre of Berlin and managed to survive all the bombing. All five women moved into the basement of the apartment block, as some of it had been destroyed by bombs. Most of Berlin had been levelled by the allies.

When the communists took Berlin, life became impossible. They were five women, on their own ,with no male protection of any kind.

The soviet troops, pillaged, raped and murdered. Women were completely helpless against them.

Evy, Gity and her cousin Gerti, were young women, around twenty years old. They boarded the basement doors and windows up and remained inside during daylight. At night the three young women ventured out to rummage through garbage cans, trying to find anything that was edible, most nights returning empty handed.

Food was extremely scarce. People were barely surviving on starvation rations. The Soviets had surrounded Berlin and nothing was coming in, or going out.

Evy's mother spoke fluent Russian. She'd been a teacher to the children of some aristocratic family before the Russian Revolution.

She wrote in large Russian letters the words Typhoid and Cholera on the walls and doors of their basement, which kept the Russian soldiers out.

But Uschi said she was pretty sure those five women had been raped during that time in Berlin.

All five women survived the Berlin Blockade, after which the city was divided into four zones. The American, British, French and Russian zones.

Evy's family happened to be in the British zone and therefore, young women, were given permits to work in the British Isles.

Uschi told me Mutti never wanted to have children. She said she didn't like them. She wasn't interested in kids and would have nothing to do with them.

Now I was beginning to understand my stepmother's aversion towards me. I was there under sufferance. She must have thought that my father would never be able to get me out from behind the Iron Curtain, but, when it happened, she wasn't able to tell him how she felt. She just had to accept the situation and live with it.

I felt pretty sad about it all. From a simplistic point of view it made sense to me, because we'd both experienced so much, we would have a common ground and therefore get on well.

Being 18 years older than me, I thought she would have some kind of motherly instinct, even though she didn't want children of her own. I thought she might have had a little compassion towards me, knowing what kind of miserable childhood, I'd had, and want us all to be a happy family. However, that was not the way my stepmother looked at it.

As time went on, it became very clear to me that Evy would never be the mother I'd hoped and longed for. The distance between us grew wider all the time. She very rarely spoke to me unless she had to.

I asked Uschi how Vati and Mutti's relationship had been before I arrived.

Uschi told me that my father was a good man. He liked people and was always ready to do things for others. Evy had no redeeming traits, as far as she could see. She was selfish and controlling. She lacked compassion for other people and was just a cold hardhearted, scheming, woman. She said people were born with certain traits and they'd never change.

Uschi said loads of people had hard times during the war, but were kind and generous, in spite of all their bad experiences.

Uschi then told me that she didn't think Evy had ever loved my father, but had married him out of desperation, rather than be sent back to Berlin, when her work permit expired. She said my father was too easy going and let Evy have her own way and wear the trousers.

Uschi told me to be patient. In a few years time, I'd meet a good man, marry and have my own life. In the meantime, she'd always be there for me and I could go and talk to her whenever I wanted.

That was a great comfort to me.

After those visits with Uschi, I felt very unsure about the future and what it held for me. My father and I got on okay, but we spent very little time together. I couldn't open up to him and express my doubts and fears. The time for being close to him and bonding with him had passed a long time ago. I felt like I didn't really know him.

He worked every day, then spent all his spare time in that little room, where I slept, sewing. He told me one day that tailoring was his passion. He'd love to do it as a full time job, but it didn't pay as well as the job in the engineering firm.

Chapter Twenty Eight

It was good to be back at school after half term. My English was improving in leaps and bounds. Ever since I'd arrived the previous November, Mutti had talked about getting a puppy. She'd been to see a German Shepherd breeder in Whittlesey and had ordered a puppy from his next litter, which was due in early spring.

I was very excited at the prospect of having a dog. I loved all animals.

We picked up our puppy just before Easter. He was eight weeks old, a beautiful ball of fluff. Mutti called him Prince and he became her prince. She treated him far better than she treated Vati or me. She spoke softly and lovingly to the puppy, which, up to that time, I believed she was incapable of doing. She took him for walks and played with him.

I adored the playful little thing and spent a lot of time with him. He chewed everything in sight, including the slippers I got for Christmas.

That spring, Vati had bought me a bike. I'd never ridden a bike, let alone owned one. I had grazes all over my legs and arms, before I mastered riding the bike.

When we got Prince, I rode all over Whittlesey with him sitting in the wicker basket attached to the front of my handlebars. It wasn't very long before he got too big for the basket, then I took him for nice long walks instead.

The mild winter turned into spring in March. I hadn't missed the waist high snow, through which I had to battle most mornings on my way to queue for milk, frozen half to death in my inadequate clothes and shoes.

At times, I thought it strange, how quickly I'd grown used to my new way of life and all the wonderful things that came with it. How I accepted things now, without a second thought, and took things so much for granted.

I was still thinking about my family back home all the time and wondered how they were. I'd written several letters, but had only had one from them. They couldn't write what they wanted and had to be very careful what they said. The letters were always opened and parts crossed out.

I'd also sent a letter to Christian, addressed to my Grandparents, but, so far, hadn't had a reply from him.

I knew he'd finish his two year apprenticeship this summer and then he'd have to go back to Kerz. My heart felt heavy. I wished he'd have the strength and courage to leave my mother and start a new life somewhere else, working at his newly acquired trade.

My father suggested I write to my mother, but I couldn't do it. I had nothing to say to her. All the bad memories were much too fresh in my mind. Maybe later on I told him.

The first few weeks, after we got Prince, he couldn't be left all day long. I'd have my lunch at school and then cycle home, which only took a few minutes.

At the beginning, I'd always come home to puddles of pee and mounds of poo. After clearing up and washing the floor, I'd take the dog for a walk and then cycle back to school.

It didn't take too long to house train Prince, so he could be left, while I was at school. I enjoyed playing in the playground with my friends during the lunch break.

The week before Easter, Mutti bought a load of eggs, which we hard boiled and coloured their shells.

Mutti and Vati gave me a big chocolate egg on Easter Sunday. I also received several more chocolate eggs from friends.

I'd eaten so much chocolate over the last few months, that I now had my fill and didn't want to eat any more. The chocolate Easter eggs hung around for weeks. I'd really had enough. I told my father not to bring chocolate home any more, as I was sick of it.

I'd also grown a little rotund. Friends were saying it was only puppy fat. The doctor said it was only natural to put on weight, after the food deprivation, throughout my childhood. If I didn't lose the weight over the following year, I was to go back and see him again.

By the time I left school the next year, I was taller, slim and willowy.

Over the Easter school holidays, I spent a lot of time taking Prince for long walks. I walked to the farm several times to see Uschi, Bruno and Brigitte. I often went to Fred and Margaret, who lived closer to home. Margaret was expecting and they were both looking forward to having a baby.

When I was with Uschi, we spent a lot of time talking and me confiding in her. I also liked playing with Brigitte and all her toys.

I always felt very much at home with Uschi and Bruno and often said how I'd like to live with them, as I didn't really feel I belonged at home.

In May, Colin, the lodger, got married. He told my parents that it was a small family affair and that was why they hadn't been invited to the wedding.

Colin had packed his belongings the week before the wedding. The day after he got married, he brought his wife to meet us all and pick up his things.

They were leaving for Southampton the next day, from there, they were sailing to New Zealand and to the start of their new life together.

Colin told me once that he'd been in the Merchant Navy for a number of years. New Zealand was the most beautiful place on the planet, he'd ever seen. It was the only place in the world, where he wanted to live.

And so, I finally moved out of the box room, with the fold up bed, and into the bedroom Colin had vacated. I now had my own bedroom.

It was a good sized room, with one window overlooking the street and another, the driveway. The bed was wider and more comfortable and I had an old wardrobe and a dressing table, where I could put all my belongings.

Vati said during the summer, when the evenings got lighter, we would redecorate the room and I could choose the wallpaper. He promised me a new divan and also new furniture.

Chapter Twenty Nine

The end of the school year was approaching. I'd made very good progress in English and was speaking fluently. I had also made several good friends and was looking forward to being around these kids and enjoying the summer.

During the past few months, I'd been going out regularly with my new found school mates. We often went to the local cinema or roller skating. It was all so new to me and a tremendous amount of fun.

I couldn't believe what a good life these kids were having and now I was part of it all.

I was aware how much I was looking forward to the summer holidays. In the past, I had dreaded the summer, more than anything and being sent to Kerz. I wouldn't have to slave from morning till night in the unbearable heat, being beaten and treated like an outcast.

I was so thankful for being here and didn't even mind that my relationship with my stepmother sucked . I had my own friends and life was good.

My parents had their annual holiday in the last week in July and the first week in August every year. Hotpoint, where Mutti worked, closed the factory for the two weeks. Vati took his holiday at the same time.

They both went to Berlin every summer, to visit Mutti's mother, sister and niece. Lilian, Mutti's niece, was about 9 years old and was born out of wedlock. The child's father had never been around.

Mutti sent several parcels to Berlin each year and took loads of presents for everybody in the summer.

This year, only Mutti would be going to Berlin. Vati was staying behind with me and Prince.

My stepmother's cousin Gerti, with whom she lived in Berlin at the end of the war, now lived in Loughborough. She was married to a Saxon, from Transylvania, called Hans. The two women were going to Berlin together.

Gerti's mother, as well as Mutti's family, still lived in the apartment block, where they'd lived during the war.

Vati rented a car for a week and we all drove to Loughborough.

Mutti and Gerti got the train to Harwich the next morning, from where they took the boat to The Hook of Holland and, from there, they went by train through the East Sector of Germany to Berlin.

Hans, Vati and I spent a wonderful week together. Hans took us somewhere different in Leicestershire every day. He always drove. He was a much better driver than Vati, who seemed very nervous, when behind the steering wheel.

Hans was a lovely man. He was much younger than my father. He was 6 years younger than his wife, who was the same age as Mutti. They had no children. Hans was tall, with very dark hair, and good looking. They had a dog, as well, and wherever we went, the dogs went with us. I had my birthday whilst in Loughborough and celebrated it for the first time in my life. It was a very special occasion. The two men took me to a little restaurant, after taking me shopping and each buying me a little gift. Vati bought me a new top and Hans bought me some lovely soaps. I had a perfect day.

After a week, which passed quickly, Vati and I returned to Whittlesey.

I enjoyed the second week of our holiday even more. Vati worked for a few hours every morning on his tailoring. I'd get lunch for both of us, which I loved doing. In the afternoons, we'd take Prince for a long walk to the river, where we all splashed around in the shallow water and had fun with the dog. Most evenings, we were invited to friends to share dinner with them.

I got to know my father a lot better during these two weeks. He was a good man, kind and gentle and liked to please.

I'd never ever seen him so relaxed. When Mutti was around, he always seemed to be on edge. She was very loud, with a voice like a fog horn, always giving orders.

Vati was quietly spoken. He would go to any length to keep the peace and please her, but it never seemed to work. Whatever he did, never made her happy. I thought she was terribly spoilt and always wanted her own way.

When Vati and I were on our own, we conversed in Saxon and, sometimes, in Romanian. When Mutti was around we all spoke German, as this was her mother tongue too. As time went by and my English improved we often spoke English as well as German at home.

My stepmother's English was much better than my father's. He still had a very strong accent. He'd often say things back to front, which amused me.

After two wonderful weeks, Mutti returned from Berlin. I noticed how the relaxed atmosphere became tense again. My father seemed more anxious and nervous.

Over the past few months, I'd heard raised voices from both of them, when I was out of the room. They were obviously arguing. I couldn't tell what it was about.

It made me uneasy. I worried in case it was my being there that caused friction between them.

I tried very hard to fit in and please Mutti. It became an impossible task. She was short and churlish with me a lot of the time and I couldn't figure out why.

During the rest of my summer holiday, I worked at making Mutti like me more. I cleaned the house, tidied up, did the ironing and took Prince for long walks, but nothing seemed to please her. She always found something to moan or complain about, saying I hadn't done this or that right.

I was glad when school started at the beginning of September. It was good to see my friends every day and have other distractions.

Prince grew into a beautiful dog. Mutti took him once a week to obedience training. She was extremely proud of him. She always took him shopping with her on a Saturday morning.

Every evening after work, Vati took Prince for a 5 mile run to the river and back . My father rode his bike and Prince ran beside him on the inside without a leash. He was a very obedient dog. We all loved Prince, but, to my parents, he became the child they never had.

School was great. I loved every moment and was now bringing home books from the school library. I had a good dictionary, which I used constantly, so my comprehension of the English language improved vastly.

I wrote home on a regular basis. I sent photographs taken on our week's holiday, with Hans. Vati said my relatives in Transylvania wouldn't recognise me, as I'd changed considerably from the fourteen year old girl, who left Transylvania.

When I arrived in England, my hair was short and straight. Uschi had permed it, which had given me loose curls all over and everybody told me I looked pretty and my new hairstyle suited me.

Now a year later, my hair had grown down to my shoulders. The perm had almost grown out and it was now straight and a shiny dark chestnut brown. I liked wearing it in a pony tail sometimes.

In the one year, I'd only had one letter from home. I felt very sad and wondered if they'd forgotten me.

Writing letters was expensive. The stamp cost a lot of money, which I knew they didn't have. Letters were often destroyed and never reached their destination. Vati said he didn't think that all my letters to Transylvania got there. I hoped they'd got the pictures I'd sent.

Mutti had a new friend at work called Doris, who was much older than her. Doris had a grown up son and daughter. Her son was married and lived in London.

Mutti and Doris often went to London for day trips to visit the son and his family. The train journey was only one and a half hours. They left early in the morning and returned late in the evening. I loved it when, Vati and I were left on our own, on a Saturday, or Sunday.

At the beginning of November, all the kids at school started talking about Bonfire Night, fireworks and parties.

My friends told me how a man called Guy Fawkes tried to blow up the English Houses of Parliament in 1605, but failed.

Guy Fawkes had been introduced to Robert Catesby, who planned to assassinate King James and restore a Catholic Monarch to the throne.

Fawkes became one of the plotters, who wanted to kill the King. They secured the lease of an underground croft beneath the House of Lords and stockpiled 36 barrels of gunpowder there.

Prompted by the receipt of an anonymous letter, Westminster Palace was searched in the early hours of November the 5th, 1605 and Guy Fawkes was found guarding the explosives. Over the next few days, Fawkes was questioned and tortured. He finally admitted to the crime.

On January 31st, 1606, Fawkes jumped from the scaffold where he was to be hanged and broke his neck, thus avoiding the agony of the drawing and quartering that followed. Fawkes became synonymous with the Gunpowder Plot and Treason, which has been commemorated in England since the 5th November 1606.

His effigy is often burned on a bonfire, accompanied by a firework display.

The week before Bonfire Night, mostly small kids were seen all over town, standing on street corners. They all had effigies of Guy Fawkes made out of old trousers and jumpers stuffed with paper, sitting in an old push chair or just leaning against a wall or fence.

Every time somebody passed by the kids would say "A penny for the Guy!" Most people would drop a few coppers into a hat and the children then spent the money on fireworks.

After dark on November the 5th, bonfires were burning in most gardens, whilst fireworks were going off.

I'd been invited to a school friend's house for the evening. My parents weren't interested in joining in. They stayed at home with Prince. Most people kept their dogs and cats indoors, because the fireworks made a heck of a racket and frightened the poor creatures to death.

I had a fabulous evening. We put potatoes on the coals to cook, roasted sausages over the fire and drank hot chocolate.

The fireworks were spectacular. My friend's father was in charge and made sure nobody got hurt. It was the first time, I'd seen fireworks. I almost felt hypnotised, as I watched the rainbow colours of the Catherine Wheels, spinning on nails, pinned to the fence, making a fantastic display.

I loved the fireworks that shot up and then came cascading down like waterfalls of gold and silver. Others, exploded high up in the sky, making a wonderful multicoloured display. There were rockets that shot high into the sky, making a tremendous noise, as they exploded.

I didn't want the evening to end. It had been a real spectacle and I was already looking forward to next year's Bonfire Night.

As it was our last year at school, all the girls in my class got to bake a fruitcake for Christmas. A week before the holidays, we decorated our cakes.

I chose pale green icing for my cake and piped dark green for trees on it with tiny red baubles hanging from the branches. I piped Merry Christmas and Happy New Year underneath the trees in red. Lastly, I tied a wide red satin ribbon round the cake. I was delighted with the result. All the cakes were on show in assembly for one morning. Every child could vote for which cake they liked best.

I won first prize and was so proud, when I took the cake home, to give to my parents, as a Christmas gift.

Hans and Gerti spent Christmas with us. They arrived on Christmas Eve on their new motorbike. It was a beauty. Hans had always wanted a big motorbike and this one certainly was huge.

Keeping the Continental tradition going, we celebrated Christmas Eve with a special meal cooked by Mutti. She had made a special effort and I'd helped her with the cooking.

After the meal and clearing up, we all sat round the open fire opening our gifts.

Vati had taken me to Peterborough, a couple of Saturdays before Christmas, and helped me pick a present for Mutti, for which he paid. I also wanted to buy him a present, so he gave me some money. While he was in the tailor shop, I went to Glasses, the department store and bought him a lovely bottle of cologne.

Mutti's present also came from Glasses, which was considered the best shop in town. Vati and I picked 6 beautiful long stemmed wine glasses. Each glass was in a different delicate colour. We both agreed they looked very elegant and were sure my stepmother would like them. I was looking forward to giving her the present.

When Mutti opened the box, she pulled a face and said ungraciously,

"Hmm, what's this? You call that a gift! It's something for the house, not me!"

I was shocked by her reaction. I'd given her something I truly believed was beautiful and she threw it back in my face. How nasty and ungrateful.

I felt bad. I wanted to run out and cry. Gerti stepped in and said she would have been delighted to have received such a lovely gift. To which my stepmother replied, she could have the glasses.

This put a real dampener on the rest of the evening and caused an uneasy atmosphere. On Christmas Day, Hans took me out for a spin on his new motorbike. We stopped by the river and he told me he was sorry for the way Evy had behaved the evening before. He told me not to take any notice of her bad manners. I told him I'd hoped she'd be the mother I never had and had tried really hard to please her, but she was a mean spirited person and there was no way I could please her.

He reassured me it wasn't my fault and she was the loser in the end.

New Year's Eve, all three of us went to a dance in Cottenham, near Cambridge. My parents belonged to an ethnic German club, which was formed by European ex POW's who remained in England after the war. The people belonging to the club were mostly Germans and Saxons.

Several times a year they all got together for a social event. The guys in the band were all German, or Saxon and played popular German music. Everybody had a lot of fun. I met a lot of men from Transylvania, who never went back.

A few days after the New Year, it's back to school. The kids were now beginning to talk about what they will do when they leave school.

Anne, the girl who's sat next to me from my first day at school, is going to work in a shop in Whittlesey. A couple of the boys are going to do apprenticeships in carpentry. Others are getting jobs in shops in Peterborough. But most of them don't seem to know what they want to do.

Ever since my flight to England, my dream was to become an air hostess, but I've never told anybody about it. When I'm asked what I want to do, I say I don't know.

The kids in my class didn't seem to be interested in learning. They were just biding their time until they could leave school at 16.

We never had exams or were given school reports. It all appeared very strange to me. These kids were given such wonderful opportunities and yet weren't taking advantage of them.

Half term came and went and then the Easter holidays.

Spring arrived early in England. Crocuses and snowdrops peeped through the ground, as early as January and February. Then by March and April, primroses, daffodils, tulips and lots of other flowers, I didn't know, bloomed in perfusion.

We had lots of blossoming shrubs and all kinds of spring flowers in the front garden. During the summer, different varieties of roses and other flowers bloomed. Mutti loved gardening. She'd rather be out there in all weathers, than indoors, doing housework.

I enjoyed cleaning and polishing the nice furniture with the lovely fragrant polishes. I liked hoovering the carpets, which was a novelty for me. Mutti had accepted my help more, as time went by, but she never ever thanked me. Still, what was new, nobody ever had.

Behind the house was the vegetable garden, where my parents grew potatoes and all kinds of vegetables. Along the fence either side, Vati had planted redcurrant, blackcurrant, raspberry and gooseberry bushes, which were laden with fruit every summer.

The house was new, when they bought it, so they planned the garden the way they wanted it. Vati had also planted a couple of apple trees and a pear tree. At the back of the house, roses climbed up a trellis. It was all rather lovely and I felt very lucky to be living here.

The last term of school started after the Easter holidays. I felt sad that school was coming to an end.

From a fairly young age, when one of my professors in Transylvania had related stories of his university days in Leipzig, Germany, I'd dreamt of going to university, myself, one day.

All the kids in my class couldn't wait to finish school, go out and do some mundane job and earn money. I would have given anything to carry on and get a good education. One day, about halfway through the last term, Mr. Burgess, the headmaster, sent for me. I wondered why he wanted to see me. Usually kids were sent to him when they misbehaved. I couldn't think of anything I'd done to warrant seeing him.

When I got to the headmaster's office, he asked me to sit in one of the easy chairs, whilst he sat the other side of the coffee table.

He asked me what my plans were for the future. I told him that I wanted to be an air hostess.

I'd have no problem there at all, he said, as I spoke three languages fluently and had all the attributes needed for the job. When I asked him what he meant, he said to be an air hostess, one had to be of a certain height, attractive and slim. He told me I'd grown into a lovely young woman and would be an asset to the air industry. I felt quite chuffed with myself.

He then asked me if I'd ever considered staying on at school and going to Grammar School in March, where the children from Whittlesey went.

I told him that going on to higher education had always been my wish.

It wasn't too late, he said, for me to carry on at school. The reports from all my teachers had been very good and I'd done extremely well to have achieved so much, in such a short time. All the teachers had told him that I was very bright and should be in Grammar School.

Mr. Burgess said he was amazed at how quickly I'd picked up English and gained command of the language. He was in no doubt that I had a real gift for languages and could make a good career as a linguist. It would be a terrible shame to waste my talent.

I felt the excitement rise up from my stomach. Maybe there was still a chance to fulfil my dreams.

Mr. Burgess then told me he'd already been in contact with the school in March and they were happy to take me in September to do A levels.

I had no idea what A levels were, but who cared, as long as I could go on learning.

The headmaster told me, he would come to the house one evening, after my parents got home from work, to tell them the good news and discuss my future with them. They should be very proud of you, he said, with a big smile.

I was so happy. I walked out of the office, in a trance like state. I was going to get another chance and go to university, after all.

I could hardly wait for my father to get home from work that evening, to tell him my good news. I thought he'd be over the moon and so proud of my achievements.

Instead he replied in a calm way, "Well, let's just wait and see what Mr. Burgess has to say."

He left me feeling quite deflated, but I hadn't given up hope.

A couple of days later, the headmaster called at the house to speak to my parents. We all sat in the living room and Mr. Burgess repeated everything he'd already told me at school.

I sat listening, quite overwhelmed with pride and a warm feeling in my entire body. I remembered the last time a teacher had pleaded on my behalf with my Grandparents to let me stay on at school. The circumstances had been very different. My Grandparents, aunt and uncle couldn't support me any longer and, therefore, further education was out of the question.

I was already fantasising about going to the Grammar School and then, to university and how wonderful it was all going to be, when I was brought back to reality by my stepmother's harsh voice saying, "She's not staying at school, she can work in the factory, if it's good enough for me, it'll be good enough for her. There's plenty of young girls working there."

I couldn't believe what I'd just heard. I felt as though I'd been smacked in the face.

Vati just sat, twiddling his thumbs, which he'd do when nervous, saying absolutely nothing. I wanted him to speak up and tell Mutti, just for once, that it would be his decision, whether I would carry on at school, or go out to work.

Mr. Burgess was taken aback by my stepmother's comment. He said it would be a terrible waste. I had so much potential, not just with languages but other subjects too.

Mutti said she didn't slave in the factory all day, so I could waste her money and time, when I could be out there, earning my own living.

Mr. Burgess told them that all the tuition in school and university was paid for by the state and I might even get a grant, then they wouldn't even have to pay for my keep.

I could see the headmaster was embarrassed. He turned to my father, who hadn't uttered a single word. "Mr. Renges, please think about this carefully. This is your daughter's future, we're talking about. Most parents would give their eye teeth to have a child bright enough to go to university."

Mr Burgess got up and said he'd see himself out and left.

I sat on the sofa near to tears. For the second time in two years, I was denied the chance of a better education, I tried to persuade them.

My stepmother said I could forget all about it. She wasn't going to let all her hard earned money pay for me wasting my time on education.

I was sitting now with tears streaming down my face, willing my father to speak up and tell Evy, that having had no part in my upbringing, he would now, at least, give me the chance to have a decent education.

Vati sat for a while longer, not a peep out of him, just staring down at his intertwined fingers and twiddling thumbs. Then he got up, walked to the window and stood there for ages looking out.

Mutti, in her agitation and looking grim, sat smoking one cigarette, after another. I couldn't understand why she was doing this and being so mean. She obviously didn't give a hoot about me.

I knew, for a fact, that my father earned much more than her. He paid the mortgage and all the bills and gave her housekeeping money every week.

What she earned was hers and she did what she liked with it. She smoked like a trooper, sent lots of parcels to Germany, bought lots of new clothes and went off to London quite often. She gave me some of her hand-me-downs, which I was glad to receive, but how could she claim I was costing her money.

I tried to speak up, once more, and point out, yet again, that they would only have to pay for my food. I said I'd get a job during the holidays and try and pay my own way.

Mutti stopped me in my tracks and told me in no uncertain terms that the discussion was over and the decision made. At the end of term I'd leave school, find a job and pay her half my wages.

I was so disappointed in my father and felt absolutely let down by him. He had no guts. Why did he let this hardhearted bitch make all the decisions?

I knew she didn't owe me anything. I wasn't her flesh and blood. At the same time I truly believed that my father should have put his foot down and told her that this had nothing to do with her. He was going to send me on to further education, whether she liked it or not.

I went over and over the discussion in my mind and just couldn't believe the outcome. My father was weak and spineless, I knew that much. This spiteful woman had him completely under her control.

My opinion of my father changed drastically for me that day. I knew I would never be able to depend on him for anything. I felt alone, deserted and unloved.

I went to my room without eating dinner. I'd completely lost my appetite. I felt enormous resentment towards my stepmother. I thought, because of her war time experiences, she might have had a little more compassion towards me and others. She was made of stone through and through.

The more I thought about what had happened, the more disappointed I was in my father.

I felt that all my life only my Grandparents had truly cared for me. My own mother had had no interest in me and treated me like a leper and now, it seemed, my father couldn't give a damn about me either.

I was nearly sixteen and had been here for eighteen months now. This had been the total time, effort and expense my father had contributed to my upbringing. I would go out and earn my own living now.

My father was a weakling. He didn't have the balls to stand up to my stepmother and tell her that a chance, like this, came only once in a lifetime. Instead, he let her dictate to him and call all the shots.

She turned out to be the archetypal wicked stepmother.

The next morning, I went to Mr. Burgess's office, after assembly. He told me he was very disappointed with the way things had gone the evening before. He asked if I'd like to see the careers people, who were now at school most days and have a chat with them. He arranged an appointment and I saw a lady the same afternoon.

She asked if I had any ideas what I'd like to do. I told her I'd like to become an air hostess. The careers woman said she'd make enquiries and get back to me the next day.

I was called back to the office the following day. The careers lady told me, from what she'd found out, I seemed to be the perfect candidate to become an air hostess. I was well above the height required, slim and very attractive and most importantly, I spoke three languages.

As I listened to her, my hopes soared.

But then, she went on to say, the only trouble is you have to be 18 years old. My heart sank once more and I wanted to cry.

It looked like my stepmother would get her wish and I'd end up working in a factory, as I had no qualifications of any sort.

The woman saw that I was close to tears and told me not to give up hope. I told her I didn't want to work in a factory. She said she'd get me an interview in an office and I could get a job, as a junior office clerk. The job would entail filing, running errands, making tea and other menial tasks. In the meantime, I could attend evening classes for typing and shorthand and eventually, work my way up to becoming a secretary.

That seemed a much better option, than working in a factory, and I told the woman I'd like that.

She also suggested I go to evening classes for French lessons, which would be good if I still wanted to pursue a career as an air hostess when I was 18.

An appointment for an interview at Newells, an engineering company in Peterborough, was arranged after the end of term. I could decide then, when to start work.

Evening classes were starting again in September, which were held in the school. They were free. I signed up for typing only, as my spelling was still very poor and, for shorthand, good spelling was essential. I could always do the shorthand later on, when my spelling improved.

I went home somewhat happier and told my father reluctantly, what my plan was. It felt as if I was letting him off the hook. He was pleased and said he didn't really want me to work in a factory. He told me he would pay for me to have private French lessons in Peterborough in the autumn. I thought he must be feeling guilty to offer private French lessons.

So, if he didn't want me to work in a factory, why hadn't he stood up for me and insisted I carry on at school and given me the chance to be educated? Thinking about it made me feel angry and resentful. I wished I'd had the nerve to tell him, how pathetic, I thought he was, for giving Evy so much power and letting her make all the decisions.

Over dinner that evening, Vati told my stepmother that I was planning to work in an office, as a junior clerk. She was not at all pleased.

"Ha!" She barked, "you'll earn a pittance in an office. You'd earn much more working in the factory."

Now it all became crystal clear to me. She'd be getting half my wage, so of course the grasping cow wanting me to earn more money, which would go straight into her pocket, as my father paid all the bills and all the household expenses.

As a junior clerk the pay was only one pound, whereas in the factory Evy said, the young girls, earned anything between 5 and 8 pounds a week.

Chapter Thirty

The last few days at school were a lot of fun. The art work and pottery, done during the last term, were exhibited in the big hall. I made a lovely summer dress in needle work which was on display with all the other things the girls made.

The dress was in a bright multicoloured fabric, sleeveless and had buttons all down the front. A belt in the same material, had been made in the local haberdasher shop, which finished the dress off perfectly.

The needlework teacher knew my father was a tailor and suggested he make the buttonholes for me, as they were the most difficult part of making the dress. My father made a real professional job and the finished result was beautiful. That dress became my favourite and I wore it for several years.

After only 18 months at school, all my teachers commended me on how well I'd done, in the short time. Neither of my parents went to the open evening, to hear how I'd got on, and my success at school.

They didn't come to my sports day either, where lots of proud parents were cheering on their kids.

This was a familiar pattern. I felt totally worthless and insignificant, and wondered if anybody, in particular people close to me, would ever truly care and appreciate me.

When I said goodbye to my form teacher, Mr. Bryant, he told me it had been a real pleasure teaching me. He told me I could really be proud of myself and that I'd grown into a beautiful young woman.

He said I wasn't just bright in the learning sense, but I'd proven myself over and over, how good I was with my hands too.

He was sorry that I had to leave school, but he was absolutely sure I'd be a great asset to anybody I worked for in the future.

He said to always be open and embrace all learning. He gave me a hug, then wished me well for the future.

If only I'd had parents like Mr. Bryant or Mr. Burgess, life would have been very different. In July I had my first interview for a junior clerk position at Newells Engineering. I was to work in the factory office, which was the same hours as factory workers. Most offices started work at 9 o'clock, but I was to start at 8 o'clock. My job began at the beginning of August. My wage was one pound.

During the rest of July I spent quite a bit of time taking Prince for walks and visiting Uschi and Bruno and Fred and Margaret.

Fred and Margaret had their baby. They named their little girl Susan. They were both completely in love with their new arrival and beamed from ear to ear every time I saw them.

Uschi and Bruno also had a second child, a baby boy; they called Brian. They were both delighted to now have a girl and boy.

I told them all that I had to leave school and would start my office job soon.

They were surprised at what I told them, as they expected me to stay on at school, because of how well I'd done.

I explained about all the things that had been going on in the last few weeks. They couldn't believe that my father hadn't stood up to Evy for once and insisted that I stay on at school.

Both couples told me, that they hoped their children would be clever enough to go to university.

In July, my parents told me that they were going to Berlin for their summer holiday, which is the last week of July and first week of August. I assumed that I'd be going with them and looked forward to the boat trip and the train journey to Berlin.

All the other kids at school were going on holiday for a week or two with their parents. About a week before the trip, my stepmother informed me that I was not going with them. At first, I thought she was kidding, but she was not a joking kind of person.

How could they do this? How could they go away for two weeks and leave me on my own? I felt so rejected. They just didn't give a damn about me.

When I asked my father about not taking me with them, he said it was too expensive for all of us to go and somebody had to stay home with Prince. I wanted to ask why they were so mean and cruel to me.

The Saturday, before they left for their holiday, Vati took me to Peterborough to buy me a present, as they won't be there for my birthday, on the 29th July.

I didn't want a birthday present, I just wanted to go to Berlin with them. But I didn't have the guts to say anything. I must be gutless like him. I have always had to accept, whatever I was given and be eternally grateful. I was never allowed to answer back and was told repeatedly to respect my elders and the decisions, they made.

Anyway, Vati bought me two lovely pairs of shoes, with 2 inch high heels. They were the first shoes, since the pair I'd been bought, when I arrived in England. They were the first high heels, I'd ever owned. I was thrilled with my present and felt it was a peace offering on my father's part. It didn't make up about the way I felt, being left at home, on my own, with Prince.

This was the old familiar pattern of rejection. When would it ever end? I was mortified. I thought everything was going to be so wonderful, once I was with my father. I'd belong and have parents, at last. I loved being in England and everything about it. I just wished I had loving parents, who cared for me and had my best interest at heart, like other parents. I was coming to the realisation that this would never be the case. I just wanted words of comfort and reassurance from my Groysie, but she was worlds away.

Standing on my own two feet, seemed the only option for me. It was going to be hard, with no other family around, in a strange country. What choice did I have? I certainly couldn't depend on my father to be there for me.

My parents left early for Peterborough, on Saturday morning, to catch the train to Harwich.

I sat lost and deflated, after they'd gone. My anger got the better of me and I did something I'd never done, or been allowed to do in my whole life.

Screaming, ranting and raving, I went through the house, protesting against the injustice and unfairness that my parents were treating me with. I wanted to pick things up and smash them, but that was going too far and would never do.

Poor old Prince kept running away from me, as he must have thought my rage was all directed at him.

I didn't even care if the neighbours could hear me. I was hurting so much and just didn't know what to do.

Eventually, I just collapsed in a chair and cried my eyes out. Prince came over to me and started whining and licking me. He had more compassion than either of my parents. I embraced him and bemoaned my lot. He was my only comfort.

Over the next two weeks, I spent a considerable amount of time with Uschi and Margaret. They often asked me to an evening meal with them. They were all disgusted and disappointed at the way my parents were treating me. I knew they felt sorry for me and didn't like it.

I spent my 16th birthday on my own. I didn't tell anybody that it was my special day, as I couldn't bear the pitying looks I would get.

Prince loved going to the river. I took him several times, while my parents were away. I met a girl, called Anne, there. I'd seen her at the river before, sunbathing and swimming. She had straight blonde shoulder length hair and was very attractive. We got chatting. She was a year older than me and attended Grammar school in March. Another year at school and then she was going to university to study art. She told me young people had a lot of fun at university. It was very different from school and she was really looking forward to going.

During that summer, Anne and I met quite often by the river and we became good friends.

She was very interested in me and my background. We could sit for hours and chat. She wanted to know all about Romania and communism, which I was happy to tell her about.

I also told her how my parents had refused to let me go on to higher education and I was starting work in an office in August.

It was a great shame she thought, as a university education would make all the difference to my future life.

Anne lived in Whittlesey, with her parents and two year old brother. They only had a council house and her father was the only one who earned a wage. She said her parents were very proud of her achievements and would do anything so she could go to university.

Anne belonged to a youth club and asked if I'd like to go with her sometime.

I was so happy to have Anne as a friend. She was so different and had much more about her than the kids, I'd known at school.

Going to the youth club, really opened my horizons. The young people there were mostly my age or older. They all seemed to be grammar school kids, with aspirations and ambitions for the future.

The youth leader arranged for me to give a talk about Transylvania and communism, one evening. Everybody was full of questions, wanting to know all about life in a country under Stalin's rule. I found the evening exhilarating, with so much interest shown.

These kids couldn't believe the poverty in which people lived, and even less so, that no one could speak freely, without fear of being arrested and disappearing. They were shocked, when I told them, we had to queue all hours of night and day for the little food, just to survive. I told of the propaganda and lies, everybody was fed, especially the school kids.

Some of these young people, including Anne, belonged to the Whittlesey drama group, which I joined as well, where plays were performed twice a year.

Doing all these new things, including evening classes, gave me a new lease of life. I really enjoyed the company of all my new friends. What was extremely important to me was the fact that they all accepted and seemed to like me. I felt very comfortable in their midst.

At home, I became more withdrawn. I distanced myself from my father and didn't feel the need to tell him things. He was not on my side, which I felt very strongly.

A handful of young people in the social circle, I now mixed in, were already going to university. They were only around during holidays. I did envy them and felt they were very lucky. The majority of the kids were at grammar school in March, which was only a 20 minute ride on the bus, and these kids were around all the time.

Albert was a young guy in the group, whom I had seen out of my bedroom window, delivering our newspaper, early in the morning, ever since I arrived in England. A lot of school kids did this before school, to earn pocket money.

It got so, that I used to listen out for him opening the garden gate, then jump out of bed and peep from behind the curtain. He was a very nice looking boy, and seemed rather athletic, the way he jumped on his bike and rode away. He was the first boy, I really liked in England, and I had a crush on him.

Albert also belonged to the drama group. He always got a main part and was a good actor. He was 19 and training to become a solicitor. I got to know him quite well. He lived just round the corner from me, so we often walked home together.

He was a nice boy. We became good friends and went to the cinema occasionally. The relationship never got beyond necking in the backseat at the pictures and a goodnight kiss at my back door.

Chapter Thirty One

I'd been at my job since the second week in August. I'd arranged it that way, as I knew my parents had their holiday at the end of July and beginning of August and I had expected to be going with them.

I quite liked working in the office, although the work was terribly boring. It was a small office and consisted of a staff of 6, including me.

Mr. Bell was the office manager and Mrs. Barnes was his secretary. They were both somewhere in their fifties. The other two women and one young man, were all in their twenties. The two women and man in the office all called Mrs. Barnes the battle axe behind her back. She was not liked.

My job was filing, getting papers out of files that had to be dealt with, running errands and taking memos to other offices, making tea on request, folding letters, addressing envelopes and taking them to the post room, at the end of each day. Generally, I was everybody's dogs body. It was easy enough, but rather mundane.

My working hours were 8 to 5, with one hour for lunch. Our office was the only one on the work floor, the rest were all in a nice building, at the front entrance to the factory. The people there worked 9 to 6. Everybody worked 5 days a week.

I had to walk through part of the factory to get to the office. Some of the lads and young men on the factory floor whistled and called out, when I walked by. I was shy and found it disconcerting. After a while though, I realised it was all just friendly banter and called back with cheeky answers.

I also had to take memos, requisitions and orders to the foremen of different departments. One place I had to go to several times a day was the tool room, where a young guy, called Jonny, often hung out, chatting to the foreman. He always gave me the eye, looked me over and smiled. His good looks didn't escape me either. A nice bit of stuff as some of my friends would say.

Next time I'm in the tool room, I asked Bill, the foreman, who the young guy was. He told me Jonny was studying to become an engineer. He was doing a sandwich course, meaning half his time is at college and the other half working in the factory. He couldn't be doing much work I thought, as he always seemed to be in the tool room chatting to Bill. Jonny was 20 years old.

As promised, my stepmother took half of my wages, which was 10 shillings, leaving me with 10 shillings, which just covered my bus fares of 2 shillings a day. I was left with nothing, not a penny.

I made sandwiches to take to work, as I couldn't afford to even buy a drink in the canteen. When Jonny's at the factory, we met for lunch in the yard and ate our sandwiches, sitting on a bench.

When it rained, Bill let us sit in the tool room and eat our lunch there.

I liked Jonny a lot and he obviously liked me too. He lived in Peterborough, but on the odd occasion he took me home on his motorbike. He met my parents. Vati said he liked him, he seemed like a nice lad.

When I was not at evening classes, Jonny came out to Whittlesey and took me for a ride to the river, or we went to a pub, where he bought me a lemonade and he had a beer. We'd been seeing each other for a few weeks, and I thought of him, as my boyfriend. One day, when I went into the tool room, Bill said he had something to tell me. He said he could see that I was getting very fond of Jonny and the longer I see him the more hurt I'll be. I couldn't think what he can possibly mean by that.

Bill said he'd asked the young man repeatedly to come clean with me, but he wouldn't. Being more like a father figure and having my interest at heart, Bill said he couldn't leave me in the dark any longer.

Jonny already had a girlfriend. He had been with her for 2 years and they were planning on getting engaged.

I couldn't believe such a nice young guy would do something so awful. I asked Bill why he was saying all this.

"Does Jonny ever see you at weekends?" Bill asks. I thought for a moment, and then told him he didn't.

"That's because his girlfriend lives in Wisbech and he spends all his weekends there with her." Bill explained.

I felt stupid, upset and betrayed. I had thought Jonny was so nice and, yet, he'd been two-timing both me, and his girlfriend.

When I saw him the next time, he tried to talk me round and said how much he liked me. I told him I wouldn't play second fiddle and how disappointed I was in him.

Chapter Thirty Two

I've been working at Newells well over two months now. Mrs. Barnes has developed the habit of giving me her mail to be sent out just before 5 o'clock, when it's time to leave work. This has been happening for a number of weeks now and I always end up missing the 5.20 and very often the 5.40 bus, as well, back to Whittlesey.

The other three in the office keep telling me to stand up to Mrs. Barnes and not let her boss me around this way. They call her a control freak and say she loves seeing me dance to her tune.

Getting the post ready, entails folding, putting the two or three dozen letters into envelopes, which I have to address by hand, then entering each letter into a ledger and, finally, taking them to the post room for stamping.

Even the girl, in the post room, who works till 6 o'clock, urges me to tell Mrs. Barnes that I will not stay on after 5 o'clock and that she must give me the mail earlier.

I've never stood up to anybody in my entire life and find it impossible to speak up.

Every evening, as my work colleagues leave the office, they egg me on to speak up and not keep taking the crap from the old bag.

One Thursday, just before 5 o'clock, the battle axe, as I've come to think of her more and more, dumps a whole pile of letters onto my desk.

I finally pluck up the courage and tell her I have to leave at 5 o'clock, because I have to be somewhere for an appointment, thinking this will make her be more reasonable.

She's so taken aback by what I say, the cigarette, dangling from her sour looking mouth, almost drops out.

I can see the others in the office, sniggering with glee, and the guy, holding up his thumb to me.

"You'd better get these letters out!" Orders Mrs. Barnes, in her hoarse voice from the constant smoking.

"I'm sorry, but they'll have to wait until tomorrow, I have to go," I tell her, picking up my bag and leaving the office, with my three coworkers.

Mrs. Barnes stands, staring at me in disbelief and giving me daggers. Then she turns and marches into Mr. Bell's office.

"Well done!" My work mates tell me, as we walk through the factory. The old cow needed telling.

The following morning, as soon as I walk into work, Mr. Bell summons me into his office. Mrs Barnes is sitting next to him behind the big desk. Clouds of smoke are already billowing from the cigarettes the pair of them smoke nonstop, all day long.

Mrs Barnes's dour, mean looking face is giving me looks that could kill. Oh boy, am I in trouble.

Mr. Bell asks what I have to say for myself.

I'm completely unprepared for this confrontation and feel utterly intimidated by these two.

I tell my boss that Mrs. Barnes is keeping me later and later at work each day and sometimes I get home as much as an hour later than I should.

Mr. Bell counters that the mail is very important and has to go out at the end of each day. Somehow I've found my voice and can't believe I'm actually coming back with answers. I tell Mr. Bell, if I was given the mail several times during the day and not all at once just before 5 o'clock, it would all go out and I'd get away on time.

Mrs. Barnes goes bright red in the face, bristling with indignation, demanding who the hell I think I am telling her how to do her job.

I wouldn't dream of telling her how to do her job, I say, but it would help me a lot to get the post throughout the day and then I could leave at 5 o'clock, I explained.

In a raised voice, she tells me I'm the junior clerk and have to do what I'm told.

I don't know what else to say. I can feel the tears welling up in my eyes and swallow hard. I don't want to give this bitch the satisfaction of getting the better of me. I'm very worried and don't know what's going to happen next.

Talk in the office has it that these two are having it off. They're both married and this horrible woman has a lot of control over Mr. Bell.

My boss lets me stand there for a while, looking down at his entwined fingers, as though he's praying. After what seems like an eternity, he puts his hands flat on the desk and looks at me.

He tells me he can't have a junior disobeying a senior in the office and, as from today, I'm sacked, with a week's wages in lieu of notice. I can work the day out.

The crow, with laryngitis, is sitting, with a smug look on her face, which I'd dearly love to slap off. She's happy, she's got what she wanted and won the day.

I'm flabbergasted. I can't speak. Tears are now welling up and start to overflow. I turn and quickly leave the office.

The others in the office can't believe that he's actually sacked me. They're calling him gutless and Mrs. Barnes all kinds of choice names under the sun.

I feel so ashamed and disgraced. How am I going to tell my parents?

After Mrs. Barnes has gone to lunch, Mr. Bell calls me into his office. He looks sheepish. He tells me he's made an appointment for me that very afternoon, to go for an interview in a shop in town.

A friend of his is the manager in a shoe shop in Peterborough and has a vacant position. The job is guaranteed, if I want it.

I'm overwhelmed with gratitude and thank my boss over and over.

I'm handed a piece of paper, with the address and the shop manager's name. Mr. Bell also hands me my week's wages and another envelope with a week's money, in lieu. He tells me I can go whenever I'm ready.

Back in the office everybody is disgusted. The spineless bastard is feeling guilty they say. He knows what he's done is wrong and he's trying to make up for it.

Ding Dong Bell has no balls, the guy in the office says, otherwise he would stand up to that brass necked controlling monster.

Another girl in the office says Bell is a coward. He's waited until Barnes has left, so she won't get to know what he did. But be sure she says, we'll find a way of letting her know about it.

I say goodbye to my work colleagues, wave to the guys on the factory floor, as I walk past and tell them I'm leaving. They all want to know why. I just say they'll find out in due course. I know full well that the word will get out and Mrs. Barnes will be disliked even more than she already is. She's a nasty piece of work and won't care anyway.

On the bus into the centre of Peterborough, I can't help but wonder, what it is with men, letting these women dictate to them and give them the power to be so obnoxious?

Mansfield is the shoe shop, I'm going to be working in. It's one of the shops I've often stood in front of, admired and longed to own one of the beautiful pairs of shoes. The shop is in Bridge Street, the main street in town.

The manager of the shop is very nice and also in his fifties. I wonder if he knows I've been sacked and why. He doesn't ask, so I don't offer the information.

We have a chat about what the job entails and am told I can start work the following Monday.

Wow! What luck! I haven't missed one day's work and my parents need never know that I was sacked.

That evening at dinner, I tell my parents that I've found another job, which pays 2 pounds, a pound more than my last job and I will start on Monday. They never ask why the sudden change and I keep quiet about being dismissed. The term sacked seems to carry the connotation of something really bad and nasty, as though it's a terrible crime. For years to come, I didn't tell anybody that I'd been let go from my first job.

Mutti only seemed to be interested in how much I would be earning. The first thing she said was that, as agreed, I'd give her half of my pay.

I now worked 6 days a week, but only half day on Thursday. My bus fares will be 12 shillings. With one pound for my stepmother, 12 shillings for the bus, I was left with 8 shillings a week. I felt rich. For the first time I had money in my pocket.

I like my new job. I'm third and last in seniority. A woman about 50 is the top sales lady and Marie is second. She's only 2 months older than me, but has worked there since leaving school in the summer. I'm the last to join the staff and therefore the dog's body, making the tea and running the occasional errand. I like both women and the manager. They're a nice bunch.

Marie lives at home with her parents and sister. She's already had a raise in her wages, as she's been there a few months. She earns 2 pound 10 shillings.

I ask Marie how much money she has to give her mother every week.

She looks at me, as though I've asked a stupid question, and tells me her mother doesn't want any money from her, as she earns so little.

She only lives a short walk from the shop, so doesn't have to pay bus fares. To me, Marie is rich. Hardly a week goes by without her buying new clothes or shoes.

Then she tells me her father often slips her a few extra shillings a week, which pays for her cigarettes.

Marie's a pretty pale skinned blonde girl. Her face is always very heavily made up. The tan pan stick is caked thick on her lovely smooth skin, but stops at a straight line at the side of he face. She wears very pale pink lipsticks, blue eye shadow and spidery false black eyelashes. Her face reminds me of a Venetian mask. Her hair is cut short, layered and heavily backcombed. Marie is slim, totters about in 4" or 5" high heeled shoes and looks just like the new Barbie doll, Brigitte got for her last birthday.

We're really like chalk and cheese. My dark shiny hair is now well past my shoulders and straight, as all the curl has now grown out and been cut off. I'm not heavily into make up. I just have a powder compact and natural lipstick, which Uschi bought for me. My green eyes complement my dark chestnut hair and olive coloured skin. The manager often looks at us, when we stand together chatting, and says what a lovely pair we make.

Marie's engaged to a boy just two years older than her. She's been going out with him since she was 14. He's the spitting image of Adam Faith, she tells me, and they're getting married next May, when she turns 17.

That's so young to tie the knot, but she's deliriously happy and doesn't stop talking about all the plans for the wedding and the white princess wedding dress she already has. She can't wait for the day to arrive.

Every morning on my way to work, I pass the upmarket and stylish ladies' shop next door, to the shoe shop. Standing in front of the huge plate glass window, I look in awe, almost salivating at the beautiful clothes on the manikins.

My taste in clothes and shoes is way beyond my pocket. I'd have to save for months from what little is left over from my wages every week to be able to buy something from this shop.

I wish I was more like Marie, who buys lots of cheap clothes and looks pretty good in them, but parting with my little bit of money is hard. I'd rather save and spend it on just one good piece of clothing.

I've been admiring a beautiful dress and matching coat in the window next door for several days. The coat is 6 pounds and the dress costs 4. I do the maths quickly in my head and realise it would take me about 8 months to save every penny after paying Mutti and my bus fares. It's a hopeless situation. Even if I did it, the coat and dress would long be gone.

One morning, as I'm standing in front of the shop window yet again, the manageress comes out and stands next to me.

"Which dress do you Like?" She asks me. I point to the dress and coat, but tell her I'd never be able to afford it.

The shop manageress must see the longing in my eyes and asks, why I don't come in during my lunch hour and try the dress on, just for fun.

What would be the point of it? I'm thinking, but just wearing such a beautiful dress for a few minutes, and seeing what it looked like on me, would be worth it. I tell the lady I'll go in during my lunch break.

I can hardly wait for the morning to pass, so I can go next door.

As I pass the window, to my horror the dress and coat have gone and the manikin is wearing something different. I feel so disappointed, but still go into the shop. Then I see the dress and coat, hanging on the door of a changing room cubicle, at the end of the shop and my heart skips a beat.

The manageress ushers me into a cubicle and hangs the coat and dress on a hook on the wall. I take off my clothes and put on the dress. I look in the long mirror and can't help admiring my reflection.

The dress is a rich tangerine, the latest colour in fashion. It zips all the way up the back to the neck. It's lined and made from a warm material, with slightly raised tiny bobbles all over. The collar is loosely rolled over around the neck and the sleeves don't quite reach the elbows.

As I walk out into the shop, the manageress is standing looking at me.

"That dress was made for you," she tells me. "It fits like a glove, and hugs your figure perfectly. The reason why it hasn't sold is because it's the smallest size, we've had in."

The woman then fetches the coat and I try it on over the dress. It's a three quarter length coat in a simple and elegant cut. When I look in the mirror I feel like a million dollars.

After I change into my own clothes, the manageress asks me to sit down for a moment. She tells me how she's watched me stop every morning and look in the window, with such longing. Then she asks me how much I can afford to pay a week.

After explaining that I only have 8 shillings a week to my name, she asks how I would feel paying 5 shillings out of that.

The dress is 4 pounds. It will all be paid off in a little under four months. That sounds pretty good to me.

My stepmother has bought stuff from a catalogue on the never never, ever since I came to England, so buying this dress, is the same kind of thing.

I tell the kind lady that I'd like to do that. She writes it all down in a book and I'm very happy with the arrangement.

She says by Christmas I'll have paid half and then she'll let me have the dress.

When I tell Marie, what I've just done, she thinks I'm completely nuts to pay that much for one dress. You could have four for that money, she says.

The coat, of course, is out of the question, although it would have been lovely and would have finished the outfit perfectly.

Two or three weeks before Christmas, Vati asks me what I'd like for a present. I tell him about the dress I've had put by on the never, never. It would be nice if he gave me a little money, instead of buying me a gift.

Coming up to Christmas, we get lots of new deliveries in the shop. Some of the shoes are really gorgeous. Marie has bought two pairs in the few weeks I've been there. Her father is always putting his hand in his pocket and buying her things.

There's one pair of shoes, in particular, that I'd love to buy. They're the latest trend, winkle pickers, with 4" stiletto heels. The pair, I really like, are in a pearlised pale tangerine, a shade or two lighter than my dress and would look just fabulous.

The discount, we get on shoes, is very generous. I ask the manager if I can put a pair by for Christmas, to which he agrees. I don't know how I'll pay for them, but I'll worry about that when the time comes.

One evening, a week or so before Christmas, my father comes to my room and hands me a 5 pound note. He tells me it's my Christmas present, so I can pay off the dress. I can hardly believe my luck. I thank him and give my father a big hug.

Now I'll be able to pay the rest of the money on the dress and for my shoes and even buy the little clutch bag to match for 10 shillings and still have a little money over for presents for Mutti and Vati.

When my father has left my room, I dance and twirl around, reminding myself how lucky I am.

I can't wait for Christmas to arrive, so I can wear my new dress and shoes. I'm going to look elegant and grown up.

I'm often told that I'm very nice looking and I know the boys like me, as they always hang around me.

When I look in the mirror, the big changes are really evident and I like what I see. Yet I struggle with the deep rooted insecurities that I still feel very strongly and lack confidence and self-esteem. That poor ugly girl in the shabby clothes is still lurking deep within me. If only I could make her go away, but it's not easy, when you've been the ugly duckling all your life.

Marie's been going on about friends of hers working in the factory at Hotpoint and earning 8 pounds a week.

She badgers me on a daily basis to go with her and get a job there. I tell her my stepmother wanted me to work there when I left school, but I didn't want to and got the job at Newells in the office. I didn't say I'd been fired, as I was ashamed to admit to it.

Eventually, I give in to Marie and lowering my standards, by being seduced into earning more money. The job in the shoe shop is going nowhere.

One lunchtime, just before Christmas, both Marie and I go to Hotpoint for an interview and both get a job.

Chapter Thirty Three

It was just past 5 o'clock on Christmas Eve, and the manager had already locked the shop door because of the holidays, we closed an hour earlier. We were all ready to leave and just wishing each other a Merry Christmas.

A knock on the glass door interrupts our jovial holiday good wishes. A young man is standing there, holding up his foot and pointing to a hole in the sole of his shoe.

The manager takes pity on him, unlocks the door and lets him in.

Marie and Mrs. Holmes both make a dash for the door, I'm left standing and have to serve the cheeky chap.

The young man is overly charming, saying to the manager, that it's really good of him to let him in, whereupon the manager retreats to the back room and leaves me to serve the customer.

The young guy's handsome looks hadn't gone unnoticed. He was very friendly and likeable.

All the men's shoes were high up on shelves, one side of the shop, where they could only be reached by getting up a ladder.

After being asked to go up umpteen times for yet another pair of shoes, which he tried on, he finally chose the very first pair I showed him.

At first, I didn't realise that every time I climbed the ladder, he got a better view of my legs, than he should have. All the time, he was engaging me in friendly banter.

He spoke with confidence and was very sure of himself. He was a real Romeo and knew exactly how to talk to a girl and charm her.

He told me I had a very interesting accent and wondered where I was from. As I was about to tell him, he stopped me and said, "Wait a minute, let me guess." And so a little guessing game started, on which he eventually gave up and I told him I was from Transylvania.

"Wow!" He said, "I have never met anybody from Dracula Country before. Are all the girls so beautiful from there and did they grow fangs after midnight?"

This had become a standing joke, whenever men found out from where I came from. It had amused me for a while, with remarks like, "I wouldn't mind you sinking your fangs into my neck, Darling." However, the wisecracks were beginning to wear a bit thin.

At the same time, I was rather flattered by the attention this young charmer was awarding me, but now all I wanted to do was go home.

After paying for his shoes, he asked that if he wasn't happy with his purchase, would I change the shoes for him, after Christmas.

I told him that, as long as he didn't wear them, the shop would change them. I asked if you would change them, he said cheekily with a wink.

I told him I wouldn't be there as I was leaving the job that very evening.

Then he wanted to know where I was going to work. I lied and told him I didn't know.

I wore my new dress and shoes with pride that Christmas. All our friends commented on how I'd grown up into a lovely young woman.

I sensed that Mutti didn't like all the compliments I was getting and jealousy was beginning to creep in.

The day after Boxing day, I sat next to Mutti on the bus going to work in the factory. She told me it was the most sensible thing I'd done so far. For her it may have been the best decision, as she was going to be pounds better off each week, getting half of my wages. I knew, for a fact that even Colin, the lodger had paid less for board and lodging than I would be paying.

I was already regretting getting a job at Hotpoint. I didn't feel I'd made the right decision at all and was determined to carry on with my evening classes and French lessons, so I could leave home and become an air hostess, at 18.

I'd arranged to meet Marie at the factory gates just before 7.30. She was already there waiting for me.

We both presented ourselves at the personnel office and were taken to the stator winder department on the second floor of a large brick building.

The whole second floor was a big open area. Several long conveyor belts ran the whole length of the big space. Women and girls were sitting in pairs, one either side of each moving belt.

I was put next to a young woman, called Glynis, who was going to teach me the ropes. Marie sat on the same conveyor belt just a few rows behind me.

The work was difficult, boring, repetitive and enough to drive you round the bend. Very fine coils of wire had to be eased and wheedled through very narrow slots into a slightly larger space, which looked far too small to accommodate the entire coil.

It was extremely hard on the finger and thumb tips. After a very short time, my fingers were red and sore. Most women had band aids wrapped round the end of their digits to stop the skin from splitting.

That evening, when I got home, there was a telegram from Hermannstadt. All it said was "Granddad has passed away."

I was mortified and beside myself with grief. The dearest man I'd known, who'd played such an important part in my childhood years, was gone and I'd never see that dear, beloved face again.

The way I remembered him over the last couple of years, was always with him standing at the railway station, tears running down his cheeks and telling me he didn't think we'd ever see each other this side of heaven. His prediction had come true and I felt sorrow and loss very deeply.

Vati said it was the best thing, as my grandfather had been ill for so long. He conveyed no sadness or grief, as he said this in a matter of fact way. It was his father, after all, didn't he feel some loss or regret at his passing?

I didn't want to be around my parents that evening. I went to my room and let my sorrow and grief engulf me.

After the first week at Hotpoint, my wage is no more than what I earned in the shoe shop and my fingers are cracked and bleeding. Everybody says my fingertips will harden and I'll get quicker and earn more.

Marie has the same problem and is already talking about leaving. We both hate the job and find most of the women working there loud and coarse. Sexual innuendo goes back and forth in the banter between them and the few men, who work on the shop floor.

Marie and I are called snobs and stuck up because we don't join in.

I feel very embarrassed and uncomfortable with the lewd and vulgar language that comes out of most women's mouths.

Glynis says I should ignore all the comments and coarse language. I've never heard people talk like that before and find it very cheap and nasty.

I carry on going to evening classes for typing and French. I enjoy going to the youth club and drama group.

I realise just what a nice bunch of young people, I mix with, so unlike those dreadful women at work, who seem to having nothing on their minds, but sex and vulgarity.

I'm embarrassed to tell my friends that I now work in the factory at Hotpoint. I make a point of telling them it's only for a short while until I'm 18, when I'll become an air hostess.

On Saturday, I usually go to Peterborough with a couple of girl friends. We just hang out at the Expresso Coffee Bar, which is where a lot of young people go.

Alcombury is only a few miles away, where the Americans have an air force base. Peterborough is full of young American G.I.'s. loads of them frequent the coffee bar we go to.

One evening, I meet a young G.I. called Ken. He seems nice enough. At least he doesn't claim to be related to Elvis Presley, like most of the others do, trying to impress the gullible English girls.

He takes me to the cinema a couple of times. He's a quiet guy and doesn't brag about everything back home, the way most other soldiers do.

Ken always brings me a gift when we meet, usually chocolates or nylons. Then one day he gives me a beautifully beaded little clutch bag. I think he's very generous, but find him rather boring, after a while.

One Saturday evening, when I meet Ken, he tells me he's borrowed a car from a mate on the base. We drive out to Alcombury to visit married friends of his, who live in the married quarters. They're a friendly young couple with a small baby.

When we're alone, the young woman tells me, how Ken smitten is with me and that he told them he wants to marry me. I've only known the guy 3 or 4 weeks and definitely don't feel the same way, but I don't say anything.

Everything we have to eat that evening comes out of a tin can or packet. I've watched with fascination, as the food is just heated up and served, making a meal in just minutes. I've never seen anything like it. I find the food very bland and tasteless. There wasn't a fresh vegetable, nor a piece of fruit, served up at the meal.

Later in the evening, Ken says he'll take me home to Whittlesey, but I tell him to drop me at the bus station. I don't know how to do this, but there's only one way. I just announce that I won't be seeing him any more. He begs and pleads with me, tells me he loves me, wants to marry me and take me back to the States.

I feel bad and tell him I'm sorry, but I don't feel the same way, besides I'm still very young. I tell him it's better to call it a day, as I don't wish to lead him on.

He remains in the car, looking sad and dejected, as I rush to get the 10.30 bus back to Whittlesey.

Marie can't stand the job any longer and tells me she's giving in her notice. Her boyfriend and parents don't like her working there after all the things she's told them. She only lasted a few weeks.

I miss her. We've stuck together and gone to the canteen at lunchtime for a bowl of soup. Neither of us have befriended other girls or women.

Now there's only Glynis left. She's quiet and doesn't have much to say. She doesn't get involved in all the antics with the rest of the women and just laughs at their behaviour.

I start going to the canteen with her most days. I could meet Mutti, but there's no way I want to be around her and I'm sure she feels the same way.

Glynis's boyfriend, Peter, meets us in the canteen most days. He works as a mechanic in the garage, servicing and looking after all the trucks.

Peter is in his mid twenties, tall, blond and good looking, very much the Tab Hunter type, whereas Glynis is plain, frumpy and quiet. I can't help but wonder how long she'll be able to keep hold of this gorgeous hunk.

Peter tells me he has a mate, who also works for Hotpoint, driving the big pantechnicons all over England, transporting washing machines and fridges. His mate's away a lot, but next time he's back in Peterborough, he'll bring him into the canteen.

Days later, when Glynis and I walk into the massive canteen and approach the table, where her boyfriend is sitting, I can't believe my eyes. There sitting right next to him, is the charmer I sold the shoes to on Christmas Eve.

I can't help thinking these two are the best looking guys I've seen at Hotpoint.

Peter's friend stands up and extends his hand to shake mine, with a huge smirk on his face. "Well, look who's here," he says. "To think, I went back to the shoe shop looking for you and here you are, you've found me."

"You know each other then?" Says Peter.

"She's the gorgeous bird, I told you about, who sold me shoes at Christmas." He turns to me, "By the way, my name is Pete."

I thought he was kidding about having been back to the shop to find out where I worked and I said so.

"No, seriously, I went back after Christmas, but the miserable old git of a manager wouldn't tell me where you went. But now here you are. You can't escape fate."

I couldn't believe that this handsome guy had gone out of his way to track me down. He asked my name and when I told him he said it was unusual, but very classy.

After lunch, we all went back to work.

Next time, we all meet up in the canteen, Pete walks me back to the building, where I work. He wants to know if I'll go out with him. I tell him no.

When I'm back at my bench, a number of women come over to me, telling me they saw me with Pete Matthews.

"So what?" I ask.

"I'd stay away from him," one of the women says, "He's trouble!"

Another one says, "He's a womaniser and married. You don't want to have anything to do with him."

From what I've learned about some of the women on my floor, a number of them are having it away with somebody or other behind their husband's back. Here they are talking, as though they're whiter than white.

I turn to Glynis and ask if what they're saying is true. She tells me Pete is married, but separated from his wife and so is her Peter, who's living with his mother.

She then says, these women are jealous and would be more than happy to have the attention of either of the two Peters, but they should be so lucky.

That evening at dinner, Mutti says that I've been seen with a certain Pete Matthews, who's got the reputation of being a no good womaniser and married, as well.

I was immediately on the defensive. "He's separated and since when is it a crime to talk to somebody?"

My father just says to be careful and not get involved with the wrong sort of guy.

I'm annoyed and can't believe my stepmother is listening to all the gossip, which is rife in the factory. What business if it of anybody, whom I choose to hang out with?

From time to time, the four of us meet in the canteen for lunch. Every time Pete sees me he pesters me to go out with him. I keep on refusing.

All kinds of people at work, even men, keep telling me to stay away from Pete Matthews, that he's a good for nothing, two timing bastard. I'm beginning to wonder if there's some truth in it.

I ask Glynis time and again, but she maintains it's all jealousy.

As the four of us are sitting in the canteen one day, Mutti comes over and I introduce her to my friends. Pete is very friendly and goes over the top with compliments. She blushes, goes all silly and giggly, like a young girl. I've seen her behave like this several times before, when she likes or fancies a bloke.

That evening Evy tells Vati that she's met this Pete Matthews.

"He's the sort of guy, who thinks he can charm the birds off the trees, but he doesn't fool me," she says.

What a lying two faced bitch, I think. She fawned all over him and enjoyed every minute of it. Her behaviour certainly suggested that she wouldn't have said no to him.

She then tells Vati that she's heard all kinds of stories about this man and they are not good.

I tell my stepmother that it's all a load of gossip and people have nothing better to do. Glynis tells me Pete is 28 years old. That's much too old for me, I'm not even 17 yet. She says age has nothing to do with it and I should go out with him if I liked him. But I still hold out and refuse to go out with Pete.

One Friday lunchtime, when we're all together, Glynis suggests we all go out for a drink after work. I agree to it, as I think there's no harm in that and I'll have Peter and Glynis with me.

We all meet up afterwards, go to the car park, where Peter's car is parked, and pile in. Glynis sits in the front on the bench seat, close to her boyfriend. Pete and I are in the back seat. I sit right in one corner, as far away from Pete, as I can. Every time he inches closer, I tell him to stay where he is. He thinks it's quite funny and says he won't bite me, but being from Transylvania, he'd be more than happy for me to bite him.

The Parson, which is how we often refer to Peter, as it's his surname, drives to a small village pub outside Peterborough.

The two guys refer to each other as Schpeedle, which sounds rather weird to me.

All the way to the pub, I sit quietly in the back, wondering what I've let myself in for. The two in the front seat haven't stopped kissing and canoodling, which makes me feel quite uneasy.

When we get to the pub, I feel relieved, now that I'm not trapped in the back seat any more with Pete.

I've been told that I'm unworldly, naive and gullible in lots of ways. No one has ever explained about the birds and bees. What little I know, Heide has told me and she's two years younger than me. In view of what happened to Annitante, I just don't want to become involved with a man. I used to think kissing could give you a baby, but at least I know that's not true.

We spend a very nice evening in the pub. The chaps have beer and Glynis drinks wine, but all I have is orange juice, as I'm still under age to drink alcohol in public.

I'm starting to relax more and quite like my friends. They're a lot of fun, joking and laughing and ribbing each other. I don't understand the jokes or what they laugh about though. Back in Romania, life was always very serious. People rarely joked and laughed. They all direct some of the fun at me and pull my leg, but I don't react the way they expect me to. They find it funny having to explain every remark they make.

I have to be home by 10 o'clock. On the way to Whittlesey, I still keep my distance from Pete. I tell the Parson to drop me just round the corner from my house, as I don't want my parents to see who I've been with.

As I'm about to get out the car, Pete grabs me and plants a long hard kiss on my lips. I'm caught completely unawares and don't even bother to struggle.

As I'm walking down the road to my house, I can still feel the pressure of Pete's lips on mine and it gives me a warm fuzzy feeling.

As I enter the kitchen, both my parents are sitting at the table. Mutti demands immediately where I've been and who with.

"Nosy parker" I think, "none of your business," but my reply is, "Oh, just some friends."

Disbelieving me, Mutti counters, "You haven't been out with that Pete Matthews, have you?"

"I told you, just some friends!" I said, a little annoyed.

"Anyway, what does it matter to you? Why do you suddenly care?"

Vati gives me a disapproving look and I just walk out of the door and go upstairs.

Chapter Thirty Four

That was the beginning of my entanglement and love affair with Pete. I fell hook, line and sinker for him. He was charming, exciting, didn't give a damn about what anybody said or thought of him and a complete law unto himself.

Pete didn't have a car, so we often went out as a foursome. We all got on very well and had a lot of fun.

Occasionally Pete and I went to the cinema in Peterborough. He always met me in the back of the auditorium. I didn't twig for a long time, the reason for meeting inside was, because he didn't want to pay for me. When it came up in conversation with a couple of girlfriends, that I met him inside the cinema, they both said he was a scoundrel and treated me badly. No decent guy would do that to a girl.

I had no idea of how a boy should behave towards a girl and didn't think much of it. Over a bowl of soup one day in the canteen, Pete said, "How about going to the Smoke?" I'd never heard the expression before and was told it was slang for London.

It didn't take much persuading the rest of us to agree to his plan. We all pooled our money for petrol and there was enough left to go to a jazz club.

When the end of the lunch siren went, we were already in the car and on our way to London.

I'd never heard about jazz, which both guys were mad about and said was the only music worth listening to.

It was late afternoon when the Parson pulled into a parking spot round the back of Oxford Street in the West End of London. We found a café, where we ate sandwiches and drank tea.

Afterwards we walked along Oxford Street looking in all the amazing shops until we came to the Marquee Jazz Club.

I'd never been anywhere like this before. The club wasn't very big and dimly lit, with small tables and chairs, around a small stage. Four or five, so called musicians were making a hell of a racket. The music had no melody and made no sense to me. It sounded as though a bunch of guys just got together and each one doing his own thing and playing a different tune.

The two Peters raved about the music and said it was fantastic. They tapped their feet and bobbed their heads, clapped and whistled, like crazy, at the end of each number. Everybody else in the room was as engrossed, as they were, in this peculiar, so called music.

Even Glynis was enjoying the din, but not quite as much as the chaps.

I was fighting to keep my sanity. All I wanted to do was scream and run out of the place. As the evening went on, I started to worry about getting home late and the trouble I'd be in. What was I going to tell my parents?

Glynis didn't have to account for where she went and how long she stayed out. She was 24 years old.

The evening dragged on and on. The musicians changed, but the music was as bad as ever.

We eventually left at midnight. Nobody cared about my concerns and getting home late. All the way home, the other three raved and talked about the music and the musicians. I was just glad I could still hear, as I was convinced I'd end up totally deaf from the noise in the club.

The Parson dropped me off at the corner of my street after 3 o'clock in the morning. I was practically wetting myself with fear and the anticipation of the terrible trouble I was heading for.

My big concern was Prince. Was he going to bark and wake the whole neighbourhood up, including my parents? Another worry hit me. Would the back door be locked?

To my relief, the door was open and Prince just came out from under the kitchen table, wagging his tail. Thank goodness, my prayers had been heard.

I didn't switch on any lights, but quietly crept up the stairs in the dark, trying to avoid the couple of creaking steps, which over the previous months, I'd got to know well, and was able to avoid.

I went into my bedroom and eased the door shut. Then let out a long sigh of relief, thinking I'd got away without being heard.

I slept in late the following morning, as it was Saturday and no work.

When I eventually got up, my father had long left, as he worked Saturday mornings. When I walked into the kitchen, my stepmother was sitting at the table, reading the paper and smoking. Without looking up she sneered, "I don't suppose there is any point in asking where you were until all hours of the morning."

I spun her some tale. She just looked at me with disdain and went back to reading the paper.

When my father got back from work, I stuck to the same story I'd told Mutti.

He obviously didn't believe a word and just told me to be careful what company I kept, because I could end up in all kinds of trouble.

I felt bad for lying to my father, but at the same time, I felt very angry towards him.

If only he would have let me stay on at school and didn't exclude me from their lives, I wouldn't be working in a factory now and trying to make a life, as best I could for myself. I liked Peter a lot. He was fun to be with and seemed to care for me, which was more than I could say for my father and even less for my stepmother.

Easter that year, Vati rented a car again and they went to Loughborough, to spend Easter with Gerti and Hans.

A couple of days before Easter, I got tonsillitis, which was something that plagued me three or four times a year, soon after my arrival in England.

I was always sick for at least a week or more, with a high temperature, ulcerated throat, feeling pretty bad and confined to bed for a few days.

I was supposed to have gone to Loughborough too, but was far too ill. They went anyway, on Good Friday, which was a holiday, through to Easter Monday and left me to my own devices.

By Easter Sunday, I was so fed up and lonely. None of our friends had called round since my parents left, as they thought we were all in Loughborough.

I found a bottle of rum in the living room sideboard and drank myself into oblivion, to be woken up by Pete standing over me.

He knew before Easter that I was sick and assumed my parents would cancel the trip to Leicestershire. He'd just popped by to see how I was doing.

He said it was completely irresponsible of my parents to leave me on my own, when I was so ill. He looked at the empty rum bottle and asked if it had been full. My slurred response was, "nearly full."

"You'll kill yourself drinking that much alcohol and taking medication at the same time."

I mumbled that I hated alcohol, but just wanted to drown my sorrows. "Anyway I'd be better off dead," I complained miserably, "Nobody cares anyway."

Sitting next to me on the sofa and hugging me, he told me that he cared. That made me feel much better. By the time he left, several hours later, I felt a lot less sorry for myself.

Several weeks later, Pete borrowed the Parson's car one Saturday, for us to go to London together.

Before we left, Parson got me on my own and told me to be careful, as

Pete had plans for me and didn't have my best interests at heart.

I asked him what exactly he meant, as I didn't believe what he was saying.

Apparently, Pete had told him he'd like to get me into a strip club in London, as he thought I'd do well and he would manage me. He reiterated that I should look out for myself and not let him talk me into anything stupid.

With no idea what a stripper was or did, I asked Pete about it on the ride to London. "They're good looking girls with nice figures, who dance on a stage and take their clothes off in front of men," he explained.

"The Parson told me that's what you want me to do."

"Well, you'd make a great stripper," he laughed, "but I was only joking."

In a raised voice, I told him, in no uncertain terms, that there was no way I'd take my clothes off in front of any man, let alone a whole room full, in a million years. I asked him how he could think so little of me and that he wanted me to do such a thing, it was no better than prostitution.

Well he was sorry and of course he didn't want any other men to gawp at me, as he liked me far too much.

The first place we went to in London was a cartoon cinema in Piccadilly Circus. I'd never seen a cartoon film before. Pete said he loved them and always went when he was in London.

The auditorium was very noisy as we entered, with everybody laughing their heads off.

We found seats and sat down. Immediately Peter joined in the crazy commotion. He laughed so much that tears were running down his face.

I looked at the screen and was completely baffled. I couldn't see anything remotely funny in these weird and strange looking caricatures. They ran around, being blown up, run over, fall down mountains and cheated death, time and time again, by the skin of their teeth, just to rise and carry on to their next adventure.

The place was so loud, everybody was in stitches.

I sat next to Pete, with not even a smirk on my face. He thought that it was as hilarious as watching the cartoons, and started to laugh at me.

Afterwards, he tried to explain why these films were so funny, but the irony was lost on me. It took quite a few years for me to understand the English sense of humour and before I started to really appreciate it.

After the cinema, we headed to the Marquee. Going to a jazz club was the main reason for the trip to London.

I dreaded the evening and the terrible noise I would have to endure. To my surprise, it was not as bad as the last time.

In fact, it sounded quite pleasant.

A young woman was singing in a somewhat strange way with a trio backing her. Her voice was quite husky and seductive, but still not the kind of music I was used to.

Throughout my childhood, all I had heard were hymns and church choirs. During the summers in Kerz, German Schlager music at the barn dances.

Mutti and Vati played a lot of German folk music.

When I was on my own at home, I liked listening to pop. Elvis was my favourite singer, I also liked Adam Faith, Pat Boon, Cliff Richard and a number of the other pop singers.

Peter told me they were all rubbish and I shouldn't be listening to any of it. Everybody was always telling me what to do, as though I hadn't got a mind of my own.

All the do's and don'ts. Everybody knows better. I wished, just for once, that people would leave me alone and let me decide for myself, what I liked and didn't like.

When I told Pete that all my friends and young people loved pop, he said they were like sheep and couldn't think for themselves. Most people just followed the trend and had no idea about what was good or bad.

None of what he said really made a lot of sense to me. I knew people who were intelligent, with good jobs and kids at university, who all loved pop and all other kinds of music, which he derided.

On a small dance floor at the Marquee, Pete and I smooched and shuffled around, cheek to cheek, to the music. This was very different from the vigorous dancing I had watched in Kerz, but I quite liked it.

It was getting on for midnight when we left the jazz club. I still worried about getting home late, but at the same time I didn't care too much any more.

The subject of my seeing Pete, which my parents know about is just avoided. They don't ask me much and I don't tell them anything.

Summer holidays are drawing near. My parents are preparing to go to Berlin again. They haven't asked me to join them. I would dearly love to see the city, which has quite a reputation.

I'll be 17, while they're away and staying at home looking after Prince.

Pete and I are seeing each other all the time now. He comes over to the house, quite often, when Mutti and Vati are away. He even stays the night sometimes.

We're both on holiday too. During the days, we go to the Peterborough swimming pool, or sometimes to the Knot Holes.

Pete picks his 5 year old son up from his estranged wife sometimes and brings him along. Richard is a cute little chap, with a cheeky face and a mop of bright red hair. Pete obviously adores him. He has another little boy David, who's 2, but he doesn't say much about him.

The Knot Holes are excavated clay pits, which have been flooded with water and made into lakes, big enough for sailing and boating. They're extremely deep and clear, inhabited by a variety of fish. Reeds grow all round the shores, providing ideal sanctuary for all kinds of water fowl.

Whittlesey is well known for its brick works. On the road to Peterborough, either side, gigantic craters are being excavated. From a double decker bus one can see right down into the bottom of these pits. The buildings and machinery at the base look like toys. Roads wind their way up around these massive holes, bringing the clay up in huge trucks. All around the craters are the brick works, with their huge, wide chimneys reaching into the sky. They belch out tons of stinking smoke and pollution, covering the surrounding brick workers' cottages in a layer of dust. The area is called Kings Dyke. Dozens of lorries, with trailers, leave the works daily, delivering bricks all over the country. The pits, that are in working progress, are a real eye sore on the landscape. They look like terrible cancerous growths invading the surrounding area of the town.

Pete is in his element in the water. He's swam since he was a small child.

Every summer, when he was very young, his parents and their friends and young families, spent the summers camping and living on the banks of the River Nene.

All these young people and their kids, loved the outdoors and the freedom camping gave them.

His Mum and Dad even had a double bed in their tent. Pete had his own little tent, next to theirs, where he slept on his own from a very young age.

Pete tells stories of how his father threw him into the river as a toddler and watched as he struggled to say afloat, only stepping in when he started to go under. He soon got the hang of it and made his way to the shore of the slow flowing and sedate river.

Pete's father was an insurance adjustor with The Royal Insurance Company. They were pretty well off and had a car. He was the only child.

All the men went to work from the camp site every day and left their families enjoying nature and all it had to offer.

When I first met Pete, he asked if I liked swimming. At the time I didn't know he'd been county swimming champion and he was in his element in the water.

Not wanting to appear stupid, I told him I loved it. I didn't want to admit that I'd nearly drowned as a kid and was quite terrified of water. Even getting my face splashed was a big deal to me and sent me into a panic.

At the swimming pool, Pete loved to show off and do all sorts of crazy dives from the high board. He spent all the summers of his youth at the pool with a gang of kids.

At the Knot Holes, he was like a fish, diving deep down and staying under the water so long, that I started worrying.

Near the edge, the water was shallow, where I could paddle or go in up to my waist. Pete ribbed and made fun of me. He reminded me of the time that I told him I could swim.

Actually, I'd never said I could swim, but that I liked swimming. He said it was all the same thing and laughed.

At the pool one day, I told Pete to watch me swim across the shallow end. I was doing breast stroke with my head way out of the water. I felt safe as long as I knew, that I could touch the bottom with my feet. As I got close to the other side of the pool, a kid jumped in and splashed my face. Panic engulfed me. I splattered, coughed and desperately wiped the water from my face.

Pete stood at the edge of the pool, laughing like a drain, telling me that he didn't call that swimming, while I felt a real idiot with swimmers looking on.

One evening after work, Pete took me to meet Daphne and Les, friends of his. They live in a council house and have three young kids.

Les works at one of the engineering companies in Peterborough. He's an addicted gambler, throws all his money away on the horses and dogs. Daphne is left having to try and make ends meet on the little money he gives her.

She does the housework for her mother-in-law, to get a little extra money, so she can put food on the table for her kids.

Daphne is small and thin. She comes across as a suppressed and pathetic creature, but very kind. I feel very sorry for her. Her husband seems a real beer swigging lout.

Pete has known the couple for quite a while from when he worked at Perkins, with Les. He tells me he's often gone round in the evening, when Les has been out gambling and listened to Daphne's troubles.

He'd often lent her a shoulder to cry on and things sometimes got out of hand and things got further than either of them had intended.

Being as naive as I was, I didn't quite understand and had to have a picture drawn. I felt cross and jealous and asked how he could do such a thing and betray a friend.

Pete justified his actions by saying he felt sorry for Daphne and just wanted to comfort her. Les was an idiot anyway.

I asked him if this was still going on between him and Daphne. When he told me it wasn't, I wanted to believe him, but couldn't.

I didn't want to go and see his friends anymore, but always wondered if he was still going and not saying anything.

Pete and I still go out with the Parson and Glynis quite often.

One evening, after dark, we drove to an adjacent field at Hotpoint. The two Peters tell us to stay and wait in the car.

Twenty minutes, or so later, they return carrying something between them that looks heavy, covered by a dark blanket.

When they take the cover off, a fridge is revealed. They manage to get it onto the back seat of the car, laying it on its side, then throwing the blanket over it.

"This isn't what I think it is, is it?" Demands Glynis. She seems very cross. I'm so green, I haven't the foggiest what she means.

"It's okay Glyn," Pete reassures her. "I've got to deliver it to a customer."

"That may well be the case, but what I want to know is how you got it."

She gets out the car, says she wants no part of this and starts walking away. The Parson goes after her and persuades her to get back in the car.

Driving over the town bridge in Peterborough, we get stopped by the police. Glynis is sitting in the front seat, practically having kittens. The Parson is nervously clicking his thumb nail against the top of his front teeth. This is something he tends to do when he feels uneasy and is playing for time.

Pete leans over the covered up fridge, grabs me, pulls me towards him and starts snogging me.

The Parson rolls down his window and starts chatting to the police officer. After a minute or so, he winds the window up, puts the car into gear and pulls away.

"Phew!" He exclaims, with huge relief, "That was close!"

Then both the guys start to laugh. By now I've cottoned on that something is wrong here.

Glynis is absolutely fuming. She shouts, telling the guys they're idiots and not to dare involve her or me in anything like that again.

A few days later, Pete is taken in by the cops and questioned. Afterwards he tells me it's one of the perks of all the lorry drivers, who occasionally flog a fridge or washing machine on the side. They all have arrangements with the store men, who cook the books, then they split the proceeds.

"But that's stealing!" I say indignantly. He tells me that it's not really the same as stealing. "How do you figure that out? To me stealing is stealing."

The stolen fridge is tracked down by the police and Pete is arrested and has to go to court. All the lorry drivers and store men at work are crapping themselves, in case Pete spills the beans to the police about the racket that goes on at Hotpoint.

Pete's found guilty, gets a 2 year suspended sentence and the sack from his job. He's taken the rap for all the other guys at work and not implicated anybody.

Pete's picture and the whole nasty episode is splashed all over the front pages of the local rag, for everybody to see and read about.

Things have gone from bad to worse at home. My father is infuriated, that I'm linked to this thief. He absolutely forbids me to see Pete or have anything further to do with him. He tells me Pete's much too old for me and I need to find somebody of my own age.

That's rich, I think. Vati is 11 years older than my stepmother, so what's the difference? Pete has a hard time finding a new job. Nobody in town will employ him.

Pete's the black sheep of the family. He's a huge disappointment to his parents. His father comes from a long line of respected naval officers.

His maternal grandfather was Mayor of Hereford, a cathedral town in the Midlands. Most of his uncles and aunts are involved in local government. One of his aunts is a magistrate in London.

At the outbreak of the Second World War, Peter was 9. He'd had a very strict upbringing, and, according to him, had felt his father's belt across his backside on more than one occasion. Although he admitted he'd been a real handful as a child and was always getting into some kind of trouble or mischief.

Pete's father joined the Navy when the war broke out and spent the whole six years of the conflict in Cape Town and Durban, South Africa.

He was in charge of the naval fleet down there and also Captain of a frigate.

The war years in the navy and the social life that went with it in South Africa, proved to be the best years Pete's dad had. After the war he almost took his wife and son and emigrated to Rhodesia.

At the onset of the war, Pete was sent to Hereford to spend time with his paternal grandmother.

Peterborough, where his mother remained, was said to be too close to Coventry, which was being bombed and therefore unsafe for a young child.

Two of his cousins, a boy and a girl from Southampton, joined Pete at his elderly grandmother's home, where they felt the children would be safer. They were roughly the same ages.

Pete loved relating stories about the year all three children spent together. They were all very naughty and badly behaved, leading the poor old girl a life of hell. They got up to all kinds of mischief: stealing from shops and throwing missiles onto passers by from the window of the third floor, where they lived. Pete and his cousins were up to no good all the time, Pete being the ring leader.

After a year, the grandmother couldn't take any more and sent them all back to their respective homes.

Pete spent the rest of the war in Peterborough, with his mother. I don't think his mother fared any better than his grandmother at keeping him under control. He more than likely ruled the roost. There were rations for certain foods, but they never went without.

Pete was 15, when his father returned from the war. He'd been King of the castle for 6 years and resented his father coming back and laying down the law. He'd become a real rebel. There was a lot of friction between Pete and his dad, but while he lived at home, he had to toe the line.

His parents had given him the best education available. He'd gone to one of the best grammar schools in Peterborough.

He was a very bright boy, good at sports, but just wanted to be out having a good time. When it came to studying, he simply did what was necessary to get through exams.

His parents wanted him to stay on at school and train for a profession. He had different ideas though. At 16 he left school and got a job in an office, which bored him to tears. He wasted his time there, doing as little as he could get away with.

According to his friends, he was wild, liked having his own way and bending the rules to his own ends.

At 18, Pete had to do his national service. He chose the RAF, against the wishes of his father, who wanted him to follow the family tradition and join the Navy.

Pete found the RAF tough. He did not take well to discipline, being given orders and generally buckling down to routine. He was often in trouble.

He was a county swimming champion, was a brilliant rugby player on the Peterborough Rugby Team.

He decided to train to become a PT instructor in the RAF and came top out of 300 men. He was also a good boxer and exceeded in any sport he took up.

Pete could have had a brilliant career in the RAF, but he hated every minute he had to spend there.

He said his freedom had been taken from him and he hated the restraint. Rather than buckle down and get on with things, he kicked against authority and always looked for ways to buck the system.

After his national service, Pete did a number of menial jobs, mostly labouring, which he found boring and just couldn't settle.

He had the chance to play rugby for a top team in the UK. He threw that chance away as well, because he didn't like the beer swilling, pompous, opinionated bores, who played the game.

He'd been going out and was engaged to one of Peterborough's beauties. Their volatile on and off relationship eventually ended.

Pete wanted to travel, but none of his friends would leave their crummy jobs and go with him. With just a few pounds in his pocket, he chucked his job and went to Paris.

There he hung out on the Left Bank and befriended a slightly older wealthy woman. Pete moved in with her and spent six weeks living the high life in a well to do social group the woman belonged to, then returned to England. He never said why he left Paris.

He then got a job at Perkins, a factory that produced all kinds of engines and machinery. His job was so monotonous and boring, that it almost sent him round the bend.

He met a girl, whom he got pregnant after a short time. He said he went out with her on the rebound, didn't love her or want to marry.

His father told him to face his responsibility for once in his life, do the decent thing and marry the girl.

On his honeymoon in London, he left his bride on their first night, looked up a stripper friend and spent the night with her.

The marriage only lasted three years. He didn't love his wife and wasn't prepared to work at the relationship. He saw a whole string of women and cheated on his wife during the three years they were together. Then he met me.

I was naive and gullible and believed he would change and mend his ways.

Pete was under a lot of pressure from his parents. They wanted him to go back to his wife and give the marriage another try. In order to get them off his back, he agreed to give it another shot.

I was devastated. How will I face my parents and all the 'I told you so's?'

On the way home after seeing Pete for the last time, I stopped at a chemist and bought two bottles of pain killers. When I got home, I went straight up to my room and swallowed the whole contents of the two bottles. "Life's just too shitty and I want out."

I was not even going to leave a note. My parents could figure it all out for themselves. All my hopes and dreams were gone. I'd had enough. There was really nothing more to live for.

I laid down on my bed, fully clothed and pulled a blanket over me. I started to feel drowsy and sleepy. I thought about my Groysie and wondered how she would take the news. Going to sleep and never waking up would be good. At least I would see my Granddad again and I hoped he would forgive me for what I had done.

I said a prayer to God and told him I was terribly unhappy and asked for forgiveness.

I was desperate to go to the loo and started to stumble down the stairs in a dreamy sate. When I got down to the hall, Peter came out of the kitchen. I was a bit too far gone and didn't know what was going on and didn't really care.

Very wobbly on my legs, I blundered along the hall bumping into the wall, as I was trying to make my way to the toilet.

Pete grabbed me and demanded to know what was the matter. I said something incoherent. He left me standing there and bounded up the stairs to my room.

The next minute, he was back down, holding the two empty pill bottles in his hand. Then all hell broke loose.

All I could think over and over was, Oh shit! Oh shit! Oh shit! ....

And then oblivion.

Chapter Thirty Five

When I came to, I was lying in a strange bed. The walls around me were all white and there were lots of beds everywhere. I was very woozy and didn't know where the heck I was. My throat and chest felt sore.

Pete said I was in hospital and I'd had my stomach pumped out. I felt very strange and confused. I just lay there, not knowing what to say. Closing my eyes, I just wanted to go back to sleep.

Pete said my father was at the hospital, but had to leave and catch the last bus to Whittlesey.

Then, Pete leant over, kissed me on the cheek, said to get a good nights rest and he would see me in the morning.

I was so glad I was on my own. I felt very ashamed. I curled up and pulled the blankets over my head, in an effort to shut the world out.

The following morning a police man and woman turned up at my bedside. The cop told me I could be charged with a criminal offence. I told them I hadn't hurt or done anything to anybody. I was shocked when he said that trying to commit suicide was a crime.

I knew it was a crime against God, but not humanity.

The female officer seemed much kinder. She stayed and chatted to me for a while. She said I was so young with my whole life in front of me, and no doubt, a lot to live for. She made me feel pretty bad.

She made me promise I would never try anything like this again, then told me they wouldn't press charges.

Neither my father or stepmother came to see me in the two days I spent in hospital. No doubt they were disgusted with me.

Pete borrowed the Parson's car and took me home.

On the drive back to Whittlesey, I was very upset and quiet, knowing this was the last time I'd see Pete.

Then he told me he'd spent a couple of nights with his ex wife and kids. "It'll never work," he says. "I don't love her and can't bring myself to touch her. What kind of a marriage would that be for her or me? It really is over between us."

Pete stayed at the house until my father came home.

My father thanked Pete for giving me a lift, then told him he was not welcome in his house. Pete told him he was sorry to hear that and left.

What happened during the last three days, was never mentioned in our house again. They didn't try and talk me out of seeing Pete, but they made it clear that I was never to bring him home. What I did outside was my business.

My relationship with my parents got even crappier, which I didn't think was possible. They never spoke to me, unless they had to. I felt like a stranger in their home.

Pete's parents had practically disowned him too. His father didn't want him to show his face round their house. His mother was a real snob and a social climber and wanted nothing to do with him either, nor his 'bloody foreign tart'.

Pete still had no job. The little money he got from social security didn't go very far. He had no home and spent nights sleeping on friends' sofas.

Pete Sandy, an old mate of his, another good for nothing layabout and out of work, is where Pete spent most nights. He had a wife and four kids. They had to be the poorest family I had met since I came to England. They lived in a council house and were on social security.

The wife was a nice woman, well spoken and was always mending and darning clothes for the children when I went round there.

All four children are of school age and seemed very well disciplined. The father merely had to glance their way and they obeyed him immediately.

I got the sense that Pete and his friend were up to no good and I told Pete what I thought. He assured me that I was wrong.

Pete said he could come to my house, sneak in after my parents have gone to bed and sleep with me in my room. I told him it was a crazy idea and he was completely nuts.

As usual, his persuasive charm won me over and I agreed to his plan.

We both caught the last bus at 10.30, back to Whittlesey, by which time my parents were in bed and the house was in darkness.

Prince knew Pete, so he didn't bark as we sneaked in the back door and up the stairs into my room. I shut the door quietly and locked it.

We didn't do much sleeping during the night and when my father knocked on my door in the morning, I almost jumped out of my skin.

I had no idea if my parents suspected anything, but my father demanded I open the door, as he wanted to come in and talk to me.

Pete grabbed his belongings and crept into the deep, built in cupboard, hiding behind my hanging clothes.

After unlocking and opening the door, yawning, stretching and looking very sleepy, Vati came into the room, looked around and then walked out again.

"So what was it you wanted to talk to me about?" I asked.

Oh, it'll keep till this evening," he replies, "I haven't got time now."

Hc must have thought I was really stupid and didn't know what he was up to. Of course, I must have needed my head examining, letting Pete spend the night with me, with my parents sleeping in the next room.

Pete was very determined. When he wanted something he was like a dog with a bone, wouldn't be told no. He pushed and pushed until he got what he wanted. I had never ever known anybody quite like him, so persistent and selfish.

I told Pete I couldn't do this anymore, I was too afraid that if my parents found out, they would kick me out and then where would I go.

One morning, after Pete had spent the night at my house, he talked me in to staying at home for the day. We lazed about in bed all morning. Round noon, I got up to make us something to eat.

Pete was in the kitchen with me, just in his underpants. He was using my father's electric razor, which he had plugged into the ceiling light, after having removed the light bulb. Outside, it was pouring with rain. I couldn't believe it, my father just walked past the kitchen window.

Both Pete and I panicked. He dashed into the hall. I heard him open the front door, then closed it, just as my father entered the kitchen through the back door. I hadn't noticed that he had left the razor hanging from the light in the middle of the kitchen.

Oh, shit!

My father walked straight through the kitchen into the hall, opened the front door and there, standing pressed flat against the wall, trying to keep out of the rain, was Pete, in his underpants.

In a calm and collected way, Vati said, "You'd better come in Pete or you'll catch a cold." Feeling completely embarrassed, I ran up to my bedroom to get dressed and get Pete's clothes. I just wanted to run out the house without facing the consequences.

When I walked back in the kitchen, both Pete and my father are standing looking at each other.

Vati looked cross and Pete had a smirk on his face.

"Get dressed!" My father ordered Pete, "and then get out of my house."

I left with Pete, but didn't know if I would get kicked out too. But the incident was not mentioned again by my father and I still had a roof over my head.

My parents didn't have a telephone. I used the red public phone box just round the corner in the next street.

Each evening, after work, I went at a prearranged time to the phone box, where Pete called me and we then made our arrangements. If the phone was occupied, he called until he could get through.

Pete had a mean streak and didn't like spending his money. He knew a way how to use the public phones without paying. He taught me how to do this, by tapping the receiver bar on the phone rapidly with just a short gap between the area code and the number.

It took me a little while to get it, but after some practice I got it off to a fine art and bingo, I didn't pay for calls any more.

On the odd occasion, when Pete has nowhere to sleep, he goes to the railway siding at the Peterborough Railway Station and sleeps in a train carriage.

One night, he must have slept very soundly. When he woke up one, he found he was on a train heading up north. After that, no more sleeping in carriages.

Pete starts hanging out at the dog track with a guy called John Beart, but better known as the Baron.

Pete's not a gambler. He's much too mean to part with his money and yet he spends quite a lot of time with the Baron.

Pete takes me to the dog track one evening to meet this guy. He's a charming, amiable character, with a twinkle in his eye, knows how to treat a woman and make her feel special and is pretty much from the same mould as Pete, and is around 30 years of age.

Later that evening, as Pete and I walk to the bus stop, I ask Peter why his mate is called the Baron.

He tells me he got the nickname in jail, where he bought and sold snout, slang for tobacco. Hence the name, Tobacco Baron.

I'm not happy at all about Peter mixing with this geezer. I'm worried they'll do things that will get him into trouble with the law.

Pete thrives on excitement and living on the edge. It's his wild, carefree ways that I'm really attracted to, after the suppressed and dull life, I've had, but I'm terrified he'll get himself into trouble and end up in prison.

The Baron is a very bad influence on him. Pete doesn't need any encouragement to do things he shouldn't and get into trouble.

Occasionally the Parson lends Pete his car for a few hours. We drive out into the countryside and spend a couple of hours under a tree or bushes, well away from anywhere. If the weather is bad, we stay in the back seat of the car.

When we're on our own, Pete thinks of nothing else but sex. He'd make love anywhere at any given time. He's very pushy and insistent and drives me nuts. I always tell him he's a sex maniac, but he just laughs and tells me it's all my fault, that he finds me irresistible. He doesn't have an ounce of self control.

When we're on the top of a double decker bus, he always insists on sitting in the back row, if it's empty. He becomes very amorous and I practically have to fight him off.

I find everything being about sex with him very wearing. I'd be just as happy to just cuddle, kiss and chat.

He's nothing like the other three boys I've had dates with. None of them ever pushed or demanded more than necking. He reminds me of the wild stone age men who dragged their women behind a bush by their hair, to get their way with them.

My other worry was always the possibility of getting pregnant. When I asked my friends, who were in relationships, how they coped with that, they told me their boyfriends used condoms.

Pete just laughed and said that would spoil his whole enjoyment and completely refused to use anything.

One day Pete met me after work in a two seater Bedford Van. When I asked who it belonged to he told me it was his.

Immediately alarm bells went off in my head.

He told me he'd bought it very cheaply with money he'd borrowed from a friend. I didn't believe him and never found out who this friend was. I was sure his new friend had something to do with this and was worried and unhappy about it.

The Baron and Pete became almost inseparable. They were both out of work, with lots of time on their hands, which was not good.

I get the feeling Pete has no intention of finding a job. He's enjoying his freedom and being a lay-about too much.

Sandy's wife has sewn small curtains for the back of Pete's van windows and behind the front seats. He papers the ceiling of his motor with dark blue paper covered in light yellow stars. A blow up air bed finishes his little love nest.

When he can't find anywhere to kip down for the night, he sleeps in his van. He's verging on being a down and out, but seems to be getting by.

Sometimes I think, what am I doing with this crazy guy? But I'm nuts about him and put up with all his weird ways.

One Saturday afternoon, Pete and I drive into the country. We drive down a deserted lane and park on the edge of a field.

We're both in the back, completely starkers, with the curtains drawn, having fun. Suddenly the back door flies open and a copper is standing there, getting an eye full and grinning from ear to ear. I immediately pull my knees up and cover my breasts, with my arms. I don't know where to look with embarrassment.

The bobby asked our names. He wanted to know how old I was. He wrote everything onto a pad and told us if the information was incorrect, we'd hear from him. Then he left. Pete said there was nothing the cop could do. I was over the legal age of consent. I worried about that business for weeks afterwards, but never heard another word from the police.

Pete had very little, or no respect, for the police or authority in general. I, on the other hand, held these people in complete awe. I was terrified and didn't want to have anything to do with them.

My fears stemmed back to Romania, where the police and authorities had absolute control and could do anything they liked. They could take you away and lock you up at any time without reason.

One evening, while we're out for a drive, Pete parks the van right on the outskirts of a small village. He tells me he has to see a man and I'm to wait in the van.

Minutes later, he comes running down the road, gets in the driver's seat and dumps a wooden drawer on my lap. He starts the engine and drives away like a bat out of hell.

The divided drawer has a few notes and some coins in it. I ask him where he got the drawer. It looks like it came out of a till.

"From a petrol Station," he replies.

A lot of the petrol stations in the countryside are in front of a workshop or house. When a car pulls up to the pumps, it drives over a wire, which sets off a bell, in the building behind. The owner will then come out and serve the customer.

There's always a small hut by the pumps where the owner keeps the till. When the door to the hut is opened, a bell also rings. A lot of these people are so trusting they leave the door unlocked.

I can't believe Pete has just brazenly robbed a petrol station. I'm absolutely terrified. The narrow country lanes are deserted and the police can easily catch us.

Pete orders me to take the notes and coins out the drawer. He shoves the money in his pocket, then opens the window and hurls the drawer over a hedge into a field.

"There, they'll never get us now," he says with confidence. "Anyway, if we're stopped, they'll never suspect a bloke who has his girlfriend with him. It's the perfect cover."

I sit there numb. I can't believe what he's just done and using me as an alibi. I tell him if he wants to lead a life of crime, that's his business, but to leave me out of it.

I ask him how he can do such a thing and not feel bad about it.

"Oh! I'd only steal from people who have insurance. Businesses are all insured and they'll claim the money back."

It all sounds very callous and flippant. "It's stealing," I tell him, "No matter how you look at it." I tell him that if he really tried, I was sure he'd get a job somewhere. "Jobs are for mugs," he counters.

It scares me. I don't wish to know what he gets up to all day. I know he's with the Baron a lot. Pete always seems to be on a high of late and has money in his pocket. He gets a kick from doing risky things. I'm sure he's breaking the law on a daily basis and doesn't give a damn.

I wish he was responsible and normal, like most other men. I love him though and am drawn to all his crazy ways. Life's never dull with him around, never knowing what to expect next. Pete being caught by the police, the longer this goes on, is becoming a real possibility. It worries the day lights out of me.

It's spring 1961. Pete has been living his life on the edge for months now. He thinks it's all a big laugh.

We've arranged to meet outside the Peterborough Cinema. I've been waiting a while. It's not unusual for Pete to be late. His motto is, "Why wait for somebody, if they can wait for you?"

Half an hour goes by and he still doesn't appear. Uneasiness sets in. I wait another half hour and still no sign of him. The feeling that something terrible is wrong comes over me.

I walk to the dog track to find the Baron. He's known by everybody there, but no one has seen him.

Then I go to the coffee bar, where we sometimes meet. No sign of him there either. Nobody seems to have seen him.

A bad feeling engulfs me and I've got no doubt that something bad has happened. I finally give up and go home.

The following evening after work, I go to the phone box round the corner from my house at the prearranged time he usually calls me, but the phone remains silent. There's no other way for me to get in touch with him. I just have to sit tight and see what happens. It's now Saturday morning. I haven't heard from Pete for two days.

Vati's at work. I'm sitting at the kitchen table having toast and tea. Mutti walks in, throws the local newspaper in front of me and walks out of the room, without a word.

Pete and the Baron's mug shots stare up at me from the paper, with the headline in big letters, which I don't remember.

I read the article below their pictures. Sure enough, the police have apprehended them after they broke into a shop, in a small place, a few miles from Peterborough and tried to spring a safe.

I run to the loo and bring up my breakfast. This is serious. Up to now it's all been petty stuff, but trying to bust a safe is a bad offence. He'll get time, that's for sure.

The Baron has already served a couple of years, for what, I don't know and have never asked.

After spending the night in the police cells and having been in front of the magistrate, they've both got bail and await trial at the end of June.

I carry on sitting at the table, feeling sick to my stomach, but at the same time, I feel relieved that Pete's life of crime, has come to an end. God only knows where it would have lead to, had they not been caught now.

My stepmother avoided me all morning and didn't say a word. The anticipation of what my father would do and say, really worried me.

When he came home from work, I was in my room. He called up the stairs and told me to come down.

When I walked into the kitchen, he was standing waiting for me. I couldn't meet his eyes and stood looking at the floor.

"I told you this would end in tears. Didn't I warn you about this lout and staying away from him? Now you can deal with the consequences and the shame. I've washed my hands of you."

I thought he had done that a long time ago. If he'd been there for me, this would never have happened.

Still not looking at my father, I didn't utter a word in Pete's, or my, defence. I knew I was completely on my own now.

Later that day, I went to Peter Sandy's, where I found Pete. I was pleased to see him and glad he wasn't hurt.

The Baron had gone through a plate glass window, trying to escape, and gashed his leg very deeply and had to have stitches.

Pete promised he'd go straight from now on and I foolishly believed him.

When I asked what he thought would happen at the trial, he told me he was pretty sure he'd get time, as he already had a suspended sentence.

After meeting me out of work one day, Pete tells me he wants me to meet a friend of his. He's been friends with Judy since his early teens.

Judy has recently returned from America, where she went, at 19, to marry her G.I. sweetheart. Her marriage was going through a rough patch, due to financial problems, so she returned to the UK with her two young daughters, to live with her mum and dad in their council house for a while, until things got better.

Judy was 27, nine years my senior. She was very slim, attractive, elegantly dressed and well groomed. She was a beautician with Elizabeth Arden and trained in the States. Judy worked on the Arden counter at Glasscs, the smart upmarket department store in town. I thought of her and her job as very glamorous.

Her two girls were gorgeous.

Candy, the five year old, was tall with long thick blonde hair and very pretty. Her strong American accent was cute.

Lisa was three. She was a much frailer looking child, with long fair hair and a very delicate, pretty little face.

They were both very nice and polite children.

Judy's parents were around sixty years old. Her father worked at Brotherhoods, one of the engineering firms in Peterborough.

Pete and I spent the evening with the family. I enjoyed their company and was made to feel comfortable and at home in their midst.

Pete felt better about going to prison and leaving me with a trusted friend, who'd be there for me if I needed somebody.

The Baron, Pete and I drove to Skegness one Saturday, a big seaside resort on the east coast. I've not been to the sea since my trip with Fred to Hunstanton, which is a little further up the coast from Skegness. The only other places I've been since arriving in England is Loughborough and London.

As we drive into Skegness, Pete notices posters all over the place, advertising a beauty contest taking place that very day. He wants me to enter the competition.

"No way!" I tell him, "I'm not going to parade in front of a load of people in my swimsuit." Pete drives to the pool anyway, to suss out the competition, he says.

He reckons I'd win if I entered. The Baron says I'd definitely win. I tell them not to waste their breath, I won't do it.

The pair of them keep badgering me and I eventually relent. I register, then go into the changing rooms and change into my swimsuit.

A middle aged woman writes down my name, measures my height and size and gives me a small square with a number on, which I have to carry.

While standing on my own, waiting for the competition to start, I look around at all the other girls.

They all stand in groups chatting. I get the feeling they must know each other. I've been told these girls go from place to place, entering beauty contests.

All the other competitors seem older than me. I'm not yet 18 and feel intimidated and unsure of myself. Oh, why was I stupid enough to agree to parade in front of all those people sitting on the pool deck?

Most of the other girls seem to be bottle blondes with permed hair, make up plastered on and long false eye lashes.

My hair is straight, hanging halfway down my back. I wear almost no make up. Pete says he prefers my natural beauty, without all the stuff plastered on my face.

There are at least 20 girls, waiting for the parade. The winner will represent East Anglia in the southern counties.

I'm extremely nervous and close to walking out and forgetting all about this whole thing. Too late. We're called out of the changing room and have to parade round the swimming pool.

We all stop in a line and then have to go in front of the judges panel, one at a time, and then return to the line up.

Spectators are sitting on benches either side of the pool, clapping and shouting as each girl parades in front of the judges.

Pete and the Baron's whistles can be heard above all the clapping and shouts as I walk up.

I've never done anything like this before. My gait and demeanour must give away how nervous I am.

After everybody has been individually presented to the panel of judges, it's round the pool once more and, thank goodness, back into the changing rooms.

I go to get changed. The woman in charge says, "No darling, you have to wait until they decide the winners and runners up."

"I won't get anywhere," I tell her.

"Oh, don't be too hasty my old duck, you're lovely."

The third runner up is called, who's a pretty blonde in a low cut swimsuit and very high heels.

I'm just standing wishing it was all over, when the next number is called.

"That's you," says one of the girls, to me. I'm not even aware what my number is.

As I walk out onto the pool side, Pete and the Baron whistle and shout like crazy. I could crawl away with embarrassment. I go and stand on the three tier podium. A man comes over, puts a sash over my head and across one shoulder, shakes my hand, hands me an envelope and kisses me on both cheeks.

The winner is a platinum blonde with a big hairdo and huge boobs. When she comes out on the pool side, she waves ecstatically at the crowd and her smile reaches from ear to ear.

Back in the changing room, a few of the girls congratulate me. Most of them are all over the winner. I think they behave like a bunch of little girls.

Relieved and happy that the circus is finally over, I quickly get dressed and go out to meet Pete and the Baron.

I open the envelope and find a 5 pound note inside. Not bad, almost a week's wages. We all go to a small restaurant for lunch and I pay the bill.

Afterwards, we walk along the promenade in the sunshine and wander through a few of the seafront shops.

When we get back to Pete's van, the Baron takes a small china figurine from under his shirt and gives it to me.

I know he's nicked it and tell him I don't want it. I'm very cross and tell him I'll never go anywhere with him again. He's an embarrassment and can't resist taking things that don't belong to him. He tells me I'm even more gorgeous when I'm cross.

It's getting close to the court case.

I've missed my period at the beginning of the month. A girlfriend tells me it could be all the upset I've had lately. I hope she's right.

When I voice my worst suspicion to Pete, all he comes back with jokingly is that it would for sure be a beautiful baby.

I'm beginning to worry about it. I've never been late. All the bad memories of my aunt and what she went through, when she got pregnant, come rushing back.

It'll be the last straw with my parents and I'm sure they'll kick me out. What on earth will I do and where will I go?

I'm thankful that my grandparents aren't around to see where I've ended up. It would hurt and disappoint them so much and I couldn't bear that.

The end of June is almost here and with it Pete's court case. He's told me he doesn't want me to go and watch the proceedings. It would be too upsetting and he'd rather I wasn't present.

We say our goodbyes the evening before. He tells me he'll write as soon as he can. I still haven't got my period and feel so miserable and forlorn.

Pete's found guilty and given fifteen months, with one third remission, for good behaviour. Neither Mutti or Vati mention the court case or any of the write ups in the local papers.

I hadn't been wrong to think Pete had been up to no good for months. At the trial, the Baron and he had 120 other cases taken into consideration.

I was shocked.

Vati must be thrilled that Pete is finally behind bars. He must feel pretty confident, with Pete banged up for the next 10 months, I'll forget him, find somebody new and get on with my life.

The relationship between my parents and me has not improved one iota. I sit on my own most evenings in my room. Occasionally, I go to the cinema with a girlfriend. On Fridays, I usually go to Judy's straight after work and spend the evening with her and her family. I haven't been attending evening classes or French lessons for a year. I got a certificate for my speed typing and, since I'd given up on becoming an air hostess, after I met Pete, I stopped going to French lessons too.

Going to the drama group and youth club had also fizzled out.

Mutti's going to Berlin, mid July, with her cousin Gerti. Vati says he's got a lot of tailoring work, so will forgo his holiday and catch up with his work.

I've missed my second period now and am becoming really desperate. I feel so alone, with no one to turn to. The only option is to see my GP.

After the examination, he confirms my worst fears. I'm over two months pregnant. I sit in the surgery, crying my eyes out. I tell the doctor I don't know what to do.

After he calms me down, he says he can help me.

The doctor makes an appointment for me to see him, a couple of days after Mutti has gone to Berlin.

It's a Monday. I go to the surgery straight from work. I sit in the waiting room until every patient and the nurse have left.

I know what the doctor is about to do, is against the law, and I'm forever grateful to him. If found out, he would lose his license.

After carrying out the necessary procedure, the doctor tells me that I will miscarry in the next 12 hours or so.

He gives me his home phone number in case something goes wrong. I can't thank him enough and then go home.

My father and I pass each other like strangers in the house, with very little to say to one another.

I go to bed early and start to wait, not having the faintest idea what's in store for me. Naively, I think I'm just going to get my period in the next few hours and all will be well.

I wake up about 2 o'clock at night with the most terrible stomach cramps. The toilet is downstairs and I go down and up several times during the night.

Terrified out of my wits, I wonder what to do if things get worse and something terrible happens. We don't have a phone. I'll have to go to the public phone box. What if I can't make it there and have to ask my father for help? That's the last thing I want.

The whole scenario is just too terrible to imagine.

Vati comes out of his room and asks why I'm up and down the stairs all night. I tell him I have a tummy bug, not to worry and go back to bed.

He doesn't seem at all bothered, goes back in his room and shuts the door. I go back to my room and lock the door.

The pain gets more intense and comes more often. I've no idea what's happening to my body. When the pain comes it feels like my gut's being ripped out of me. I sit on the bed, then I pace the floor. I lie down to try and rest. I'm exhausted.

This has been going on for about two hours now and just getting worse. Oh, God, when will it end?

The time between the pain is getting closer and closer. It's becoming excruciating and unbearable. I want to scream and shout, but have to bite back and swallow the deadly pain, gripping my whole being.

I'm on my hands and knees. My lower body's burning up with pain.

Suddenly, blood starts to gush from below. The lower part of my nightie is saturated and the rug on the floor is covered in a congealed mass of blood. I remain on all fours and the blood keeps flowing.

The pain has eased at last. What a relief!

When the blood flow starts to ease off, I get my sanitary belt and put on a pad. I'm in a hell of a mess and so is the rug and the floor.

Thank heavens Mutti's not here.

I feel so weak. All I want to do is crawl into bed and go to sleep, but I have to clean up this mess.

It's already 5 o'clock and quite light outside. Vati will be up in a while. I really must get on with it and clean up before he finds me and the mess.

I go downstairs quietly, fill up a bucket with water and liquid soap in the kitchen, grab some old newspapers and old rags and head back upstairs and lock my door.

The mess on the floor is making me feel sick. I look at the congealed lumps of blood and know there's a baby in there somewhere. I feel very bad and upset.

I scoop up the mess on the rug up with my hands and put it on newspaper, then wrap it all up tightly.

The rug is badly stained. With the scrubbing brush and soapy water, I work on the stain. I'm so dog tired and weak, sweat is pouring off my face and body.

After the third bucket of clean water, the rug is as clean as I think

I'll get it. Luckily it's patterned with quite a lot of rust, so the stain is not too obvious.

I take off my nightie, drop it in the bucket, then take it down to the kitchen with the paper parcel.

I put the newspaper parcel in the stove that heats the water and set it alight. I shove in a load more newspaper to make sure everything is burnt. I rinse out my nightie and leave it in the bucket to wash later. I haven't got the strength to do anymore.

I'm so relieved to have survived the terrible ordeal. I really thought, at one stage, that I was going to die.

The minute I hit the sack, I'm out like a light.

At 6 o'clock my father knocks on the door and says it's time to get up.

I've only had about an hour's sleep, but I get up anyway. My mind is like a fog and I'm not thinking straight at all and don't even consider staying at home and sleeping.

When I walk in the kitchen, Vati says that I look like death warmed up. I tell him that I've been throwing up all night, but I'm okay and will go to work.

I don't know how I managed to get to the bus that morning, let alone to work. By midday, I'm almost falling over and decide to go home, where I go straight to bed and sleep practically twice around the clock.

There are only three more days before the factory shuts for the holidays. Mutti's finished work a week early, as she's decided to spend three weeks in Berlin this year.

Since Pete was arrested and gone to prison, the women at work have been giving me a rough time. I still sit next to Glynis, which is okay, but I'm not even remotely friendly with anybody else there.

Some of the women are okay to my face, but slag me off behind my back and call me all sorts of choice names.

I see all the accusing looks and feel like I've committed a crime and been convicted for it. These people remind me of the mob that turned up for public executions, shouting obscenities and throwing rotten stuff at the prisoners, knowing full well they could be next in line for the chop.

This rabble are the very ones, who wouldn't turn down or be averse to buying something that had fallen off the back of a lorry. Most of them were a bunch of hypocrites. I'd seen plenty going on, while I worked there.

Married men and women getting up to all kinds of things they shouldn't, but that was all right as long as you weren't found out.

I just wanted to get away from this place and have some anonymity.

At lunchtime I went to the office and handed in my notice, which felt really good.

I knew Mutti wouldn't be pleased. I'd never managed to earn 8 pounds a week, but usually went home with 6 pounds in my pay packet, half of which, she got. She'd done all right in the last 19 months from me, I'd certainly paid my fair share.

The next week, I went to the labour exchange in Peterborough to find a new job.

The idea of becoming an air hostess still appealed to me, although Pete had managed pretty well to talk me out of it.

He told me London wasn't a safe place to be on my own. He said I'd soon forget him if I went away and he didn't want to lose me. At the time, I thought he cared and was genuinely concerned about me, not realising he said all these things for his own selfish reasons.

I was now very lonely. At home we went our separate ways. How could things have gone so terribly wrong?

All the wonderful pictures my aunts had painted back home about the life awaiting me in England, had turned to dust.

My father had obviously not considered the responsibility my arrival would mean. He never brought up a child and must have thought that, after school, they would be independent.

He was never there for me to guide and point me in the right direction.

When I arrived at the age of 14, I was very naive and immature in many ways. I had so much growing up to do and needed to learn all about my new surroundings, ways of life and how to cope with things.

My parents had no idea how to guide and show me the way. Letting me stay on at school would have achieved all that, helped me mature and lead me in the right direction.

It was all too late. I just had to get on and make the best of my life.

At 18 and with no qualifications, apart from typing, there weren't many jobs for me out there. The woman at the job centre told me that being a cashier in a butcher's shop, was my best option.

It was going to be hard earning just 2 pounds a week again, which meant 1 pound for my stepmother, 12 shillings for the bus and the grand total of 8 shillings left for me.

I'd got into the bad habit of smoking. Everybody smoked. In fact my first cigarette was offered to me by my own father, at a small gathering of their friends at a wedding, a few months previously.

A pack of 20 cigarettes was 2 shillings, they lasted me all week, just having the occasional one in the evening or round Judy's.

During the two weeks' summer holiday, I biked to the river most days, just to get out of my father's way at home.

I very rarely visited Uschi and Bruno or Fred and Margaret. I felt ashamed about being connected with Pete. I didn't know what they thought about the whole business and they were my parents' friends, when all was said and done.

A lot of the young people, I'd been mixing with at the youth club and drama group, were often at the river.

Most of them were now at university, including my friend, Anne. Some had finished education and were in good jobs. I seemed to be the only one with no education or goal in life. I felt very sad and disappointed at the way things had turned out for me.

Chapter Thirty Six

Three weeks had passed. There had been no news at all from Pete. Perhaps he'd decided not to keep in touch and let everything drift and dwindle. I thought at least he could let me know if that was the case.

Judy's house was my refuge once a week. I felt safe and comfortable with her and her family. She was the only person I could confide in. When I told her Pete hadn't been in touch and I thought he'd given up on me, she reassured me that wasn't so. She was pretty sure there was a good reason for him not writing.

Judy said he'd told her time and time again that he loved me and was nuts about me. At the end of an evening at her house, I always felt better and went home happier.

Chapter Thirty Seven

Judy's older sister and brother-in-law also lived with her parents. They'd been there for a number of years, ever since they got married, while saving their money to buy a house.

Jack and Mary were just about to move into their brand new bungalow in a new and very upmarket suburb of Peterborough.

Judy asked if I'd like to go and see Mary and Jack's new house the following Sunday. I was more than happy, as the alternative was being at home moping.

Jack picked Judy, the girls and me up from the house in his VW Beetle and took us to Orton Longueville, where their new home was.

The 2 bedroom place was like a show home, furnished very tastefully in the latest G.Plan furniture throughout.

The kitchen and bathroom were installed with all the latest mod cons.

Judy said all the houses in America were like that. I'd never seen anything as modern and lovely.

The garden was all landscaped with lawns, shrubs and flowerbeds. It was a real dream home.

As we were all sitting having a cup of tea, the phone rang. Mary answered it. She seemed surprised and listened intently, then said, "Where are you Pete?"

My ears pricked up, at the mention of the name. Pete was a very common name, so I thought nothing more of it.

Then Mary says, "Yes, she's right here," and hands me the phone.

It's so good to hear Pete's voice the other end, I can hardly believe it.

"Ursy," which is his nickname for me, "I've been beside myself. Why haven't you answered my letters?"

"What letters?" I say, "There's been no letters and I've been worried sick." I ask where he sent them and when he tells me to my house, I know exactly what's happened.

My parents have obviously intercepted the mail and kept Pete's letters from me.

In future he'll send all the mail to Judy's house, where I can pick it up every week. The prisoners are only allowed to send one letter a week and have one visit a month.

He's already sent one visiting order, which I haven't received, but he'll go and explain to the head screw what happened and hopes they'll issue a new one for him.

He tells me how much he loves me, thinks about me all the time and can't bear the thought of losing me.

I'm so happy, I want to dance with joy.

Mary and Jack had paid for the phone at Judy's house, so when they moved they took the number with them.

It was such a coincidence that I was there when Pete called. It was the only time I ever went to their house and that was the only phone number Pete knew.

My reaction was to confront my parents about the letter. But why give them the satisfaction and letting them know how hurt I was?

The best thing was to let it be. Let them believe that he stopped writing, which would, perhaps, make life a little easier for me.

I was very wrong in thinking I'd get away from Hotpoint and all the people who knew Pete and my connection to him.

Everywhere I went, people knew Pete Matthews, or about him. He'd been very active in all kinds of ways during his youth and twenties and had had many different jobs. After Pete's latest escapades, nobody had a good word for him.

The manager of the butcher's shop lived in Whittlesey. One of the young lads in the shop, also from Whittlesey, got a lift to and from work with the boss. They suggested I join them and instead of paying 12 shillings in fares, it would only cost me 10 and I was 2 bob better off.

This worked well for a few weeks. The manager was a man in his 40's with a wife and young kids.

One evening after work, the young chap said he was staying in Peterborough to meet a friend.

When the boss took the long road out of town, which went by the river, I asked why he was going that way.

He told me there were road works on the main road to Whittlesey, which caused long hold ups.

I didn't give his explanation another thought.

The back road to Whittlesey was rarely used by motorists.

Halfway along the dirt road, with the river on the right and fields as far as the eye could see on the left, the manager pulled the car off the road into a field.

I ask him what's wrong and why he's stopped.

With a big smirk on his face, he turns to me in his seat, "Come on now," he says, "you're not stupid, lets have a bit of fun!" And he grabs my upper arms.

I tell him to get off. He grabs me harder and starts pulling me towards him. I try to get his hands off me, but he's very strong.

He tells me to stop struggling, otherwise he'll hurt me.

Screaming and shouting, I tell him to let go. I'm terrified.

He shouts back at me, telling me not to play so hard to get. After all I'm only a jailbird's bit of skirt on the side, no better than a whore or tart.

I pull and tug, but can't free myself from the mans grasp. He leans over, opens my car door and pushes me out, then leaps on top of me, pinning me to the ground.

We're by the side of the car, hidden from the road. Even if a car comes by, we won't be seen.

I scream, kick, bite and do everything in my power to free myself from his grip. It feels like I'm fighting for my life.

Struggling like a wild thing, trying to keep this monster off me, I manage to kick him in the groin with my knee.

Swearing, cursing and writhing in agony, he releases his hold on me to clutch at his privates.

I manage to get out from under the brute. I'm up and running like crazy along the road, looking up and down, but there's no car or human in sight.

Back at the car, that murderous swine's getting back into the driver's seat. I've got to get out of here, but how? I run as fast as my legs will carry me, but he'll catch me up in no time at all.

I know this stretch of road from the times I've spent at the river with friends. There's a place, very close, where the water only comes up to my waist in the middle of the river.

With my shoes already in my hands, so I could run quicker, I wade into the water, as I'm pulling my dress over my head.

The bastard has pulled the car up onto the bank where I'm crossing. He starts shouting and telling me to come back, that he won't touch me.

"Like hell he won't," I'm thinking.

Hoping he won't follow me in the water, I keep going. The water's getting deeper and is reaching my armpits now. If it gets any deeper, I know I'll panic and then I'll be in real trouble.

Luck is on my side. A little over halfway, the water becomes shallower and I finally reach the bank on the other side.

As I'm getting out of the river and look back, that degenerate's car is disappearing in the distance.

It's mid October. The water is pretty cold. The swimming season's long over.

Standing on the riverbank, in my underwear, I'm shaking from head to toe, not merely from the cold water, but from the traumatic experience I've just had. There's not a soul in sight. Dusk is falling, it won't be long before it starts to get dark.

I'm in shock. I sit with my arms wrapped around my knees, shaking like a leaf and crying my eyes out.

I've heard stories and read about rapes and how some even end up in murder.

I wonder if all men look at me as easy pickings, just because my boyfriend's in jail and that makes me worthless.

After a while, I compose myself, tell myself I'm very lucky and need to get home. I take off my wet underwear, slip the dress over my head and put on my shoes. At least I've managed to keep them dry, holding them high over my head, whilst crossing the river.

I walk across grass fields and stay off the road, until I reach the outskirts of Whittlesey. I'm debating whether to go to the police and report the incident, but decide against it. Who would believe me anyway? It'll be my word against his. I'm the one with the thief as a boyfriend.

I thank my lucky stars that I've escaped with just a few bruises and go home. The next morning, I go into town by bus.

The head office for the chain of butchers I work for is above the shop, accessible along a passage and stairs at the side. I go straight up there to tell the manager about the attack on me the evening before by the manager of the shop and also to give in my notice.

As soon as I walk in, even before I have a chance to speak, the office manager says, a complaint has been made against me by the manager of the shop.

The accusation against me is that I've been stealing from the till, as there's very often a shortfall at the end of the day.

So shocked by having been called a thief, I stutter and stammer for words, but just manage to say it's all a lie.

The office manager says he's been told that I have criminal connections. I know however much I protest, his mind's made up that I'm guilty.

I stand there blubbering that I've never stolen a thing in my life, that I've had a good Christian upbringing.

As I regain my composure, I tell him to look to his manager in the shop as the culprit. Most days the guy has his hand in the till, taking out a few bob here and there, before going to lunch.

The office manager hands me my cards and pay packet, with wages until the end of the week. "No pay in lieu of notice," he says, "for those who steal and tell lies. Consider yourself lucky I'm not bringing charges."

No point in telling him about the attack on me, he won't believe me anyway.

I walk out of the office, with tears of outrage, anger and frustration, streaming down my face.

I feel utterly degraded and want to shout about the injustice. I'm the victim here and can't believe how it's all been turned around to make me into the villain.

I've no one to turn to. My father's the last person I would tell. He's never been on my side before and has never stood up for me and fought my corner, so why would he now? I go straight to the employment agency. They arrange an interview, there and then, for a junior typist position in the works office at Brotherhoods.

I'm surprised to get the job. Maybe word hasn't got back to the employment agency about me getting the sack. I'm 18. Have had the sack twice and am on my 5th job. What will become of me?

I hang around town for the rest of the day, then go round Judy's in the evening. Both Judy and her mum can't believe what I tell them. They both think I should have gone to the police about the attack.

I point out to them that things wouldn't look too good for me with Pete in jail. I'm pretty sure the police would be more inclined to believe a shop manager, who's an upstanding citizen with an unblemished record.

They both agree that looking at it from that perspective, the likelihood of being believed are very slim.

Chapter Thirty Eight

Pete's already served three months of his sentence. He's due out at the beginning of May. He's in an open prison in Sudbury, Derbyshire. Most first time offenders end up in these type of jails, unless the crime is extremely serious.

I've been to Sudbury twice to visit him. It's a long way and cost a lot of money, which I don't have. I had to save every penny I had left with from my month's wages, just to pay for the train fare.

I couldn't wait to see him the first time I went. I had no idea what to expect. I imagined all kinds of scenarios; high walls, prisoners behind bars, striped clothing for inmates. I'd seen too many films.

I took the long train ride from Peterborough to Derby, then a bus to Sudbury.

I'd been up since five that morning, bathing, washing my hair and wanting to look my best for Pete.

I caught an early train, so I'd be there in plenty of time. Visiting was from 2 to 4 and I didn't want to miss a minute of it.

As I was getting off the bus, outside the prison gates, with a motley lot, the driver's comment, as I passed, was "What's a nice girl like you doing, going to a place like that?"

I ignored the wisecrack and quickly got off the bus.

The prison is nothing like I expected. There's no high wall around the place. Barriers, similar to those at a level crossing, stretch across a wide entrance. A large board above the entrance has H.M. Prison, Sudbury, written in large letters.

I follow the crowd from the bus through the open gate. Beyond the entrance there are numerous single storey buildings. Behind them I can see large open fields.

Signs direct visitors to a building with open double doors. The wardens I've seen so far, don't carry guns or any other type of weapons.

I enter a big hall with lots of tables and chairs. I find an empty table and sit down. About 10 minutes to go, I can hardly contain myself.

One by one, the prisoners come in through a door at the end of the room, where a couple of wardens, with hands clasped behind their backs, stand either side of the entrance, facing the visitor's hall.

As the eager, smiling inmates come through the door, friendly banter is exchanged between them and the screws.

Pete is one of the first men to come in. He scans the open space and notices me almost immediately. With a sure and confident step, he walks over to my table. We embrace and share a long kiss, then he takes a seat on the opposite side of the table from me. We're not allowed to sit side by side.

Pete holds my hands in his across the table and looks at me for a long time, before he tells me I look more beautiful than he remembers.

He looks great, suntanned and handsome in his pale blue shirt and dark trousers. He looks as though he's just come back from a beach holiday.

He tells me everything that's happened since he was convicted. Both he and the Baron were taken to a closed prison, where they spent the first night in a cell. The next day, he was driven to Sudbury with a bunch of other guys. The Baron remained at the closed prison, as he was a second time offender and had to serve his time there.

Pete said the prison was better than the RAF camp had been. The food was great. The inmates got a lot of free time and played a lot of football and rugby. During the evenings, they spent time watching TV or going to the camp cinema. They all slept in dorms.

The prison ran all kinds of courses. Pete had signed up for a diploma course in motor mechanics, which he'd finish by the end of his sentence.

He said he'd met some really nice and interesting guys. The screws were mostly decent men and friendly. They had a league going in football and rugby, playing against the wardens.

To me, it sounded more like a holiday camp than a prison, with which Peter agreed.

The only drawback was having your freedom taken away and not being able to step beyond the barbwire fences, surrounding the prison. If anybody was caught outside, they pretty well risked losing their remission.

Pete then told me he'd taken a real chance to call me at Judy's sister's house. He'd been so desperate and didn't care if he got caught.

The phone box was just outside the front gates, opposite the warden's houses. He knew he was taking a hell of a risk, but just couldn't think straight anymore.

"When you're locked up like this, one can go crazy, not knowing what's going on outside," he said. "So don't ever leave me," he begged.

Anyway, he got away with it. I told him I loved him more than anything and to never do anything so foolish again.

As soon as he'd gone to Sudbury, Pete had asked for a transfer to Oakham, an open prison not far from Peterborough, where it would cost less for me to visit.

I told him I'd left Hotpoint and worked as a cashier at the Dewhurst Butcher in town.

He said I deserved a better job than either, but was pleased I didn't work at the factory any more.

The two hours went by very quickly, being completely engrossed in each other, declaring our undying love for one another and chatting.

When the final bell announced the end of visiting, with everybody around us hugging, kissing and saying goodbye to their loved ones, it was hard to leave.

The wardens urged all the inmates to make haste. Pete as usual pushed the limits. A warden finally came over to us and told him jokingly, he could see why it was so hard for him to drag himself away from me.

Pete embraced and kissed me one last time and then walked to the open door, turned and waved, then disappeared.

As I stood and watched him go, I felt sad, but reassured that he was in such a good place, with all kinds of things to do, which stopped him from getting bored.

They had access to a good library, snooker tables, chess and a number of other things. It really did seem like a holiday camp and hardly like punishment.

Knowing Pete though, losing his freedom and independence, was punishment enough. Having to obey rules and regulations and knuckle down to hard work, was not his idea of living.

I only visited Pete once more in Sudbury, before he was transferred to Oakham, Leicestershire, only half an hour by train from Peterborough.

Pete's dream had always been to become a musician. He wanted to travel the world playing trumpet, like his friend Bas, who was a brilliant musician and was currently playing trumpet in the band on the Queen Mary, going back and forth to the States.

Pete had bought a trumpet a number of years ago and had a few lessons, but had not pursued his ambition. His mother had taken his trumpet to him on her only visit.

He was happy being allowed to play the instrument as much as he liked in his spare time.

Pete's father never went to see him in prison and would have nothing to do with him.

The first time I visit Pete at Oakham prison, I tell him about the attack and near rape I experienced and my dismissal from the butcher's shop, after my attacker made an accusation against me for stealing.

Pete's outraged at the dirty and unfair treatment against me. He says he'll track the guy down and beat the living daylights out of him when he's released.

I tell him he'll only get into more trouble. I wish I hadn't said anything. Hopefully he'll have calmed down sufficiently enough to let it all go when the time comes, otherwise he could end up in prison again.

In spite of the lax regime and easy going life in prison, Pete really feels like a caged animal. He's written to the Parson and asked him to come with me the next time I go to see him.

The Parson took me in his car for the next visit.

Pete's reason for wanting the Parson to visit was for a scheme he had.

He wanted the Parson to drive to the prison in the evening at a prearranged time, park his car in a country lane, adjacent to the wire fence of the jail, and then make himself scarce for an hour or so.

Pete was going to sneak out from the compound and meet me, while the other inmates watched a film in the camp cinema.

The screws never stayed once the film started. They just counted the prisoners in before the beginning and again after the movie was over.

Pete said he'd watched for weeks now and given it a lot of thought. He was pretty sure it would work.

Both the Parson and I thought this was another stupid and crazy idea of Pete's.

He begged us both to go along with his plan. The place was driving him completely insane. He didn't know if he could stand another 5 months. It would help him get through the rest of his confinement.

This was Pete all over. Blackmailing and frightening me into doing his bidding, even though I didn't feel right about it or wanted to do it. That was the way he operated. Push and coerce until he got what he wanted.

He really put the pressure on when he said I might as well go, as he would be there waiting.

He knew just how to push my buttons. I was easily talked into things and always gave in and let him have his way.

He told me once, when I was visiting him, that something was put in the morning porridge to suppress the prisoner's sex drive. I thought they needed to put in tons more to calm down Pete's oversexed nature.

Reluctantly, I agreed to his mad plan.

On the way home, the Parson thinks I've done the right thing. Pete's so wilful, he'll do what he wants anyway. If I'm not there, he might just do something stupid.

On the rearranged evening, the Parson drives me to the prison and leaves me in the car on my own.

Pete is already near the fence waiting. The time we spend together, I feel almost as though I'm being devoured alive. All he ever thinks about is himself and his needs.

Afterwards he disappears, through the fence and into the dark.

The Parson and I drive back to Peterborough. He jokingly says he half expected to just find a skeleton in the back of the car. I think it's quite funny and we laugh. He knows Pete pretty well too.

I nervously await Pete's next letter, telling me that everything went well. When the mail arrives and my fears are allayed, I can finally relax again. But there's no way I'll let him talk me into something that stupid again.

My father took a week off from work and went with a bus tour to the VW Works in Germany. His dream was to own a brand new VW Beetle, which would be his first car. Whilst at the factory, he ordered a burgundy Beetle, which was delivered shortly before Christmas.

He'd had a brick garage built at the end of the drive, for his long awaited car.

He was absolutely delighted and proud of his new toy.

At first he washed it every day after getting home from work. Then it became a weekly ritual. First the washing, then the polishing, until he could see his reflection in the bodywork. The car was as clean as a button inside and out.

First Prince and now the car became his pride and joy. It seemed like his life revolved around them.

Both my parents went out quite a lot more now, visiting friends. On the very rare occasion when I was in the car, being given a lift, Vati blew his horn whenever another Beetle passed him and then waved. Apparently this was some sort of secret code all Beetle owners used. I thought it odd and rather peculiar. It was like little boys playing games.

I spent a lot of time at home on my own in the evenings. They never asked me to join them when they went out. I was glad about it.

I didn't want to be in their company anyway.

I like my new job at Brotherhoods. There are four of us in the office.

Jean and Daphne are both secretaries to bosses on the shop floor and the personnel manager, who is in the office next door. They are both somewhere in their mid to late twenties and married to engineers, also working at Brotherhoods.

Jean and Daphne both live a short walk from the factory in very nice semi-detached houses.

Jean's husband often works away from home for short periods. She sometimes asks me to go and stay with her, as she doesn't like being on her own and also enjoys my company.

I liked Jean a lot. We got on very well. It was always a lot of fun staying at her house. The other good thing was not having to spend an hour at the end of every day, travelling to and from work.

Daphne's mother lived also very close to Brotherhoods, where Daphne and her husband went for a cooked lunch every day. He also worked away from home sometimes, then Daphne would ask me to join her and her mum for a meal.

The third person in the office was Mr. Andrews, who looked quite ancient. He was a lovely old boy, quite frail and walked with the aid of a stick and stooped over.

Mr. Andrews desk was quite different from all the rest. It was more like a draughtsman's table, so he could sit upright and work without bending over. He sat all day entering things into ledgers by hand.

I'd been told that he was long past retirement age. He desperately wanted to stay on at work, so the company had let him. He was married, but had no children. He always said he liked being busy and enjoyed being in the company of young people, they kept him youthful.

Mr. Andrews and I often sat together in the office during the lunch break, eating our sandwiches. He rarely talked about himself, but was very interested and always asking questions about Romania and communism. I told him stories about life and hardship there and how I came to be in England. He never got tired of listening to me.

One day, he told me I was a very sophisticated and interesting young woman, especially for one so young.

I had no idea what sophisticated meant. When I looked it up I felt very flattered to be called that, but didn't really think it applied to me.

Every Friday, after work, I go to Judy's house, to pick up my letter from Pete and spend the evening with them all.

Judy's such a lovely mum to her two girls. She's so loving and gentle with them. It's so obvious that she absolutely adores her children.

Life's not easy for her, without a husband, but she's lucky to have such a supporting family around her.

As a beautician, she doesn't earn a lot. Judy always prepares some food for the girls, me and herself. It's always toast with either baked beans or tinned tomatoes. On the odd occasion, she makes sandwiches from a small tin of salmon.

Judy's been a very good friend to me, for which I'm really grateful. I've become very fond of her and the girls.

I like Queeny, her mother, too. She never says much, seems unhappy and downtrodden. I feel sorry for her. She's a very nice woman.

Percy, Judy's father, has always had an eye for the women. I think that's a lot of the problem between him and his wife.

The toilet in their house is just outside the back door. On more than one occasion, when I've gone out there, Percy has lingered outside, grabbed and tried to kiss me.

I find it totally disgusting and manage to get away.

Judy can sense that something's wrong. I'm very reluctant to tell her about her dad, but in the end I do. She calls him a lecherous old sod and accompanies me to the toilet every time I need to go, or sends Candy her older daughter with me. I'm not the first young friend of hers he's accosted, she tells me.

Pete never misses a week without writing. He's only allowed one letter per week and it's always to me.

He writes very well and has a really good command of the English language. All his poems and love letters are very special to me.

He tells me some of the blokes in the nick are almost illiterate and they ask him to dictate what to write to their wives and girlfriends. He says he does it sometimes, as he feels sorry for these guys.

He always writes about his fears and insecurities in prison. He always begs me to stay true to him and never give up on him, as life without me would be nothing.

He tells me some of the men inside get Dear John letters.

He explains they're letters telling them that their loved one has found somebody new and the relationship is over. He talks of the devastating effect this has on these guys and how betrayed and helpless they feel.

He wants reassurance that I will never do that to him.

Every letter I send, I promise to stay true and faithful and that I'll always love him. To make him feel better, I tell him I never go anywhere, apart from seeing Judy, and that I'm just not interested in any other man.

I don't ever tell him that I get asked out by young men all the time. It would only make him feel even more insecure and he'd be wondering if, one day, I'd be tempted and go out with somebody else.

My work colleagues never pry or say anything to me about Pete, but I know they would like to see me go out with other boys and find somebody really nice.

I'm 18 and never go anywhere.

The annual Christmas works party is coming up.

I tell Daphne and Jean I won't be going. Several very nice young men have asked if I'd go to the party with them. I've refused every one of them.

Jean and Daphne try their hardest to persuade me to accept a date. I keep telling them, no.

Then they suggest I go with them to the Christmas party. Eventually I agree to their suggestion. I enjoy the evening very much.

I dance with lots of different lads, but go home with Jean and spend the night there.

Chapter Thirty Nine

We've got a newcomer in the office, a 16 year old girl called Luba. She and her parents haven't been in the country very long. I spend a couple of weeks, showing her what her job entails. I've been the junior in the office until now, doing all the running around and menial tasks.

From now on, I'm in the office all the time and Luba can walk all over the factory doing errands, being whistled at and flirted with by the men.

My parents go off to Loughborough to spend Christmas with her cousin. They take Prince with them. I'm at home on my own and very happy to be so. I spend my Christmas Day with Judy and her family.

Pete's over half way through his prison sentence. Only 4 months to go.

Countdown has started for the beginning of May.

Pete and I have talked about that day, every time I visit. He doesn't want to stay in Peterborough. His life is over there. He doesn't stand a chance of getting a job anywhere. I've told him I'll go with him, wherever he goes.

A call comes from the personnel manager in the main offices, that requests me to go and see him. I always think the worst when I'm summoned like that.

I've never met the guy before. He asks me to sit down, then explains that a delegation from Romania is in the factory for a few days. He says he's been told that I'm from there and speak the language. He wants to know if I'm fluent. I tell him that I grew up there and still speak Romanian fluently.

He then asks me if I'd like to accompany the three Romanian visitors and three of our own engineers to dinner that evening. It will just entail socialising and chatting with the Romanian men and doing some translating.

It sounds wonderful to me and I tell the personnel manager I'd love to do it.

One of the English engineers is called to the office and he explains a little more in detail about the evening. He tells me that, during the day, they have a translator for the technical jargon, but it would be much nicer to have an attractive young woman, who could converse in both languages, joining them for the evening.

After arranging where to meet up later, I go back to my office. Excited about the prospect of going to a posh restaurant, I tell everybody in the office about it.

Daphne asks how much I'm being paid for doing it. I tell her I don't know, that I haven't even thought about it.

She asks if I know how much translators get paid. I tell her I haven't the foggiest. "Plenty," she says and you should be paid too.

I'm allowed to leave work an hour early to go and get ready.

I'm really looking forward to the evening. I've never been to a restaurant, only to cafés, on a handful of occasions.

When I get home, I have a bath and wash my hair, taking care with my make-up and putting my best dress on, which is still the tangerine one I bought when working in the shoe shop. Then I head back into Peterborough and the French restaurant, which I was told is the best eating place in town.

The six guys are already there, standing near the bar having a drink. The man I met earlier, introduces me to the other five in the group. They range in age perhaps from late thirties to mid fifties. They're all very charming and make a fuss of me.

I've never been in the company of six grown men before, all giving me their undivided attention and making me feel quite special and grown up.

When we get called to our table by the waiter, the oldest English guy in the group takes me under his wing and explains all the different meals on the menu. I've never even seen a menu before. In cafés, the meals available are always written up on a board on the wall.

I'm told if I like meat, I should order the fillet steak, which is the best.

There are a number of starters. I just opt for soup, which is really good. Then I do have the fillet. I've never eaten meat that's so tender and tastes so fantastic.

A dessert trolley is wheeled over with the most wonderful looking sweet delights. I choose one and the taste is like being in seventh heaven.

"I could easily get used to this kind of food," I tell the guys.

Everybody's had wine and I've enjoyed a glass too. Now the men all sit over coffee and brandy, smoking cigars. I'm offered a cigarette by one of the English men and join them in a small liqueur and coffee.

What a memorable evening it has been.

One of the men offers to take me to Whittlesey, but I decline, telling him I don't want to put anybody out and will catch the 10.30 bus, which will get me home just as quickly.

I'm very reluctant to get in a car with a relative stranger after what happened with the butcher.

When I tell the girls at work about my evening and how wonderful the food was, Daphne said, it would have been the best. She said all the food and drinks for the whole evening would have been on expense account. She had to explain what that meant.

Then I tell them I'll be going out that evening again, as the Romanians were here until the following day and they all wished me to join them again, as they'd enjoyed having such a beautiful young woman chatting to them all evening.

That evening we all met up at yet another one of Peterborough's top restaurants. The cuisine here was Italian and every bit as scrumptious as the French food.

The men were as attentive as ever and told me I looked very elegant. I was wearing my grey skirt and matching three quarter length coat, my father had made for me, from a picture I'd seen in Judy's Vogue magazine.

The next day I was full of myself, telling everybody at work what a fabulous evening I'd had.

Daphne said I'd done the company a good service and she hoped I'd get some payment for it.

There was not a penny more in my next pay packet. My work colleagues were quite disgusted. Yet I didn't care. I'd had a great time, eaten the best food ever and hoped I'd be asked again if there was a next time.

There were a couple more occasions when I went out with a German delegation of engineers and some of our own. They all turned out to be as enjoyable as the first.

The girls at work told me I was being taken advantage of. I should stand up for my rights and what I was entitled to. They told me not be such a push over.

I looked at it differently. If I demanded pay for my time and language skills, they might not ask me. Then I'd be losing out on a great evening, the best food and getting to talk to very interesting people.

Anyway, what would I have been doing? Sitting at home on my own, no doubt. Apart from going round Judy's once a week and staying at Jean's occasionally, I rarely went anywhere.

As May draws closer, anticipation and excitement grow more with each day. The weather's getting warm. I'm so elated, I feel like singing and dancing.

I know for sure that Pete will wait outside the big factory gates at 5 o'clock on that special day. I can hardly wait.

I make an extra special effort to look my best that day.

On the day, as the time draws near for leaving work, my nerves are getting the better of me. All kinds of thoughts go through my head. What if something has happened, or what if he's lost his remission? The waiting is really getting to me.

I'm ready to go and watching the office clock. The moment the second hand hits the twelve, I'm out of the office like a shot, across the big courtyard and through the open factory gates.

Then I spot him, leaning easily and relaxed against a brick wall on the other side of the road.

Pete's face is tanned and he looks very handsome. He doesn't move, but just remains leaning on the wall watching me cross the road. Then we're in each other's arms, embracing and kissing madly, not wanting ever to let go of each other.

I'm overwhelmed with joy and happiness.

With arms round each others backs, looking into each others eyes, we start walking slowly down Lincoln Road to Judy's house.

Pete could be very romantic. He loved putting his feelings into words.

He said he'd chosen to stand the other side of the road from the factory, so he could watch me and drink in my loveliness, before finally embracing and kissing me. He wanted his senses to explode when he finally held me in his arms, as a free man.

Judy made tinned salmon sandwiches for everybody and we all spent a lovely evening together.

Pete took me to catch the 10.30 bus to Whittlesey and he went and spent his first night at a friend's house, as his father wouldn't have him at home.

Soon after Pete got out of jail, I came down with tonsillitis again. My doctor said it was time to arrange for me to go into hospital and have my tonsils removed, as I was being sick too often.

I was in a ward at the Peterborough hospital with a bunch of little kids, who were also having their tonsils out.

The following morning, I was the first to be operated on.

When I came to after the surgery, I felt absolutely awful. All the little kids around me were sitting up in bed and eating ice cream.

I couldn't face anything and kept throwing up. I couldn't utter a word, my throat felt as if it were on fire.

The next day, all the little kids went home. I had to stay in hospital another five days!

I couldn't eat. Drinking was like swallowing razor blades. The pain was excruciating. The doctor said that the operation on young children was almost pain free. For adults however, it was one of the most painful things to go through.

Mutti and Vati only visited me the evening of the operation, when Pete was there. They could barely bring themselves to say hello to him, in spite of him being friendly towards them. They didn't visit again. I wasn't bothered, as Pete was by my bedside, every evening, during visiting time.

My recovery from the operation took much longer than I thought. I couldn't eat any solids for 2 weeks and the weight fell off me. Pete said I needed fattening up, I was getting too skinny. I was very slim to begin with and couldn't really afford to lose more weight.

Pete and I spoke endlessly about what to do and where to move to. There was no way he'd stay in Peterborough he said. I'd be 19 at the end of July and more than ready and happy to move away and start a new life.

One day in early June, Pete told me he was going down to the southwest coast to see if he could find some work in a seaside resort. As soon as he got a job, he would send for me.

After a couple of weeks, I received a postcard from Torquay, saying he hadn't found anything yet, but was still looking for work.

Knowing Pete the way I did, I thought it was more likely that he was sunning himself on a beach all day and not making too much effort finding a job. However, I remained hopeful.

There was no forwarding address for me to write to, so I just had to wait for news from him.

His second postcard arrived about three weeks after the first. He still wasn't working. When I told Judy that Pete couldn't get a job, she didn't believe it. There were all kinds of jobs in a seaside resort, she told me, Pete's always been lazy and will carry on being lazy. I bet anything he's not even tried to find work, she said.

She then told me how Pete had always been very unreliable, selfish and irresponsible. I'd be better off to ditch him. She thought, in the long run, he'd make me very unhappy.

Feeling deflated and having mixed feelings after what Judy had said, I just didn't know what to do next.

Living at home had become impossible and I just wanted to get away. But what would I do and where would I go, that was my biggest problem.

It's towards the end of July and I've not heard anything from Pete for quite a while. It looks like I'll be spending my 19th birthday on my own.

My birthday's been and gone and still no word from Pete.

As I'm eating some toast before going to work one morning, my father walks in the kitchen with a grim face. He throws the newspaper in front of me.

"Read that," he commands.

I stare at the paper, lying in front of me. There on the front page of the Peterborough Gazette, Pete and the Baron's faces, stare straight back at me.

My father gives me the most contemptuous look.

"Once a thief, always a thief," he spits, then leaves the room.

I sit with my eyes fixed to the paper, unable to take it all in. I'm completely undone. What now?

Pete promised he wouldn't have anything more to do with the Baron and all the time he's been in Torquay with him. The lying, cheating bastard, how could he?

I feel very angry, but most of all, betrayed. What else has he been up to and lying about? My parents go off to work, but I stay at home. I can't face people at work, I'm too ashamed.

The Baron was a bad influence on Pete, but Pete was no angel. He had a mind of his own and knew exactly what he was doing. He was just a scoundrel and a thief. Always looking for trouble and excitement, just for the sheer hell of it. He didn't give a damn who he hurt in the process.

Then I sat and read the article. They'd already been in front of the judge, been found guilty, sentenced to probation and were being sent back to Peterborough.

Judy's words came back to me. Pete was no good and would always make me unhappy. I'd really believed him when he told me he wanted to make a fresh start. Was this the way things were going to be, with me always wondering when the police would come knocking?

The news article stated that the pair of them had been arrested for stealing an old woman's handbag.

How degrading I thought! You couldn't sink much lower than that. Other offences had been taken into consideration.

Both Pete and the Baron had walked along the beach each morning giving out fake tickets to people using community deck chairs and collecting money.

When the guy, whose job it was to give tickets out and collect the cash from the customers, found out, day after day, that people had already paid, the authorities started to watch out for the culprits.

The stunts the two of them pulled, were so demeaning and low, it was beyond belief.

That evening, I call Judy. She tells me Pete's been at her house all afternoon and wants to see me.

I tell her I'm gutted and disappointed with him. I don't ever want to see him.

Then Pete gets on the phone, full of excuses. He begs me to see him and give him a chance to explain.

I have to sort this out, one way or another. It's still early, I catch the bus into Peterborough and go to Judy's house.

Pete's full of recriminations. It's all over between him and the Baron. He'll never see him again. I'm the only person he loves and wants to be with. On and on it goes.

"Lets just leave this dump and go to London," he says. "Plenty of work there and new chances."

All I see in Judy's face is scepticism and disbelief. But she doesn't say anything.

All his smooth talking finally wins me over and I agree to go to London with him. There's nothing left for me here either. Maybe if we're away from here, we can make it work somewhere else.

I meet Pete in town the next day. He goes to Brotherhoods with me and waits outside the factory while I go in, give in my notice and pick up the money I'm owed.

Then we head into town, where I go to a pawn broker and pawn a gold ring my father bought me for my 18th birthday.

I have a total of 12 pounds in my purse - 5 for the ring, another 5 for two weeks holiday pay and a couple of pounds for the few days wages. Pete has no money at all.

I arrange to meet him at the Peterborough bus park the next morning, and then I go home.

That evening, I sit in my room for the best part, wondering if I'm making a huge mistake by going off with Pete. I'm also trying to figure out how I'm going to tell my father about leaving the next morning.

What a dilemma!

I sit and think about the past few years. The happiness I'd experienced when I first arrived. The hopes and dreams I'd had of a new and wonderful life, with good, loving and supportive parents.

Where had it all gone so wrong? I'd tried so hard, done my very best, but had failed miserably.

My stepmother had made it clear from the beginning that she'd rather I hadn't come. I thought my father was a good man, but very weak, not standing up to his wife and letting her call all the shots.

The last thing I wanted to do, was hurt my father, but I wanted more from life than I was getting from him. I pinned my hopes on Pete and that he would sort himself out and fly straight.

I decided to go to bed without telling him and get up early in the morning to write a letter before leaving.

It was the cowardly way out, but I'd never stood up to anybody in my entire life. I didn't want to see the disappointment, regret or loss on my father's face. Or would it be relief and indifference?

After a very restless night, I sat in the kitchen with Prince once my parents had gone to work and wrote the letter. I addressed it to my father.

I told him I was very grateful for everything he'd done for me since arriving in England. I was extremely sorry the way things had turned out.

I was going to London with a friend to find work and make a new life for myself. I would write as soon as I settled down.

Then, I packed my few belongings in a small case I found in the box room. I hugged and said goodbye to Prince, then left the house to catch the bus to Peterborough.

All the way into town I wondered how my father would take it. Would he write to my Grandmother and the family and tell them what I'd done?

I'd never made any mention, when writing home, that things had gone quite sour between me and my parents.

They had enough problems just staying alive, without worrying about me.

I came to the conclusion that my father wouldn't say anything either. He wanted to keep faith and not have fingers pointing at him for failing in his duty and responsibility towards me, as a parent.

Pete was already at the bus station waiting for me. As ever, he seemed carefree and happy and tried to cheer me up. We got a bus to the A1, where we got off. Pete stuck out his thumb and pretty soon a lorry pulled up. Pete opened the passenger door.

The driver asked, "Where to mate?

Pete replied, "The Smoke."

Pete helped me up into the cab, then got in after me. He and the lorry driver chatted most of the way to London.

Very confused and unsure, I sat quietly with my own thoughts about how the future was going to pan out. Deep down, I was still questioning whether I'd done the right thing, or made the biggest mistake of my life, going off with Pete? Only time would tell.

I didn't feel sad leaving, but somewhat guilty about the way I'd done it.

I was willing to give him the benefit of the doubt, that he'd perhaps tried his best. Perhaps too much time had been lost to build a meaningful and loving relationship between us.

There was no way to bridge the gap over all the years we'd missed, during which he hadn't been there for me.

Chapter Forty

Looking back on my life as an older, mature woman, I can see things so much more clearly. I've tried to make sense of my life and seek to understand people, who have been a big part of my life, and the reason why they've behaved in certain ways.

Having suffered so much physical and emotional abuse, being rejected, humiliated and degraded, has turned me into the person I've become. I go to any length to please others, keep peace at any cost, and submit to their demands.

Most of all, I seek acceptance, wanting to belong and be loved.

I will always be deeply grateful to my Grandparents, who were the only people who truly loved me and my brother during my growing years.

They could easily have turned their backs on us and let us be put into an orphanage.

I can't imagine the depth of despair my grandparents went through during the two world wars.

Then losing everything they possessed, being thrown into poverty and deprivation, living like paupers for the rest of their lives.

They became second class citizens in the land that they, and their forefathers, built and shaped into the rich and prosperous place it became.

My Grandparents were the most wonderful people. Their religion and strong faith got them through all the tough times.

My Grandmother played the biggest role in my life. She was extremely kind, generous and loving.

I never knew her to be unkind to anybody and she always reached out a helping hand, whenever it was within her power to do so.

They both taught me a lot. Without the love they gave me, I can't imagine where I'd be today. They will live in my heart forever.

Over the years I've fought with so many conflicting thoughts and emotions about my mother. I've tried to visualise her life in the Russian labour camps, the brutality, hardship and inhuman treatment she and all the other prisoners received.

Then being crushed physically and emotionally and having to face the future, bringing up two children in poverty, on her own.

My mother became embittered, angry and frustrated, when most of the men returned from the war, but her husband failed to do so.

My father knew that Transylvania was under Stalinist rule and yet he abandoned us, to our miserable fate, to save his own skin. The selfishness of the man is just beyond me.

The misery, despair and suffering that followed, must have been unbearable for my mother. She turned all her animosity and resentment on my brother and me.

My mother lived the rest of her life with bitterness and hatred, which ate away at her and poisoned her body and mind.

"Without forgiveness, the soul can't heal," my Grandmother used to say.

I've tried very hard to come to terms with that part of my life and forgive my mother. As a mother myself and knowing how I feel towards my children, I find it very hard to forgive completely.

If she'd treated the children from her second marriage the same, it would have been easier to understand and put it all down to what happened. But she loved and cherished her two little boys and didn't subject them to the beatings and cruelty my brother and I had to endure.

All I ever wanted was to be loved by my mother. But she couldn't even bear to have me around and look at me. She seemed to get some perverted and sadistic pleasure, by inflicting so much pain and misery. Being excluded and ostracised from her family was very hard to take and extremely damaging.

Being pushed from pillar to post as a child, learning to be compliant and do everybody's bidding, became my second nature. I learned to become this submissive and meek creature, who became everybody's doormat.

I thought I'd get a second chance when I went to England. I always felt a certain guilt for being the one to get out of Romania, and my brother having to stay behind.

But my father never turned out to be the father I'd hoped he'd be.

He was never really there for me or my brother. So I clung to the first man who came along and showed me affection and what I took to be love.

I was too naive and gullible.

My brother's life and suffering went on in Romania. When he was diagnosed with a brain tumour in his mid forties and was given just months to live, we managed to get him to England for treatment.

During the four and a half months Christian was in London with Pete and me, my father only visited once. He had the chance to do something for my brother and help with the twenty odd thousand pound hospital bill we had to pay.

My father was comfortably well off, but didn't make as much as a penny contribution. I felt pretty disgusted.

When I first went to London with Pete, I thought he'd be the man who would finally be there for me. We'd make a life together and raise a family.

It soon became evident that this wasn't the case.

Pete was lazy and didn't like to work. He wasn't a drinker or gambler, just a womaniser. His name should have been Casanova.

He always singled the young, good looking women out, flirted and was all over them like a rash. Most of the women were flattered by his attention and responded to his charm. If I said anything and got upset and told me I was over sensitive and just imagined things.

Pete would deliberately pick arguments with me, storm off and then threaten not to come back, leaving me heartbroken. When he came home the following day, after being out all night, he'd act as though nothing had happened. I was too scared to say anything, in case he cleared off again.

He pulled so many dirty stunts, then charmed his way out of what he'd done. I was always ready to believe and forgive him, and give him the benefit of the doubt.

But most of the time, I found telltale hints on his clothes, lipstick, perfume or love notes and women's hankies in his pockets. The heartache and degradation he caused me was devastating.

Pete was so brazen about the way he carried on.

He was either completely insensitive or didn't give a shit about how much he hurt me and how badly he treated me. Maybe he thought I was so stupid and gullible, he could get away with anything. But, in the end, I allowed it and did nothing to end the relationship.

At the beginning I was captivated by Pete, but after living with him for a little while, I stopped believing all his excuses and lies.

I was terrified of being in London on my own and felt trapped. I always lived in the hope that things would change for the better.

When we first arrived in London, we went to a young guy's house he'd met in jail.

He lived in Hendon, North London with his family. We were only there for the weekend as his wife and child were away visiting her parents. We had to leave before she returned. His mate gave Pete an address in East

London, where we could both get a job.

The next three nights, we slept in the waiting room at Liverpool Street Station in the City of London, as we had nowhere else to go and no money to pay for a hotel.

The place we'd been sent to for jobs was a dingy office. The job entailed driving out to wealthy suburbs, in a van with other people, selling blankets and carpet shampooers door to door.

The other workers were all East End types, brash and crude. Pete seemed to enjoy their company and all the flirting and innuendo became a regular thing between him and a young woman in the group.

Not being the pushy type, I never managed to make a sale and Pete didn't do much better either.

One of the women let us sleep on her living room floor for a couple of nights.

I couldn't stand the way we were living and the way Pete was behaving around these other women, so I got a job in an office at Tower Hill in the City, as a typist.

We got a room off Mile End Road, where we had no cooking facilities and shared the bathroom with several other people.

My wages just about paid for the room, but didn't leave much over. We survived on egg and chips, once a day, at the local cafe.

Pete earned hardly anything and would often bugger off and hitch a lift back to Peterborough for a few days, leaving me on my own. He'd scrounge off different people whilst up there.

Very often, I only ate once a day and went hungry the rest of the time.

A young guy, from New Zealand, rented a room in the same house. He was in England for a couple of years, studying.

He felt sorry for me. When I was left on my own, he'd ask me if I wanted a hot drink, which he made with an electrical element he put in a mug that heated the water. How I envied that simple little gadget.

On a couple of occasions he asked me to go to the cafe with him, where he bought me egg and chips.

He asked me what a lovely girl like me was doing with a loser like Pete. I didn't know what to say. He said I should ditch him and find somebody else. He said he was engaged to a girl back in New Zealand, otherwise he would have snapped me up.

He was a nice, decent guy.

I kept on working in the City, whilst Pete was wasting his time driving around the suburbs of London, bringing home pennies.

He often came home with tales about the guys who ran this so-called business. He'd seen all kinds of things - guns and clubs in their desks drawers, which they didn't hesitate to use. He'd seen another guy cower in the corner of the office, having a gun pointed at him, begging for his life. These people were crooks, had served time for murder and GBH and were part of the London Jewish Mafia.

These stories really scared me and I kept begging Pete to leave and find another job. We looked for another place to live and found two rooms in a house in North London. Here we had a sink and stove.

At least I could cook a meal.

My money covered the rent, my train fare into the city and what was left over was just about enough for cereal and beans on toast every day.

Pete still wouldn't look for another job.

Three other families lived in the house - each one in two rooms like us. The one bathroom and toilet was shared by all.

I befriended the young woman in one of the ground floor rooms. They had the use of the garden. She lived there with her husband and little boy. The husband worked and they were saving to buy a house. A mere dream for me.

Pat was the only person I knew in London. She told me time and time again that Pete was a no good useless bastard and I should leave him. She said there were plenty of young men out there who'd be very happy to go out with me.

I told her I had nowhere to go and was terrified of being alone in such a big city.

I never confided in my work colleagues. Living with a man in the early sixties, was not something a decent girl did. The people I worked with all came from good backgrounds. They lived in the lovely suburbs of London in nice homes, either with family or husbands. None of them were aware of what kind of life I led, and I didn't want anybody to know about it as I was ashamed.

Pete's debauchery carried on.

It was like an incurable disease. Some of the things he did were low, even by his rock bottom standards.

I lived in hope that he would change once we had children, but his womanising never ceased. Nothing changed and I was too scared to rock the boat. It was a matter of rather the devil you know...

Then I got pregnant a second time. Pete said if I wasn't prepared to get rid of the baby, he would leave me. After the experience of my first abortion, I was terrified, but I was scared stiff to be left alone as well. I felt I had no choice and agreed to see a backstreet abortionist, as the procedure was still illegal.

It was a pretty horrible experience. Pete had no compassion or feelings for me. I had no idea that all this could jeopardise my chance of having children later on.

The abortion didn't work. Three months later I had a miscarriage.

I was rushed into hospital, having lost a lot of blood and remained there for 2 weeks. The doctors knew that I'd attempted an abortion and questioned Pete. He denied knowing anything. The baby was apparently damaged. It had been a little boy and I was mortified and swore I would never go through anything like that again.

Pete wasn't at all remorseful. I was beginning to realise more and more what a selfish, flawed man he was.

When I fell pregnant for the third time and refused to have an abortion, he told me he wouldn't marry me. He'd been married once and that was enough.

I told him I needed to think about my situation and would go and stay with a friend for a couple of days. I stayed with Pat on the ground floor.

He didn't waste any time. That same evening he brought his Latin American tart back to the rooms, with whom he'd been carrying on for some weeks.

Shortly before that, he'd even had the gall to ask a friend to pretend she was his girlfriend. We all went to the cinema. His friend sat like a statue throughout the film, with me at the other end, whilst Pete and his brazen hussy, where all over each other in the middle.

I felt humiliated and betrayed.

Wasn't it enough that he was carrying on, but to take me to witness his antics and rub my nose in it, was just cruel.

I was 3 months pregnant with his child at the time.

Pete denied any wrong doing. He told me to stop being jealous and just let him be himself. But several years later, the friend and his wife, who became good friends, admitted that he'd just come along as a favour to Pete.

Pete tried to justify what he'd done by saying that we were just living together and weren't married. He certainly had a twisted and weird take on life.

When I was 4 months pregnant, Pete agreed to marry me.

I was still nuts about him, in spite of all the rotten things he'd done. I was very happy and thought once we had a child he would change and become responsible and a nicer person.

I carried on working until I was 8 months pregnant. I told my colleagues that I had gotten married and was now expecting a baby. I wore a corset throughout the rest of my time at work, trying to hide the fact that I was pregnant when I got hitched.

Pete never stopped playing away from home. I knew him so well and always knew the signs when he had somebody else. He kept breaking my heart time and time again. He never showed any regret or guilt for putting me through hell.

He was a complete controller and I submitted to his will most of the time. He even told me what books to read and what music to listen to. Anything he didn't approve of was rubbish.

He'd always been condescending and sarcastic, enjoying making fun of people and ridiculing them, including me. He often derided people with disabilities and problems and thought it was okay to laugh at them, that what they didn't know didn't hurt them.

It was a mean and nasty trait, which I always hated about Pete.

For the first 18 months in London, Pete had so many jobs.

The first one was the door to door selling, which made no money and lasted from September to January. I was earning just enough to keep us from starvation, which he seemed happy with.

Then, a succession of driving and other menial jobs came along, where he only lasted a week or two at a time. He always maintained he was not cut out to work for other people. The trouble was that he was bone idle and hated taking orders. He preferred going to the park or the swimming pool and laying in the sun.

The biggest joy of my life, has always been my children.

When my son was born, I was 21. The first time he was put into my arms and I looked at that precious little face, no words could explain how I felt. I was overwhelmed with such love for this little being, I thought I would burst with happiness.

It was then I thought of my mother for the first time in years. I wondered if she'd ever felt like this? I felt the need to know. I promised myself if I ever saw her again I would ask her.

Three years later, I had a beautiful little girl. The feelings of joy and happiness I felt for her were every bit as strong as they had been the first time round.

I knew no matter what, that my love for both my children was boundless and immeasurable. There was nothing that I would not be prepared to do for them. From now on, it was for them that I lived. I wanted to keep them safe, shower them with love and give them all the things and opportunities I'd never had.

Pete had been working as a lifeguard at a couple of different swimming pools. This brought with it its own problems, due to all the girls throwing themselves at him, which he obviously loved.

Pete remained unreliable and still hated work. I held a job down for a while between having the two children, then again when my baby girl was six months old. I kept on working until I was 60.

When we went out with friends to places where there was dancing, they all danced with their partners. Pete was always off dancing with some young girl he'd taken a fancy to, leaving me sitting on my own at the table.

I knew our friends felt sorry for me, but no one ever said anything. Pete just couldn't stop humiliating and degrading me.

We made several road trips to Transylvania when my children were growing up.

This particular summer when, they were 2 and 5 years old, we took a large tent with us and camped in the foothills of the Carpathian Mountains by a stream.

Annitante, Nickitante, Hansuncle and my cousins all came with us.

Renate, the eldest of my cousins, was 16 going on 17.

Pete couldn't even control his urges with my family around. He targeted Renate with his charm.

She was obviously smitten with this handsome, debonair Englishman, who gave her so much attention and made her feel very special.

On several occasions during the camping trip, they would both disappear into the woods and return ages after.

In the evening, Renate would sit on Pete's lap by the campfire. He was 39 and she was a stupid, young 16 year old.

I asked Pete to stop what he was doing. He said it was all in my imagination.

"Yes, like all the other times," I said.

I was amazed that Renate's parents didn't say something to her. Maybe they didn't want to rock the boat and cause a scene by bringing attention to what was going on.

I just couldn't bring myself to confront Pete and my cousin in front of the whole family. It made me feel sick to my stomach, watching Pete take advantage of an impressionable, infatuated young girl.

Pete and I built up a business in manufacturing lampshades.

For a number of years, we worked 12 to 18 hours a day, 7 days a week. The work was hard and backbreaking, especially for me, sitting at a sewing machine all the time. Pete had the much easier jobs, seeing buyers etc. The business became very successful.

But, as always, Pete managed to sabotage what we built by not wanting to work and letting other people do the jobs he should have been doing.

I continued working long hours.

Pete preferred spending his time on the squash court now, chasing a ball and a pipe dream. He wanted to be Britain's best squash player in his age group.

Eventually, the business went into liquidation and we lost everything.

Pete was completely useless in the home as well. He hated any kind of manual work. He never even changed as much as a plug on an electrical item. I had to learn how to do everything including, painting, decorating and other jobs around the house.

His idea of fixing something was to glue it together with chewing gum. His antics became a joke to our friends.

I watched as he made one disastrous decision after another, and got us deeper into debt.

I'd stopped loving him a long time ago and had lost every last ounce of respect for him too.

I'd been on the verge of calling it a day many times.

We'd been in London about 13 years. Throughout that time Pete had been unfaithful and I'm pretty sure he'd played around from when I first knew him.

I'd been on the verge of leaving him on more than one occasion. Each time, I had to think what was best for my kids. The split could have a shattering effect on them. It could rob them of a good education, which I so desperately wanted them both to have. I'd never ever been unfaithful to Pete or even looked at another guy.

Then, a young guy we both knew asked me out for a drink one evening.

Pete found out and went absolutely ballistic. He went around the house smashing things, calling me all kinds of choice names. He told my children that their mother was a whore and didn't love them.

The nerve and double standards of the guy, bewildered me. All the dirty rotten things he'd done to me over the years, were conveniently forgotten and he was now lily white.

He made my life hell for 6 months, flying into rages and throwing his weight about, accusing me of things I wouldn't dream of doing. If I was 10 minutes later than he thought I should be when I went shopping, he'd maintain I'd been with somebody. He was obviously judging me by his own rotten standards.

Life was unbearable.

When I threatened to leave, he'd beg and grovel and tell me he couldn't live without me. Within minutes, he'd have another outburst and start treating me as though I'd committed the crime of the century.

It all came to a head when we went away for a few days to Cornwall with the children, where we stayed in a B&B.

The children were already in bed and I followed soon after, leaving Pete watching a football match.

I dreaded being on my own with him. He'd just look at me and become very mean, call me names and goad me.

When he came up to bed, I lay very still and pretended to be asleep, as I didn't want him to start a fight, especially as we were in somebody else's home.

He got into bed, started to call and needle me. He was really vile and started pushing me around.

I got out of bed and said I was going downstairs, as I didn't wish to be there and put up with all his crap.

He jumped out of bed and blocked my way. Screaming abuse at me, he started throwing punches. As he backed me into the corner of the room, still throwing his fists, I cowered down, trying to protect my head and face with my arms. He was out of control and really hurting me. I was scared stiff, crying and moaning, begging him to stop.

Seconds later, my son walked in the room with my daughter close behind. The kids were 11 and 8 years old. What a thing for them to witness.

The blows kept coming. My children must have been very frightened, seeing their father beating me like this. My son shouted at my husband to stop. My little girl was crying. I tried to comfort them and tell them everything was all right.

It was too late, they'd seen it all.

I told them both to get dressed and quickly put on my own things.

The landlady had heard the commotion and was coming up the stairs to see what was going on.

I asked her to get a cab for me, that I was leaving with the children and going to the station.

She said there were no trains this time of night.

I would wait at the railway station until the morning, I told her. Pete was now very remorseful and begging me not to go.

I was at the end of my rope and just couldn't take any more of his abuse. He cancelled the cab and said he'd take me to the station himself.

The minute I get back to London I told him, I would see a solicitor and file for divorce.

In the end, he talked me into us all driving back to London together. I sat all through the night not saying a word to him. He babbled, cried and begged for my forgiveness.

I really despised him.

I told him I just couldn't go on living like this. He started to bring the kids into the argument and saying how much they'd lose if we split up.

My concern for my children and what would happen to them was his saving grace and I agreed to give him another chance. I told him if he ever laid another finger on me, I would take the kids and go. I would also go the police and file a complaint against him for physical abuse.

I never felt the same about Pete after that. He'd killed the last bit of love or respect I had for him.

My marriage was dead.

I made up my mind there and then, that when the children were old enough and left home, I would go as well.

Our friends knew that our marriage was going through yet another rough patch. I didn't discuss my problems with anybody, just concentrated on my kids and work and biding my time.

I'd mended some bridges with my father and stepmother after my son was born, but didn't see them much at all. They would have been the last people I would have confided in and asked for help.

My parents were never there for me. When I had my babies, I could have done with a little help, but it was never offered or given and I didn't ask.

As a family, we did have some good times, as the children were growing up. We made three or four road trips through Europe to Transylvania. Summer camping holidays on the Costa Brava and Winter ski holidays in the Alps.

But they never made up for all the infidelities, physical and emotional abuse I suffered at Pete's hands.

Pete was a good father, especially to our son. He thinks women are inferior and only good for one thing. He never treated his only daughter with the same respect as his son, and always made it evident whom he favoured.

Both my children were now in their mid and late twenties and had been living with their partners and away from home for a while.

Chapter Forty One

At the age of 50, I finally found the strength to walk away from my marriage. Times were very hard. Pete fought tooth and nail to make things difficult. He was losing his housekeeper and cook. The divorce dragged on and on and cost a small fortune.

I made ends meet by cleaning houses and working part time as a physiotherapy assistant.

Unable to sell our house and not having the funds to set up separate homes, we had to carry on living under the same roof.

Life became unbearable.

I never knew what nasty or dirty trick he'd come up with next.

The divorce proved to be extremely acrimonious. I began to fall apart and went into deep depression.

I was told by somebody close to me, that I needed to sort myself out and they paid for one session for me to see a councillor.

The counselling session lasted 4 hours. The counsellor sat and listened to me patiently for nearly the whole time, while I poured my heart out.

The counsellor told me that to have lived the life I had and come through it all and still held on to my sanity, showed a very strong will and spirit.

She said, in her opinion, the person who'd sent me to her had the real problems and needed help.

It was no wonder that I let everybody crap all over me. I'd been conditioned from early childhood, through all the abuse, degradation and undermining I'd had, which had carried on through later years and into my marriage and adulthood.

All I'd ever been taught and learnt was how to be submissive and let people dominate and control me. It had become second nature to me, to always be agreeable and yield to everybody's wishes, leading me to believe that this would make people like me.

She said I'd always been an enabler and pleaser and didn't know how to demand respect from others and say no.

"Unfortunately, plenty of people will take advantage of your weaknesses and kind nature. They're mean and nasty individuals, who take pleasure in humiliating and diminishing others in any way they can. These people are pretty useless. By putting others down, it makes them feel better about themselves. Never having had anybody to fight your corner, instead, the people who should have stood up for you, gave the abuser and bully power over you. Finally finding the courage to leave your husband was a huge step for you."

To have survived and come through all the adversities throughout my life, showed that I had a lot of inner strength, which was still there. I just needed to learn how to use it and stand up to the bullies and nasty people in my life.

It wasn't any wonder that I always felt inferior and worthless, when all my life I'd been put down, by most of the people around me.

I had to learn to put myself first for once - love and value myself and stop saying yes and being everybody's doormat.

I told the counsellor that, after a lifetime of conditioning, this would not be an easy thing for me to do. However, I would try really hard to achieve the goals she'd set.

Pete is, or chooses to be, totally oblivious to the past. He sails through life in complete denial of any wrongdoing, pain or suffering he's caused to so many.

If at all possible, he's become even more narcissistic, selfish, self-absorbed and self-righteous. If a conversation isn't about him, he loses interest and walks away. Pete will never do anything he doesn't want to, not even to please somebody else.

In his latter years Pete's come to think of himself as an upright and law-abiding citizen. He's become holier than thou. Rants and raves and sits in judgement of other peoples behaviour, so much so that one might think his life has been whiter than white.

He sits and brags to his newly acquired friends, about the good old days and the fantastic business he once had and built single handed.

Whenever he talks about our business to anybody, I'm never mentioned or given the credit for all the hard work or my part in it.

Pete lives in his jazz dreamworld, surrounded by jazz singers and musicians, who are revered by him and the only people worth their salt, as far as he's concerned.

Over recent years I've often asked myself if I ever liked Pete? The answer to that is a definite NO! But I did love him.

It was his charm, sense of fun and devil may care attitude that attracted me to him. After my abusive, suppressed and miserable childhood, he was a breath of fresh air and like an opiate.

Looking back, I don't think anybody ever really liked Pete. His bohemian and unaccountable behaviour and antics, were amusing to onlookers, as long as they weren't involved with him.

I don't think he can count on any real friends. Over the years they've all fallen by the wayside.

His mother said a strange thing to Judy on her deathbed. "Why did no one ever like Pete?"

That's a very sad thing for a mother to say about her son.

My life has been one huge roller coaster with many more downs that ups.

I've always considered myself very lucky to have escaped the tyranny of Communist Romania.

I feel extremely blessed having two wonderful children and four beautiful grandchildren. They all make life worth living and I love them more than words could ever express.

Over the years, I have gained strength from the adversities and hardships, I've had to endure. I try to understand human nature and why people behave the way they do.

It's been a hard and long journey of discovery and learning.

I hope the road will become easier and go on for a while longer yet.

"When we honour the gate of suffering, what arises is the wondrous power of compassion"

The Truth about Suffering - Jack Kornfield

About the Author

Ursula Matthews was born in Transylvania, in 1943. Her story; this story, covers European historical events, which shattered her family and community.

Her father was conscripted into the German Army in WW2 and became a POW in England. When Ursula was six months old, her mother was snatched off the street, pushed into a lorry and sent to a Russian Labour Camp where she was forced to work in a coal mine. Her two children went to their paternal grandparents, who owned a farm.

Their rural life soon devolved into harsh poverty and their lives depended on family love and loyalty, amidst the cruelty of a despotic regime and racist hierarchy.

Her story is of a family's struggle, sorrow, heartache and above all, love and hope. Ursula writes with a straight forward, descriptive style, which the reader will find adds substance, rather than self-pity, as her childhood unfolds.

As an adult, Ursula has created an amazing family life and the love, trust and loyalty between her and her two adult children and grandchildren are palpable.

Unsurprisingly, her own health has deteriorated in recent years, yet, with underlying appreciation, a sharp humour and ready smile, her remarkable courage, stamina and determination shine through.

Many people will be inspired and informed by reading Ursula's story, which tells a family's journey through European history and topically addresses the realities of war, abuse of power, immigration and their consequences.

Editors Note

In keeping with the author's unflinching honesty in the writing of this memoir, I shall be equally honest: this was the hardest book I've ever hard to edit. Not, I hasten to add, because it was badly written, even though English is the writer's third language. Rather, what Ursula Matthews has related within the preceding pages actually happened, and is far worse than any horror fiction writer's efforts to appal us. Sitting in a modern comfortable, warm, and cosy suburban or rural home as most of us do, it is as well to be reminded that just under 80 years ago (the span of a human lifetime) things were very different for some people, where deprivation and poverty were tangible, observable facts, affecting large swathes of the world. Parallel to that is the undeniable fact that man's cruelty towards his fellow men lies just beneath the surface, prompted by differences of race, religion, political ideology, or social status. The post-second-world-war years of Ursula's young life happened to coincide with the rise of the communist Eastern Europe under the malign expansionist aegis of Stalin's Russia, and we're all too aware of his legacy.

Broad historical texts, necessarily limited because of space issues, paint only a tiny aspect of the picture – the major personalities, the battles and their outcomes, and the major consequences of those actions: in other words, the macrocosmic. Here, in Shattered Spirits, Broken Hearts we delve into the minutiae of small lives, the microcosmic: queueing for the most basic of foodstuffs, the collectivisation of agriculture and the nationalisation of housing, the scarcity of materials, the discrimination shown to those of a different ethnic disposition or language, the stratification between those with (party members and their families) and those without (everybody else), between 'pure' Romanian and Saxon. Here also is the abject abuse of the human soul on a societal level (the Communist regime), and the abuse of trust between mother (Maria) and daughter (Ute, as Ursula was then known). It defies common sense, dignity, and our sensibilities, and yet this is a human reaction.

Ursula's memoirs are written simply, without artifice or exaggeration. As editor, I have attempted to keep it as the writer has told it: in this way it will stand as a powerful testament to two fundamental facets of humanity. One, the infinite capacity of mankind to inflict misery and suffering upon those of its own kind, and Two, the equally infinite ability of people to transcend their afflictions and rise above them, to retain compassion and heart even in spite of their experiences. Ursula has shown us here that forebearance and love can defeat the meanest and pettiest of actions, and that spirit itself is stronger than armies and nations.

We should be grateful that people of the calibre of Ursula Matthews survived so that they could tell us their stories. The past always informs the future, and the past written about here with such clarity serves as both a warning for our future and as a history. Read it well, and understand.

Printed in Great Britain
by Amazon

54180279R00237